# The
# Age of Chopin

# The
# *Age of Chopin*

## Interdisciplinary Inquiries

Halina Goldberg

*Editor*

**INDIANA**
University Press

Bloomington & Indianapolis

This book is a publication of

Indiana University Press
601 North Morton Street
Bloomington, IN 47404-3797 USA

http://iupress.indiana.edu

Telephone orders     800-842-6796
Fax orders     812-855-7931
Orders by e-mail     iuporder@indiana.edu

© 2004 by Halina Goldberg

The paper used in this publication meets the minimum
requirements of American National Standard for Information
Sciences—Permanence of Paper for Printed Library Materials,
ANSI Z39.48-1984.

MANUFACTURED IN THE UNITED STATES OF AMERICA

**Library of Congress Cataloging-in-Publication Data**

The age of Chopin : interdisciplinary inquiries / Halina Goldberg,
editor.
    p. cm.
"The present collection grew out of the interdisciplinary
conference that took place at Indiana University–Bloomington
during the 1999 sesquicentennial commemorations of Fryderyk
Chopin's death"—Pref.
    Includes bibliographical references and index.
    ISBN 0-253-34319-4 (alk. paper)—ISBN 0-253-21628-1
(pbk. : alk. paper)
    1. Chopin, Frédéric, 1810–1849—Congresses. 2. Music—
Poland—19th century—Congresses. I. Goldberg, Halina, date
    ML410.C54A48 2004
    786.2'092—dc21

2003013822

1 2 3 4 5 09 08 07 06 05 04

# Contents

# Preface

The present collection grew out of the interdisciplinary conference that took place at Indiana University–Bloomington during the 1999 sesquicentennial commemorations of Fryderyk Chopin's death. The original conference and this resulting volume were built on the premise that bringing together voices of scholars from various fields will allow us to better perceive the various facets of Chopin's music and personality, and will enhance our awareness of the various contexts that shaped Chopin's mind and art as well as the reception of his music.

The studies contained in this volume engage the fields of music theory and musicology, in addition to contributions from history, literature, art history, aesthetics, dance history, and audiovisual media theory. Some articles represent a single mode of inquiry or methodology, giving fresh perspectives, new interpretations of sources, or introducing important new information. Other articles adopt a truly multidisciplinary approach, in which the authors cross the boundaries of their individual specializations in order to better understand Chopin's cultural frame of reference and the readings (or misreadings) of his compositions by his contemporaries and succeeding generations.

In Daniel Stone's introductory essay Chopin is presented within his own historical context, the Polish Kingdom during the pre– and post–November Uprising (1830) years, to be compared and contrasted with a hypothetical Chopin born 140 years later and growing up in Communist Poland. Such juxtaposition provokes the exploration of uncharted cultural and sociological terrain and allows some unexpected conclusions.

Part 1, entitled "Memories, Images, and Dreams," includes essays that address a variety of aesthetic and philosophical topics. The art-historical essays explore ideas surrounding the two familiar images of Chopin: the celebrated portrait by Delacroix, found in almost every book on the composer, and Poland's favorite Chopin icon—the monument in Warsaw's Łazienki Park. While Waldemar Okoń delves into the aesthetic dilemma of presenting a non-corporeal concept (music) through a materially confined medium (sculpture), John Nici regards the well-known portrait of Chopin as an example of "Romantic transference." The Romantic aesthetics of alienation and homelessness—particularly pronounced in the Polish émigré community—is addressed in Bożena Shallcross's article, in which the various homes the Polish composer inhabited and his own descriptions of these spaces are viewed as revealing more about Chopin's mind and the spirit of the time than about his actual surroundings. My own article examines Chopin's links to messianic philosophy and addresses the perception of Chopin as Mickiewicz's heir to the role of *wieszcz:* a poet, bard, seer, and prophet—the nation's spiritual leader.

Part 2, "Analytical Perspectives," includes essays that provide theoretical interpretations of Chopin's music in Schenkerian, interdisciplinary, and multimedia contexts. Using the A♭ Major Mazurka op. 24 no. 3 as a primary focus, Carl Schachter examines the unusual temporal features of the Chopin mazurka style, in which unpredictable metric events are set against the apparent dance-like rhythmic regularity. Eric McKee's article, after discussing Chopin's involvement with social dancing, considers the musical structure of Chopin's waltzes from the standpoint of the dance patterns that generated it. Marianne Kielian-Gilbert explores twentieth-century settings of Chopin's music in audiovisual media (ballet, film, and television) and the significance of varying material contexts for particular analytical accounts of the music, thus addressing music's transgressive values and openness to subjective meaning.

In part 3, "Gender, Genre, Genius," James Parakilas investigates the gendered origins of the piano nocturne genre, focusing specifically on the Parisian tradition of the vocal nocturne, in which at least one singer was a woman (thus differing from the German tradition of "the serenading man"). He then discusses the stylistic manifestations of this tradition in Chopin's nocturnes. Whitney Walton's essay analyzes gendered representations of George Sand and Chopin, explaining the diverse imaging of gender and genius as mirroring the aesthetics of the early nineteenth century.

Modes of the reception and dissemination of Chopin's music are discussed in the last part, "Chopin Appropriated." The first three articles concentrate on topics relating to Chopin's reception in Poland. Zofia Chechlińska contrasts the reception of Chopin in Polish periodicals in the nineteenth century with the views of Chopin's music presented abroad (Germany, in particular). The responses in Chopin's homeland to his first biography, Liszt's *Frédéric Chopin,* are surveyed by Irena Poniatowska. Maja Trochimczyk's article, drawing on the writings of prominent Polish musicians (Paderewski, Noskowski, Żeleński, and Szymanowski), examines the effect of Polish nationalist ideologies on early-twentieth-century constructions of Chopin's musical identity. The final essay of the book, by Sandra Rosenblum, takes us to the New World and carefully maps the history of Chopin's performance in the United States, as well as the patterns of its dissemination and critical reception.

It is our hope that by presenting previously unexplored sources and perspectives, as well as familiar material viewed in a different light, this volume will prompt a reassessment of various aspects of Chopin, the man and his oeuvre. Ultimately we wish to inspire the reader to hear Chopin's music with a fresh ear.

Halina Goldberg

# Acknowledgments

Support and funding for the original 1999 conference at Indiana University–Bloomington, which instigated this book, came from the Polish Studies Center, Russian and East European Institute, Office of International Programs, School of Music and The Multidisciplinary Ventures and Seminars Fund at Indiana University, as well as the Polish Ministry of Culture and the Kościuszko Foundation in New York. I am particularly indebted to my colleagues at Indiana University who participated in and encouraged this project: Edward Auer, A. Peter Brown, J. Peter Burkholder, Denise Gardiner, Roy Gardner, Timothy Wiles, Patrick O'Meara, and especially Bożena Shallcross, who was the co-author and co-organizer of the conference. Most heartening were the enthusiasm, inspiration, and assistance provided at every stage of this event by my students at the School of Music.

A research grant from the University Graduate School at Indiana University–Bloomington assisted the book production. I want to thank my remarkably competent and reliable assistants, Amanda Mae Palmer and Katie Lundeen, who helped with various research and editing tasks, never failing to brighten my day with a smile as a bonus; Mariola Nałęcz, the Head of the Music Collection at the National Library in Warsaw, who with generosity typical of her manner suggested the original idea for the cover page; Gary Smokes who expertly prepared the musical examples; and Jennifer King for her work on the index. The competence and forbearance of copyeditor Rita Bernhard and managing editor Jane Lyle were invaluable in completing the volume. I am particularly thankful to sponsoring editor Gayle Sherwood for her help and patience in guiding me around various obstacles during the publication process.

My greatest gratitude goes to my parents, Maria and Zenon Goldberg, for their faith in me and for their unremitting affection. To them I dedicate this book with love.

Grateful acknowledgment is made for permission to reprint the following material:

**Oliver Cromwell**

# The
# Age of Chopin

*Introduction*

---

# Chopin Then and Now:
# A Fantasy

### DANIEL STONE

With this essay I would like to fantasize about Chopin's life—surely an appropriate approach for this collection. Let us imagine a modern Chopin, born in 1950, shortly after the Communists solidified their hold on Poland, instead of the actual date of 1810. His death would have occurred in the last year of Communist rule in Poland, 1989, not 1849. Let us then examine the relationship between Chopin and his society in his actual historical experience of 1810–49 and compare it with a hypothetical experience, as if he had lived between 1950 and 1989—a life coterminous with Communist rule. By readjusting the dates in this manner I hope to make Chopin's experience more immediate and accessible. For those readers who visited Poland as tourists, exchange students, lecturers, research scholars, and performers, or followed the last few decades of political developments there from afar, the analogy may help bring together two strands of experience—the sense of Polish history and personal memories. In a more general sense, it is an attempt to provide a clearer view about relations between Poland and Russia in both the nineteenth and twentieth centuries by presenting a variety of factors: political institutions, economic opportunities, nationalism, cultural trends, and emigration.

## Political Institutions

In Chopin's real lifetime, at the end of the Napoleonic wars, Russia incorporated approximately three-fifths of Poland into her empire, increasing the possessions she had taken in the three partitions at the end of the eighteenth century. Despite Russia's rule, Poland was still, legally and institutionally, an autonomous part of the Russian Empire. For a mixture of libertarian, humanitarian, and hard-headed diplomatic reasons, Tsar Alexander I created the Kingdom of Poland, commonly called the Congress Kingdom, out of the former Duchy of Warsaw. He made it, at least on paper, the most liberal state on the European continent. Poland enjoyed more political freedom than Bourbon France or any of the German states, not to mention Romanov Russia—free elections, free campaigning, and free speech in parliament—even if issues of national security, as defined by tsarist officials, were off-limits. These included the borders of the Kingdom and control over the Polish army.

The Constitution of the Kingdom of Poland drew primarily on Napoleon's Duchy of Warsaw. Alexander crowned himself king of Poland, exercising executive authority through five ministers and a secretary of state, grouped in an Administrative Council. Following older Polish practice, administrative committees of local landowners ruled in the countryside, and committees of property owners ruled in cities. A Crown appointee presided to ensure that patriots did not use the committees to seek independence.

In theory, the bicameral parliament continued to share power with the king much as it had before the partitions. A Senate consisted of royal nominees, as before, with the addition of members of the Russian imperial family. Like the U.S. Senate, the new Polish Senate initiated legislation, and, like the British House of Lords, it served as a high court for political and administrative cases. The lower chamber, the Sejm, was much larger and, like the U.S. House of Representatives, enjoyed full legislative rights.

Because government practice is more important than statements written on paper by constitutional lawyers, autonomy of the Kingdom of Poland was implemented with mixed success. Obviously there were significant limitations on freedom. Alexander vested supreme power in his brother, the Grand Duke Constantine, who commanded the Polish army, imposing Russian military traditions while building a modern, well-trained instrument. Constantine's character was a major irritant. He was devoted to Poland in his way—especially after a morganatic marriage to a Polish noblewoman, Joanna Grudzińska, that removed him from first place in the line of succession to the Russian throne—but he was erratic, choleric, and punitive. His outbursts of rage on the parade ground drove at least a dozen officers to suicide. However, Constantine played little part in civil politics or administration. Alexander appointed General Józef Zajączek as viceroy, bypassing his former close personal friend, Adam Jerzy Czartoryski. A radical, so-called Jacobin in the 1790s, Zajączek was now a loyal servant of the tsar. All that remained of his radicalism was an abiding distrust for Czartoryski and other rich nobles. Czartoryski, a Pole, had served Alexander as foreign minister at the Congress of Vienna, but his views on the Congress Kingdom did not match Alexander's. The strongest issue separating the two men was the disposition of the eastern lands: Lithuania, Belarus, and parts of Ukraine that Russia had absorbed in the partitions. Tsar Alexander had no intention of returning these to Polish rule. Czartoryski, to the contrary, worked to extend the borders of the Kingdom of Poland as much as possible and give the new state full autonomy. Occasionally Nikolai Novosiltsev, a third extra-constitutional figure, acted as Alexander's personal representative, undercutting all semblance of Polish autonomy including Grand Duke Constantine's military initiatives.

As a result, the limitations of democracy in the Congress Kingdom were starkly apparent. Progressive educational reforms were abandoned, and relatively innocent dissent was punished with imprisonment and exile. Constantine and Novosiltsev fought the liberal opposition, illegally stripping its leaders of their seats in parliament. Dissent went underground where Novosiltsev's secret police sought it out. When Alexander died in 1825, his brother, Nicholas I, returned to the constitutional governing system that his brother had almost abandoned. Relations became strained, however, after Russian state security services uncovered Polish sympathizers with the Russian Decembrist Revolt that had tried to block Nicholas's accession to the throne.

This was the atmosphere of Chopin's formative first twenty years. Poland represented a kind of halfway house between nineteenth-century democracy and authoritarian rule, between independence and subservience. Russian domination, although irksome, permitted some legal dissent and tolerated, just barely, extra-legal dissent. Chopin would have been acutely conscious of these strains as he grew up, and, like most Poles of his generation, he became a patriot who prized Polish independence. He was, however, indifferent to the form of government that prevailed so long as Poles, rather than Russians, ruled according to legal standards, and his dissatisfaction with Poland's circumstances did not prevent him from taking the steps necessary to furthering his pianistic career.

Let us now imagine that Chopin had been born in 1950. This modern Chopin would have had many similar experiences, though he certainly would have had many sharply different experiences as well. He would have narrowly missed the most severe discrimination in the harsh Stalinist period of 1949–54, when, as a child of a mother from minor nobility and an intelligentsia father, he might have been passed over for admission to the Warsaw Conservatory, and, if admitted, he still might have been ignored if school authorities needed a young star to perform for visiting Soviet dignitaries. However, the modern Chopin would have been fortunate, because, in 1956, a near-revolution installed Władyław Gomułka as head of the Communist Party and put an end to the most punitive forms of Communism. If nothing else, at least the regime stopped throwing citizens in prison for imaginary crimes and permitted new artistic forms that the Stalinists had forbidden. Stalinist social realism yielded to experimental forms of modern music in the annual Warsaw Autumn [*Warszawska Jesień*] festival, and art galleries hung abstract paintings. In this fashion, the atmosphere came to resemble that of Chopin's actual youth.

Despite these improvements, Gomułka's Poland remained harsher than the Congress Kingdom of Chopin's formative years. It maintained a Communist ideological monopoly that rejected so-called bourgeois civil rights and denigrated religious expression, if less cruelly than the Stalinists. The constitutional position of Communist Poland—the Polish People's Republic—was better than that of the Congress Kingdom, but the reality was worse. Despite wartime fears that Poland would be incorporated into the USSR as a Soviet Republic, post–World War II Poland remained an independent country. Nevertheless the Soviet Union called the tune, and the Poles had to dance. The Soviet army and security police retained a far greater presence than in the tsarist empire before 1830, and, during the Stalinist years, the Soviet ambassador gave marching orders to the Polish government on daily affairs while orders on major matters were delivered in person by summoning President Bierut and others to Moscow. After 1956 Gomułka acquired greater freedom of action, but he still consulted closely with Soviet officials. Moreover, as a Communist, he was committed to the Soviet system. No Polish political figure of Chopin's youth, not even Viceroy Zajączek, approached Gomułka in his conformity to a foreign way of life.

Gomułka's Poland supported parliamentary forms and permitted a slight measure of choice through multi-candidate ballots (an innovation the USSR finally adopted under Gorbachev), but the Communist parliament enjoyed less independence than under the Congress Kingdom. Elections were neither competitive nor free.

## Economic Opportunities

Since music, like society in general, runs on money, it was lucky that the nineteenth-century Polish economy developed rapidly in Chopin's historical youth. Poland recovered rapidly from the economic ravages of the Napoleonic wars and ensuing postwar heavy indebtedness. The Congress Kingdom profited both from inclusion in the Russian customs area and from a measure of economic autonomy that Finance Minister Ksawery Drucki-Lubecki used to enact protectionist measures stimulating new Polish industries. The state also helped to turn the small village of Łódź into a "Polish Manchester" by placing orders for clothing for the Polish and Russian armies. Rural prosperity was assured by supplying state credits to landowners who adopted modern techniques. Unfortunately modernizing often meant expelling the peasants, taking over their fields, and cultivating industrial crops such as potatoes and sugar beets with hired labor.

Chopin was probably not aware of these economic problems. He came from a secure home and, thanks to his musical genius, was adopted by the social and economic elite. The enrichment of the Polish aristocracy and the emergence of a new banking-industrialist elite provided the funds that supported musicians' careers during Chopin's early years. Rich Poles and Warsaw-based Russians had the funds to pay performers for salon appearances, and to frequent concert and opera performances. The stable economy also fostered the growth of musical and educational institutions—among them the Warsaw Conservatory, where Chopin received extensive musical training during his last years in Poland.

The modern Chopin, born in 1950, would also have encountered state-directed economic development, in its much more extreme Communist form. Driven by ideology more than the exigencies of postwar recovery, the Polish People's Republic nationalized all industry and most commerce, imposing a crash program of industrialization financed by restricting personal incomes and holding living standards to distressingly low levels. Peasant land ownership was allowed to continue, although collectivization loomed on the horizon until 1956.

After 1956 the more liberal Gomułka government allowed small-scale private trade and handicrafts. It also devoted a higher percentage of government industries toward consumer goods such as housing, clothing, and electronics. The general economic improvement peaked in about 1963 and stagnated until Gomułka fell from power in 1970. Living standards improved slowly and erratically until 1989.

Not entirely devoid of public spirit, the Communists rebuilt Old Warsaw (destroyed by Nazi bombardments), including the Kazimierz Palace, where Chopin lived during most of his Warsaw years. They also devoted substantial sums to cultural expression in education and the arts (though expression was distorted by ideology). For instance, they provided funds to build concert halls and opera houses, and developed a network of specialized primary and secondary music schools, as well as conservatories, in which the modern Chopin would have studied. Given low prevailing economic standards, prominent native artists could earn relatively high fees for concerts across the country, but even stars suffered from the prevailing shortages.

## Cultural Nationalism

The historical Chopin was in the forefront of cultural nationalism in an age when national identities formed and revived across Europe. Nationalism is peculiarly difficult to distinguish from its predecessor, "national consciousness," which had existed in Poland for centuries as illustrated by Mikołaj Rej's mid-sixteenth century comment that Poles should write in Polish instead of Latin because, as he put it, "Poles are not geese and have their own language." The growing awareness of folk culture in the later part of the eighteenth century led to a European-wide movement to collect folk poetry, songs, and melodies, and use them in musical compositions, although many composers felt free to adopt the tunes of several different countries. In the nationalistic nineteenth century, peasants, who remained outside cosmopolitan experiences, were held to represent the best qualities of the nation, and a musical vocabulary credited to them became the central inspiration for many composers, including Chopin.

In the nineteenth century, national identity became a preoccupation of political leaders and ordinary citizens across Europe as they tried to align their political borders with their ethnic consciousness. While Poland sought to regain the political identity it had lost in the partitions and Hungary sought to regain the autonomy it had lost within the Habsburg Empire, most Eastern European peoples—Czechs, Slovaks, Romanians, Croatians, Serbs, Greeks, Bulgarians, and Albanians—yearned to create, re-create, or expand their national political identity—along with Western Europeans such as the Italians and Germans, who achieved national unity, and the Irish, Scots, Welsh, Catalans, Bretons, and others whose national movements enjoyed less success.

In addition to being a cultural nationalist, the historical Chopin was also a celebrated Romantic along with contemporary Polish poets Adam Mickiewicz, Juliusz Słowacki, and Zygmunt Krasiński. In Poland, as elsewhere in Europe, Romanticism replaced Classicism as the dominant mode of expression in the early nineteenth century and, in time, gained general approval. The Russian court and society had no objection to Romanticism as such, even though a number of its practitioners committed political indiscretions. For example, Alexander Pushkin spent some time under Tsar Nicholas's personal supervision and more years in provincial exile for his Decembrist sympathies, but Nicholas personally approved publication of Pushkin's nonpolitical poems. Mickiewicz was arrested and exiled to Petersburg for his part in the Philomat Society in Wilno, but his poetry escaped censorship. Russians, like everyone else, loved Chopin's works, along with the music of other Romantic composers, and, by and large, his compositions were not censored.

The modern Chopin of the 1950s and 1960s would have been gratified to see the reemergence of Poland and the creation of other national states, but he probably would not have adopted a national musical style to express his Polish identity. The age of Romantic nationalism was long gone, and artists' interest in folk culture declined sharply along with the view of peasants as exemplars of national identity. Remnants of the rural myth can still be observed from time to time but more from the point of view of the country gentry than that of the peasantry.

Paradoxically Communist endorsement of nationalist forms put the finishing touches to folk-based Polish nationalism. Emphasizing their alleged support for the peasants and urban working class, Communists endorsed folk music and dance. State-subsidized folk troupes appeared in virtually every village and town, reaching a high artistic level in national ensembles such as *Mazowsze* and *Śląsk*. In the earlier years of Communism, folk music also permeated the concert hall, since composers, anxious to avoid accusations of "bourgeois formalism," introduced folk tunes to apply socialist-realist canons and appeal to the average listener.

With folk culture irremediably tainted by Soviet rule, Polish patriots returned to the cosmopolitan intellectual and artistic trends that their teachers had practiced before the war. When the Polish October (the 1956 Gomułka takeover) made it possible to move on, Polish artists asserted their independence through dissonant modern music, jazz, and abstract art. New schools of Polish achievement emerged, exemplified by Krzysztof Penderecki and Witold Lutosławski. The modern Chopin, born in 1950, would have expressed his nationalism by writing atonal music or, because of his love of melody, playing jazz riffs on the piano. "Folk" themes might even have seemed anti-Polish at this time—in contrast to the period of the historical Chopin.

## Emigration

The historical Chopin left Poland in 1830 on a concert tour and never returned. For all his national sentiment, he probably welcomed the opportunity to settle in Paris, the cultural center of Europe, although he might have returned home if the November Uprising of 1830 had not broken out and failed, leaving Poland's autonomy all but gone.

Despite his absence from Poland, Chopin still spent much of his time in Polish society. The Great Emigration—some nine thousand Polish émigrés, two-thirds of them nobles, who left Poland after the failure of the November Uprising—settled mostly in Paris. Patriotic rather than political, Chopin established good terms with all the bitterly opposed factions. He gladly accepted invitations to play for aristocrats such as Prince Adam Czartoryski, Tsar Alexander's one-time friend who had reluctantly headed the insurrectionary government of 1830–31. But Chopin also remained on good terms with the Polish radicals who felt that social revolution was not only just but also the best way to achieve independence. Chopin even had nothing against the Russians in Paris, and among his pupils were Elizavieta Chernishev, Anna and Elizavieta Shermietiev, and Viera Kologrivov (who later married Rubio).

It is hard to imagine the modern Chopin retaining this degree of equanimity in exile after 1970. Actually we cannot even speak of a Polish emigration in contemporary times in the same sense as in the nineteenth century. There certainly was a post–World War II emigration with centers in London, Paris, and New York. Its strength was both augmented and diluted by its relationship with the larger group of Polish immigrants who had mostly arrived before World War I. The trickle of political émigrés in the 1960s, 1970s, and 1980s was similarly augmented and diluted by the flood of economic migrants. There are parallels with the 1830s, however. Exiles and migrants retained strong feelings about their native land and enthusiastically attended concerts given by Polish artists—like our hypothetical modern Chopin. There are differences as well. Whereas the Polish situation worsened after the November Uprising of 1830, Polish Communism continued to liberalize throughout the 1970s and 1980s, thanks, in part, to the weakening Soviet control. Even the suppression of Solidarity failed to halt the evolution of Polish Communism toward more liberal forms with greater acceptance of dissent, foreign contact, and private enterprise. That would have made it easy for the modern Chopin to entertain friendly relations with Polish diplomats in New York, London, or Paris and even to visit Poland from time to time.

## Conclusion

In this fantasy I have explored political, economic, and cultural factors that determined the direction in which Fryderyk Chopin's genius emerged. As we all are, Chopin was a product of his times. A patriotic Pole (seemingly an unchanging quality in European history), he became a Romantic composer and pianist who used inspiration from folk dances to express his ideas. Because of political and economic circumstances, he developed much of his career abroad. The degree to which his experience reflected his times is highlighted by the hypothetical construction of a modern Chopin, born in Stalinist Poland in 1950 and perhaps emigrating to New York in 1970. Equally gifted, this modern Chopin would have faced Russian domination, political repression, artistic censorship, and economic hardship. Artistically, this Chopin would have followed different models. He might have been an atonalist or a jazz pianist. Patriotism, however, would have remained a guiding force.

It is remarkable how much Polish cultural life owes to foreign domination, though one can scarcely expect Poles to be grateful for this kind of stimulation. Much of what Chopin and others accomplished was influenced by difficult political situations. Samuel Johnson is said to have remarked that one's imminent execution concentrates the mind. The partitions "executed" Poland, and Chopin's mind was profoundly concentrated on expressing the prevailing patriotic sentiment that, at his time, adopted a Romantic and folk orientation. We are drawn to his music because he expressed it so beautifully.

# *Part I*

---

## Memories, Images, and Dreams

# 1

## Chopin at Home

### BOŻENA SHALLCROSS

I have been united with this house as if one body, and
this house gives me pain as if it were a part of my body.[1]
—Zygmunt Krasiński

The Romantics tended to understand the relationship between
artist and home in terms of an unavoidable, but nonetheless desir-
able, state of homelessness, positioning the artist as an alienated
and dispossessed self. Their vision continues to affect both the popular perception and literary/cultural representation of an artist as
either an uprooted or eternally suffering exile. Yet the Romantics
also developed an entirely different topophilic attitude,[2] that of a
very close attachment to one's domestic environment, which often
resulted in a self-identification with the surroundings.

I propose to show that Romanticism, as a philosophy of indi-
vidualism—powerfully represented in literature, music, and the visual arts—opens for artists the concept of the home as a new mode
of self-expression and a sphere particularly conducive for experimentation.[3] What is deemed poetic, mysterious, sublime, and exotic is displayed in the objects of acquisition, the choice of decor,
and the aura of the abode, which distinctly manifest these particular
Romantic traits and speak of their owner's/inhabitant's identity.

Since Théophile Gautier's memorable description, in his *His-*

*tory of Romanticism*, of Victor Hugo's apartment, the notion of the home as an independent textual creation has been radically refor-mulated.[4] Since then, home has been understood as a *text* governed by strict aesthetic principles that reflect not only the inhabitant's identity but also his taste, preferences, and idiosyncrasies. "We speak of the keeping of a room as we would of the keeping of a picture," Edgar Allan Poe wrote in his "Philosophy of Furniture," "for both the picture and the room are amenable to those undev-iating principles which regulate all varieties of art; and very nearly the same laws by which we decide on the higher merits of a paint-ing, suffice for decision on the adjustment of a chamber."[5] If an apartment can be arranged as a picture, it can also be perceived as a picture or, as I put it, as a pictorial text. How, then, did Fryderyk Chopin invent his home as a Romantic pictorial text? And how is his persona represented in such a text?

Although Chopin was the most refined dresser among Polish émigré artists—like his friend Eugène Delacroix, he created for himself the image of a dandy—the degree of aestheticism toward home that Poe advises can be seldom detected in what we know about Chopin's apartments. His letters, either those written to his family or those addressed to his close Polish friends, Grzymała and Fontana, are dominated by the rather practical considerations con-ditioned by his poor health, his need of a well-heated interior not-withstanding. Yet, for a reader whose critical lens focuses on his correspondence, one thing is clear: Chopin views and describes his intimate interior space in a manner that fuses the representation of his home furnishings and paraphernalia with his state of mind. His place speaks of his frame of mind, while his frame of mind colors the perception of his surroundings.

For instance, during the summer of 1844 Chopin was in No-hant with George Sand, her children, his sister, Ludwika Jędrze-jewicz, and his sister's husband, Kalasanty. Seemingly he was closer than ever, at least since he left Poland, to the notion of the home as a family hearth. Several letters to his sister after her departure to Warsaw articulate an acute sense of alienation caused by her absence:

> I feel strange this year; often in the morning I glimpse in the adjacent room, but nobody is there.—Therefore [ ... ] I placed the piano differently—against the wall where there used to be a settee with a small table at which Ludwika was embroidering my

slippers and the Lady of the House was working on something. The desk on which I am writing stands in the middle, on which to the left are several of my musical papers. [ . . . ] In front of me this timepiece, which you have mailed me [ . . . ] Roses and carnations, quills and a piece of sealing wax left by Kalasanty. With one leg I am always with you, with the other in the neighboring room where the Lady of the House is working, but [I am] not at all here[6] at this moment, only as usual in some strange space. This must be *espaces imaginaires*, but I am not embarrassed by it.[7]

Enhancing the remarkable degree of visualization of this Romantic pictorial text is Chopin's descriptive care of details, spatial organization and placement of furniture. The reader of his letter could easily reconstruct the room's new arrangement meant to control its inhabitant's nostalgia. We know where the piano, the desk, and all minute paraphernalia were. We know where the mistress was. But where exactly was the author of these words?

Admittedly, sitting at his desk in Nohant, Chopin felt the strangeness of his familiar ambience. The pervasive memory of his family that had left for Poland seems to contribute to his split sense of the present moment, while the penetration of this instance makes the composer aware of his estrangement from his immediate surroundings. Chopin's being partly with his family, partly with George Sand, and partly *elsewhere* leaves nothing of his actual presence in his own room. His letter translates the Romantic longing for other, often distant, places into a desire for a different domestic space. This vaguely imagined territory, perhaps suitable for another family happiness and reunion, offers a glimpse at Chopin's inner life as *he* verbalized it by embedding the French expression "*espace imaginaire*" into his letter. Granted, unembarrassed by his nostalgic feelings, he is aware that such space does not exist, that it is only an invented idea of a space. Chopin's *elsewhere* does not simply appease his nostalgia but, like Victor Hugo's "*maison visionée*," gives his topophilic anxieties a concrete visual form and articulates them in a manner that eventually develops into a certain mental pattern.

More often an outsider than an escapist, the composer, in his letter to his sister, controls his wandering mind and attempts to focus on material objects. This shift from the intelligible to the tangible invokes a whole range of meaning. Thus, in general, his letter manifests how our domestic material culture has changed, but it also allows a simple object to acquire a metonymical function: the mention of sealing wax, quills, or *répéter*[8] speaks in the language of fragments of the past sojourn with Chopin's sister and brother-in-law.

The letter reveals a self-portrait that is continued in another characteristic instance in which he mentions his sister's room in Nohant:

> Often, when I enter, I am seeking whether there is something left by you and I only see the same place next to the couch, where we drank chocolate . . . —More is left after you in my room—on the table is Your embroidering of the slipper wrapped in English wrapping tissue—on the piano the tiny pencil, which used to be in Your little wallet and now ideally serves me.[9]

Again, the stark contrast between presence and absence prompts Chopin's nostalgic feelings. In this instance, however, the objects serve as vestiges of his sister's presence that he seeks around his place. I ascribe the metonymical role of objects displayed in Chopin's room to the Romantic cult of a *pamiątka*, a memento. Such keepsakes write the text of the composer's personal history with intimate details that attest to his past joys and sorrows. An old piece of wax, a lock of hair, and a red ribbon that binds a packet of letters inform a rich language of traces, the grammar of vestiges and echoes, in which Chopin, as a quintessential Romantic, is quite skilled.[10]

## *"The Most Poetic Home on Earth"*

Our house is very political as well as poetical.
—Mary Shelley, *Letters*

Chopin's dream of an ideal and peaceful domicile has many facets; some of them are defined by his poor health, which, at one point, made George Sand convince him to spend what turned out to be a rather disastrous winter in Majorca. Repeatedly Chopin's expectations regarding Valldemosa, his destination point on this island, assumed in correspondence an aestheticized shape of the Great Elsewhere. In this respect the composer shared his hopes with George Sand, who perceived their home in the Valldemosa monastery in terms of its aura and aesthetic qualities as "the most poetic home on earth."[11]

Indeed, from Chopin's perspective, the place in Valldemosa represented something akin to a catalogue of Romantic motifs and clichés:

I shall probably lodge in a wonderful monastery, the most beautiful situation in the world; sea, mountains, palms, a cemetery, a crusaders' church, ruined mosques, aged trees, thousand-year-old olives.[12]

Listed as an inventory of aspects most appealing to an eye of the Romantic, the infinite space of the sea, the nearby cemetery, time petrified in trees and time triumphant in ruins, history and exoticism, as well as the poetic aura emanating from this whole imagined scene contributed to Chopin's pictorial portrayal of his future abode. In fact, this type of house and its locale would fit the expectations of many Romantics, be it Chateaubriand, Eugène Delacroix, Lord Byron, Alexis de Tocqueville, Zygmunt Krasiński (or even James Fenimore Cooper during his stay in Europe), for they all sought and reveled in the mystique of a place. But could one, and Chopin in particular, live in such a mysterious dwelling? And what did his home in Valldemosa provide in terms of more practical expectations?

It's a huge Carthusian monastery, stuck down between rocks and sea, where you may imagine me, without gloves and hair curlers, as pale as ever, in a cell with such doors as Paris never had for gates. The cell is the shape of a *tall coffin*, with an enormous dusty vaulting, a small window, outside the window orange-trees, and palms, cypresses, opposite the window my bed on rollers (?) under a Moorish filigree rosette. Beside the bed is a square *claque nitouchable* for writing, which I can scarcely use, and on it (a great *luxe* here) a leaden candlestick with a candle . . . my scrawls, and (not my) waste paper—*silence—you could scream—there still would be silence. Indeed, I write to you from a strange place.*[13]

The much-desired enchantment of the abode was quickly gone, replaced by the quotidian and its disappointing elements. The monk's cell provided shelter from the elements but no comfort. Hence Chopin found himself among several domestic contradictions: the door was too large for the narrow shape of his room; the view from his cell was splendid, but the window was too small to contemplate the enchanting panorama that appeared in some of Maurice Sand's drawings; and the otherwise highly valued poetic effect of a flickering candlelight did not provide enough light. The coziness of a fireplace and the modicum of comfort offered by the upholstered furniture, portrayed in some of Chopin's Parisian flats, expose, by contrast, the Spartan conditions of the Valldemosa monastery that Chopin had traveled so far to enjoy.[14] And, most important, the silence pervading the place is *not* of the inspiring but of the deadening type.

Again, the passage from Chopin's letter presents a description of a place as well as a state of mind. The monastery, located between the immensity of rocks and sea, held within it not a home but a metaphorical tomb devoid of color, light, and warmth. Chopin did not find in his cell that which he sought, yet its representation did not articulate mere disappointment. Since he could not identify with this cell in any meaningful way, its space spoke of Chopin's displacement and, to a certain degree, his homelessness. And yet, from the tension between disappointment and positionality a creative moment occurs, which prompts the working of the "transfiguring perceptual imagination,"[15] to use Samuel Coleridge's concept. In Chopin's description, the cell's aura sharpens and acquires Gothic features. The recollection of the old monk, the previous tenant of the cell whose image haunts Chopin, his coffin-like room, and its *dead* silence suggest the horror of someone buried alive, or perhaps dying in solitude. Under Chopin's pen, the room turns into quite a different Romantic creation, into a symbol of emptiness and death. It is remarkable how, in his letters relating his sojourn in Majorca, Chopin's perceptual trajectory of the Valldemosa monastery changes from the intimations of the poetic to the projected deletion of the self.

## The Most Romantic Place in Paris

James Fenimore Cooper once observed: "There is an instinctive tendency in men to look at any man who has become distinguished."[16] Houses of great artists are a part of this phenomenon, and visits paid to their houses constitute its variant. During Romanticism, every cultivated man and woman rushed to Goethe's house in Weimar; this habit later spread rapidly throughout Europe, where houses of artistic celebrities became tourist attractions and destination points for secularized pilgrimages.[17] In this spirit one could argue that visits to late writers' homes signify secular veneration of the dead.[18]

However, the appeal of an artist's place may have diverse motivations. One of them is to pay homage to a living artist. This opportunity allows one to see each object of the artist's interior firsthand, to sense the spirit of the place, and ultimately, if one is lucky, to observe behind-the-scenes activities: what impels the artist's creation. Matters concerning everyday life and the inhabitant's creative efforts are frequently enacted in the same room. From the cultural habit of visiting artists' residences evolves another habit— that of recording impressions of these homes. For many, it is serious duty to bear witness by portraying their visits in images or depicting them in words.

It is Liszt's description[19] of Chopin's apartment on Chaussée d'Antin in Paris that transforms the private into the public. Curiously, as one of the first depictions that introduced Chopin's lodging to the wider audience, this text represents an ultimate Romantic creation of this composer's domestic space. Here, the notion of the "Temple of Creation" and intimate sanctity conflate in one superbly dynamic image:

> His apartment . . . was lit up by some wax candles grouped around a Pleyel piano which he liked so much. . . . The corners of the room were left in obscurity so that all idea of limit was lost, and there seemed to be no boundary to darkness of space around. A tall piece of furniture draped in white revealed itself in this dim light—a form indistinct, as if a specter lifting itself to listen to the tones calling it forth. The light concentrated around the piano, and falling on the floor, glided like a spreading wave until it reached and mingled with the fitful flashes from the fire, from which the orange-lined plumes rose and fell, as if some shifting gnomes attracted to this spot by mystic incantations in their own language. A single portrait of a pianist . . . seemed as if invited to be a constant auditor of the ebbing and flowing tide of sound which sighed, moaned, murmured, broke, and died upon the instrument near which it always hung. By a curious coincidence, the polished surface of the mirror reflected, in such manner as to double it to our vision, that beautiful oval with silky curls drawn by so many pencils.[20]

This description, indeed a brilliant ekphrastic performance in itself, evokes the place miraculously transformed during one of Chopin's improvisations. Although no Romantic painting parallels this pictorial text,[21] this image owes inspiration to the Romantic style of painting, in particular to Delacroix and his nonlinear treatment of the contour of objects.[22] In this dynamic mélange of light, darkness, motion, and sound, Chopin's drawing room is completely transformed into an enchanting yet domestic sanctuary. The dynamics of this image takes momentum from the memory of a creative instance, from the pure spirituality of Chopin's improvisation.[23]

But one has to ask what is missing in this evocation of image. Where, then, is the improviser? Indeed, as we follow the appearing and disappearing waves of music, we do not catch a single glimpse of the musician. Once again, Chopin's actual presence is suspended, if not erased. Instead, in yet another metonymical gesture, the reader is offered Chopin's visual substitute in the form of his portrait, doubled by the mirror. While the wave of light interplays with that of the music, the reflection in the mirror echoes the concept Delacroix used in his portrait of Chopin with the composer's features indistinctly repeated on the piano's lid. Thus the inhabitant's otherwise negated presence is transposed to the realm of art, and in that realm to be immortalized.[24]

In the three different instances invoked here, the projection of the inhabitant's emotional state on his immediate surroundings— a quintessential Romantic behavior—subordinates the interior space to further change. Paradoxically, what ensues is Chopin's persistent alienation from his surroundings—opposing Krasiński's bodily unity with his home—which takes the form of his actual or projected absence.

## NOTES

1. Zygmunt Krasiński, Letter from Nicea, 8 August 1846, in *Letters to Delfina Potocka*, ed. Zygmunt Suchodolski, 3 vols. (Warszawa: Państwowy Instytut Wydawniczy, 1975), 3:52. If not stated otherwise, all translations in this article are mine.

2. For an elaboration on topophilia, see Yi-Fu Tuan, *Topophilia: A Study of Environmental Perception, Attitudes, and Values* (Englewood Cliffs, N.J.: Prentice Hall, 1974).

3. I fully elaborate this concept in *Dom romantycznego artysty* (Kraków: Wydawnictwo Literackie, 1992).

4. Théophile Gautier, *Vente du mobilier de Victor Hugo en 1852 Histoire du romantisme du suivie de notices romantique et d'une étude sur la poésie française 1830–1868* (Paris: Charpentier, 1877), 88.

5. Edgar Allan Poe, "Philosophy of Furniture," in *The Complete Works*, 5 vols. (New York: Collier, 1903), 5:10–11.

6. In the original, "*u siebie.*"

7. Fryderyk Chopin, Letter to his sister Ludwika Jędrzejewicz, *Korespondencja Fryderyka Chopina z rodziną*, Krystyna Kobylańska, ed. (Warszawa: Państwowy Instytut Wydawniczy, 1972), 141.

8. In the original "*repetier.*"

9. Chopin, Letter to his sister Ludwika Jędrzejewicz, *Korespondencja Fryderyka Chopina z rodziną*, 138.

10. To mention only Walter Scott's Abbotsford where, after his death, his family scrupulously kept the vestiges of his demise for public viewing in what was designated in his residence as the museum.

11. George Sand, Letter to Mme Marliani, *Correspondance*, ed. Georges Lubin, 27 vols. (Paris: 1968), 4:532.

12. Fryderyk Chopin, *Correspondance de Frédéric Chopin, l'Aube 1816–1831*, ed. Bronislas Sydow, Suzanne and Denise Chainaye, and Irène Sydow, 3 vols. (Paris: Richard-Masse, 1954–60), 2:265. See also the excerpt from another letter to Fontana: "I shall lodge in a huge, old ruined monastery of Carthusians, whom Mendisabel expelled, as if especially for me" (2:274).

13. Chopin, *Correspondance de Frédéric Chopin*, 2:282.

14. Chopin's places if turned into a museum participate in a completely different type of discourse—that of the public creation and display of an artist's image. For example, the lack of any resemblance between Chopin's description of his apartment in Valldemosa and the present arrangement in the museum is quite striking. The coffin-like cell was turned into a light and cozy room; decorated with the red and white Polish national flag as well as red and white carnations, the room, for the sake of tourists, is a showcase of the Spanish understanding of Polishness. With all the intimacy gone, the room participates in a shift to a different type of discourse—that of the public creation of an artist's image.

15. Samuel Taylor Coleridge, "Biographia Literaria," in *The Critical Tradition: Classic Texts and Contemporary Trends*, ed. David H. Richter (New York: St. Martin's, 1989), 306.

16. Thomas Carlyle, "Sir Walter Scott," in *The Harvard Classics*, ed. Charles W. Eliot, 50 vols. (New York: Collier, 1909), 25:409.

17. On this subject, see Kenneth Hudson, *Museums of Influence* (Cambridge: Cambridge University Press, 1987), 145–46.

18. See also Beth Holmgren, "At Home with Sienkiewicz," in *Framing the Polish Home: Postwar Cultural Constructions of Hearth, Nation, and Self*, ed. Bożena Shallcross (Athens: Ohio University Press, 2002), 219–36.

19. I am aware that Liszt's authorship of *Life of Chopin* has been questioned.

20. Franz Liszt, *Life of Chopin*, trans. John Broadhouse (London: William Reeves), 98–99.

21. Probably the one that comes closest would be the canvas by Carus, *The Artist's Studio at the Moonlight*.

22. The drawing of Chopin's parlor in his apartment on Chaussée d'Antin—a rather unimaginative rendering devoid of any traces of the room's inhabitant—further reveals the gap between the verbal representation of the composer's homes, including his own, and the visual ones.

23. Liszt's description of Chopin's improvisation as a spiritual and theatrical experience seems to parallel Adam Mickiewicz's notion and practice of improvisation. On Chopin's improvisations and their relationship to Mickiewicz's concept of *wieszcz*, see Halina Goldberg's essay in this volume.

24. For an insightful discussion of Delacroix's portrait of Chopin, see John Nici's essay in this volume.

# 2

## Delacroix's Portrait of Chopin as a Surrogate Self-Portrait

### JOHN B. NICI

In Nathaniel Hawthorne's "The Artist of the Beautiful" a sensitive woman named Annie is spellbound by a hand-made mechanical butterfly. She asks the artist, Owen Warland, if what seems so real is alive or whether it is his creation. He responds, "Alive? Yes, Annie; it may be said to possess life, for it has absorbed my own being into itself."[1]

Eugène Delacroix's portrait of Fryderyk Chopin (1838, Louvre/Paris), perhaps the most famous portrait of a composer ever painted, is challenged for that honor only by the same painter's portrait of Niccolò Paganini (c. 1831, Phillips Collection/Washington, D.C.). Today it is considered the quintessential Romantic portrait, officially enthroned in nearly every edition of H. W. Janson's *History of Art*, in which the painting has been thought to embody the very essence of "Romantic agony."[2] In fact, few commentators can resist coupling the painting with the word *Romantic*[3] (Figure 2.1).

Introductory music texts are no less enthusiastic in enshrining the portrait as both an image of a famous composer and the embodiment of the essence of Romanticism.[4] Perhaps for that reason the painting has acquired the stature of being the official portrait of Chopin, even though a number of other portraits exist by less familiar artists, including the 1836 portrait by his one-time intended, Maria Wodzińska (National Museum/Warsaw), and a drawing by George Sand (Aurore Dudevant) (Music Division, New

Figure 2.1. Eugène Delacroix, *Frédéric Chopin*, 1838, oil on canvas. Louvre, Paris. Copyright Réunion des Musées Nationaux/Art Resource, New York.

York Public Library/Lincoln Center). There are photographs, too, including an especially memorable one taken shortly before Chopin's death by Louis-Auguste Bisson.[5]

Given the popularity of Delacroix's portrait, one would assume that it is a complete rendering of the artist's intentions, but this portrait is only a fragment of a much larger canvas that was to include Chopin and George Sand and was never completed. The composition the artist intended can perhaps be understood by examining a preliminary drawing now housed in the Louvre. Sand seems to be seated behind Chopin as he plays the piano (Figure 2.2).

Figure 2.2. Eugène Delacroix, *Chopin and Sand*, 1838, pen and ink sketch. Louvre, Paris. Copyright Réunion des Musées Nationaux/ Art Resource, New York.

The double portrait was begun sometime after George Sand introduced Delacroix to Chopin, although the circumstances behind the commissioning of the painting have never been ascertained, if indeed the painting were commissioned in the ordinary sense of the term. About all that is known is that a piano had to be borrowed from the firm of Pleyel so that the painting could be executed in Delacroix's studio[6] but, ironically, that piano never figured in any of the finished head fragments. Unfortunately the painting was never finished, nor was the incomplete painting given to Chopin. It remained in Delacroix's studio until the artist's death and afterward passed into the hands of the Dutilleux family. Subsequently the salable portions were cut away from the larger canvas and submitted to the art market.[7] The Chopin bust found its way into the Louvre, and the Sand is now in the Ordrupgaard Museum in Copenhagen.

The Sand portion of the painting is fascinating mostly because it does not function as a typical portrait but more as a counterpoint to Chopin. Depicted largely in shadow with more emphasis on emotion than image, the portrayal of Sand differs markedly from

Figure 2.3. Eugène Delacroix, *George Sand*, 1838, oil on canvas. Ordrupgaard Museum, Copenhagen.

most of Delacroix's other portraits, as well as nearly all early-nineteenth-century portraits. The full-faced and formal *Charles de Verninac* (1827, Sachs Collection/Paris) is more typical of Delacroix's portraits. Here we see Delacroix's and his subject's concern with showing as complete a visage as possible. In his rare full-length portraits, as in *Baron Schwiter* (1827, National Gallery/London), the figure is again nearly full-faced and rather static (Figure 2.7). But Sand is anything but static, as she reacts with passionate intensity to Chopin's playing. Her presence is less an individual portrait than a response to Chopin's genius. Swept away by a Chopin melody, she, with eyes virtually closed, is captivated by his playing. This is not the great nineteenth-century novelist but the impassioned companion of the great nineteenth-century composer (Figure 2.3).

The portrait of Chopin, a three-quarter pose and facing right, does not need the interaction of Sand to be complete. Indeed, the painting survives quite well as an independent work: perhaps this is why it is so often quoted out of context. Conventional wisdom seems to place it squarely in the tradition of Romantic portraiture. In fact, it is often viewed as a descendant of Antoine-Jean Gros's *Napoleon at Arcole*, a 1796 portrait depicting the then twenty-seven-year-old general leading his troops into battle in northern Italy[8] (Figure 2.4). The bravura brushwork visible in both the Gros and the Delacroix enhances its Romantic spirit. Both portraits capture their sitters as heroic individuals—dashing, young, and energetic. As leaders in their respective fields they are at once inspired and inspiring. When Delacroix came to paint Chopin, he may have had Gros's portrait in mind, but there is enough evidence to suggest that the connection between artist and subject was much deeper: that Chopin's image is a reflection of Delacroix himself.

## Delacroix's Representations of Himself

Delacroix was not one to shy away from representing himself in his paintings. A number of self-portraits exist including an 1837 *Self-Portrait* in the Louvre (Figure 2.5) and an 1821 *Self-Portrait as Hamlet* (Musée Delacroix/Paris), a character with whom Delacroix had a particular affinity. Delacroix, Hamlet, and Chopin all perceived themselves as exiles, even while at home.[9] The painter's "lifelong sympathy for spiritual loneliness"[10] is perhaps most pronounced in his representations of *Christ on the Cross* (1846, Walter's Art Gallery/Baltimore), *Tasso in a Madhouse* (c. 1830, Reinhart Collection/Winterthur), *Ovid in Exile among the Scythians* (1859, National Gallery/London), and *Michelangelo in his Studio* (1851, Musée Montpellier/Fabre).[11]

Delacroix's depiction of Tasso locked in the madhouse and the numerous references to the Renaissance poet in his journals suggest a sympathy for a fellow artist, whose patrons treated his psychotic illness in a cruel and unfeeling manner.[12] In the Michelan-

Figure 2.4. Antoine-Jean Gros, *Napoleon at Arcole*, 1796, oil on canvas. Versailles, France. Copyright Réunion des Musées Nationaux/Art Resource, New York.

gelo image a number of autobiographical elements occur. A heavy scarf, the type Delacroix wore because of his frequent throat ailments, is wrapped around Michelangelo's neck. The brooding gloom, consistent with Delacroix's Romantic vision of Michelangelo, suited his own manner. The useless sculpting tool lies at his feet in the manner of Dürer's vision of *Melancolia*, another favorite image of the Romantic era.

Figure 2.5. Eugène Delacroix, *Self-Portrait*, 1837, oil on canvas.
Louvre, Paris. Copyright Réunion des Musées Nationaux/Art
Resource, New York.

Contemporaries believed that Delacroix's most famous statement of self-portrayal is in *Liberty Leading the People* (Louvre/Paris),
the 1830 manifesto against the Bourbon rulers of France. The
painting is filled with allegory, from the bare-breasted figure of
Liberty to the street child armed with two pistols. To the left of
center is a man with a black plug hat and a sawed-off musket.
According to early observers, this is Delacroix himself, aligned with
the forces of Louis Philippe in the movement to establish the self-
styled "Citizen King." Such a placement of the artist in a group
scene is a time-honored tradition. Indeed, works as famous as
Raphael's *School of Athens* (1510–11, Vatican/Rome) and Velázquez's
*Las Meninas* (1656, Prado/Madrid) immediately spring to mind.

Figure 2.6. Eugène Delacroix, *Liberty Leading the People*, 1830, oil on canvas, Louvre, Paris. Copyright Réunion des Musées Nationaux/Art Resource, New York.

But what is striking about *Liberty Leading the People* is the artist's daring: his direct attempt to place himself at the forefront of a political movement (Figure 2.6).

Great political paintings only a generation earlier, such as Francisco de Goya's *Third of May 1808* (1814, Prado Museum/ Madrid) and Gros's *Napoleon in the Pest House of Jaffa* (1804, Louvre/Paris), are conspicuously without the artist's presence. While we know that Goya's sympathies were with the Spanish and that Gros enjoyed enhancing the Napoleonic myth, neither artist puts himself directly into the action, either physically or allegorically. In *Liberty Leading the People*, one does not get the sense that the painting depicts an actual event but rather the combined sympathies of the revolutionaries and the ideas they fought for. Some of the details of the fallen soldier's uniforms and the traces of Notre Dame in the distance lend themselves to placing the action in a certain place and time, but Delacroix reaches beyond actuality into an allegorical space in which he has emotionally placed himself. Some experts have challenged the attribution of this self-portrait, providing alternate Frenchmen as possible heroes.[13] However, as we shall see, the fact that the figure looks like Delacroix, even if it is not the artist himself, turns out to be significant for understanding his image of Chopin.

Late-eighteenth and early-nineteenth-century painting fostered the depiction of the artist as a tortured, Romantic soul. In this tradition artists portrayed themselves as misunderstood and fiery individuals, whose art drove them to an inexplicable passion for their work. This consuming fire is seen in Francisco de Goya's *Self-Portrait* of 1815 (Prado/Madrid), Jean-Dominique Ingres's portrait of the sculptor *Paul Lemoyne* of c. 1819 (Nelson-Atkins Gallery/Kansas City), and, most convincingly, in Jacques-Louis David's *Self-Portrait* of 1794 (Louvre/Paris). In the latter we see a tempest-tossed painter, his hair flying about, evincing a self-absorbed and penetrating stare. David signed his painting "David in Vinculis," an allusion to his political incarceration during the French Revolution, as well as his artistic isolation—outside his jail, rival painters were setting up a guillotine for his anticipated execution.[14] In comparison with his agonized and incisive self-portrait, how coolly David painted images of Napoleon! Though this tradition is by no means universal in this period—Ingres's imperturbable and official-looking *Portrait of Paganini* (1819, Louvre/Paris) and Benjamin West's *Self-Portrait* of c. 1770 (National Gallery/Washington, D.C.) show more worldly success than passion—Delacroix, when choosing a mode of expression for Chopin and for himself, opted for capturing the emotion rather than the sophisticated success.

## Delacroix and Chopin: Friendship and Affinities

Despite the stereotype of the impetuous Romantic, neither Delacroix nor Chopin indulged in public displays of extreme emotion. Dry and reserved, Delacroix saw high society as a necessary evil. Although he did not seek to become the darling of the social world, nor did he count influential people among his intimates, he understood and respected the power of those in charge of official commissions, to whom he was polite, decorous, and diplomatic; on matters of passion, he allowed his work to speak for him. Charles Baudelaire's oft-quoted remark summed him up aptly: "A volcanic crater artistically concealed beneath a bouquet of flowers."[15] Similarly Robert Schumann captured the spirit of Chopin's music by declaring, "Chopin's pieces are like guns buried in flowers."[16]

Certainly Delacroix had a profound interest in Chopin. For

with Chopin he was in the presence of a genius at least equal to his own; this formed the basis for much of their relationship. At the time of Chopin's portrait, 1838, Delacroix was a highly successful artist who exhibited in many of the Salons of Paris. Twelve years older than Chopin, he was about to form a lasting friendship with this up-and-coming composer and music master, who, although already well known to the Parisian musical circles and high society, only recently received official recognition by giving a concert for Louis Philippe. Chopin still had much of his great music ahead of him.

Delacroix's interest in music stems from his childhood, when he trained as a violinist. Throughout his life he continued to develop this interest, leaving behind hundreds of journal pages and hundreds of letters assessing the entire Parisian musical scene. He knew Rossini, Cherubini, and Meyerbeer personally. His artistic affinity with Berlioz would seem natural, given both men's political inclinations: Delacroix's *Greece Expiring on the Ruins of Missolonghi* (1826, Musée des Beaux-Arts/Bordeaux) and Berlioz's *Les Troyens* were both inspired by the Greek war for independence. Rare was the opera opening in Paris that Delacroix missed. In fact, in a 1998–99 exhibition of Delacroix's work in the Philadelphia Museum of Art, the museum took the opportunity to issue a compact disc that catalogued Delacroix's musical interests.[17]

But no one inspired Delacroix as Chopin did. And Chopin, who was notoriously reluctant to discuss his music,[18] saw in Delacroix a knowledgeable understanding person who knew and truly understood great music:

> During the day, he talked music with me, and that gave him new animation. I asked him what establishes logic in music. He made me feel what counterpoint and harmony are; how the fugue is like pure logic in music, and that to know the fugue deeply is to be acquainted with the element of all reason and all consistency in music. I thought how happy I should have been to learn about all this—which is the despair of the common run of musicians. That feeling gave me an idea of the pleasure in science that is experienced by philosophers worthy of the name. The thing is that true science is not what is ordinarily understood under that term, that is to say, a department of knowledge which differs from art. No, science, looked upon in the way I mean, demonstrated by a man like Chopin, is art itself, and, obversely, art is no longer

what the vulgar think it to be, that is, some sort of inspiration which comes from nowhere, which proceeds by chance, and presents no more than the picturesque externals of things. It is reason itself, adorned by genius, but following a necessary course and encompassed by higher laws.[19]

One can only imagine that Delacroix's own interests in music were considerably heightened by his interaction with Chopin. When the composer wrote to a friend that Delacroix "adores Mozart—knows all his operas by heart,"[20] he was granting Delacroix the highest possible praise. In the days before recordings, Delacroix's breadth of musical knowledge was far-reaching. And if his tastes in music differ from the accepted orthodoxy of the early twenty-first century (for example, "All I have in my head is the harmonies of Cimarosa. What varied genius, supple, and elegant! Decidedly he is more dramatic than Mozart")[21] then his understanding at least comes from a well-schooled opinion and not one he arrived at capriciously.

Whereas understanding the basis for Delacroix's interest in Chopin is easily construed, it is somewhat more difficult to comprehend the interest Chopin had in Delacroix's work. Although an amateur artist, Chopin had little interest in discussing painting with Delacroix. In his voluminous surviving letters and journals, bare mention is made of Chopin's philosophy concerning Delacroix's painting. Indeed, little of Chopin's tastes in painting have come to light at all. All we know of the subject is gleaned from George Sand, who, years later in 1873, commented in *Impressions et souvenirs* that Chopin "has plenty of wit, subtlety, irony but he cannot understand painting or sculpture at all. Michelangelo frightens him, Rubens horrifies him."[22] Jean-Jacques Eigeldinger has commented that the presumed dislike Chopin had for art, and especially for the work of Delacroix, is not well documented and exists only in Sand's reference. He seems convinced that Delacroix was able to discuss and interpret his paintings with Chopin and proposes that Chopin's Prelude op. 45 is, in fact, an attempt to apply Delacroix's principles of color reflection to music.[23]

But even if Chopin detested Delacroix's work, the two had more than just music and art to sustain their relationship. Chopin seems to have admired the artistic dandyism that Delacroix encouraged. Delacroix's *Self-Portrait* of 1837 (Figure 2.5), reflecting his direct and magnetic stare, his aloofness, his artistic persona, confronts us forcefully, just as the actual Delacroix must have affected the considerably younger and more impressionable Chopin.

Their common interest in fashion seems also to have bonded them. Delacroix's admiration for clothes, tailors, and fabrics found its match in Chopin. Friends often joked that the two men were brought together because of their love of clothes.[24] Fashion was a lifelong preoccupation with Delacroix. Unfailingly he painted his sitters, who rarely paid him, in dapper and fashionable clothes. Baron Schwiter, for example, is rendered with great attention to detail (Figure 2.7). Everything matches, from the black bows on the shoes to the double-breasted, high-collared jacket. His vest is neatly parted at the bottom, with just one button undone. Charles de Verninac, painted in the same year (1827), is wearing a similar outfit, with some color changes for variation.

In addition to their common interests, both men had similar lifestyles, including the fact that both were plagued by poor health their whole lives. At times they spirited themselves away to sunnier climates to aid their recuperation, as was the tradition in the nineteenth century. On occasion they even vacationed together. For Delacroix, it was lingering fevers. In looking over his chronology it is hard to find a year in which some illness does not afflict him. At age twenty-four, in the journal entry of 22 October 1822, he complained, "I am nearly always ill; I cannot speak for a long time."[25] In 1842 an attack of laryngitis, probably tubercular, seriously crippled him and lingered hauntingly through the rest of his life. Strangely Delacroix found his illness a stimulant to work, although severe bouts would keep him idle months at a time.

Chopin, too, was no stranger to illness. In 1835, while passing through Heidelberg, Chopin had a major bronchial attack so severe that reports of his death were circulated and later printed in the Warsaw press.[26] His health, in all probability, played a great role in the decision by his betrothed's family to cancel his engagement to Maria Wodzińska. Nearly every year after that, especially in winter, Chopin had serious bouts of bronchitis and consumption, until his health finally collapsed in 1849. One of the chief mourners at Chopin's funeral was Delacroix, who appeared hatless, following the coffin all the way to the cemetery. The night after the burial, according to tradition, Delacroix was moved to sketch Chopin in the guise of the great poet Dante, who is the unofficial poet of the hereafter and the poet who inspired so much of Delacroix's own work[27] (Figure 2.8).

Figure 2.7. Eugène Delacroix, *Baron Schwiter*, 1827, oil on canvas. Copyright National Gallery, London.

In light of these many similarities in Chopin's and Delacroix's experiences, tastes, interests, and artistic paths, as well as Delacroix's established tradition of identifying himself with his heroes, it is compelling to see Delacroix's portrait of Chopin in the context of the Romantic aesthetics of transference. Parallels with literature from this period provide an illuminating counterpoint.

Figure 2.8. Eugène Delacroix, *Chopin as Dante*, 1849, pen and ink sketch. Musée Eugène Delacroix, Paris. Copyright Réunion des Musées Nationaux/Art Resource, New York.

## *The Romantic Transference in Literature and Painting*

Romantic biography, as never before, stressed the affinity the subject had with the author. Eighteenth-century biographies—for example, Boswell's *Life of Johnson*—contain numerous insights and discoveries that only an intimate could render. But at the same time Boswell does not put himself on the same plane as Johnson, nor does he attempt to see himself in Johnson's reflection. With the advent of influential works, however, such as Goethe's *Dichtung und Wahrheit*, the hermeneutics shifts to representation of the self and the reflection of the self in others. This trend, particularly in Romantic autobiography, achieves an apotheosis of selfhood, as, say, in Jean-Jacques Rousseau's *Confessions* and Adam Oehlenschläger's *Ungdomserindringer.*[28] This is not to say that Romantic authors were unfaithful to their subjects or modified their subject's lives to fit a prearranged ideology; it is to suggest that their choice of subject, as well as the subtle highlighting of selected events, casts their subject in a favorable philosophical light.

So-called transcendental biographies by Thomas Carlyle and Ralph Waldo Emerson fall into this category. Kenneth Marc Harris has noted that "Carlyle always strove for identification with his subject, and the greater his sympathy, the more completely he tried to merge himself with his hero."[29]

The most relevant example of Romantic transference in biography is the attempt by Honoré de Balzac to fictionalize the life of Delacroix in the 1847 novel *The Black Sheep*. Balzac had a passing acquaintance with Delacroix but saw in him a series of parallel autobiographical convictions: as the injured innocent, the isolated gloomy genius, and the artist convinced of his own greatness.[30] Through an elaborate working of this complex novel Balzac achieves a fictional narrative that is both a biography and a portrait of its author.[31] In light of literary and philosophical research, art historians are now beginning to speak about the connection between sitter and subject in the late eighteenth and early nineteenth centuries.[32] This approach provides a persuasive interpretation of the figure of the partisan in *Liberty Leading the People:* if it is Delacroix, then he has taken up the Romantic cause to react against oppression; if it is someone else, it is someone who so resembles the artist that one could be mistaken for the other. This vicarious placement of a look-alike in Delacroix's place gives the artist a chance to express his political vision through a surrogate.

Understandably Delacroix's varied approaches to his sitters stemmed from his feelings for them. We know that Baron Schwiter (Figure 2.7) was Delacroix's childhood friend[33] and mention is made in Delacroix's journals that Schwiter was an amateur painter who discussed painting on an equal footing with Delacroix.[34] Schwiter had even been named one of the executors of Delacroix's will. Yet for all this intimacy, the portrait is filled with reserve. Schwiter's gaze is an unnerving tentative glance. Here Delacroix, instead of identifying with Baron Schwiter, is portraying the sitter's nature as independent from the artist's.

The same is true of Charles de Verninac (c. 1826, Arthur Sachs Collection/Paris), who was Delacroix's nephew. This portrait is sensitive and sentimental, but the sitter is neither emotionally charged nor possessed by a creative spirit. In his paintings of both Baron Schwiter and Charles de Verninac, Delacroix sets himself apart.

How different his portrait of Chopin! The emotional turmoil Delacroix has captured in the painting makes it an apt companion not to any of Delacroix's other portraits but to his own *Self-Portrait*. Everything about these two paintings suggests a similar approach: from the matching but plain backgrounds, which focus our attention on Delacroix and Chopin, to the visible and animated brushwork, which makes these sitters appear spontaneous and yet solid. Even though these works are on a small scale, the forms are rendered in such a way as to make the subjects seem monumental. This monumentality reinforces their position as cultural heroes whose accomplishments match their depicted dignity and stature. Both paintings are done in earthy, subdued color tones that negate the fashion-plate image each man publicly garnered throughout his life.

The mutual personal and professional respect these men had for each other is mirrored in the similarities in these paintings: their love of music, their sense of exile, their coping with persistent illnesses, and their reluctance to face the public. Therefore it should come as no surprise that both portraits are alike in their execution, artistic fervor, and emotional sensibility. In his portrait of Chopin, Delacroix has depicted a surrogate self-portrait: his identification with his subject is so complete that he has rendered Chopin with the same "Romantic agony" he reserved exclusively for himself.

### NOTES

I am indebted to Halina Goldberg for the opportunity to present this paper, and Carol Lewine for the much needed advice on its execution and delivery. Joseph Canzoneri, my "surrogate self-portrait," worked on the manuscript diligently for me. And to all things, I thank my wife, Judy Nici, for her long-suffering forbearance in projects like this.

1. Nathaniel Hawthorne, "The Artist of the Beautiful," in *The Portable Hawthorne*, revised and expanded by Malcolm Cowley (New York: Viking, 1969), 237.

2. H. W. Janson, *History of Art*, 4th ed. (New York: Abrams, 1991; Englewood Cliffs, N.J.: Prentice Hall, 1991), 636.

3. Lawrence Cunningham refers to Chopin's life as being "almost too Romantic to be true" (Lawrence Cunningham and John Reich, *Culture and Values*, 4th ed. [New York: Harcourt Brace, 1998], 433).

4. The painting appears as the sole illustration of Chopin in three basic music texts: Martin Bernstein and Martin Picker, *An Introduction to Music*, 4th ed. (Englewood Cliffs, N.J.: Prentice Hall, 1972), 388; Roger Kamien, *Music: An Appreciation*, 5th ed. (New York: McGraw-Hill, 1992), 326; and Joseph Machlis and Kristine Forney, *The Enjoyment of Music*, 6th ed. (New York: Norton, 1990), 307.

5. Bisson, a distinguished photographer who learned the process of daguerre-otype from its inventor, rendered Chopin as a man who now appears physically and mentally exhausted and near the end (1849, Chopin Society/Warsaw). This is entirely different than Delacroix's painting.

6. Ruth Jordan, *Nocturne: A Life of Chopin* (New York: Taplinger, 1978), 192.

7. Alfred Robaut and Ernest Chesneau, *L'Œuvre complet de Eugène Delacroix* (Paris: Charavay Frères, 1885), 180.

8. H. W. Janson, *A Basic History of Art* (New York: Abrams, 1971; Englewood Cliffs, N.J.: Prentice Hall, 1971), 286.

9. See the essay by Bożena Shalcross in this volume.

10. David Gervais, "Delacroix's Hamlet," *The Cambridge Quarterly* 13, no. 1 (1984): 45.

11. Ibid.

12. William Conger, John E. Gedo, and Mary Mathews Gedo, "Autobiography, Biography, Fiction: A Symposium," in *Psychoanalytic Studies of Biography* (Madison, Wis.: International Universities Press, 1987), 387.

13. Lee Johnson, *The Paintings of Eugène Delacroix: A Critical Catalogue* (Oxford: Clarendon, 1981), 148.

14. Kenneth Clark, *The Romantic Rebellion* (New York: Harper and Row, 1973), 32.

15. Charles Baudelaire, "Curiosités esthétiques," in *Œuvres complètes de Charles Baudelaire* (Paris: Michel Lévy, 1868), 860.

16. Robert Schumann, 1836 review of Chopin's newly published Concertos in *Neue Zeitschrift für Musik*.

17. *Music, Romanticism, and Delacroix*, Philadelphia Museum of Art, 1998.

18. Jordan, *Nocturne*, 192.

19. *The Journal of Eugène Delacroix*, trans. Walter Pach (New York: Grove, 1961), 194–95, journal entry for 7 April 1849.

20. Jean-Jacques Eigeldinger, "Placing Chopin: Reflections on a Compositional Aesthetic," in *Chopin Studies 2*, ed. John Rink and Jim Samson (Cambridge: Cambridge University Press, 1994), 122.

21. *The Journal of Eugène Delacroix*, 165, journal entry for 5 May 1847.

22. Jordan, *Nocturne*, 193.

23. Jean-Jacques Eigeldinger, "Chopin and 'la note bleue': An Interpretation of the Prelude op. 45," *Music & Letters* 78 (1997): 233–58.

24. Jordan, *Nocturne*, 192.

25. *The Journal of Eugène Delacroix*, 43, journal entry for 22 October 1822.

26. Jim Samson, *Chopin* (New York: Schirmer, 1996), 131.

27. Although there is no documentary proof of this assertion, it has been inspired by the fact that Delacroix inscribed the Louvre portrait of Dante/Chopin with the words "cher Chopin." In the years 1840–46 Delacroix was working on a monumental series of frescoes in the Luxembourg Palace in Paris. Some critics suggest that, in Delacroix's epic *Parnassus*, the figures of Virgil and Homer distinctly resemble Chopin and Delacroix. Others, with more foundation, see the figure of Dante in the cupola of the Luxembourg as a portrait of Chopin, and the passionately etched sketch as a preparatory study (Frank Anderson Trapp, *The Attainment of Delacroix* (Baltimore, Md.: The Johns Hopkins University Press, 1971), 280–81.

28. Helene Hørup, "Romantic Self-Representation and Aesthetics in Adam Oehlenschläger's *Ungdomserindringer*," *Scandinavian Studies* 74, no. 4 (winter 2000): 435.

29. Kenneth Marc Harris, *Transcendental Biography: Carlyle and Emerson,*

*Studies in Biography* (Cambridge, Mass.: Harvard University Press, 1978), 101. Emerson's *Memoirs of Margaret Fuller Ossoli* is another illustration of this genre.

30. Conger, Gedo, and Gedo, "Autobiography, Biography, Fiction," 397, 398.

31. Ibid., 397.

32. John Singleton Copley's portrait of *Paul Revere* has already been called a surrogate self-portrait (Susan Rather, "Carpenter, Tailor, Shoemaker, Artist: Copley and Portrait Painting around 1770," *Art Bulletin* 79, no. 2 [June 1997]: 289).

33. Rene Huyghe, *Delacroix* (New York: Abrams, 1963), 415.

34. *The Journal of Eugène Delacroix*, 482, journal entry for 31 August 1855.

# 3

## The Monument of Fryderyk Chopin by Wacław Szymanowski: Concepts and Reality

WALDEMAR OKOŃ

Musik: Atem der Statuen. Vielleicht:
Stille der Bilder. Du Sprache wo Sprachen
enden. Du Zeit,
die senkrecht steht auf der Richtung
vergehender Herzen.[1]
—R. M. Rilke

In a poem written toward the end of World War I entitled "Music," Rainer Maria Rilke compares the art so dear to Chopin to the "breath of statues" and the "silence of paintings," to "language in which everything becomes silence," to "time in which hearts, moved by music, disappear." In this poem, which provides the central theme of this essay, man is overwhelmed by music, but, at the same time, music emerges as a power whose source derives from man's most hidden, subconscious essence. This energy both surrounds us and becomes our inner self, this mysterious "other side of the air" in which, according to the poet, "we cannot dwell."

The artistic concept and atmosphere of Rilke's poem closely resemble those evoked by another work, the Warsaw monument of Fryderyk Chopin sculpted by Wacław Szymanowski. This monument attests to the sculptor's attempt to achieve the impossible, since the essence of music cannot be rendered in words. We cannot carve both the figure of the artist and his work, assuming that the "breath of statues" can be given a tangible fin de siècle form, while the "silence of paintings" and the "audible landscapes" of Rilke's poems appear in a dynamic but calm, almost classical shape.

Let us leave the heights of poetry for now and proceed with a brief account of the monument's history.[2] The idea of commemorating the most distinguished Polish composer with a monumental sculpture had already been proposed by the Warsaw Music Society in 1876. However, a ban issued by the tsar allowed only for a marble plaque by Leander Marconi, unveiled in 1882, to be set in one of the pillars of the Holy Cross Church in Warsaw, marking the place where Chopin's heart was laid. The Founding Committee for Chopin's Monument [*Komitet Budowy Pomnika Chopina*] was established in 1901, with Count Aleksander Dienheim-Szczawiński-Brochocki as its first chairman. Over the twenty-two years that the committee was in place, its makeup changed several times as it faced numerous financial problems as well as obstacles posed by censorship. After Count Brochocki's death in 1907, Count Maurycy Zamoyski was elected chairman.

The Russian imperial authorities originally selected Warecki Square for the location of the monument. Despite the various controversies concerning space limitations and the proximity of high buildings, as well as protests from both the committee and artists, it was this site that was proposed for the 1908 publicized competition to determine the design of Chopin's monument. Sixty-six designs were entered in the competition. Extensive commentaries that included photographs of the awarded works were published in the current press, as were articles touting the artistic accomplishments of the foreign jurors—the French sculptors Albert Bartholome and Antoine Bourdell. One journalist wrote: "The 15th of May will become a great day in the history of Polish sculpture. The competition for Chopin's monument has become a great manifestation of our national art, a cheer to celebrate our national genius."[3]

Wacław Szymanowski had contemplated the concept of such a monument much earlier, in 1902, six years before the competition was advertised. In one of his letters to the famous Polish painter Teodor Axentowicz he wrote:

> You wonder whether it would not be right to entrust Rodin with the task of Chopin's monument. The answer is simple. Still, I prefer to answer with a question. Would you be content if an-

other painter, even the greatest, was entrusted with a job you
would be able to accomplish? You demand inhuman sacrifice
from me and as I am frank and feel myself to be an artist so I
answer what I think . . . anyway, I am working on a design of
Chopin's monument and the concept, I guarantee you, is new.[4]

Szymanowski's first sketches date back to 1903, and, in 1904,
he created a 1:8 model in plaster (84 × 82 × 57.5 cm). The artist
presented his model in 1905 at the third exhibition of the society
"Art" in Kraków. In 1909, at almost the last minute, he entered his
work, already known to art critics, in the official contest. Later the
sculptor wrote: "I sent my design without any hope for a favorable
verdict, as I believed that its original form would become an in-
surmountable impediment."[5] Contrary to his expectations, on 15
May 1909 the jury unanimously awarded Szymanowski first prize,
emphasizing his project's formal merits, originality of design, and
stylistic homogeneity. The first design included an architectonic
concept of the surroundings by Franciszek Mączyński. The monument was to be situated by a pool of water, with two huge fin de
siècle frogs perched on the edge. The inclusion of the frogs was
controversial from the very beginning, with members of the jury
advising their removal.

　　Not everyone, of course, welcomed the outcome of the contest.
The well-known Polish critic of art and literature Antoni Sygietyński, a musicologist who praised naturalism in art, wrote bluntly:

> The public, somehow inspired by the Warsaw press, eager to
> celebrate the hundredth anniversary of Chopin's birth, has grad-
> ually and silently agreed on a monument designed several years
> ago by Wacław Szymanowski. And it must be added that this
> monument wants poetry, artistic merit and the grandeur expected
> from monumental art. It is some affectionate novelette light-
> heartedly cast in plaster . . . a novelette worthy of an enamored
> devil in a split willow and not Chopin, the subtlest musical ge-
> nius. The rendering is entirely non-monumental and fails in
> sculptural terms, not to mention those frogs on the edge of the
> pool ridiculing, by their mere presence, not only the whole con-
> cept but also the very figure of Chopin, a figure so poorly
> sketched and badly posed that it is unclear how it is seated and
> on what.[6]

Prior to its execution, the chosen design had to be accepted by
the Imperial Academy of Fine Arts in St. Petersburg. Here it en-

countered numerous obstacles of both artistic and ideological nature. But through Szymanowski's tenacity and the power of favoritism (which, in the Russian Empire, opened all doors), Tsar Nicholas II granted his permission for the sculpture's realization, overriding the strong objections voiced by the Academy. On 14 May 1914 a contract for the execution of a bronze cast was signed with Fulda, a Parisian foundry. Unfortunately shortly thereafter, on 1 August 1914, World War I erupted. The full-scale model of the monument was divided into two parts: one stayed in Kraków, while the other, which was sent to France, was believed to have been irretrievably lost. Fulda went bankrupt, and the fin de siècle design itself, having already had numerous enemies since its inception, became—according to Hanna Kotkowska-Bareja—"outdated" in 1918.[7]

After the war half of the monument was found in a shed in Kraków; the fate of the part left in France remained unknown. By 1923 the Founding Committee no longer existed, and, were it not for the persistent efforts and determination of Szymanowski himself, the final realization of the monument might never have been accomplished. As a result of his and his supporters' perseverance, a second Founding Committee for the creation of Chopin's monument was established. In June 1926 a bronze cast, based on the two joined parts of the model that Szymanowski had created before the war, was finally made at Barbedienne in Paris. Apparently both parts of the model, the one deemed lost in France and the one in Poland, miraculously survived the war. After numerous disputes it was decided that the monument would be located in a former orchard, in a part of Łazienki next to Belweder.[8] The pedestal of the monument was lowered, and the original granite was replaced by red sandstone. The unveiling of the monument was set for 14 November 1926, a date chosen deliberately as it marked the twenty-fifth anniversary of the Warsaw Philharmonic. The unveiling ceremony lasted more than two hours and was celebrated with grandeur. As the well-known critic and expert on sculpture Jan Kleczyński wrote on that day in *Kurier warszawski*

> It is only in the proper monumental size that the artist's concept can be fully appreciated. It was a thing conceived in large scale from the very beginning. Warsaw has received a wonderful decoration; Chopin, a permanent sign of his genius; and the whole nation has been granted an exceptional work of art praising the name of Poland and [the monument's] creator.[9]

Neither the participants of this jubilant event nor Wacław Szymanowski, who died in 1930, could at this moment foresee the
tragic and unusual fate of his most outstanding work.

Following the outbreak of World War II the German authorities in occupied Poland censured Chopin's music. The name of
Chopin was removed from repertoires, German musical publications, and radio programs. Musical scores already published were
withdrawn from sale. Monuments commemorating the composer
were destroyed: the first to suffer, in October 1939, was the monument in Poznań, sculpted by Marcin Rożek. The wooden model
of Szymanowski's monument, called the "Chopin Group," which
the artist had offered to the Museum of Greater Poland in 1920,
was chopped up; only the head survived. The monument in
Łazienki was destroyed in 1940. *Polska żyje*, the publication of the
Polish resistance movement, wrote: "The destruction of monuments began with Chopin's . . . which was blown up on May 31,
cut into pieces, and removed. The terrifying list keeps growing."[10]

After World War II ended the artist's sons recovered a tiny
model of the monument, cast in Bastianelli's workshop in Rome in
1923, which had survived in the ruined basement of Szymanowski's house in Mokotów, Warsaw. This model, as well as other
remaining parts of the monument, provided the basis for its re-
construction. First modeled in clay, it was then cast in bronze by
a Warsaw cooperative, Decorative Bronze [*Brąz dekoracyjny*], in
early 1958. The monument was unveiled once again on 11 May
1958 and has now been standing for more than forty years in the
place its creator originally envisaged. The work's continued existence seems to affirm the decision of the 1909 jury whose verdict
professed that "Szymanowski's idea appeals by its simplicity, im-
pressive monumental quality, and exceptionally good concept. In
the movement of its body and head, the figure of Chopin homo-
geneously expresses an immersion in music and atmosphere"[11]
(Figure 3.1).

Several years after the jury's decision was made public, in a
short story entitled "The Stone Guest" and published in 1913, a
former opponent and critic of Szymanowski raised the problem of
monumental art once again. This time Sygietyński uses the hero,
a sculptor, as his spokesman articulating the doubts:

> How to sculpt Chopin's monument? . . . One figure? That is not
> enough to satisfy our dilettante sense of art. . . . A group of fig-

Figure 3.1. Wacław Szymanowski, Monument of Fryderyk Chopin, Łazienki, Warsaw. Photographed by the author.

ures? This is already baroque and abuses the sense of grand style in sculpture . . . perhaps Chopin's figure? A figure? Chopin suits a caricature better than a statue. The case is lost. The Muse? Yes and no. . . . More of a symbol—but of which Chopin? The patron of angelic-idyllic poets or of romantic spinsters . . . Chopin's muse! Yes, it is the power of spirit cast in bronze harmony or rather spellbound in a bronze form of harmony . . . the fluid melodic line supported by colorful harmony still fails to grasp the whole of Chopin.[12]

I quote these fragments from Sygietyński to underscore the range of expectations expressed by contemporary critics and by artists themselves. They cherished the belief voiced earlier by the famous sculptor David d'Angers: "The idea is the criterion of genius. The idea itself, even without a strict form, means much. However, form without an idea means nothing."[13] This attitude rendered monumental sculpture impossible throughout the nineteenth century and continued through the fin de siècle era. Art never had the slightest chance of rendering the greatness of the idea it was expected to represent; it drifted, inevitably, toward eclectic allegory or anecdote that undermined the "noble simplicity and quiet greatness" it was to achieve. An acute disparity between the humble means of expression sculpture had at its disposal and the gravity of tasks it was expected to face emerges both from discussions on monumental art and the outcome of competitions advertised in this field. The results were perceived as not being fully successful: in the eyes of critics, the absolute idea surpassed art, which was tainted by its material being as well as by the quality of the very material used.[14] Just as it was impossible to sculpt the greatness of the poetry of either Adam Mickiewicz or Juliusz Słowacki, it was impossible to render Chopin's music or the feelings related to this music in sculptural terms. This stemmed from the fact that sculpture, at that time, was a concrete art, immersed in a highly realistic model of representation, and most efforts aimed at its liberation failed. Sculptors remained unable to render abstract rhythm, harmony, melody, or counterpoint, and, at their best, they presented the artist surrounded by allegories whose function was to explain his greatness to the viewers. They could also provide a portrait-like, stylized modernistic figure as an embodiment of the work itself. This option was used for "Mickiewicz" by Antoine Bourdell, Auguste Rodin's "Balzac,"[15] and also for Szymanowski's "Chopin," where the old allegorical model (the willow as a symbol of Polishness) is blended with the symbolic rendering of Chopin listening to the wind in the willow (Figure 3.1). Thus, figuratively, it shows the indebtedness of national art to local nature, as some contemporaries have noted:

> Over the figure of Chopin, whose face shows some painful longing and creative immersion in music while his hand listlessly follows the rhythm, the wind whispers in the bough of a Polish willow bringing the melody of the artist's native fields, a thread he will follow to weave the charm of his songs.[16]

Figure 3.2. Wacław Szymanowski, Monument of Fryderyk Chopin, Łazienki, Warsaw. Photographed by the author.

Szymanowski was the sculptor of an earlier, academically "correct" monument to another bard of Polish art, Artur Grottger, and of the *Improvisation of Mickiewicz,* Rodinesque in style, which he completed in 1898. In the Chopin sculpture he tried to depart from accepted conventions by introducing a form both static (the figure of Chopin) and dynamic, or fluid—the tree "bending" over the artist. Consulting contemporary and earlier symbols associated with this image provides additional dimensions to this interpretation. Already in the ancient world of symbols the tree was the most excellent product of vegetation; the willow, in particular, being among the first to develop leaves in the spring, became the symbol of renewed life. Similarly the belief in a special relationship between man and tree is ages old, relating to the possibility of transferring the forces of nature from one living creature onto another. The shape of Szymanowski's willow is reminiscent of a hand extended over the composer, and, indeed, since antiquity the hand has been associated with divine power or the creative forces of nature: for instance, for Rodin, one of Szymanowski's masters, hands become a "Cathedral" sheltering what is sacred.[17] In Chopin's monument, the hand-shaped willow is a fragment of the familiar landscape, almost a home in whose shadow the artist can feel safe, protected against a foreign world. The willow and Chopin's figure form the outline of a harp and thus suggest the creation of music—music of the harp symbolizing joy, gratitude, and adoration. This motif also alludes to the Bible where people are compared to harps, the instruments of God who remains the greatest among composers.

The sculpture is placed by a man-made lake, which was executed especially for this project (Figure 3.2). The doubling of the image produces an impressionistic dizzying effect. It has been said that, depending on the light, weather, and season, the setting produces an additional quality:

> The mirror-like surface of the pond creates a picture within a picture and becomes a central point of reference. Those luring "eyes of the earth," the legates of earth's mystery, bestowed the landscape frame with a deeper, symbolic dimension.[18]

The search for symbols in the organic world led Szymanowski to the idea of the frogs perched at the edge of the lake; they were ultimately removed from the design. Frogs belonged to the favorite motifs of fin de siècle ornamentation and decorative art. More significantly, their presence was associated with water, the familiar landscape, and evening concerts. Further, the frog awaking from the winter sleep in mud expresses the idea of eternal life and resurrection. One can argue that such an analysis constitutes over-interpretation. Still, considering our knowledge of other works by the same sculptor and his predilection for symbols and national historiosophy,[19] we can assume that, in the work devoted to Chopin and his music, these elements applied in a very precise way, as a homogeneous symbolic language focusing, on the one hand, on the idea of eternal duration and continuity of life (including the life of the nation) but, on the other hand, on the local and national character of the work of the greatest Polish Romantic composer.

There was yet another requirement which a monument, devoted to the composer of polonaises and mazurkas, was obliged to meet: the artistic expression had to correspond to the biography of the musical genius, already heavily mythologized in the time of Szymanowski. The rhetoric of the work and its potential readings were to be analogous to the rhetoric of Chopin's music itself, or at least of the well-established images of the artist and his importance for Polish culture.

> Blessed be the generation from whose womb he was born; blessed be the earth which lulled him with its songs, nourished with its

bread and, having added a new gift to these, offered him to the people! Rich are the lands around the Vistula River if such be their fruit; full of life are the people, their prophets lead those of other nations towards the great . . . knowledge of the future. And these are the best riches! Everyone can use them; and they will grow like the wine at the wedding in the town of Cana, in Galilee; they will multiply like the five loaves in the desert. Since the times of the Piast it is not the first miracle for Polish affluence and, God speed, not the last one.[20]

This quotation comes from the 1849 article "Wspomnienie Chopina" ["A Recollection of Chopin"] by Józef Sikorski, and was used as a motto in Ferdynand Hoesick's monumental biography of Chopin, contemporary with Szymanowski's monument.[21] Comments of this type abound in nineteenth- and twentieth-century writings.[22] Such a nationalist reception of the artist was further intertwined with the dominating romanticized view of the composer and his music as being ethereal and otherworldly. Hence the difficulties in sculpting the monument of that "Aeolian harp," the "Ariel of the piano," and the necessity of transgressing the limits imposed by traditional nineteenth-century monumental art. In this respect Rodin's inspiration was particularly important. However, such experiments can also be found in earlier Polish sculpture, most notably Antoni Kurzawa's *Mickiewicz Awaking the Genius of Poetry* (1889–90), Bolesław Biegas's *Chopin's Funeral March* (1902), and Szymanowski's already mentioned *Improvisation of Mickiewicz* (1898).[23]

A related set of interpretations of Szymanowski's work is best articulated in the words of Charles Baudelaire from his famous 1861 article, "Richard Wagner et Tannhäuser à Paris":

> Things have always been expressed in terms of analogies since the day God created the world as a single, complex but indivisible whole, and therefore it would be most surprising, indeed, if the timbre of music was unable to suggest color, if the colors were unable to bring a melody to mind, and if sound and color were incapable of expressing thoughts.[24]

In its sense of "multiplicity in unity," monumental character, and a clear transgression of the properties of sculptural material—which were imposed on contemporary art at that time a priori—Szymanowski's work belongs to the few successful realizations of the Wagnerian idea of a *Gesamtkunstwerk* of that period, a human response to the unity of the world created by God.

On 25 March 1902 Max Klinger completed a statue of Bee-thoven; this work, unlike other works by Klinger, immediately stirred emotions. When the sculpture was displayed at the Four-teenth Fin de Siècle Exhibition in Vienna, it became a peculiar manifestation of the theory of a "total work": the architectonic background for the sculpture was designed by Joseff Hoffman, the frescos were executed by well-known fin de siècle painters, such as Gustav Klimt, and Beethoven's Ninth Symphony was directed by Gustav Mahler. The press wrote: "Never has there been sensed such a solemn atmosphere, the public experienced an almost reli-gious spiritual stimulation, art was perceived as the world power of life."[25] In his work Klinger inscribed a complex system of mean-ing related not only to Beethoven's music but also to a more gen-eral reflection on both spiritual and material sources of artistic cre-ativity.[26] But let us consider the statue of the composer separately.

Beethoven appears as one of the Olympian gods seated on a broad throne, his naked body covered only by a robe draped on his knees. The composer's head, with its characteristic, recogniza-ble features, was formed on the basis of a mask made while he was still alive. Spiritual tension marks his face; the powerful internal life bears a resemblance to *Moses* by Michelangelo. It is the mys-terious energy, the illusory quietness, immediately preceding an explosion of creativity. The critics proclaimed, "This is the fore-father," and compared Beethoven to an embryo about to burst with new life and to a lion ready to attack.[27] In Beethoven's tight fist, one of the main accentuated points of the sculpture, Klinger con-tained the elemental expression of spiritual concentration and power. The composer's eyes are turned toward infinity, the first cause of all being. They constitute the "dominant" of the com-position, commanding the tight fist, and extending their control—through their determination—over the whole statue. The inhuman steadfastness and determination grow from a mystical depth, close to art. The sculptor of this monument believed that the composer was the "master of integrity and honesty who taught people how to live and die";[28] through those like him humanity rediscovered its revelation and redemption.

Although both sculptures were designed at about the same time, the concepts engendered by Beethoven's face and hand are quite distinct from those captured by Chopin's facial expression and the slightly sentimental gesture of his right hand, following music born in the familiar willow. Chopin, as rendered by Szymanowski, is neither a rebel nor a legislator of his created universe but rather an outstanding lyricist enchanted by nature, an embodiment of humbleness and faith in the poetry of the universe.

Rainer Maria Rilke, in sonnet 15 of the cycle entitled *Sonnets to Orpheus*, encourages the dancing lasses to "dance an orange." He writes:

> Tanzt die Orange. Die wärmere Landschaft,
> werft sie aus euch, dass die reife erstrahle
> in Lüften der Heimat! Erglühte, enthüllt
>
> Düfte um Düfte. Schafft die Verwandtschaft
> mit der reinen, sich weigernden Schale,
> mit dem Saft, der die Glückliche füllt![29]

I do not know whether the girls succeeded in dancing the orange. Perhaps the poet was too demanding. However, I am convinced that both Wacław Szymanowski and Max Klinger succeeded, in their monuments of Chopin and Beethoven, in grasping the essential internal quality of their music, what Rilke calls the "silence of paintings," the "breath of the monuments," the "audible landscape," and the "silenced speech."

NOTES

1. Music: breathing of statues. Perhaps:
   stillness of pictures. You speech, where speeches
   end. You time,
   vertically poised on the courses of vanishing hearts.
Trans. J. B. Leishman (London: Hogarth, 1957), 234.

2. An essential study on this subject is Hanna Kotkowska-Bareja, *Pomnik Chopina*, published in the Zabytki Warszawy series (Warszawa: Państwowe Wydawnictwo Naukowe, 1970). Another helpful source on the works of Wacław Szymanowski is the catalogue of an exhibition organized by the National Museum in Warsaw in June–July 1981: Hanna Kotkowska-Bareja, ed., *Wacław Szymanowski, 1859–1930* (Warszawa: Muzeum Narodowe w Warszawie, 1981) (henceforth referred to as *Catalogue*).

3. The journalist was Henryk Piątkowski, and his opinion was published in *Tygodnik ilustrowany*. After Kotkowska-Bareja, *Pomnik Chopina*, 18.

4. Kotkowska-Bareja, *Catalogue*, 16.

5. Kotkowska-Bareja, *Pomnik Chopina*, 13.

6. Ibid., 19.

7. Ibid., 33.

8. Warsaw's Łazienki Park is a complex of eighteenth-century buildings and gardens that originally were the residence of Poland's last king, Stanisław August; today a public park and museum buildings surround Belweder, the residence of the Polish president.

9. Kotkowska-Bareja, *Pomnik Chopina*, 43. Kleczyński was one of the most outstanding Polish experts on sculpture. On Kleczyński, see Andrzej Pietrzak, "Poglądy estetyczne Jana Kleczyńskiego," *Roczniki humanistyczne* 4:46 (Lublin, 1998). Extensive remarks on Kleczyński can be found in an essential study on Polish sculpture at the turn of the nineteenth century, namely, Piotr Szubert, *Rzeźba polska przełomu XIX i XX wieku* (Warszawa: Semper, 1995). The unveiling of the monument also provoked negative reactions. For example, Wacław Husarski commented on the monument in the influential periodical *Wiedza o Polsce* as follows: "Chopin's monument, a kind of fin de siècle ashtray enlarged to a monstrous size, was placed in the Ujazdowski Park in Warsaw to commemorate one of the worst moments in the history of art, a moment blending all the failures of impressionism with all the mistakes of the symbolic fin de siècle style" (quoted in Kotkowska-Bareja, *Pomnik Chopina*, 63).

10. Ibid., 50.

11. Ibid., 20.

12. Antoni Sygietyński, "Gość kamienny," *Sfinks* 4 (1913): 32–33.

13. David d'Angers (1788–1856) was a French sculptor most famous for his "Aux Grands Hommes La Patrie Reconnaissante," the pediment of the Parisian Panthéon (1831–37). I make more extensive comments on this dilemma when analyzing the sculptural rendering of the Polish king who ruled in the twelfth century, Bolesław the Brave. See Okoń, "Pomnik Bolesława Śmiałego w sztuce polskiej pierwszego dwudziestolecia XX wieku—interpretacje," in *Wtajemniczenia. Studia z dziejów sztuki XIX i XX wieku* (Wrocław: Wydawnictwo Uniwersytetu Wrocławskiego, 1996). Also see Szubert, *Rzeźba*.

14. Piotr Szubert, "Pomnik Adama Mickiewicza w Krakowie—idea i realizacje," in *Dzieła czy kicze*, ed. Elżbieta Grabska and Tadeusz Stefan Jaroszewski (Warszawa: Państwowe Wydawnictwo Naukowe, 1981). See also, by the same author, "Pomnik Adama Mickiewicza w Wilnie," Blok-Notes (Muzeum Literatury im. A. Mickiewicza, 1988).

15. Rodin's "Balzac" was made in the years 1891–98. The design of Bourdell's monument for Mickiewicz was ready in the spring of 1912, although, as a result of financial difficulties, it was only finally unveiled in 1929.

16. Stosław [A. Chłoniewski], "Z pracowni Wacława Szymanowskiego," *Świat* 13 (1907): 5. The tree under which Chopin is seated caused numerous controversies. Some believed "this design is poorly composed and makes the impression of something anti-artistic, especially the tree and the minor figures around the pool. . . . The tree in the sculpture is improper, even redundant if one considers that the monument is to be surrounded by plants" (Kotkowska-Bareja, *Pomnik Chopina*, 26). As the author of this book remarks, "the trunk of this strange botanical phenomenon created by Szymanowski for his own purpose is a trunk of an ordinary willow [*salix fragilis*] while the tree top was borrowed by the artist from a weeping willow [*salix alba*] because the trunks of the weeping willows are too thin and fragile" (ibid., 70). If I can add anything to this dispute, the willow in Chopin's monument is simply the Polish willow, synonymous with our native landscape.

17. Monique Laurent writes: "Rodin was fascinated by Gothic architecture. He believed that in the hands raised in prayer he discovered the source of pointed arch and therefore he called his work 'Cathedral.' The 'Cathedral' was completed in 1908" (Monique Laurent, *Rodin*, trans. Kazimiera Bielawska [Warszawa: Penta; Elpol, 1991], 138).

18. Petr Wittlich, *Secesja. Sztuka i życie,* trans. Andrzej Borowiecki (Warszawa: Wydawnictwa Artystyczne i Filmowe, 1987), 38–40. On the symbolic aspects of Chopin's monument, see, for example, Manfred Lurker, *Słownik obrazów i symboli biblijnych,* trans. Kazimierz Romaniuk (Poznań: Pallottinum, 1989); Dorothea Forstner, *Świat symboliki chrześcijańskiej,* trans. and ed. Wanda Zakrzewska, Paweł Pachciarek, and Ryszard Turzyński, commentary by Tamara Łozińska (Warszawa: Pax, 1990), s.v. *harfa, woda, żaba.*

19. These symbols are to be found, in particular, in the monumental design, Szymanowski's lifework—*The Procession to Wawel.* See my comments in the study of the image of Boleslaus the Brave, "Pomnik Bolesława Śmiałego." For more information, see also Kotkowska-Bareja, *Catalogue.*

20. Józef Sikorski, "Wspomnienie Chopina," *Biblioteka warszawska* 4 (1849): 510–59; quoted after Ferdynand Hoesick, *Chopin. Życie i twórczość,* 4 vols. (Kraków: Polskie Wydawnictwo Muzyczne, 1962), 1:21.

21. The first three-volume edition of Hoesick's monograph appeared in the years 1910–11, preceded by the 1907 single volume, which covered only the years 1810–31. The second, somewhat abbreviated edition of 1927 was the basis of the 1962 modern edition.

22. See essays 10 and 12 on the reception of Chopin (Chechlińska; Trochimczyk) and essay 4 on the messianic context of Chopin's music (Goldberg).

23. For extensive comments, see Szubert, *Rzeźba.* The problem requires further detailed analysis and careful differentiation, so it is only mentioned here.

24. Charles Baudelaire, "Richard Wagner et Tannhauser à Paris" (Polish translation by Anna Baranowa, "Wagner, Gesamtkunstwerk i moderniści," in *Roczniki Humanistyczne,* 103). This work offers a very detailed analysis of the Wagnerian "total work" in relation to the essential idea for the period of "the correspondence of arts".

25. Ludwig Hevesi, *Acht Jahre Sezession* (Vienna: Konegen, 1906; rpt. Klagenfurt: Ritter, 1984), 24. A color model of the sculpture already appeared in 1886. At that time Klinger lived in Paris, where he worked on his graphic cycle, *Love. Op. X,* and on his painting, *The Judgment of Paris.* In 1888 the artist left for Rome. In Italy he sought inspiration not only in the art of *quatrocento* but also in various sculptural material applied in a masterly manner in such works as *Beethoven.*

26. Wilhelm Lübke and Friedrich Haack, *Die Kunst des XIX Jahrhunderts und der Gegenwart,* 2 vols. (Esslingen: Neff, 1925), 2:142.

27. Hevesi, *Acht Jahre Sezession,* 26.

28. Hans Wolfgang Singer, ed., *Briefe von Max Klinger aus den Jahren 1874 bis 1919* (Leipzig, 1924), 178.

29. Dance the orange. Throw its warmer landscape
out of yourselves, let the ripeness shine
in its native air! Peel away, radiant

fragrance on fragrance! Create a kinship
with the pure and reluctant rind,
with the juice that loads the ecstatic fruit!

R. M. Rilke, *Sonnets to Orpheus,* trans. David Young (Middletown, Conn.: Wesleyan University Press, 1987), 31.

# 4

## "Remembering that tale of grief": The Prophetic Voice in Chopin's Music

### HALINA GOLDBERG

And ever louder grew the music's roar,
And you could hear the tramp of marching, war,
Attack, a storm, the boom of guns, the moans
Of children, and a weeping mother's groans.
So splendidly the master's art resembled
The horror of the storm, the women trembled
Remembering with tears that tale of grief.[1]

In these poignant tones the Polish-Jewish bard, Jankiel—one of the most cherished poetic characters created by Adam Mickiewicz—narrates the last episode of the Kościuszko Uprising: the 1794 massacre of thousands of civilians in the Warsaw suburb of Praga by Aleksandr Suvorov's Russian forces. Jankiel's "Concert of Concerts," a musical narrative portraying the key events of Polish history between 1791 and 1812, is among the most celebrated verses of Mickiewicz's epic poem, *Pan Tadeusz*, a nostalgic masterpiece written during his exile in Paris in the 1830s. In it the Polish poet remembered his homeland from the time of the Napoleonic conquests: its fears and its hopes.

At the end of the eighteenth century, in a series of three partitions, the sovereign state of Poland was dismembered by its neighbors—destined to be absent from the maps of Europe for more than a century. The doomed nation had some glimpses of hope: the Constitution of the Third of May, the Kościuszko Uprising, the formation of the Polish Legion under General Henryk Dąbrowski, the brief period of joy spurred by Napoleon's promises of independence, and afterward the limited liberty within the Congress Kingdom—a tiny Polish state under the rule of tsarist Russia. All these hopes were crushed with the fall of the November Uprising in the summer of 1831. The country's economy was devastated; its bravest sons and daughters dead or banished, their property confiscated; its culture halted; and its bards exiled. Poland became a wasteland.

It is the earlier part of this "tale of grief" that Jankiel, the Jewish innkeeper, a patriot, and a master dulcimer player, retells through his music. And it is during this concert that Jankiel undergoes a spiritual transformation, an apotheosis, the becoming of a *wieszcz*.[2] A *wieszcz*, which does not have a suitable English equivalent, is a poet or bard, but he is also a seer and a prophet, one who guides his people to other spiritual and temporal realms.

In light of the later Polish veneration of Fryderyk Chopin as the nation's musical *wieszcz* and the lasting association between Chopin and Mickiewicz, it is tempting to believe that Chopin was the model for Mickiewicz's Jankiel. There is no explicit evidence to support this claim.[3] More importantly, Jankiel is Mickiewicz's own elliptic alter ego, and, like many of the poet's heroes who undergo a spiritual transformation and find their prophetic voice, he represents the messianic messenger, the *wieszcz*, who guides his flock toward the revelation.[4]

This essay examines the circumstances surrounding the articulation of Chopin's role as a *wieszcz:* his political and patriotic attitudes, and his contacts with the messianic philosophy; the earliest public and private pronouncements of his prophetic destiny; and Chopin's musical contributions that allowed the audiences this perception. The essay argues that Chopin's listeners heard Polishness and the "prophetic" message in his musical orations not just in his dances but also through clearly recognizable topoi and affiliations with Polish patriotic songs; it also contends that Chopin, well aware of these musical allusions, allowed them to speak directly or as concealed suggestions. Finally, it searches for any signs, verbal or musical, of the reticent composer's reaction to his live canonization into the Polish messianic Parnassus.

## Polish Political Messianism

The Polish political messianism has found much of its inspiration in the German philosophy of Friedrich Schelling, but, more significantly, it was very closely intertwined with the nineteenth-century French messianic trends represented by Charles Fourier, Henri de Saint-Simon, Joseph de Maistre, Pierre-Simon Ballanche, and Pierre Leroux. Their messianic concepts permeated many aspects of French philosophical, political, and social thought and found their manifestations in countless literary works, including those by George Sand, Victor Hugo, and Alphonse de Lamartine. But at no point did the French philosophy of political crucifixion and redemption match the intensity and centrality of Polish messianism. The messianic principles could be found in almost every major work of Polish Romanticism, not just works by Mickiewicz but also those by his eminent contemporaries, Juliusz Słowacki and Zygmunt Krasiński, and by the many lesser poets, several of them Chopin's close friends (especially Bohdan Zaleski and Stefan Witwicki).[5]

At the heart of Polish messianism was the belief that the country was an innocent victim crucified by foreign powers: Christ among the nations; a sacrifice which would serve as expiation for the world's sins and would bring about universal salvation and rebirth. In the most explicitly messianic of his works, *Books of the Polish Nation and Its Pilgrimage* (1832), Mickiewicz wrote:

> The Pole on his pilgrimage has not yet name of his own, but that name will be given to him later, just as name was given to the confessors of Christ later.
>
> But meanwhile the Pole is called a pilgrim; and since he hath made a vow to journey to the holy land, the free country, he hath vowed to journey until he shall find it.
>
> But the Polish Nation is not a divinity like Christ, therefore its soul on its pilgrimage over the abyss may go astray, and its return to the body and the resurrection may thus be deferred.
>
> Therefore, let us read diligently the Gospel of Christ, and those teachings and parables which Christian pilgrim gathered from the lips and writings of Christian Poles, martyrs and pilgrims.[6]

Messianic principles were not relegated to philosophical treatises and high art: they lived in every stratum of Polish civilization,

Figure 4.1. Polish Postcard, n.d. (before 1914). Author's collection.

from the most sublime poetry and music to the familiar realms of religious and popular culture. Messianism fed and sustained Polish culture throughout the pain-filled nineteenth century and persisted in elements of twentieth-century Polish thought—it defined, and to some degree continues to define, modern Poland. No better evidence of the prevalence of messianic thinking can be offered than its inclusion in the most commonplace mode of disseminating images: the postcard (Figure 4.1).

Built on a strong Marian tradition, in which the concepts of the Virgin/Mother/Poland existed in close proximity, Polish messianic imagery freely combined religious and national symbols. This imagery is apparent on the postcard, probably dating back to the last decade of the nineteenth century, representing the shackled Virgin/Mother/Poland kneeling at the foot of the cross in the arms of Christ (in the messianic iconography Poland is never depicted as Christ, but invariably as a woman, often with Christ's or the Virgin's attributes). The rim of her garment has dates representing the four major uprisings (1794, 1830, 1848, and 1863); the three dates on the left (1772, 1793, and 1795), affixed on a spear, correspond to the three partitions that led to the destruction of independent Poland. In the background the two historic residences of Polish kings can be seen: the Royal Castle in Warsaw, on the left, and the older Royal Castle in Kraków, on the right. The latter is radiating a skyward light containing the sign "May 3." The dates on the two arms of the cross, 1791 and 1891, mark the creation and the hundred-year anniversary of the Constitution of May 3, the document that reformed the principles of Polish governing in an attempt to halt further seizure of Polish lands by its neighbors. The inscription on the banner further elucidates the messianic significance of the whole composition: "The moment of expiation has not yet arrived."[7]

Mickiewicz's messianism, in particular, assumed the agency of chosen individuals, higher spirits capable of receiving divine inspiration. It needed a *wieszcz*, and Mickiewicz—incarnated as Konrad, the poetic hero of *Forefathers' Eve*, Part III—was the Chosen One:

> Now is my soul incarnate in my country,
> And in my body dwells her soul;
> My fatherland and I are one great whole.
> My name is million, for I love as millions:
> Their pain and suffering I feel.[8]

Mickiewicz carried his calling with all seriousness, perhaps with more zeal than the typical supporter of this doctrine was prepared to accept. Once he crossed that boundary, his status as the nation's indisputable spiritual leader was unsettled.[9]

Along with the concept of the messianic messenger, political messianism adopted numerous other elements from Judaic thought, especially from Talmudic mysticism and the Hebrew prophetic tradition. This lineage explains, at least in part, Mickiewicz's choice of Jankiel, a Jew, a musician, a master dulcimer improviser, as his poetic *wieszcz*. The contemporary views emphasized that ancient Hebrew music had a sacred function, and thus, in his ency-clopedia article, Oskar Kolberg asserted: "For Hebrew writers the musician, the sage, and the prophet were one and the same; teaching and prophesying were done in the form of poetry with music."[10] Furthermore, Poles alleged a long-standing native tradition in which the poet, the teacher, the prophet, and the musician were one.

Whereas *wieszcz* was the term usually applied by the Romantics to the messianic guide (*wieszczba* was the old-Polish term denoting the art of poetry), there was another related term, *guślarz* [*guslar, guslarz, gęślarz*] (derived from the same root as the old-Polish word *gędźba*, the art of tones). The folk celebration of the departed forefathers, which opens Mickiewicz's *Forefathers' Eve*, Part II, was officiated by a *guślarz*, a poet and a priest, whose traditional instrument was *gęśl* (a native dulcimer). In "The Instruments of Old Native Music," Prince Adam Czartoryski—father of the Czartoryski/Zamoyski clan that led the Polish political and cultural scene during Chopin's time—defines *gęśla* or *gęśl* as

> one of the oldest musical instruments, which is still used; had no more but three wire strings. Lying flat, they are hit, with mallets, meaning wooden sticks, and make different sounds. It is probable that this simple instrument, in Slavic named *huszle* or *guszle*, was used by soothsayers, and gave raise to the word *gusła* [visions, also superstitions], *guślarz* [soothsayer, poet, priest, musician], etc.[11]

According to the *Orgelbrand* article:

> The folk—dazed by the melody and words that touched the very core of their hearts—attributed magic powers to skilled musicians of this kind, who at the same time improvised and sang with the accompaniment of *gęśle*, and often consulted them as oracles.[12]

Jankiel's famous dulcimer improvisation related directly to this ostensible folk model but went a step further, for Jankiel no longer needed words to reach his audience: he spoke to them and was clearly understood through purely instrumental idiom. In light of this tradition, it was therefore natural, perhaps even more ideal, for a great musician, a great instrumental improviser, one who spoke in a native musical language, to be cast in the role of the *wieszcz*. The path was already chosen for Chopin.

## Chopin's Political Stance

Fryderyk Chopin was very much in the center of the messianic historiosophy. Many of the creators and proponents of these ideas were his friends and acquaintances before he left Poland: during his university years he mingled with the Romantic literary avant-garde in Warsaw, among them Goszczyński and perhaps Krasiński, whose later works embodied Polish messianism. He frequented the favorite haunt of Warsaw's young rebellious intelligentsia, the *Honoratka* café, where the plot of the November Uprising was conceived; and Lelewel and Mochnacki, the core conspirators, were among his closest acquaintances (particularly Mochnacki, who penned several reviews of Chopin's performances).[13]

The eruption and tragic fall of the November Uprising left a deep mark on Chopin, as attested by several letters and the so-called Stuttgart Diary. In particular, the distressed entries, which he had jotted in the diary upon learning about the fall of the November Uprising, have an ardent, passionate tone, often compared to sections of Konrad's "Grand Improvisation" from Mickiewicz's *Forefathers' Eve*, Part III.

Chopin, *Stuttgart Diary:*

> Oh God, are you there?!—You exist and you do not avenge?!—Are the Muscovites' crimes still not enough—or—or you yourself are a Muscovite![14]

Mickiewicz, *Forefathers' Eve*, Part III:

> VOICE: Then hear me, Lord!
> [ . . . ] yet all your plan
> Of wheeling worlds and planets, every star,
> Shall rock, as my voice shot throughout creation
> From generation unto generation shouts you are not the father . . .
> [VOICE OF THE DEVIL]: But the tsar![15]

I am not suggesting that one influenced the other or that it is even remotely possible, but the common spirit in the two fragments is striking.

After his arrival in Paris, Chopin moved with apparent ease among diverse social groups, which included Polish and foreign aristocrats, artists, and intelligentsia, as well as the local upper bourgeoisie. Although he did not take an active part in any political events, he was well aware of the political tensions and the role of the various political parties in Paris. Shortly after his arrival in Paris he wrote:

> The lower classes are infuriated to the quick, and take every opportunity to hold counsel on how to change the state of their misery, but, unfortunately, the government is very careful about these things, and the smallest gathering of the masses is dispersed by mounted gendarmes. . . . you must know that each political group is differently dressed (I speak here about the extremists): the Carlists wear green vests; the Republicans and Napoleonists [Bonapartists], meaning the *"jeune France"* dress in red; the Saint-Simonians—that means the new Christians creating new religion and drawing large numbers of proselytes—who are also for equality, are attired in blue.[16]

About a year later he made a lighthearted comment: "I love the Carlists, I cannot stand the Philippists, and as for myself I am a revolutionary, therefore I don't care about money but about friendship."[17]

Chopin did not appear to be involved in any of the political camps of the Polish émigré community: judging from the apparent pleasure he took, on an earlier occasion, in bringing together the opposing factions of Warsaw's musical world, his inclination was to avoid this kind of divisiveness.[18] However, he remained profoundly committed to his Polishness and to his country's pursuit of independence; he was intimately associated with Polish poets, political activists, historians, and heroes of the uprising in the Polish émigré circles; and the enthusiasts of messianic philosophy were among his closest friends.[19] Many of his non-Polish friends (George Sand, Marie d'Agoult, Franz Liszt, among others) were also concerned with politics, often pursuing French branches of messianism,[20] and were sympathetic to the Polish plight.

During 1840 Chopin's political awareness seemed to have intensified: with George Sand, he began attending Collège de France to hear Mickiewicz's lectures on Slavonic literatures containing the essence of messianic historiosophy.[21] At the same time Sand and Pierre Leroux, whose utopian socialism hinted at messianic concepts, published an alternative journal, *La Revue Indépendante*. When, on 1 October 1840, Sand wrote to her coworkers about asking Mickiewicz for an article on Poland, she told them of Chopin's extraordinary enthusiasm for the project. Rather than reacting

with his typical reserve and reason, Chopin supported and pro-
moted the idea, notwithstanding Mickiewicz's increasingly more
frequent transgressions into mysticism and cultism.[22]

Two other events of that summer might have reinforced Chopin's political impetus. In July 1840 Paris was commemorating the
tenth anniversary of the July 1830 revolution.[23] Some weeks later,
in September, after the brutal police raid on the streets of Paris,
Sand remarked to her son, Maurice: "Chopin, who did not want
to believe anything, finally got the certainty and evidence."[24]

This growing political awareness was timely, since the following year brought about changes that placed Chopin at the center
of Polish political eschatology. On 21 May 1841 the venerated Julian Ursyn Niemcewicz died. Niemcewicz was a writer, a poet, and
a politician; a coauthor of the Constitution of May 3; and the poet
of the *Historical Chants* [*Śpiewy historyczne*], a collection of songs
that nurtured the patriotism of Chopin and his peers. A generation
that remembered independent Poland departed with Niemcewicz:
an entire epoch was gone.

At the same time Mickiewicz, along with the poets Słowacki
and Goszczyński, was drawn into the circle of the mystic philosopher Andrzej Tomasz Towiański, who critiqued all philosophy
based on reason and, after his second revelation of 1839, uncon-
ditionally rejected an institutionalized Church. Mickiewicz's anti-
Church attitude and his wholehearted involvement in the religious
mysticism of Towiański distanced him from his audience and his
supporters, ultimately causing his suspension from his position at
the Collège de France. Gradually he began losing his role as the
national bard, the prophet, the *wieszcz*. At first Chopin responded
to Mickiewicz's follies with disbelief:

> Are we still returning to our homeland?! Did they go completely
> mad?! I am not worried about Mick[iewicz] and Sob[ański], be-
> cause they have strong heads and can survive a few more exiles
> without losing their faculties and energy.[25]

But only a week later Chopin was alarmed: "Mick[iewicz] will meet
an awful end, unless he is mocking you."[26]

It is during this period that Chopin completed a group of extraordinary compositions: Polonaise op. 44, *Allegro de Concert* op.
46,[27] Ballade op. 47, Nocturnes op. 48, and the F Minor Fantasy
op. 49. These works, the Fantasy in particular, radiate an intensely

patriotic feeling, a Polishness that resides in the echoes of patriotic and popular songs and employs musical topoi which would have been readily understood by his compatriots—contemporary and future.[28] While it is not my intention to map out a program or a specific narrative path for the work, I will argue that for Chopin's audiences (Polish in particular) the Fantasy's narrative, growing out of Chopin's improvisational practices, was clearly set in a hermeneutic context, and that this and other compositions engaging the patriotic topoi helped to establish the composer's role as the Fourth *Wieszcz*.

## Polish Patriotic Songs and Chopin's Improvisations

Chopin's early fame already rested in part on his extraordinary ability as an improviser—a skill expected of a virtuoso performer. Sometime after 1835, however, the nature of Chopin's improvisations changed: he entirely gave up public virtuoso extemporizations on popular themes and improvised most often on Polish national tunes, preferably among friends, typically in émigré circles.[29] The occasions for these performances were private and often very patriotic, for instance, several were specifically intended to benefit the veterans of the November Uprising.[30] The contemporary descriptions of these improvisations almost invariably use the language of Polish historical, and often specifically messianic, narrative, and engage topoi or even actual references to Polish patriotic song literature.

Musicological literature, especially outside Poland, has placed most emphasis on the Polish dances—mazurka, krakowiak, and polonaise—as determinants of Polishness in Chopin's music.[31] Nineteenth-century reactions, however, attest to a coexisting tradition of hearing nationality through non-dance topics. Already in 1821 professor Kazimierz Brodziński, Chopin's neighbor, whose lectures on literature Chopin attended at the university during 1826, argued for the importance of religious songs and Polish masses in encouraging national "thinking and feeling." Brodziński, the mentor of Warsaw's restless Romantics, believed that religious chants were a primeval expression of every nation, and he reported that Warsaw's two chief composers of the time, Karol Kurpiński and Chopin's composition teacher, Józef Elsner, consented to compose appropriate national-religious tunes for his religious poems.[32] Indeed, Elsner went even further in realizing these principles: in his 1818 opera, *King Łokietek* [*Król Łokietek*], the legendary king's central aria and the ensuing *scena*, during which the humble pilgrim reveals himself as the savior of Poland, are quoting and developing the then well-known religious hymn "I Stand at Your Door, O Lord" ["U drzwi Twoich stoję Panie"].[33]

In a lengthy aesthetic essay entitled "On Music" (1843),[34] Józef Sikorski (renowned music writer, Chopin's younger conservatory colleague, and, like him, a student of Elsner) asserted that "nationality" in other arts is more tangible, but in music it speaks to emotions. As a result,

> the musician can arrange sounds at will, but very few will understand him, unless he employs supporting gestures, or even expressions, that mentally mark the kind and degree of emotion. In such a state, it is difficult for music to be national; it is even more difficult to tangibly, so to speak, present this nationality.[35]

Sikorski explained that folk music falls into two categories: worldly and religious, and that although the second kind has fewer characteristic traits, "these chants . . . the solemn religious music, are national music."[36]

> We can observe how the national melody, freed from the narrow forms of mazur, krakowiak, and polonaise (under whose guises many still exclusively seek national music), enlivens spacious forms well known to the musical world. Examples are found in the Symphony, Quartet, and Fantasy by Dobrzyński, but, if we examine them closely, we also find them in all works by Chopin.[37]

The question of how to indicate nationality in music was already addressed two decades earlier by the above-mentioned Karol Kurpiński, the director of Warsaw's opera theater, a composer, and a conservatory professor during the years Sikorski, Dobrzyński, and Chopin were students there. In an article entitled "On Musical Expression and Mimesis" Kurpiński asserted that music can speak to the listener by recalling tunes that have a certain meaning. This is particularly true in stage music but can also be achieved in compositions without words by means of "arias, which—nested in everyone's memory through frequent repetitions—allow diverse allusions."[38] Kurpiński stressed that "these are only reminiscences, but therefore they speak stronger to the heart," and he gave the example of a march tune evoking in the listener the image of "national troops."[39]

Some years later Kurpiński provided an illustration of this method in his "Lithuanian Song" ["Litwinka"], one of the most important nineteenth-century patriotic songs, which is central to our discussion of Chopin's op. 49 below. In this patriotic song, composed in 1831 during the November Uprising and published before the fall of the insurrection as "The Hymn of the Lithuanian Legions," Kurpiński undeniably alluded to the refrain of "The Hymn of General Dąbrowski's Polish Legions" also known as the "Dąbrowski Mazurka," or "Poland Has Yet Not Perished," a patriotic song from Napoleonic times etched into the heart of every Pole. In the original 1831 edition of "Litwinka" Kurpiński offered a very specific description of this musical allusion: in an annotation to the fifth line of the fourth stanza, which reads, "The joyful sound penetrated a thousand hearts," Kurpiński explained: "This line became the reason for the composer to recall the tune of the 'Dąbrowski Mazurka' in this spot"[40] (Examples 4.1a and 4.1b).

It is not only unusual that the composer's own testimony of such design would come down to us; it is also remarkable that Kurpiński demonstrated his method by linking the "Dąbrowski Mazurka" and "Litwinka," the two songs that were at the heart of Polish patriotic repertory.

Like all Poles of his generation, Chopin drew strength and hope from a group of songs that defined Polish patriotism: the "Dąbrowski Mazurka," the religious hymn "O God, Thou Who Hast Graced Poland" ["Boże co Polskę"], and the medieval chant

Example 4.1a. Karol Kurpiński, "Litwinka," poem by Cywiński, after original edition (Warsaw: Brzezina, 1831). Warsaw, Biblioteka Narodowa, *Mus. II 18.506 cim.*, mm. 36–39.

Example 4.1b. Anonymous, "Dąbrowski Mazurka," poem by Józef Wybicki, mm. 9–12.

"Mother of God" ["Bogurodzica"]—all three being one-time con-
tenders for the role of Polish national anthem;[41] Kurpiński's two
insurrectionary songs, "Litwinka" and the "Warsaw Song" ["Warszawianka"]; and Niemcewicz's *Historical Chants*. Contemporary
sources provide documentation of Chopin's involvement with
nearly all these songs.

Chopin improvised on the "Dąbrowski Mazurka"—which ultimately became Poland's national anthem—at least on two occasions: in September 1835 in the Dresden salon of the Wodzińskis
(the family of his fiancée Maria) and in February 1844 on the occasion of Bohdan Zaleski's birthday.[42] A description of the 1835 soirée makes the political force of his improvisations quite apparent:

> Among others, he played "Poland Has Yet Not Perished" or the
> "Dąbrowski Mazurka" and his own variations on this tune . . .
> next day I was called to the Russian embassy and asked: "How
> could you have stayed in a house, where patriotic, revolutionary
> songs were sung? . . . If you want to be a loyal subject of our
> Monarch, and sojourn abroad without being considered a rebel,
> you should have thrown out a demagogue like Chopin!!! Or at
> least silenced him yourself."[43]

Sometime during the 1835 trip Chopin also wrote a piano arrangement of the "Dąbrowski Mazurka's" refrain into the *Stammbuch* of
an unknown owner in Karlsbad.[44]

Chopin's *Largo* in E♭ (title derived from the tempo marking) is
clearly a setting of "O God, Thou Who Hast Graced Poland," a
religious hymn that was central to the creation and preservation of
Polish national identity, which Chopin would have played as a
weekly conclusion of the Sunday mass during his early years as an
organist at the Visitation Nuns' Church[45] (Figure 4.2). Interestingly, like Kurpiński's "Litwinka," this hymn (in Kaszewski's original and Chopin's setting) also cites the "Dąbrowski Mazurka."[46]

The largest and perhaps most influential group of patriotic
songs were the *Historical Chants* to poems by Niemcewicz. In 1806,
as one of the endeavors aimed at maintaining and re-creating Polish national identity, the Society for the Friends of Learning invited Julian Ursyn Niemcewicz to begin work on a cycle of Polish
historical poems. During the next few years, these works—known
as *Historical Chants*—were set to music by Polish amateurs and professional composers, thus becoming the pillar of national patriotic
culture. Many generations, growing up after the collection was first

# 1. Modlitwa

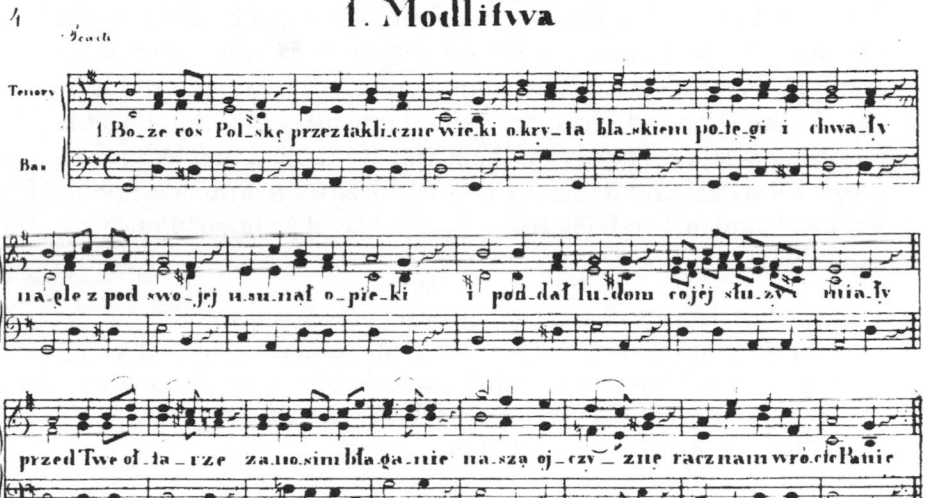

11
*Modlitwa*
(druk litografowany)

Figure 4.2. Jan Kaszewski, "O God, Thou Who Hast Graced Poland" ["Boże coś Polskę"], the November Uprising version. Poem by Alojzy Feliński (Philadelphia [!], 1835).

published in 1816, were raised on the *Historical Chants*, and the political power of these musical works became such that in 1827 Russian authorities forbade teaching them for they "awoke patriotic feelings."[47] Chopin was a child of the first generation raised on *Historical Chants:* he would have sung these songs at home, with his friends, and later, in Paris, through these songs he would remember Poland. Liszt tells us that when Chopin improvised on *Historical Chants* in the presence of Niemcewicz, his music captured "crash of arms, the chant of vanquishers, festive hymns, complaints of the illustrious prisoners, and ballads over dead heroes."[48] According to another report on 24 December 1836 Chopin played, sang, and improvised, while Niemcewicz was recounting for the children the time of the Four-Year Sejm.[49]

The patriotic songs popular during Chopin's life represent several thematic groups; among them, of greatest interest to us are themes characteristic of the historical/messianic narrative: the funeral processional, the military and triumphal marches, and religious hymns. In the Polish nineteenth-century tradition, the function of religious chorales is not merely devotional, since, in the nationalist context, their sacred tones stand for Christianity as defining Polishness (specifically Catholicism, in contrast to the Russian Orthodoxy and Prussian Protestantism) and echo Poland's messianic destiny. The text of the hymn "O God, Thou Who Hast Graced Poland" and its nearly two-hundred-year history of political involvement[50] embody this very essence of religious Polish patriotism:

> Oh God! Thou, who through long centuries hast graced Poland with the glow of glory and then suddenly withdrew Thy protection, giving Poland into servitude to nations that were to be its servants. In front of Thy altars we bring our prayers: deem to return our homeland to us, O Lord![51]

Several of the *Historical Chants* adopt the religious topos: for instance, Maria Szymanowska's "Jan Albrycht" with its chordal, chorale-like textures, somber melody, and *Maestoso e lento* character exemplifies this tone. Appropriately the poem centers on this fifteenth-century king's thwarted attempt to battle the Turks, thus dramatizing and underscoring Poland's sacrificial role in protecting Christendom from Muslims (Figure 4.3).

The chorale topos is present in many of Chopin's works, including the G Minor Nocturne op. 15,[52] the G Minor Nocturne op. 37, the C♯ Minor Scherzo, and C Minor Prelude op. 28 no. 20, as well as the works composed in 1841: the C Minor Nocturne op. 48 and the op. 49 Fantasy. Given the patriotic connotations of religious hymns, his chorales must be understood within the Polish historiosophic framework, as capable of conveying messianic significance and patriotic yearnings to Chopin and his audiences.[53] Antoni Marceli Szulc, Chopin's future biographer, for instance, in his 1842 review, said of the C Minor Nocturne's *Poco più lento* chorale: "[It is] poised, vigorous, proud, like a man of iron will, who stubbornly resists dangers and obstacles. He is attacked by hordes of devils, a thousand monsters, but he stands unshaken, invincible, immaculate."[54]

Another group of national songs speak through the sounds of funeral march and lament. In the Polish patriotic tradition a lament would most clearly relate to the last and most popular of the *Historical Chants*: "The Funeral of Prince Józef Poniatowski." This poem, commemorating the tragic death of the idolized nephew of Poland's last king, was set to music by Franciszek Lessel, one of the most talented composers of pre–Chopin Poland and a pupil

Figure 4.3. Maria Szymanowska, "Jan Albrycht," poem by Julian Ursyn Niemcewicz. From *Historical Chants*, 5th ed. (Lwów: Kajetan Jabłoński, 1849).

of Joseph Haydn. Prince Józef, who died surrounded by enemy forces during the Napoleonic campaign, was an archetypal military Romantic hero, and, for the rest of the century, his act of self-sacrifice served as a patriotic symbol of the nation's desperate plight. In Lessel's song he is bemoaned through a slow ceremonial tempo and the minor mode accentuated by plaintive chromaticism. The solemn mood of mourning is further emphasized by the presence of falling melodic motives and elegiac rhythms, in Poland particularly associated with the genre referred to as *duma, dumka,* or Polish elegy[55] (Figure 4.4).

Chopin's youthful C Minor March and the *Marche funèbre* from op. 35 Sonata are the best-known examples of funeral marches, but funereal tones also echo in the *Tempo di marcia* of op. 49, several songs, and the opening of the C Minor Nocturne op. 48. The jagged, sobbing, recitative-like melodies of the Nocturne's opening and the songs "Leaves Are Falling" and "Melody," in particular, recall most effectively the narrative qualities of a lament: an elegy on the death of a hero and the nation.

Military marches are numerous among Polish patriotic songs—both "Warszawianka" and "Litwinka" as well as several of Niemcewicz's poems are set in this manner. The heroic type can be illustrated by a song, "Zawisza Czarny," in which the brisk tempo, resolute rhythms, fanfare motives, and bright diatonic sonorities depict the great deeds of the fearless, victorious fifteenth-century knight, Zawisza Czarny. These military tones resonate in Chopin's work, once more, most noticeably in the Fantasy op. 49 and in the song "Leaves Are Falling." The heroic connotations of this topic elucidate its role in Chopin's narratives as both reminiscence of the glorious past and a seed of messianic hope (Figures 4.5 and 4.6).

These familiar topoi—the hymn, the lament, the military march, all embedded in struggle—must have been common in Chopin's improvisations, for they are reflected in his contemporaries' reception of his music. Bohdan Zaleski (1802–1886), a Romantic poet, a revolutionary who fought in the November Uprising, and Chopin's close friend, having heard Fryderyk's 1844 improvisation on the "Dąbrowski Mazurka," described it as an unambiguously messianic musical narrative: "Chopin called all the voices pleasant and painful from the past, moaned through the cries of *dumkas* and finally concluded with "Poland Has Yet Not Perished" in all tones, from militant to children and angels."[56] By the time of this performance, and certainly by the time Zaleski's ac-

Figure 4.4. Franciszek Lessel, "The Funeral of Prince Józef Poniatowski" [Pogrzeb Xcia Józ. Poniatowskiego], poem by Julian Ursyn Niemcewicz. From *Historical Chants*, 5th ed. (Lwów: Kajetan Jabłoński, 1849).

Figure 4.5. Lithograph representing Zawisza Czarny. From
*Historical Chants*, 5th ed. (Lwów: Kajetan Jabłoński, 1849).

count was posthumously published in 1899, Mickiewicz's *Pan Tadeusz*, with its "Jankiel's Concert" being one of the most beloved
passages, was ensconced in Polish national culture as the emblem
of an idyllic and heroic national past. At the culmination and conclusion of his improvisation, quoted at the end of this essay, Jankiel
intones a melody instantly recognized by all in attendance, "a poor
old song, to Polish troops so dear!" This being none other than
the "Dąbrowski Mazurka," played by the Jewish bard in the presence of General Dąbrowski himself, is a gesture of remembrance
and reverence. Thus in his ekphrastic narrative (the multifold mirroring which involves depictions by Jankiel, Mickiewicz, Chopin,
and Zaleski invites a separate discussion), Zaleski places Chopin's
improvisation in the heart of Polish messianic tradition, and, if we
are to trust Zaleski's report, Chopin himself must have been keenly
aware of the association with the literary Jankiel that such improvisation had to invoke. Although the Polish composer must have
given performances of this sort on many occasions, the only acknowledged musical record of such improvisations exists in the
song "Leaves Are Falling."

Figure 4.6. Franciszek Lessel, "Zawisza Czarny," poem by Julian Ursyn Niemcewicz. From *Historical Chants*, 5th ed. (Lwów: Kajetan Jabłoński, 1849).

According to Julian Fontana, in 1836, when a volume of Wincenty Pol's insurrectionary poems was published in Paris under the pseudonym "Janusz," Chopin improvised songs to these new poems "from open book" in the company of close friends.[57] Some twelve songs were composed, of which "Leaves Are Falling" ["Leci liście"], originally entitled "Chant from the Tomb" ["Śpiew z mogiły"], is the only one known, written down from his recollections of Chopin's improvisation by Fontana.[58] The song must have had particularly strong patriotic connotations since the manuscript, which survives in Fontana's hand, and the *Stichvorlage*, in another copyist's hand but annotated by Fontana, bear the date 3 May 1836—commemorating the supreme moment of Polish hope: the Constitution of May 3. This moment, so dear to the memory of the homeless Polish exiles, was traditionally remembered with private performances of national songs. Chopin was undoubtedly a participant of such commemorations, and on another occasion, in a letter of 1849 to his close friend Konstanty Gaszyński (a poet who fought in the November Uprising), he fervently highlighted the date of May 3.[59]

The lengthy text of "Leaves Are Falling" centers on the November Uprising of 1830. Remembering the triumphant events from the early days of the uprising, the poet reflects on the destruction of land and loss of life in the aftermath of this tragic episode in Polish history. This song betrays its improvisational origins in its rhapsodic, narrative tone and flexible, open structure. The music follows the text responding perceptively to the imagery with readily understood musical topoi. The dominating funereal tone signified by lamenting downward melodies and elegiac rhythms is interrupted by two moments of victory and hope—the first is a triumphal march that, in proud soaring lines, recalls the expectations of the uprising; the second reflects on a better time, when Poland's sons would be building their homeland rather than dying for it (See Examples 4.2a, 4.2b, and 4.2c).

## Fantasy op. 49

The generic characteristics that define the musical plot of "Leaves Are Falling" correspond closely to those of the Fantasy op. 49. Many writers have remarked on the powerful narrative features of this piece: the funereal opening, the struggle between the two keys, the victory of A♭ major over F minor, the triumphal celebration,

Example 4.2a. Chopin, "Leaves Are Falling," op. 74 no. 17, poem by Wincenty Pol, mm. 1–8.

Example 4.2b. Chopin, "Leaves Are Falling," mm. 43–46.

Example 4.2c. Chopin, "Leaves Are Falling," mm. 85–92.

the meditative, hymn-like character of the *Lento sostenuto*, and the
ethereal, almost angelic conclusion.[60]

The work opens with an unmistakable funeral march, expressed
through the modality, the tempo, and the solemn dotted rhythms.
The generic classification is further underscored by the presence
of the descending Phrygian tetrachord, an explicit attribute of the
lament. This beginning clearly echoes the tone of Lessel's "The
Funeral of Prince Józef Poniatowski." Moreover, Mieczysław Tomaszewski's comprehensive study of op. 49 lists a number of other
*Historical Chants* that belong to the same type and calls attention
to the remarkable affinity between Chopin's opening theme and
Kurpiński's "Litwinka"[61] (Examples 4.3a, 4.3b, and 4.3c).

It is significant, however, that Chopin's recollection of this
well-known tune generates a different meaning than that of the
original. Kurpiński's song, composed and published during the triumphal days of the uprising, is conceived in the heroic genre, as a
military march; Chopin's allusion has the quality of reminiscence,
a sorrowful remembrance of the insurgents' expectations and the

Example 4.3a. Chopin, Fantasy op. 49, mm. 1–4.

Example 4.3b. Chopin, Fantasy op. 49, mm. 21–24.

wio - nął wiatr bło - gi na Le-chi - tów zie - mię

Example 4.3c. Karol Kurpiński, "Litwinka," poem by Cywiński, after original edition (Warsaw: Brzezina, 1831). Warsaw, Biblioteka Narodowa, *Mus. II 18.506 cim.*, mm. 18–21.

event's tragic conclusion. The opening, which reiterates the initial gesture of the song in F minor, transforms "Litwinka" into a lament, whereas the ensuing F major march is more of a memory than a quotation of Kurpiński's spirited march.

The heroic topos finally does make its appearance in the guise of a triumphal march, first in E♭ major and later in A♭ major. The two victorious moments, each preceded by *agitato* episodes that embody struggle and longing, flank the B major *Lento sostenuto* chorale, which resonates with the realm of the patriotic religious hymns discussed earlier ("O God, Thou Who Hast Graced Po-

Example 4.3d. Chopin, Fantasy op. 49, mm. 199–206.

land" and "Jan Albrycht") (Example 4.3d). The second march, reasserting itself after the pensive repose of the *Lento sostenuto*, categorically establishes the victorious key of A♭ major and restores the promise of triumph. Thus the narrative of the Fantasy ushers the listener through a network of recognizable patriotic musical topics, alluding to national death and resurrection.

Chopin's contemporaries immediately noticed the national allusions. In his 1842 review of the Fantasy, Szulc emphasized the national character of the chorale:

> Its themes are national, full of sweetness and lyricism, namely the melody on page 15 (B major, *Lento sostenuto*), whose fleeting, almost unintentional recollection toward the end of the composition makes a unique impression.[62]

Sikorski, in his earlier-quoted essay "On Music," used the Fantasy to exemplify how nationality in music can be represented through means other than national dances:

> Already in the march, which opens the Fantasy, turns of phrase characterizing our music are found here and there, but the main theme begins on page 4 [correction: page 3 of the original edition—H.G.]. Step out into Warsaw's outskirts, and you will be

Example 4.3e. Chopin, Fantasy op. 49, mm. 294–302.

surrounded by the familiar melody; a seemingly humble idea transformed by Chopin's genius into a mighty tree that spreads its roots deeply into the foundations of this work, here and there allowing smaller plants to flourish under its care.[63]

Sikorski believed that every melody of this work has Polish character but that "it is particularly evident in the section beginning on page 10 [the "heroic" march in E♭ major—H.G.], where the melody placed in the bass [lower register—H.G.] grabs the heart."[64] For Chopin's contemporaries there was an unambiguous national reading of the Fantasy and the other works completed in 1841—they needed no words to elucidate the narrative. However, Chopin's strongest proclamation of musical Polishness came in the guise of his last song.

## "Melody"

Several of Chopin's songs engaged or hinted at patriotic themes: "The Wish," "Twofold End," "Sad River," and "The Warrior."[65] The most explicitly messianic of Chopin's works, however, is the last of his songs, "Melody," to the words of Zygmunt Krasiński, one of the three poets on whom the Poles bequeathed the honor of *wieszcz*. Krasiński's poem was so overtly messianic and politically provocative that in the original Parisian edition of the poem (1847) and in the first edition of the songs (Breitkopf & Härtel, 1859) the poet of "Melodya" had to be identified as anonymous.[66]

> From the mountains, as they bore the burden of the awe-
>    inspiring crosses,
> They saw in the distance the Promised Land.
> They saw the radiance of the blue rays,
> Toward which their tribe below was heading,
> Yet, they will not enter this realm!
> They will not partake in the feast of life,
> And perhaps they may even be forgotten.

The poem, in its imagery of the exiled tribe's pilgrimage to the Promised Land, embodies the messianic suffering and hopes of the Polish pilgrims. Fontana's inscription in the *Stichvorlage* indicates that the song was composed in 1847, and, according to Fontana's and Jane Stirling's correspondence, it was written into the *Stammbuch* of Delfina Potocka.[67] Delfina was known for her enchanting voice, trained in accordance with the principles of bel canto. Chopin much enjoyed her singing, and in his last hours, at his request, Delfina comforted him with arias by Rossini and Bellini.[68] She was one of the most important women in Chopin's life, and a friend who remained by his side till the very last moment, but she was also Krasiński's life-long lover and muse. A gift of Krasiński's poem, set to music by Fryderyk, bestowed on a talented singer, must have been of great significance to both, the dedicatee and the composer.

The concept of peregrinations is central to Chopin's setting, defined by unsettled tonality and meandering harmonies; the only harmonically stable section of the piece is in a distant key and conveys the poetic image of the faraway Promised Land—illuminating the pilgrims' path but unattainable to the messianic guides. Although Chopin creates a sense of dramatic recitation in the outer sections of the song and gives the central section a lyrical quality, the thematic fabric of the vocal line is surprisingly homogeneous throughout, and the contrasting emotions are achieved in most subtle ways. All through this piece Chopin makes use of mostly stepwise melodic lines cast into the rhythms of *duma* or Polish elegy, typical among the funereal *Historical Chants* and found, among other works, in his own songs "Dumka" and "Twofold End." In fact, Tomaszewski's charts listing rhythmic patterns typ-

Example 4.4a. Common rhythmic patterns in *Historical Chants*, based on Mieczysław Tomaszewski, *Muzyka Chopina na nowo odczytana* (Kraków: Akademia Muzyczna, 1996), 87.

Example 4.4b. Common rhythmic patterns in *Historical Chants*, based on Mieczysław Tomaszewski, *Muzyka Chopina na nowo odczytana* (Kraków: Akademia Muzyczna, 1996), 88.

ical of *Historical Chants* include thirteen that correspond precisely to the rhythms of the outer parts of Chopin's song and seven that are the variant used in the song's middle section[69] (Examples 4.4a, 4.4b, 4.5a, and 4.5b).

Chopin's most painful reflection on Krasiński's text is found in the last section of this song. The character of this section parallels the first part of the song, but the style of declamation is more impassioned: the lines are almost invariably moving downward in lamentation, and they are often punctuated by large dramatic leaps. Here, in two instances, Chopin repeats words of the original text: first he uses the word *even* [*nawet*] in measures 33–34, and a moment later he utters the word *forgotten* [*zapomnieni*] three times to a haunting, melodically awkward figure (see the leap of a dimin-

Example 4.5a. Chopin, "Melody," op. 74 no. 9, poem by Zygmunt Krasiński, mm. 5–8.

Example 4.5b. Chopin, "Melody," mm. 15–20.

ished 7th in measure 36). By emphasizing the word *forgotten*, Chopin draws attention to the last line of the poem, making his reading
more poignant. The threefold utterance of *forgotten* (mm. 36, 38,
and 41–42) with the motive attempting to move sequentially upward and returning to original pitch in rhythmic augmentation
(mm. 41–42); the ever longer pauses breaking up the narrative
(mm. 28, 32, 37, 39–40); and the fading piano accompaniment and
delayed arrival of the tonic through solitary vocal elaboration (mm.
43–44) allow Chopin's music to follow Krasiński's poem into bit-
terness, doubt, and resignation (Example 4.5c).

## Chopin as a Wieszcz

The messianic features of Chopin's improvised and composed musical narratives must have spoken very loudly to his contemporaries. When placing Chopin among the six most illustrious compos-

Example 4.5c. Chopin, "Melody," mm. 33–45.

ers of the modern times, Kolberg considered prophecy to be the single most important feature of Chopin's musical achievement:

> During the last three hundred years of evolution, six names shine prominently, like six stars on the musical horizon that sending rays from its core ignited other geniuses into action. They are: Palestrina (austere solemnity), Bach (faith), Händel (might), Mozart (grace), Beethoven (poetry), Chopin (prophecy).[70]

This perception of Chopin as a *wieszcz* was established sometime in the early 1840s. Already in 1841, in a review of opp. 35–
42, Szulc wrote:

> If the opinion that only with Mickiewicz native poetry was cre-
> ated is correct, than, by the same token, one might say that Cho-
> pin created national music. . . . He sings out our misery most
> woefully; he best recounts our past magnificence; our hopes. . . .
> He alone, as if prompted by the whisper of a *guślarz*, knows how
> to stir the play of passions and how to sooth it with melodious
> song; he is one of the most dignified representatives of our na-
> tionality. We salute and thank him![71]

In the spring of 1842, when, to most Poles, Mickiewicz's voice
started to sound distant, in the above discussed review of Chopin's
opuses 44–49, Szulc proclaimed Chopin to be Mickiewicz's heir,
the new *wieszcz*, the spiritual leader of the nation:

> Given our present situation, Mr. Chopin's position is more dis-
> tinguished than anyone else. Our warrior, who until now led our
> *wieszcz* hosts, trampled his *guśle* and remains persistently mute.
> Chopin inherited his power, and he keeps alive in our hearts the
> torch of nationhood. He translates most expressively the thoughts
> of the nation; his works are a holy shrine, the ark, as Mickiewicz
> said, in which the treasure of native music is kept. In it is hidden
> the most noble, beautiful, and exalted that reverberates in the
> Polish heart: the thread of popular thought, the legacy and the
> heritage of several centuries, the proud testimony of the poetic
> aspirations of our nation.[72]

Following a discussion of Chopin's individual compositions, Szulc
concludes his article by calling Chopin's music "the voice of the
prophet" and claiming that he

> belongs exclusively to our nation; the nation should, therefore,
> know about him. As someone once said to a foreigner, that there
> is no Pole that would not know a few *Historical Chants* by heart,
> so a time will come when Chopin's masterpieces will permeate
> the nation, for they are native, immaculate, and purely Polish.[73]

This context was not just privy to Polish ears. Wilhelm von
Lenz wrote: "Chopin was the only political pianist of the time.
Through his music he imparted Poland; he composed Poland."[74]
Blanchard called Chopin "the bard of his homeless homeland."[75]

Mallefile's excessive description of Chopin's "Polish ballad" where "the Old Man" advises the young to "keep their weapons for the day of the resurrection," concluded "To you, Poland! Saint Poland! Tomb of our forefathers! Cradle of our children."[76] Another clear gesture of Chopin investiture in his prophetic role came from his admiring French friend, the celebrated painter Eugène Delacroix. Delacroix's choice to represent the composer as Dante in a sketch (see Fig. 2.8) and possibly in the monumental fresco at the Palais de Luxembourg was rather striking, since the Romantics saw Dante, through his artistic visions of the other world, as a prophetic guide into the unfamiliar regions of imagination and mysticism.[77]

To comprehend just how strongly the tradition of reading Chopin's music through national topoi persisted into the twentieth century, suffice it to lend an ear to Ignacy Jan Paderewski, who, in a discourse delivered at the opening of the Chopin Centenary Festival in Lviv/Lemberg/Lwów (at the time still under Austrian control) on 23 October 1910, said of Chopin's prophetic voice:

> Chopin alone was not forbidden to us. And yet in him we still could find the living breath of all that was prohibited; . . . he gave all back to us, mingled with the prayers of broken hearts, the revolt of fettered souls, the pains of slavery, lost freedom's ache, the cursing of tyrants, and exultant songs of victory.[78]

Chopin himself seems to have become aware of his historic destiny sometime while composing the Fantasy. On 21 October 1841 he wrote to Fontana:

> Today I finished the fantasy—the sky is beautiful, my heart is sad—but it doesn't matter. If it were different, perhaps my existence would be of no use to anyone. Let us save ourselves for after death.[79]

How closely do these words resonate with Mickiewicz's lectures at the Collège de France:

> A man who best developed his spirit opens up a channel to heaven, through which God's revelation pours down, and thus he becomes an oracle. He is not just a passive tool, for he must be deserving and capable of making sacrifices; he should "push aside his own affairs, his individuality, his ego."[80]

During his final years Chopin provided an explicit artistic testimony of his resignation to this noble but tragic destiny by setting Krasiński's poem to music. The haunting text of "Melody" epitomizes the messianic idea, but, more significantly, the poem and Chopin's musical setting underscore the self-sacrifice that is expected of the *wieszcz*, the isolation and suffering that the messianic messenger must endure. For he must bear the cross of his nation's tragedy; in the darkest of the night he must see the divine light of hope ahead; and, like Moses guiding his tribe to the Promised Land, he is not destined to attain it.

Chopin again expressed the necessity for sacrifice in his last lengthy political commentary in a letter to Julian Fontana, written just before embarking on the devastating voyage to England and Scotland. Responding to the events of the Springtime of the Peoples, more particularly to the formation in Poznań (20 March 1848) of the Polish National Committee [Polski Komitet Narodowy], which aimed at securing administrative and military independence of the Great Duchy of Poznań from Prussia, Chopin wrote: "There is no way horrifying events can be averted, but in the end of it all is a splendid, great Poland; in a word: Poland."[81]

Chopin was never a devoted messianist, but the visions of Poland's past glory, its suffering and death, and hopes for its resurrection surrounded and touched him. Being reserved, unwilling to commit himself to any "-isms," and seldom expressing his most passionate thoughts in words, he would let his music speak instead. And it was through his music that he would most eloquently express, for everyone to hear, his dreams of Poland past and future, perhaps not unlike Jankiel's musical visions:

> A poor old song, to Polish troops so dear!
> The soldiers recognized it, crowding near
> Around the master; listening, they recall
> That dreadful hour when o'er their country's fall
> They sang the song, and went to distant climes;
> And to their minds came memories of those times,
> Of wandering through frosts and burning sands
> And seas, when oft in camps in foreign lands
> This Polish song had cheered and comforted
> Such were their thoughts, and each man bowed his head.[82]

NOTES

1. Adam Mickiewicz, *Pan Tadeusz*, trans. Kenneth R. Mackenzie (New York: Hippocrene, 1992), 566. Unless otherwise indicated, all translations in this essay are mine.

2. Bożena Shallcross, " 'The Wondrous Fire': Adam Mickiewicz's *Pan Tadeusz* and the Romantic Improvisation," *East European Politics and Societies* 3 (1995): 523–33.

3. Among others, Josiek Guzikow, the Jewish straw fiddle virtuoso and improviser, amazing audiences in Poland and abroad, has been advanced as a plausible candidate.

4. Shallcross, " 'The Wondrous Fire.' "

5. On Polish messianism, see Andrzej Walicki, *Filozofia a mesjanizm. Studia z dziejów filozofii i myśli społeczno-religijnej romantyzmu polskiego* (Warszawa: Państwowy Instytut Wydawniczy, 1970), 9–88.

6. Adam Mickiewicz, *Konrad Wallenrod, and Other Writings of Adam Mickiewicz*, trans. Jewell Parish, Dorothea Prall Radin, George Rapall Noyes, et al. (Berkeley: University of California Press, 1925), 113.

7. Depictions of this kind are quite common on postcards and prints. Predictably the image that adorns the title page of the Parisian first edition (1832) of *Books of the Polish Nation and Its Pilgrimage* follows the same model.

8. Adam Mickiewicz, *Forefathers' Eve*, Part III, in *Polish Romantic Drama*, trans. Harold B. Segel (Ithaca, N.Y.: Cornell University Press, 1977), 108.

9. In July 1841 Mickiewicz met Andrzej Towiański and soon became the main propagator of his mystic ideas, which led the authorities to suspend Mickiewicz as a professor in May 1844. Following Towiański's program, he organized a legion, which fought in Italy until July 1849. In 1855, during the Crimean War, he went to Turkey to support the organization of a Polish legion for the struggle against Russia. He died, probably of cholera, in Istanbul on 26 November 1855.

10. O[skar] K[olberg], "Muzyka," *Encyklopedia powszechna Orgelbranda*, 28 vols. (Warszawa: Orgelbrand, 1859–68; reprint, 1984–88), 19:108. Oskar Kolberg, Poland's most celebrated ethnomusicologist of the nineteenth century, was responsible for many articles in the prestigious *Orgelbrand Encyclopedia*. He was also Chopin's childhood acquaintance (though Chopin was appalled by Kolberg's first collection of arranged folk tunes). The Chopin and Kolberg families were neighbors, and Fryderyk was very close with the oldest boy, Wilhelm. See Halina Goldberg, *Music in Chopin's Warsaw*, forthcoming from Oxford University Press.

11. Adam Czartoryski, "Narzędzia dawnéy muzyki kraiowéy," in "Słownik wyrazów niektórych polskich mniéy używanych. . . ." After 1800. Biblioteka Ossolińskich, *Ms. 496*.

12. S.v., "Guslar, guslarz," *Encyklopedia Orgelbranda*, 11:45.

13. For a detailed discussion of Chopin's involvement with literary Romanticism during his Warsaw years, see Halina Goldberg, "Chopin in Literary Salons and Warsaw's Romantic Awakening," *The Polish Review* 45 (January 2000): 53–64.

14. Stuttgart, after 8 September 1831, from Chopin's *Album-Diary*, in *Korespondencja Fryderyka Chopina*, ed. Bronisław Edward Sydow, 2 vols. (Warszawa: Państwowy Instytut Wydawniczy, 1955), 1:185.

15. Mickiewicz, *Forefathers' Eve*, Part III, 108–9.

16. Fryderyk Chopin to Tytus Woyciechowski, Paris, 25 December 1831, *Korespondencja*, 1:207–8.

17. Fryderyk Chopin to Dominik Dziewanowski, Paris, mid-January 1833,

*Korespondencja*, 1:223. The Carlists were the supporters of Charles X, who abdicated as a result of the July Revolution of 1830; the Philippists were those who backed Louis Philippe, duc d'Orléans, who replaced him.

18. He reported on the subject of inviting the quarreling sides to attend a rehearsal of his E Minor Concerto at his house: "It is without precedent that these gentlemen be seen together, but I can accomplish it and will do it for my delight" (Fryderyk Chopin to Tytus Woyciechowski, Warsaw, Wednesday morning, 22 September [1]830, *Korespondencja*, 1:141).

19. Jolanta Pękacz argues that Chopin was altogether apolitical, not interested in political causes ("Deconstructing a 'National Composer': Chopin and Polish Exiles in Paris, 1831–49," *19th-Century Music* 24 [2000]: 161–72). The present article, although agreeing with some of her observations, argues otherwise. A number of specific statements Pękacz uses to support her view invite closer scrutiny. She claims that Chopin never played benefits for Polish émigrés (Pękacz, "Deconstructing," 172), but there are records of several such performances (on public and private performances for the veterans of the November Uprising in Paris and in London, see notes 29 and 30 below). The list of compositions dedicated to Poles (completed during his early and mature years) includes more than twenty-four names, hardly justifying the statement that he dedicated only a handful of pieces to Polish dedicatees (168). The assertion that he set only pieces by minor Polish poets (171) is neither entirely accurate (he set two texts by Mickiewicz and one by Krasiński, the "high priests" of Polish Romanticism), nor does it reinforce her thesis: although the poets Chopin preferred might have been second tier, they were not at all apolitical; Wincenty Pol, Bohdan Zaleski, and Stefan Witwicki were ardent patriots, who viewed their own poetry as a vehicle through which to further the national cause—and, as discussed below, several of their texts that Chopin set to music are fundamentally patriotic.

20. On the political writings of George Sand and Marie d'Agout, see Whitney Walton, *Eve's Proud Descendants: Four Women Writers and Republican Politics in Nineteenth-Century France* (Stanford, Calif.: Stanford University Press, 2000); on the connection between Hector Berlioz, Henri Reber, Franz Liszt, Ferdinand Hiller, Adolphe Nourrit, and Felix Mendelssohn-Bartholdy, all Chopin's acquaintances, and the Saint-Simonian movement, see Ralph P. Locke, *Music, Musicians, and the Saint-Simonians* (Chicago: University of Chicago Press, 1986).

21. Mieczysław Tomaszewski, *Chopin* (Poznań: Wydawnictwo Podsiedlik-Raniowski i Spółka, 1997), 88–89. Tomaszewski's encyclopedic compendium is an invaluable reference tool, essential for any serious student of Chopin.

22. Ibid., 92.

23. On 26 July 1840 Chopin and Sand attended the dress rehearsal of Berlioz's *Symphonie funèbre et triomphale*, composed to commemorate the victims of the July 1830 French revolution on the tenth anniversary of the event (Hector Berlioz to Fryderyk Chopin, Paris, before 26 July 1840, *Korespondencja*, 2:11). Berlioz's note had a ticket enclosed. Incidentally the three movements of Berlioz's rather uninspired *Symphonie funèbre et triomphale*, which Chopin disliked, are *Marche funèbre*, *Oraison funèbre*, and *Apothéose*, and they explore the same topoi as the works of Chopin discussed below.

24. Tomaszewski, *Chopin*, 88. In 1840 the increased protests and demands for electoral reform and suffrage for the National Guard were repressed by Thiers. This is probably what Sand and Chopin were responding to. See Philippe Vigier, *La monarchie de Juillet* (Paris: Presses Universitaires de France, 1962), 91.

25. Fryderyk Chopin to Julian Fontana, Nohant, 11 September 1841, *Korespondencja*, 2:36.

26. Ibid., 18 September 1841, *Korespondencja*, 2:37.

27. Op. 46, most likely first conceived during his early years in Paris as an opening movement of his third concerto, was published only in 1841 as a solo piano piece. On the provenance of this work, see John Rink, *Chopin: The Piano Concertos* (Cambridge: Cambridge University Press, 1997), 89–92. However, the publication of this piece in 1841, along with opp. 47, 48, and 49, seems very timely in the context of the particular fondness Chopin seems to have had for this work. According to an indirect report, Chopin said: "This will be the first piece that I will play in my first concert in free Warsaw upon my return to the country" (Marceli Antoni Szulc, *Fryderyk Chopin i utwory jego muzyczne* [Poznań: Żupański, 1873], 81). Similarly, as he sent Julian Fontana the manuscript of op. 46, he instructed him: "Respect my manuscript and do not wrinkle or stain it, or tear it (all [these are] things that you are not capable of doing, but I write it because I so much love my written tedia)" (Fryderyk Chopin to Julian Fontana, Nohant, 18 October 1841, *Korespondencja*, 2:44).

28. A number of articles have highlighted the national readings of Chopin's music, most notably Karol Berger, "Chopin's Ballade op. 23 and the Revolution of the Intellectuals," in *Chopin Studies 2*, ed. John Rink and Jim Samson (Cambridge: Cambridge University Press, 1994), 72–83; Jeffrey Kallberg "Hearing Poland: Chopin and Nationalism," in *Nineteenth-Century Piano Music*, ed. Larry Todd (New York: Schirmer, 1990), 221–57; and idem, "Rhetoric of a Genre: Chopin's Nocturne in G Minor," in *Chopin at the Boundaries: Sex, History, and Musical Genre* (Cambridge, Mass.: Harvard University Press, 1996), 3–29.

29. Numerous accounts of Chopin's improvisations on, and involvement with, Polish patriotic songs have come down to us. For the most complete list, see Krystyna Kobylańska, "Improwizacje Fryderyka Chopina," *Rocznik Chopinowski* 19 (1987): 69–92.

30. For instance, 4 April and 24 December 1835, 20 February 1846, and 16 November 1848. See Mieczysław Tomaszewski, *Muzyka Chopina na nowo odczytana* (Kraków: Akademia Muzyczna, 1996), 38.

31. With the exception of the ballades, the "national" status of which has never been doubted, and which have generated continuing attempts at semiotic and hermeneutic interpretation. The history of the reception of Chopin's ballades, plagued by its own set of national legends and interpretational conjectures, is a colossal study in itself that cannot be undertaken here.

32. Kazimierz Brodziński, "Uwagi nad potrzebą wyboru poezji dla młodzieży, zbioru pieśni duchowych i narodowych," speech delivered at the meeting of the Warsaw Society for the Friends of Learning, 12 March 1821; in *Kazimierz Brodziński. Pisma estetyczno-krytyczne*, ed. Aleksander Łucki, 2 vols. (Warszawa: Z Zasiłku Funduszu Kultury Narodowej, 1934), 1:222–32. It is important to note that both composers already headed societies devoted to national religious music: Elsner was one of the founders of the Society for the Friends of Religious and National Music (1814), and Kurpiński founded the Gathering of the Aficionados of National-Religious Songs (1821).

33. See Alina Nowak-Romanowicz, *Józef Elsner* (Kraków: Polskie Wydawnictwo Muzyczne, 1957), 154. This intensely patriotic opera was well known to Chopin. Though forbidden by the censor after 1822, it was remembered throughout the 1820s and revived on the national stage during the November Uprising. See Halina Goldberg, *Music in Chopin's Warsaw*, forthcoming.

34. Józef Sikorski, "O muzyce," *Biblioteka warszawska* 2 (1843): 665–73.

35. Ibid., 667.

36. Ibid., 668.

37. Ibid., 672. Ignacy Dobrzyński, a prominent composer of the Polish Romantic generation, was another conservatory colleague of Chopin.

38. Karol Kurpiński, "O expresji muzycznej i naśladowaniu," *Tygodnik muzyczny i dramatyczny*, no. 6 (16 May 1821): 21–22.

39. Ibid.

40. Karol Kurpiński, "The Hymn of the Lithuanian Legions" (Warszawa: Brzezina, 1831); Warsaw, Biblioteka Narodowa, *Mus. II 18.506 cim.*

41. See Maja Trochimczyk, "Sacred/Secular Constructs of National Identity: A Convoluted History of Polish Anthems," in *After Chopin: Studies in Polish Music*, ed. Maja Trochimczyk, Polish Music History series, vol. 6 (Los Angeles: Polish Music Center at University of Southern California, 2000), 246–68.

42. Tomaszewski, *Muzyka Chopina*, 39.

43. This description in Tomaszewski, *Muzyka Chopina*, 39, published after A. Simonówna, *Polski rocznik muzykologiczny* 1 (1935): 105, is a report by Count Józef Krasiński in his *Pamiętnik czyli wspomnienia i znaczniejsze wypadki życia mojego*.

44. Warsaw, The Frederic Chopin Society, *M/1960*. Józef Michał Chomiński and Teresa Dalila Turło, *A Catalogue of the Works of Frederick Chopin* (Kraków: Polskie Wydawnictwo Muzyczne, 1990), 239.

45. The hymn, which in our century contended for the role of the national anthem, in Chopin's youth was a praise of tsar Alexander, the king of Poland. During the subsequent century and a half the text changed many times: for the duration of the November Uprising and the painful period that followed its collapse, it became a prayer for a free Poland. See Bogdan Zakrzewski, *Boże coś Polskę Alojzego Felińskiego* (Wrocław: Ossolineum, 1983).

46. Tadeusz A. Zieliński, *Chopin. Życie i droga twórcza*, 2nd ed. (Warszawa: Polskie Wydawnictwo Muzyczne, 1998), 403–4 and 639–40.

47. Fryderyk Skarbek, *Pamiętniki* (Poznań: Żupański, 1878), 136.

48. Franz Liszt, *Chopin*, ed. Nicole Priollaud (Paris: Liana Levi, 1990), 93.

49. Report by Januszkiewicz in Kobylańska, "Improwizacje Fryderyka Chopina," 90.

50. The modern version of this hymn is still sung today, and in the 1980s it lent strength to the anticommunist movement.

51. The translation is mine. The November Uprising version of the text is after Zakrzewski, *Boże coś Polskę Alojzego Felińskiego*.

52. This work was eloquently set in national context by Jeffrey Kallberg in "Rhetoric of a Genre: Chopin's Nocturne in G Minor."

53. Węcowski searches, with mixed success, for quotations of religious tunes in Chopin's compositions. See Jan Węcowski, "Religious Folklore in Chopin's Polish Music," *Polish Music Journal* 2 (1999). http://www.usc.edu/dept/polish_music/pmj/issue/2.1.99/wecowski.html, accessed 31 July 2002.

54. Marceli Antoni Szulc, "Przegląd ostatnich dzieł Chopina," in *Tygodnik literacki*, nos. 10–11 (7 March 1842; 14 March 1842): 76–77, 82–83.

55. For a brief discussion of early-nineteenth-century examples and a survey of literature, see Alina Nowak-Romanowicz, *Klasycyzm, 1750–1830 Historia Muzyki Polskiej* series, vol. 4 (Warszawa: Sutkowski, 1995), 202–8. The *duma/dumka* is the least discussed musical signifier of Polishness. Much of it has to do with its relationship with Ukrainian songs and later developments in the concept of Polish national identity. Chopin's Poland was multiethnic and multicultural, and the earlier writings on music took this reality into account. For instance, Sikorski's essay, "On Music," states that Polish national music has varying character depending on the province of origin, and next to the "central lands" he enumerates the Lithuanian, Ukrainian, Cracovian, and Cossack types (670). The nineteenth century produced an ideal of culturally homogenous Poland, in which the status of the *duma/dumka* became predictably awkward. For a good general description of this historical process, see Norman Davies, *God's Playground: A History of Poland*,

2 vols. (New York: Columbia University Press, 1982). See below for Zaleski's description of Chopin's improvisation on the "Dąbrowski Mazurka" and for further discussion of this genre in Chopin's own compositions.

56. After Tomaszewski, *Muzyka Chopina*, 39. The event took place on 2 February 1844 (on the occasion of Zaleski's birthday) (Bohdan Zaleski, "Dziennik," in *Przewodnik naukowy* (1899). There have been efforts to trace motivic links between the "Dąbrowski Mazurka" and the op. 61 *Polonaise fantaisie*, but the argument is not convincing enough; see Ferdinand Gajewski, "Jeszcze Polska nie zginęła: The Apotheosis of the Dąbrowski Mazurka," *Studi musicali* 19 (1990): 407–18.

57. Julian Fontana, preface to Fryderyk Chopin, *Zbiór śpiewów polskich*, Posthumous Works, part 2 (Warszawa: Gebethner i Spółka, 1859).

58. This title is found on the Julian Fontana copy (Warszawa: The Warsaw Music Society, *21/Ch*) and in the *Stichvorlage* (Vienna: Österreichische Nationalbibliothek, Musiksammlung) (Krystyna Kobylańska, *Rękopisy utworów Chopina: Katalog*, 2 vols. [Kraków: Polskie Wydawnictwo Muzyczne, 1977], 2:470–72). In the nineteenth-century Breitkopf & Härtel edition this song is entitled "Polens Grabgesang" ["Śpiew Grobowy"] (Friedrich Chopin, *Lieder für eine Singstimme mit Begleitung des Pianoforte: nachgelassene Werke*, in *Friedrich Chopin's Werke: Erste Gesamtausgabe* [Leipzig: Breitkopf & Härtel, 1880], vol. 14).

59. Fryderyk Chopin to Konstanty Gaszyński, Paris, 3 May 1840, *Korespondencja*, 2:8.

60. For a full list of critical responses to this composition, see Tomaszewski, "Fantazja F-Moll Op. 49: Struktura dwoista i drugie dno," in *Muzyka Chopina*, 73–93. Many of my observations about this work are indebted to this exhaustive essay.

61. Ibid.

62. Szulc, "Przegląd ostatnich dzieł Chopina," in *Tygodnik literacki*, no. 11 (14 March 1842): 82.

63. Sikorski, "O muzyce," 673.

64. Ibid. Tomaszewski believes that Chopin is here referring to "Marsz obozowy," another composition by Kurpiński (Tomaszewski, "Fantazja F-Moll," in *Muzyka Chopina*, 91–92).

65. According to the unconfirmed report in Szulc's biography (1873), Chopin's settings of insurrectionary poems by Konstanty Gaszyński (*Songs of the Polish Pilgrim* [Paris, 1833]) and Maurycy Gosławski (*Poems of the Polish Uhlan* [Paris, 1833]) existed at one time. Szulc also reports that Chopin intended to set Krasiński's poem "I Know That Poland Will Fight the Victorious Battle, That It Did Not Perish, and Never Will Perish," which was found among his posthumous papers (after Tomaszewski, *Muzyka Chopina*, 40).

66. This manner of publication was typical of Count Zygmunt Krasiński (1812–1859), whose almost entire output was historiosophic in nature. He maintained anonymity because of his infamous father's prominent social and political position in Warsaw, as well as to preserve his own ability to make intermittent trips to Poland. The original poem carried no title, serving as a motto to a longer poem entitled "The Last One" ["Ostatni"].

67. The whereabouts of this *Stammbuch* are not known, but it still existed in the beginning of the twentieth century. The *Stichvorlage* is in an unknown copyist's hand, annotated by Fontana (Vienna, Österreichische Nationalbibliothek, Musiksammlung) (Kobylańska, *Rękopisy utworów Chopina*, 2:454–55).

68. Wojciech Grzymała to August Léo, Paris, end of October 1849, *Korespondencja*, 2:324.

69. Tomaszewski, *Muzyka Chopina*, 87–88.

70. Kolberg, "Muzyka," in *Encyklopedia Orgelbranda*, 19:115.

71. Marceli Antoni Szulc, "O najnowszych utworach Chopina," *Orędownik narodowy*, no. 26 (1841): 211.

72. Szulc, "Przegląd ostatnich dzieł Chopina," in *Tygodnik literacki*, no. 10 (7 March 1842): 76. Stanisław Tarnowski (1871), on the authority of Marcelina Czartoryska, officially inducted Chopin as the fourth *wieszcz* (the other three were Mickiewicz, Słowacki, and Krasiński) (Tomaszewski, *Chopin*, 752).

73. Szulc, "Przegląd ostatnich dzieł Chopina," in *Tygodnik literacki*, no. 11 (14 March 1842): 83.

74. Wilhelm von Lenz, *Die grossen Pianoforte-Virtuosen unserer Zeit aus persönlich Bekanntschaft* (Berlin: B. Behr, 1872), 86.

75. Henri Blanchard in *Revue et gazette musicale*, 12 March 1843; after Tomaszewski, *Muzyka Chopina*, 86.

76. Félicien Mallefile, "A.M.F. Chopin," *Revue et gazette musicale de Paris*, 9 September 1838, 562–64; after Berger, "Chopin's Ballade op. 23," 82. In his article Berger addresses the messianic context of Chopin's Ballade op. 23. Similarly, foreign composers who were sympathetic to the Polish cause responded with pieces featuring the earlier-discussed Polish patriotic songs. Among these are Wagner's Overture *Polonia* (1836), inspired by hearing these songs on an anniversary of the Constitution of May 3, and Liszt's *Salve Polonia*.

77. On Delacroix's view of Chopin, see John Nici's essay in this volume.

78. Ignacy Jan Paderewski, *F. Chopin* (Warszawa: Stowarzyszenie Bibliotekarzy Polskich, 1991), 48. Also see the excerpt from Sikorski's "A Recollection of Chopin," quoted in Waldemar Okoń's essay. For more on the twentieth-century reception of Chopin, including that of Paderewski, see Maja Tochimczyk's essay in this volume.

79. He continues, "N.B. not in the sense of Le Roux, because then the younger one gets killed, the more right he is," referring to the radical elements in the messianic social utopia of Pierre Leroux's—George Sand's collaborator (Fryderyk Chopin to Julian Fontana, Nohant, 20 October 1841, *Korespondencja*, 2:45).

80. Adam Mickiewicz, *Literatura słowiańska*, trans. Leon Płoszewski, *Dzieła wszystkie*, ed. Julian Krzyżanowski, 16 vols. (Warszawa: Czytelnik, 1955), 10:409–10.

81. Fryderyk Chopin to Julian Fontana, Paris, 4 April 1848, *Korespondencja*, 2:239.

82. Mickiewicz, *Pan Tadeusz*, 566–68.

# Part II

---

## Analytical Perspectives

# 5

# Idiosyncrasies of Phrase Rhythm in Chopin's Mazurkas

CARL SCHACHTER

## *Introduction*

The brilliant American author Guy Davenport writes the following in one of his short stories: "Parmenides is wrong: the nothing he will not allow to be is time itself. Time is the empty house that being inhabits."[1] Davenport's seemingly contradictory metaphors—time both as "nothing" and as an "empty house"—are a wonderful evocation of time in tonal music, for the metrical divisions of time that help make music comprehensible—the walls of the empty house—are not part of the sonic structure. Instead, the listener imagines them as one facet of his or her response to the pattern of durations built into that structure. In a sense these temporal divisions are indeed nothing, but, if listeners could not infer them, music as we know and feel it would not exist; there would be no house for it to inhabit.

Standard musical notation is designed to indicate the smaller units of the metrical patterns found in music—beats, divisions of beats, and measures. The larger units—consistent groups of mea-

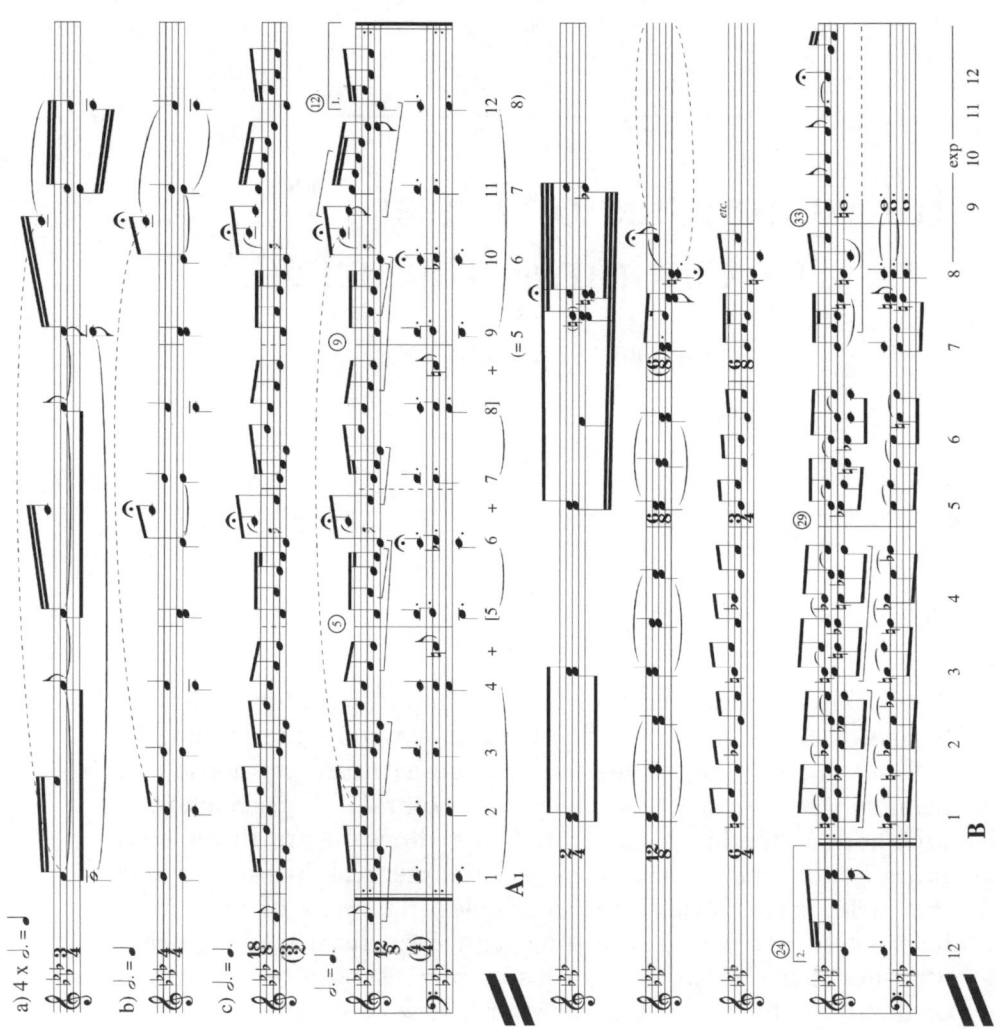

Example 5.1. Chopin, Mazurka in A♭ Major op. 24 no. 3, durational reduction

sures, or hypermeasures—are very seldom notated at all: Beethoven's "*ritmo di tre battute*" in the Ninth Symphony or Liszt's "1–2–
3–4" starting with an empty bar at the beginning of the first
*Mephisto Waltz* are very much the exception to normal notational
practice. Some years ago I wanted to try out my approach to large-
scale rhythm and meter on a significant body of works with common stylistic and generic features. I chose the Chopin mazurkas
largely because they unite in seeming paradox Chopin's characteristically uniform four-bar groups with highly varied and unpredictable patterns of accentuation, both within the bar and within
the larger durational units.[2] It is this work that I am going to discuss here, concentrating on two idiosyncratic features and one
piece. The features are (1) delayed initial tonic chords, and (2)
twelve-bar phrases; the piece is the A♭ Mazurka op. 24 no. 3. Example 5.1 consists of a multilevel durational reduction (tonal and
rhythmic analysis) of this mazurka.

   Before going on to the phrase rhythm, I shall discuss briefly
the large-scale melodic contour and the motivic design of the mazurka. There is a typically Chopinesque bel canto profile to the
melody of the A section, with a wonderfully gradual rise to $c^3$ as
the climax and a quick fall to the original register for the cadence.
Example 5.2 presents Schenker's graph of the A section in *Free
Composition*. He shows the ascending motion as a tonic arpeggiation
up to the high C as $\hat{3}$; rather curiously, in my view, he does not
show the lower C of bar 2 as a structural melodic note transferred
up an octave through the arpeggiation. In his graph, however, the
$\hat{2}$ and $\hat{1}$ at the end fall in the lower octave. In addition, the entire
B section unfolds in the lower octave and the coda comes to rest
on the $c^2$ from which the arpeggio originated.[3]

   And now I shall address a salient feature of the motivic design.
In Example 5.3 I try to show how the descending fourth A♭–G–F–
E♭ permeates the entire piece. As Example 5.3a indicates, the
meaning of this fourth varies according to the context. At first the
G is the emphasized note, moving back to A♭ after a detour; in
bars 5 and 6, however, the G is a passing tone down to an emphasized F, which in turn resolves to E♭. Example 5.3b and 5.3c
add further variations in meaning. At the beginning of the middle
section (5.3b), the fourth is filled in chromatically, the interior
notes moving in an unbroken line from A♭ to E♭. And at the end
of this section (5.3c), the fourth seems to end on the wrong note—
E♮—until the E♭ of the reprise completes and "corrects" the mo-

Chopin, Mazurka op. 24 no. 3

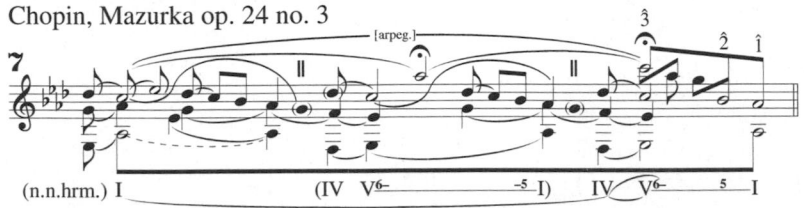

Example 5.2. Chopin, Mazurka in A♭ Major op. 24 no. 3, graph of the A section from Heinrich Schenker, *Free Composition*, trans. and ed. Ernst Oster (New York: Longman, 1979), Figure 40,7.

tion. Particularly ingenious are the registrally expanded presentations in the cadential bars (5.3d) and the final echo of the motive at the very end of the coda (5.3e).

## Non-Tonic Beginnings

Note that the first chord in op. 24 no. 3 is a $V^{7}$, preceded by the tonic note as an unharmonized upbeat. As I mentioned before, many mazurkas delay the advent of the first tonic chord. Most often, as in opus 24 no. 3, it appears in bar 2, following a V in bar 1. The delayed tonic is somewhat more frequent in the later mazurkas than in the earlier ones. Of the twenty-nine composed in the 1830s, from opus 6 through opus 33, twelve have delayed tonics. Of the twelve pieces from the 1840s, from opus 50 to opus 63, as many as five have delayed tonics. Thus the combined total is seventeen out of the forty-one mazurkas Chopin himself published (more or less two out of five)—a very high number for a comparatively unusual feature. In these figures I did not include the mazurkas whose initial tonics appear in the first bar of a phrase following an extended introduction, for this type of delay does not impinge on the normal phrase rhythm. In the ones I am considering, the avoidance of a tonic on the metrically strong first bar of a phrase sets up a conflict between harmony and meter, denying metrical emphasis to the governing harmony. This lack of correspondence between metrical accent and tonal structure is one of the sources of the remarkable rhythmic fluidity of these mazurkas.

In trying to understand these non-tonic beginnings, we must at least consider the possibility that the first bars should be heard as upbeats, with the first complete four-bar group dating from bar 2. After all, the feeling of forward movement into the tonic of the

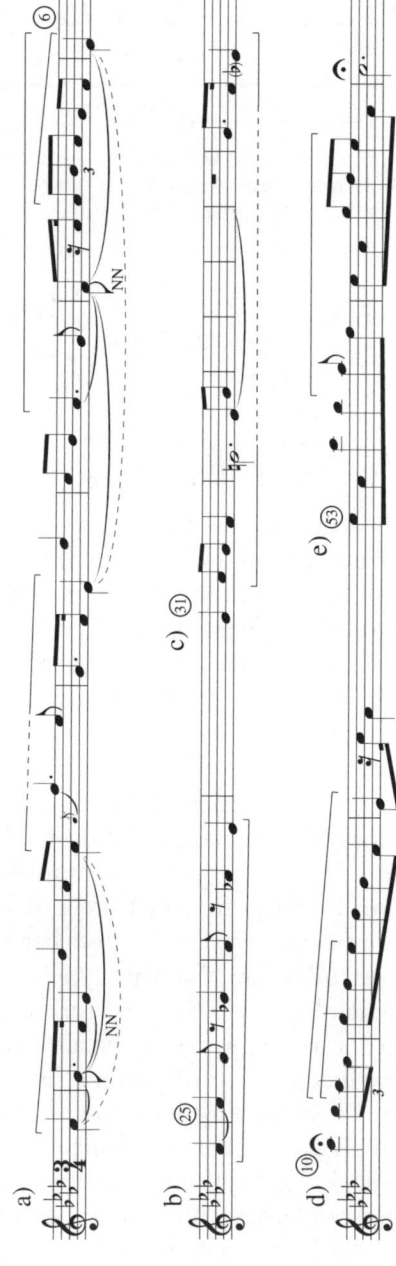

Example 5.3. Chopin, Mazurka in A♭ Major op. 24 no. 3, fourth motive

second bar does give bar 1 something of the feeling of an upbeat. In op. 24 no. 3, all the tonic chords in the A section fall on even-numbered bars—2, 4, 8, and 12—and striking $^6_4$s on cadential dominants occupy bars 6 and 10. This regular periodicity of important tonal arrivals could speak for hearing the even bars as strong. Against this, however, are Chopin's slurs and accent signs in bars 1–4, which tell us to bring out the first beats in the odd bars. Moreover, the B section must be read in fours starting with its first bar; the hemiola rhythms that begin it and the four "extra" bars at the end permit no other possibility. These last four bars clearly lead into a hypermetrical downbeat on the first bar of the reprise, which corresponds to bar 1. So it is clear that the four-bar groups throughout the mazurka date from bar 1. The emphases produced by harmony conflict with the hypermeter, setting up a rival schema—what Frank Samarotto calls a "shadow meter."[4] Only in the coda does a metrical reinterpretation finally allow the tonic chord to come to rest on a downbeat bar.

## Twelve-Bar Phrases

Let us now turn to the second general feature I wish to discuss: twelve-bar phrases. Although not nearly as common as the delayed tonics, they nonetheless form a rather prominent stylistic feature of the Chopin mazurkas, often appearing as the opening strain of a piece. In every instance the twelve bars can be parsed as three fours, producing a triple meter on a very large scale—a triple hypermeter, if you will. But none of these large phrases are simply 3 × 4. Let us look at the end of the B section of our A♭ Mazurka, bars 29–36, as represented in the durational reduction of Example 5.1. Let me explain how the reduction works. In level c I show each four-bar group as a measure of $^{12}/_8$ and each measure of the music as one beat within that measure. In level b I use more or less the same rate of reduction, but I eliminate a good deal of local detail to concentrate on larger melodic and rhythmic shapes. And, in level a, I carry this process of reduction still further, so much so that four bars of music become a quarter-note beat within a bar of $^3/_4$. In this way, the large-scale rhythmic and metric organization of the phrase becomes more readily visible. Now looking at the representation of bars 29–36 in level c, you can see that I regard the twelve bars of this phrase as resulting from the expansion of an underlying eight. This expansion is of the simplest kind, extending the duration of the goal C-major harmony (III♮) in a kind of composed fermata, while the right-hand repeated notes bring back a clear expression of the ¾ time, which had become obscured through the pervasive hemiola rhythms of the preceding music. One can leave out the "extra" four bars of the expansion without removing any essential element of melody or harmony, but the rhythmic shape, of course, would become quite different. In most of the twelve-bar phrases of the mazurkas, one can feel an underlying eight-bar idea, which becomes twelve by means of an expansion.

Not all Chopin's twelve-bar phrases, however, result from expansion. In *Free Composition*, Schenker discusses the opening strain of our A♭ Mazurka op. 24 no. 3, and says the following: "A 12-measure group, comprising three 4-measure groups, is found in Chopin's Mazurka op. 24 no. 3 (Figure 40,7). The triple ordering arises because, in the arpeggiation up to $c^3$, $a♭^2$ has its own 4-measure group."[5] If you will turn again to the durational reduction of my Example 5.1, level c, you will see that $c^2$ is established in the first four-bar group together with a rise to $e♭^2$. The second group of four bars brings in the $a♭^2$ (with the fermata) to which Schenker refers. And the third group reaches the $c^3$ and concludes the twelve bars with a cadence. Let us now turn to levels b and a of my durational graph. In these levels, which show only the broad outlines of melody, harmony, and rhythm, the "triple ordering" of which Schenker speaks becomes very clear—most especially in level a. Those who are familiar with Schenker's work on rhythm will understand that he does not regard these twelve bars as arising from expansion. In his terminology the unusual number of bars grows organically out of a diminution (or melodic figure)—in this case the arpeggio up to the high C.

Because the $a♭^2$ forms an integral element of this arpeggio, Schenker is surely correct in implying that the twelve bars do not simply result from a durational expansion. Compare this opening phrase with the twelve-bar group at the end of the B section, whose last four bars could fall away without taking any essential tonal element with them. And yet my ear persists in telling me that in perhaps some different sense there is a kind of expansion going on here. That is because bars 7–10 are an exact repetition of bars 3–6—exact, that is, with the crucial exception of the high C in bar 10. One can easily imagine an eight-bar phrase consisting of bars 1–4 and 9–12. An important melodic element—$a♭^2$—would be missing, so the eight-bar phrase would not be simply a compressed version of the twelve bars. Rhythmically, however, the two halves of the phrase would balance perfectly. Perhaps they would balance too perfectly: part of the charm of these twelve-bar groups is precisely their subversion of a felt bilateral symmetry underlying the phrase. As a tonal entity, therefore, the twelve bars do not contain an expansion, but, as a durational unit, maybe they do. This leads me to believe that Schenker's rigidly formulated distinction between phrase rhythms modified by expansion and those growing organically out of a diminution needs to be loosened up a bit. Sometimes it might be a case of both/and rather than either/or.

The unique rhythmic character of the opening idea of op. 24 no. 3 deserves a closer look. First, there is the near repetition in bar 3 of the contents of bar 1. There is nothing very unusual about this; the same thing happens in quite a few mazurkas, not to mention other kinds of pieces. Here, however, the feature becomes something special because of the way it interacts with two other elements: the fermata in bar 6 and the near repetition in bars 7–10 of bars 3–6. This first fermata creates a halt in the forward motion of the phrase, which raises the possibility of hearing bar 7 as a new beginning. And when bar 7 repeats bar 3, it is also coming very close to repeating bar 1, the real beginning. As a result, the rhythm and design produce a strong articulation midway through the phrase, between bars 6 and 7. This articulation divides the phrase into two segments, 1–6 and 7–12, a duple division of 6 + 6 that cuts across the threefold grouping into 4 + 4 + 4. One can think of it as an enormously extended rhythm of two against three that stretches over twelve bars of music. The most detailed level of my durational reduction (Example 5.1c) attempts to depict this remarkable rhythmic situation by means of a separate stave added above the main one. It also shows that both the four-bar and the six-bar groups can be subdivided into 4 + 2 + 2 + 4.

A question to consider is whether the two rival groupings—6 + 6 and 4 + 4 + 4—are of equal significance. I think that they are not; for the mazurka, the division into three four-bar groups is surely the primary one. This is partly because the genre itself is characterized by groups of four bars as the norm. In addition, the division into three such groups is deeply embedded in the compositional fabric of this twelve-bar phrase. This comes across quite clearly in the durational reductions of Example 5.1, where the threefold division persists in all levels from the most immediate to the most remote, whereas the division into two sixes disappears as soon as the surface detail is eliminated. Even if I had made a reduction based on six-bar units, the contour of the melodic line with its three-stage rise—first to E♭, then to A♭, and finally to C—would fight against the analysis and would suggest that the division into four-bar groups is the more natural. Thus Schenker was profoundly right in stating that a "triple ordering" of four-bar groups grows out of the melodic structure.

In this mazurka the middle section forms a sharp contrast in character to the opening strain. And yet there are important links. Curiously enough the middle section also has an implicit two-against-three rhythm, less grandiose than the one in bars 1–12 but more easily perceptible. The hemiola pattern that runs through most of the section sets up a division of every two-bar group into three, a division that cuts across the two notated ¾ bars and thus conflicts with the listener's memory of the A section. Another, more subtle, link is found in the durational expansion of the section's final C-major chord, with its melodic halt on $c^2$. This stasis recalls the fermatas that are so striking a feature of the opening section. And, of course, the most important link of all is the descending fourth from A♭ to E♭. Since the B section closes on a C-major chord with E♮ as its third, the motive is not fulfilled until the V chord at the beginning of the reprise introduces the goal tone E♭. Thus the chromatic move from $ab^1$ to $eb^1$ that completes the motivic descending fourth also bridges over the formal articulation. This motivic completion across a sectional boundary is one type of what Schenker called *Knüpftechnik* or linkage technique. Some have cited Chopin's liking for simple, sectionalized designs such as this ABA as evidence of his alleged incompetence in matters of form. But, to the contrary, his ability to individualize and breathe life into these designs in ways I have shown here reveals a mastery unsurpassed by any composer.

The beginning of the coda is the only place where Chopin openly breaks his self-imposed rule of four. The first bar of the coda replaces the weak last bar of the A section with a strong first bar of the following group. In other words, the normally weak twelfth bar becomes reinterpreted as a strong first bar. As level c of the durational graph shows, I take the entire coda to be the expansion of the last bar of the mazurka's main theme—one bar expanded to eight. Because of the metrical reinterpretation, elements of the theme now appear with reversed metric accentuation.

Bar 48, which corresponds to weak bars in the theme—bars 10 and 12—is converted into a strong bar, and bar 49, which corresponds to bar 11, is converted from strong to weak. Through these changes the mazurka's conflict between metric accent and harmony is now resolved. The tonic occupies a strong bar and the dominant a weak one.

A few other features of the coda deserve mention. The final descending melodic line from high C to low C traces in reverse the contour of the opening theme's rising arpeggiation, at the very end bringing in the descending fourth that forms the mazurka's primary motive. In so doing, the coda suppresses the structural ab¹—the final goal of the structural melodic line—for the A-flats that do occur are surely surface ornamentation rather than structural goals. Thus the mazurka ends without an explicit resolution to its final melodic goal; the $\hat{1}$ is present only as a memory of its earlier appearance before the repeat. The holding of $\hat{3}$ creates a feeling of melodic stasis despite the descending arpeggio through the octave and the descending fourth at the end. This stasis is perhaps a final reference to the fermatas that are so striking a part of the mazurka's melodic and rhythmic design. The fermata effect is enhanced by Chopin's long pedal—through the last five bars—that casts a veil over every melodic shape, converting melody into an indistinct ripple within the sustained harmony.

NOTES

1. Guy Davenport, "The Death of Picasso," in *Eclogues* (San Francisco: North Point, 1981), 15.

2. I did this work in collaboration with David Stern, who was then my student. Some of his ideas have undoubtedly found their way into this article.

3. Heinrich Schenker, *Free Composition*, trans. and ed. Ernst Oster (New York: Longman, 1979), Figure 40,7.

4. Frank Samarrotto, "Strange Dimensions: Regularity and Irregularity in Deep Levels of Rhythmic Reduction," in Carl Schachter and Hedi Siegel, eds., *Schenker Studies 2* (Cambridge: Cambridge University Press, 1999), 235–37.

5. Schenker, *Free Composition*, 120.

# 6

## Dance and the Music of Chopin: The Waltz

### ERIC MCKEE

No other Romantic composer of art music was more devoted to the composition of dance music than Fryderyk Chopin (1810–1849). From the irregular rhythms of the mazurka to the pulsating drive of the waltz, nearly half of Chopin's works are dances, and a large portion of the remaining works incorporate dance elements within them. Despite the prominence of popular dance music in Chopin's compositions and within his social world, musicologists and theorists have been reluctant to view his music in light of the urban social dance practices his compositions are based on.[1] The devaluation of popular music, the feminine association of the salon, the ideology of autonomy, and, in the case of the mazurka, the "myth of the folk"[2] are all elements that have diverted attention away from the feet of the well-heeled dancer.

This study attempts to provide new analytical insights into the waltzes of Chopin by viewing them in light of early nineteenth-century urban dance practices as found in Europe and specifically in Warsaw. The underlying premise of this study is that in order to understand fully the musical structure and expressive meaning in Chopin's dance music, it is necessary to be aware of the bodily rhythms and social contexts of the dances they are based on. Only in this way can one adequately establish their influence as a primary compositional motivation.

The article is divided into three sections. The first section presents an overview of social dancing in Warsaw from roughly 1800 to 1830 and discusses the reception of the waltz in Warsaw. The second section examines Chopin's involvement with social dancing both as a dancer and a dance musician. The third section discusses the choreography of the waltz during the years 1820–1840 and examines Chopin's waltzes as a musical vision of the dancers on the ballroom dance floor.

## Social Dancing in Chopin's Time

Despite political unrest, Warsaw, the city where Chopin grew up and spent his first twenty years, was a robust cosmopolitan center in the midst of a cultural renaissance and economic boom. Importantly for Chopin, Warsaw was well connected to the social and artistic trends of Vienna and Paris, and, as in other European capitals, ballroom dancing was deeply woven into the warp and woof of its social fabric.[3] Foreign dancing masters, largely French, kept Warsaw's elite abreast of Europe's most current dances, dance steps, and dance etiquette. Two of the most popular ballroom Polish dances were the mazurka and the polonaise. Although both these dances have their roots in regional folk dances, by Chopin's time they had been transformed into stylized urban dances for the upper classes.

In his two books devoted to statistical, historical, and social descriptions of Warsaw, the historian Łukasz Gołębiowski (1773–1849) provides the first detailed account of social dancing in Warsaw during the second half of the eighteenth century and into the first quarter of the nineteenth century.[4]

Gołębiowski reports that *redutas* (small dance parties held in rented halls or palaces) were given at least three times a week from October to Lent.[5] Certain entrepreneurs became well known for the splendor and opulence of their *redutas*, which also included, in addition to dancing, eating, drinking, and gambling.[6] Gołębiowski observes that at one such dance party more than ten thousand złotys changed hands, a considerable amount even by today's standards.[7]

Balls, a general designation for a dancing occasion larger and more formal than *redutas*, were the most common form of dance entertainment in Warsaw. It seems that almost any occasion warranted a ball. There were charity balls, friendly balls, children's balls, balls for old people, birthday balls, almond balls, professional assembly balls, saint's day balls, balls for foreign dignitaries, balls for the commemoration of historical events, military balls, political balls, and special balls organized for the lower classes. Masquerade balls, first introduced by King August II (1670–1733) in the first half of the eighteenth century, were a particular favorite of the upper classes.[8] According to Gołębiowski, they owed their popularity to an enticing combination of music, dancing, theater, gambling, and the thrill of appearing incognito.[9] Exorbitant amounts of money were spent on lavish costumes. An entertainment writer for the *Kurier warszawski*, Warsaw's daily rag, describes the various costumes worn at a masquerade held at the National Theater on 1 January 1830:

> Of masks, we can mention a wise *Pilgrim* and of an old *German*, who with his constant movement entertained all. Also there was a *Man from Cracow* coupled with a *Greek Woman*, a *Spaniard* with a *Warsaw Woman*, a joyful *Squire*, a very polite *Hunchback*, and a *Shepherd Girl* in dark trousers, etc.[10]

In the 1820s, when Chopin became active in social life, public balls were regularly held in four halls: the Merchant's Resursa, the New Resursa, the Variety Theater, and the National Theater, which, apart from the main theater, also had a hall specifically designed for dancing. The main halls of the Variety and National theaters could easily accommodate large numbers of dancers as there were no permanent chairs and their main floors were flat, not pitched, as is customary in modern halls.[11] Many palaces such as the Royal Palace, Łazienki Palace, and the Branicki Palace also contained their own dance halls. During the summer months there were dancing entertainments in the parks and gardens in and around Warsaw (e.g., Saxon Gardens and Tamka).[12] Gołębiowski also tells of dancing at casinos, at picnics, and at concerts.[13]

The main venue for social dancing in Warsaw, besides the public and private dance halls, were salons, the private entertaining rooms of the middle and upper classes. According to Halina Goldberg, "Warsaw had over 40 significant salons, just as splendid and socially refined as their counterparts in Paris, and direct evidence of Chopin's musical presence can be established in most of them."[14] Although Chopin received a comprehensive formal musical education at the Warsaw Conservatory under the direction of Józef Elsner (1769–1854),[15] it was in the salons where he perfected his ability to improvise, both freely and for the pleasure of the dancers.

The most intense period of dancing in a given year occurred during carnival season, which was celebrated in Warsaw from Epiphany to the beginning of Ash Wednesday. Warsaw, which was predominantly Roman Catholic, celebrated carnival with no less zeal than did Vienna or Paris.[16] Indeed, a significant part of Warsaw's economy was built around carnival season. Warsaw's newspapers were filled with advertisements and notices for the latest costumes or for costume ornaments, such as flowers, ribbons, feathers and exotic fabrics, for the rental of dance halls, for musicians to provide the dance music, for caterers who would provide choice food and beverages, and for various perfumes, which were doused on the dance floor not only to mask unpleasant odors but also to keep the dust down.

The newspapers also carried notices for dancing parties held in apartments or rented halls [*redutas*]. During Carnival it was not uncommon for Warsaw to have ten to fifteen dancing parties in one night, these in addition to dancing in the four main theaters and in private salons. For a small entrance fee (no charge for ladies), one could have access to an entire night of alleged good music, adequate dancing space and lighting, and hospitable service, including food and beverages. Many writers of such notices exercised creativity in appealing to the public to attend their dancing parties. One such notice reads:

> While in attendance . . . at a noble house where quite a number of people were present, I heard one of my friends telling the ladies about an evening dancing party that was to take place that same day in a house called the Gdańsk Cellar; as the name of this house was unknown to most of the guests . . . and as the expression "party at the Gdańsk cellar" was enjoyed by the young ladies, they, guided by their curiosity, sent me immediately to that place in order that, when I returned, they would have even more fun. Obeying their orders, I went. But when faced with well-furnished rooms, music the same as played in the Resursa, buffets full of delightful food and drink . . . I almost forgot the purpose

of my trip; and choosing a beautiful dancing partner, I began a mazurka, and then came other dances. With full delight I enjoyed the party until daybreak. . . . The next day I clarified the confusion of my curious ladies, explaining to them how much enjoyment could be had by one wrongly understood word [cellar]. I am, what is more, publishing this account in order that the good master of this house, looking after the best of company as well as to their comfort, will not suffer financial losses when, on the demand of his friends, he will give a party again next Saturday. . . . He undertakes this effort in order to support an unfortunate family.[17]

Largely because of the strong patronage of Poland's last king, King Stanisław August Poniatowski (ruled 1764–95), French ballet was visibly present in Warsaw at the end of the eighteenth century into the beginning of the nineteenth century. In 1776 a ballet school was founded on the estate of Count Antoni Tyzenhauz in Grodno (about two hundred miles northeast of Warsaw). In 1784 Tyzenhauz hired the most influential dancer in the early history of Warsaw's ballet, François Gabriel Le Doux (1755–1823), a former dancer with the Paris Opera and student of Gaëtan Vestris.[18] The ballet school not only offered a curriculum designed to prepare dancers for a professional career, it also offered instruction for amateurs. After the death of Tyzenhauz in 1785 the ballet company came under the aegis of King Stanisław August, who moved Le Doux and company to Warsaw and renamed it His Majesty's National Dancers. During its existence His Majesty's National Dancers premiered approximately one hundred ballets including the works of Charles Le Picq and Jean-Georges Noverre.[19] Le Doux remained active as a choreographer and ballet master until 1805, during which time he founded several more ballet schools. Le Doux's obituary mentions that toward the end of his career he was especially active in teaching dance to the children of Warsaw.[20]

Polish ballet and court dancing in the first quarter of the nineteenth century continued to be dominated by French dancers, choreographers, and ballet masters, including Louis Duport, Louis Thierry, Maurice Pion, the Volange family, and Alexander Debrey.[21] Gradually, however, the emergence of a specifically Polish ballet complete with Polish topics, costumes, music, and dances made it possible for native Polish dancers, choreographers, and composers to assert a greater influence.[22]

During the eighteenth century, social and theatrical dances were closely related; the same techniques used on stage were used on the ballroom floor; and it was common for dancing masters, such as Le Doux, to teach both professional ballet and social ballroom dancing. During the opening decades of the nineteenth century, however, ballet increasingly became more virtuosic, and the technical division between theatrical and ballroom dance increased to a point where each discipline began to develop its own technique and protocol.[23] Increasingly ballet masters no longer taught ballroom dancing, and as a result a new breed of dancing masters emerged. An 1829 statistical report for the city of Warsaw lists ten dancing masters who specialized in the instruction of ballroom dances.[24] Such dancing masters typically began to advertise lessons in September in preparation for the upcoming carnival season. For example, in 1830, between September 5 and October 28, seven dancing masters ran notices in the *Kurier warszawski* advertising dance instruction.[25] One of the most active among them, Jakub Zieliński, held weekly classes and parties during carnival in his Warsaw apartment. A notice of Zieliński's that was published in the *Kurier warszawski* reads:

> J. Zieliński, dancing master of social dancing, announces that on the 3rd of January, i.e. Sunday, in his apartment . . . he will give a *Dance Party* called *Casino*, and that he will give similar parties on every carnival Sunday. Persons that are unknown to me, if they wish to make their presence known to me, which would be my honor, are kindly asked to inform me beforehand. At the same place one can rent various ballroom costumes.[26]

Instruction in ballroom dancing was also part of the curricula in Warsaw's public schools and military training schools.[27] One cadet complained: "One of the faults of our education was that we were used by the upper classes. We played at comedies and learned to dance. We were taken to balls at all the best houses."[28] An important outcome of such training was that, upon graduation from military school, these polished military cadets disseminated Polish dance practices across Western and Eastern Europe, especially during the Napoleonic military campaigns when Polish soldiers served in the Polish Legion, France's largest foreign contingent. The Polish composer Michał Kleofas Ogiński (1765–1833) writes:

After the formation of the Duchy of Warszawa, the Polish soldiers who served with Napoleon first introduced the mazur at
Parisian Balls. It was danced in the highest circles by 1809–10.
It was the rage and common throughout this most elegant of
capitals. Not only due to the merits of the dance itself but also
because it was popularized by the most loved unit of Napoleon:
the officers of the Polish lancers—the Emperor's Guards.[29]

The economic sector that most benefited from Warsaw's passion for dancing was the music publishing industry, which thrived
on the publication of dance music.[30] As Gołębiowski sadly observed: "Should future generations want to judge the present state
of music in Poland based on printed musical works, how demean-
ing would their opinion of us be if they found only waltzes, mazurkas, gallops, polonaises, and those composed mostly by amateurs."[31]

Typically orchestras were the first to perform dance music at
public balls. Afterward, one had only to wait a short time before
the hits of the dance floor became available as sheet music for the
piano. Such works were often marketed as musical souvenirs that
allowed the performer (typically female) to recapture memories, in
music, of an enchanted evening. Much information can be gleaned
from the title pages of these publications. Figures 6.1 and 6.2 show
the title pages of two dances. The first is from a waltz by Aleksander Świeszewski published in Warsaw in 1830 by Józef Kośmiński.
In a letter written while Chopin was in Vienna in 1830, Chopin
refers to Świeszewski and his brother as the Lanner and Strauss of
Warsaw.[32] The title page reads:

Waltz
composed by
A. Świeszewski
transcribed from the Orchestra
for the
Piano-Forte
for four hands
played for Soirées at the Resursa
can be found at A. Brzezina, C. Magnus,
F. Klukowski and at many other
Music Shops
in Warsaw

Figure 6.1. Title page of a waltz composed by Aleksander
Świeszewski. Kraków: Jagiellonian Library.

Typical of Warsaw dance publications of the first quarter of the
nineteenth century, the text is in French, the language of Warsaw's
high culture. One foreign traveler observed that while visiting
Warsaw in 1818 it was his experience that in good society only
French was spoken and that Polish was spoken only to children
and domestics.[33] As national sentiment increased during the 1820s,
however, dance publications increasingly appeared in Polish. The
fashions of the waltzing couple are French. The long, loose-fitting
dress of the woman, sans corset and ornamented with ribbons, accentuates her whirling movements. The two dancers return our
gaze as if to invite us into their waltz.[34]

The second example is a title page from a polonaise by Karol
Kurpiński (1785–1857), an influential Polish composer of opera
and the music director of Warsaw's National Opera Company from
1810 to 1840. The title page provides a full context for the ball at
which it (presumably) was first performed:

Figure 6.2. Title page of a Polonaise composed by Karol Kurpiński. Jagiellonian Library, Kraków.

Polonez
Composed on the eighteenth day of December in the year 1828
as an annual Celebration of the exalted Name Day of
His Most Gracious Majesty Emperor of Russia and King of Poland
NICOLAUS I
Performed on this very day by the Great Orchestra
of the Regiment of Grenadiers of the Polish Guard
and
arranged for Pianoforte
by
K. KURPIŃSKI
Kapellmeister of the Court of the Kingdom of Poland
Publishing House of A. Brzezina, Warsaw

Although the tsar was not present in Warsaw for his name-day celebration, he did arrive several months later on May 17 to be crowned the king of Poland. It is likely that Kurpiński's polonaise was quickly published and marketed with the upcoming coronation in mind.[35]

In concluding this section I wish to stress two points concerning social dancing in Warsaw during Chopin's youth. First, the importance of dance in Warsaw cannot be overestimated: it was a vibrant and ubiquitous activity deeply woven into the social and economic fabric of Warsaw's society.[36] The population of Warsaw in 1827 was approximately 123,000, of which 16,000 were of noble descent [*szlachta*].[37] This group was increased by the ranks of the innumerable intelligentsia and bourgeoisie (artists, merchants, administrators, teachers, etc.) who could not claim noble birth but most certainly participated in Warsaw's dance events. When one considers that, during carnival, dancing was present in Warsaw's private salons, palaces, in dozens of rented halls, and in four large theaters, it is not unreasonable to assume that the only people who were not dancing during any given week of carnival were those physically unable to do so. The second point I wish to emphasize is that ballroom dancing in Warsaw, through cultural and political ties to France and through the presence of French dancing masters, was strongly influenced by French tastes.

### THE WALTZ IN WARSAW

During the first half of the nineteenth century the waltz ruled as the most popular ballroom dance in Europe. A whirling dance that, in part, developed out of German regional dances, the waltz fed the needs and passions of a growing middle class.[38] It was relatively easy to learn and therefore did not require expensive lessons from a dancing master; it allowed for a greater number of dancers on the floor; and it was scandalous. Although it may seem tame by today's standards, the waltz created a social outrage in Chopin's time, for it was the first ballroom dance that permitted dancers to embrace face to face, torso to torso, for an extended period of time. Moreover, the centrifugal force created by the spinning motion required a firm and tight grasp; to avoid vertigo, dancers gazed directly into each other's eyes. The constant spinning motion visually blurred the couple's perception of the world around them; the only objects they could see clearly were each other. The dancers thus were able to construct an intensely intimate and private world within a crowded public space.

The historian Kazimierz Władysław Wójcicki (1807–1879) reports that the waltz was first introduced to Poland during the Prussian occupation (1794–1806).[39] Given the early popularity of the waltz in Berlin, Wójcicki is probably right. Just two years before the beginning of the occupation, a Berlin journal reported that "waltzes and nothing but waltzes are now so much the fashion that at dances nothing else is seen; one need only be able to dance the waltz and everything is all right."[40] The following year the waltz made its entrance to Berlin's high society. Princess Louise Hohenzollern, the niece of Fryderyk II and the future wife of Prince Antoni Radziwiłł, recalls that, at a ball held at the Prussian Royal Court, "the King admired their waltzing. This dance had hitherto been forbidden at Court. . . . However, as the dance was much in vogue in the Imperial dominions, the King now sanctioned it.[41]

Although the king greatly enjoyed the whirling spectacle, the Queen Mother was not impressed: "The Queen was duly shocked at this indecency, and to see her daughters-in-law introduce a dance she disapproved of. She reiterated her prohibition to her daughters and averted her eyes to avoid seeing her daughters-in-law waltzing."[42]

When Prussia took control of Warsaw in 1794, only Germans were placed in government positions.[43] The influx of Prussian families, many of great wealth and influence, resulted in a visible presence of Prussian culture, including their favorite dances.

Polish society did not immediately embrace the waltz, however. As Wojciech Tomaszewski's research on Warsaw's music-publishing industry shows, in the opening years of the nineteenth century the polonaise was by far the Poles' favorite dance, constituting an amazing 96 percent of the published dance works for piano.[44] During the years 1815 to 1825, however, the waltz gradually overtook the polonaise in popularity. And after 1820 the waltz enjoyed a surge of popularity as Warsaw became yet another European city to fall victim to the throes of the "waltz craze." The publishing market was flooded with a tidal wave of waltzes, a great many written by amateurs and, consequently, a great many of low artistic quality. Indeed, composing waltzes became fashionable among the cultural elite as a type of parlor game. One publication by Józef Damse went so far as to make the following fantastic claim: "A million waltzes or a way to compose a million waltzes even for those who know nothing about music."[45]

The extreme popularity of the waltz and its saturation into Warsaw's social life allowed it to be used as a normative background from which to measure the bizarre, unusual, and extraordinary. For example, within the span of only two months the *Kurier warszawski* ran the following stories: in a show of strength a Polish strongman dances to the waltz from *Der Freischütz* with two Turkish men standing on his shoulders;[46] a beautiful Spanish woman, born without arms and legs, knits stockings and with her nose plucks out a waltz on the piano;[47] at a ball in Madrid a woman waltzes flawlessly even though she was blind from birth;[48] in Istanbul, Turkish women are prohibited at public gatherings, so at balls Turkish men waltz with Christian women;[49] and at a Parisian ball for the elderly a seventy-year-old woman cannot find a waltz partner because all the men are too drunk to dance.[50]

## Chopin as a Dancer

Chopin's contact with authentic peasant dance music and the purported influence that it exerted on his music—especially his mazurkas—has been greatly exaggerated.[51] The type of dance Chopin had most contact with while living in Warsaw was not the dance of the peasants but rather the urban ballroom dances of the upper classes.

Dance was considered an essential part of the education of the cultural elite, and all children who were physically able took dance lessons. Instruction in dance not only included knowledge of current ballroom dances, but it also encompassed such basic physical activities as sitting down and standing up, walking across a room, stepping in and out of a carriage, and, most important, making gestures of greeting. The manner in which one moved signaled one's social/economic position and allowed those of the upper classes to identify with one another and exclude those who had neither the money nor time to learn such social codes. By all accounts Chopin was a gentleman who moved comfortably in high aristocratic circles: he had great personal charm, exquisite manners, and an extremely refined sense of noble ease. Such attributes do not come naturally but are learned at a very young age.

As a child Chopin would have had the opportunity to learn proper conduct, and to dance at children's afternoon tea parties and costume balls given by his benefactors Countess Zofia Zamoyska, Princess Izabela Czartoryska, and Countess Aleksandra Potocka.[52] Such events were common throughout Warsaw in the homes of the upper class, especially during carnival season. By his fifteenth year Chopin appears to have acquired a fair amount of skill—or at least confidence—as a dancer. At an impromptu dance party in Szafarnia, Chopin took it upon himself to lead the opening dance, a waltz, with a young cousin of the host.[53] Customarily only the very best dancers were given, or attempted to undertake, this privilege.

Chopin's letters clearly indicate that he eagerly and actively took part in Warsaw's ball scene, especially during carnival. But while Chopin notes his attendance at various balls and soirées, he only mentions dancing if something unusual or unexpected occurred during the dance. This suggests that dancing was such a common activity for Chopin that it was not noteworthy in its own right. For example, in 1825 he committed to verse a night of wild dancing where he spent half the time playing for the dancers and the rest of the time dancing. Toward the end of the evening, while dancing the mazurka, he slipped and sprained his ankle.[54] In a letter from November 1829 he brags about an evening party where a beautiful woman asked him to be her partner in a mazurka, and, moreover, she had only just refused to dance with a Polish general.[55] And on another occasion, while dancing the mazurka at a soirée in December 1830, one of his friends took to the floor pretending to be some sort of sheep.[56]

Although Chopin rarely commented on performing for dancers, his friends and acquaintances did. By all accounts he was not only a consummate dance musician but also an enthusiastic one. Józefa Wodzińska recounts that Chopin enjoyed entertaining his younger friends either by playing pranks on the piano or playing waltzes, polkas, gallops, and mazurkas for them to dance to.[57] Occasionally after improvising, according to another report, Chopin "would turn into a lusty musician and start thundering out mazurkas, waltzes and polkas until, tired of playing and eager to join in the dancing himself, he would cede the keyboard to a humbler replacement."[58] Although accounts of his dancing activity decline after Chopin left Warsaw, partly because of his progressing illness, they do continue. The latest account I have found dates from November 1847 when Chopin played for dancers at a soirée given by the Czartoryskis in Paris.[59]

Chopin kept abreast of what was being played in the ballrooms of Warsaw and who was doing the playing. In a letter to his close friend, Jan Białobłocki, Chopin compares the work of his sister to the general fare: "Ludwika has written an excellent mazurka, such as Warsaw has not danced to in a long time. This is her *non plus ultra*, and really it is a *non plus ultra* of its kind—vivacious, pretty; in a word, for dancing to and, without flattery, of a rare quality. When you come I will play it for you."[60]

In another letter to Białobłocki, Chopin modestly writes: "Do let me know whether you received the music. As a matter of fact, instead of my own poor efforts, I sent you some of Rembieliński's waltzes. They ought to please you."[61]

Figure 6.3. Waltz by Aleksander Rembieliński. Published by
Andrzej Brzezina, Warsaw, 1828. Jagiellonian Library, Kraków.

Aleksander Rembieliński was an amateur pianist whose fluid
and relaxed technique Chopin greatly admired.[62] Figure 6.3 shows
one of only three extant waltzes that Rembieliński composed. In
its virtuosic pianism, rhythmic subtleties, and melodic and tonal
organization, one can perhaps understand Chopin's attraction to
Rembieliński's work. In the opening three measures, the repeating
three-note arpeggiation of the melody creates a 3 + 3 grouping
against the um-pah-pah accompaniment.[63] Rembieliński rhythmically varies the arpeggiation motive upon its return in measure 9.
The rhythmic variation creates a melodic connection between the
highest notes of the arpeggiation, G and F. In measures 13–14
Rembieliński restates the G–F motive in a new rhythmic config-
uration. The successive development of an opening motive belies
a compositional sophistication quite uncharacteristic of most Warsaw dance publications.

Rembieliński's long-necked melodies avoid the standard four-
bar segmentation. In the first reprise of the first waltz the large
arching contour, which explores the extreme high register of the
piano, and the lack of any tonal articulation in measure 4, unifies
the eight measures as a single gesture. In the second reprise the
melody's 3/2 hemiola in measures 12–13 rhythmically veils the var-

Example 6.1. Bass-line sketch of Rembieliński's waltz.

ied return of measures 9 and 10 in measures 13 and 14. (The motivic parallelism suggests that at an underlying level the reprise is conceptually based upon a 4 + 4 model.)

Also noteworthy is Rembieliński's maverick tonal design. The standard tonal procedure of Warsaw waltzes was extremely conservative: simple diatonic progressions without modulation. Here each of the four reprises establishes a different key: the first, E♭ major; the second, B♭ major; the third, D major; and the fourth, A major. Taken as a whole in a conventional da capo layout (e.g., waltz 1—waltz 2—waltz 1),[64] Rembieliński provides large-scale continuity by joining the waltzes together in the statement of a large tonal progression: I–III–IV–V–I (Example 6.1). Notice that the opening waltz does not begin squarely in the tonic key of B♭ major; it first establishes E♭ major, the subdominant of B♭, which then progresses to V–I in the second reprise. This tonal procedure of beginning a piece off tonic, often referred to as an auxiliary progression, is a trademark tonal technique of Chopin.[65]

Finally, in establishing Chopin's role as a dance musician, it should not be overlooked that Chopin, throughout his life, was not averse to performing music as an accompaniment to other activities. He often accompanied singers and instrumentalists; he apparently was quite good at mimicking other pianists for comic relief; and, according to some sources, which are not completely reliable, in his younger years he was fond of playing musical games and improvising music to spoken stories.[66] The latter gains support by his pivotal role in the creation of the marionette theater at Nohant. According to George Sand:

> [Chopin] improvised at the piano while the young people performed different scenes together with comical dances. . . . As soon as Chopin noticed a performer, he immediately, and with incredible skill, adapted to his role the content and form of the music.[67]

The foregoing evidence suggests that Chopin's conception of dance music grew directly out of his experience with urban ballroom dancing both as a dancer and dance musician. Both Franz Liszt and Robert Schumann also identified the source of Chopin's inspiration for his waltz music within the movement of the dancers on the ballroom dance floor. In his biography of Chopin, Liszt writes:

> Through the mediation of [Princess Czetweryńska] he had the honor of being presented at the home of Princess de Lowicz, and here he was brought together with Countess Zamoyska, Princess Radziwill, Princess Thérèsa Jablonowska, enchantresses all. . . . It was [Chopin's] lot, while still young, to play the piano for their dancing. At these parties . . . he was able to discover, many times perhaps, the secrets of excited and tender hearts fleetingly disclosed in whirling rounds. . . . Did no group, like frolicking nymphs, to wheedle some waltz of dizzying speed, shower him with smiles which taught him to merge with their merriment?[68]

I suggest that many of Chopin's Warsaw waltzes and mazurkas may have originated on the dance floor as dance improvisations and were only later committed to paper. It has been reported, for example, that two of Chopin's earliest mazurkas had first been improvised in the salon of Samuel Linde and only later, at the suggestion of Oskar Kolberg, committed to paper.[69] It follows that an important source of inspiration for Chopin's music may be found in the physical movements of the dance itself. Through critical examination of Chopin's waltzes I will attempt to show that Chopin was not only receptive to the needs of the dancers but was also able to translate their bodily motions into an artistic musical vision. Or, to put it in Liszt's terms, at an early age Chopin learned how to "merge with the merriment" of the dancers. Only after he left Warsaw in 1830 did Chopin begin consistently to introduce nondance elements into his waltzes. Two elements clearly indicate a shift in function: musical devices that disrupt the meter and the increasing emphasis given to global musical closure. Even so, many of Chopin's Viennese and Parisian waltzes are eminently danceable, and the distinction between functional and stylized was largely a matter of how they were used in their social context.

## Chopin's Waltzes as a Musical Vision of the Dance

Figure 6.4 provides a list of all Chopin's known waltzes, eight of which Chopin published; nine were in completed form but inten-

Figure 6.4. Chopin's Waltzes (KK = Kobylańska, *Katalog*)

|  |  |  | Composed | Published |
|---|---|---|---|---|
| **Published by Chopin** | | | | |
| op. 18 | E♭ | Grande Valse Brillante | 1831–32 | 1834 |
| op. 34/2 | a | Grande Valse Brillante | c. 1834 | 1838 |
| op. 34/1 | A♭ | Grande Valse Brillante | 1835 | 1838 |
| op. 34/3 | F | Grande Valse Brillante | 1838 | 1838 |
| op. 42 | A♭ | Grande Valse | 1840 | 1840 |
| op. 64/1 | D♭ | Valse | 1847 | 1847 |
| op. 64/2 | c♯ | Valse | 1847 | 1847 |
| op. 64/3 | A♭ | Valse | 1847 | 1847 |
| **Left Unpublished by Chopin** | | | | |
| op. 69/2 | b | Valse | 1829 | 1855 |
| op. 70/3 | D♭ | Valse | 1829 | 1852 |
| KK 1207–8 | E | Valse | c. 1829 | 1871 |
| KK 1209–11 | A♭ | Valse | 1830 | 1902 |
| KK 1213–14 | e | Valse | 1830 | 1868 |
| op. 70/1 | G♭ | Valse | 1832 | 1855 |
| op. 69/1 | A♭ | Valse | 1835 | 1855 |
| op. 70/2 | f | Valse | 1842 | 1852 |
| KK 1238–39 | a | Valse | 1847 | 1955 |
| **Lost** | | | | |
| KK 1266 | a | description only | 1824 | |
| KK 1248 | C | incipit only | 1824 | |
| KK 1249 | C | incipit only | 1826 | |
| KK 1250/1268 | A♭ | incipit only | 1827 | |
| KK 1252 | d | incipit only | 1828 | |
| KK 1251/1267/1270 | A♭ | incipit only | 1829 | |
| KK 1253/1267/1270 | E♭ | incipit only | 1829 | |
| KK 1295 | | description only | | |
| KK 1308 | | description only | 1832 | |
| KK 1316 | | description only | 1845 | |
| KK 1245 | B | description only | 1848 | |

tionally left unpublished; eleven more are known to have existed but are now lost. In this section I interpret these waltzes as musical visions of the dancers on the ballroom dance floor. I shall attempt to show that Chopin, by translating physical motions into musical gestures, was not only receptive to the wishes of a body in motion but that these musical gestures became compositional source material of a sort whose potential was developed on many different levels of musical organization, from the smallest to the largest.

Another issue I develop during the course of this section is the nature of the musical differences between the waltzes Chopin chose to publish during his lifetime and those he intentionally left unpublished. I shall argue that those he left unpublished are, in most cases, not somehow incomplete or inferior in quality but, rather, constitute a separate category of waltzes that were conceived by different compositional motivations than those he chose to publish.

### THE WALTZ AS DANCED, 1820–1840

The standard dance form of the waltz that dominated European dance floors from 1820 to 1840 was the *Valse à trois temps*.[70] As shown in Figure 6.5, it requires the dancers to traverse the dance floor in large circles, counterclockwise, while at the same time revolving in small clockwise circles. The smaller revolutions are completed in a five-step sequence corresponding to two measures of music: the first measure initiates the first half of the revolution, and the second completes it.[71] Figure 6.6a illustrates how the steps of the man and woman are aligned with the meter. Figure 6.6b shows the characteristic rhythms of the five-step sequence in musical notation. It is extremely important to note that the man and woman *do not* perform the same steps at the same time. In the first measure the man executes a pivot turn or twirl, as it is sometimes called. The second measure is completed with three steps. The woman reverses this two bar pattern; she first performs three steps and then follows with a twirl. The defining feature of the *Valse à trois temps* is the twirl, which is what distinguishes it from other styles of waltzing. As such, the twirl is conceptually marked in relation to the more commonly found three-step sequence. In his dance treatise, *Dances of the Salon*, the French dancing master Henri Cellarius provides instructions for the twirl:

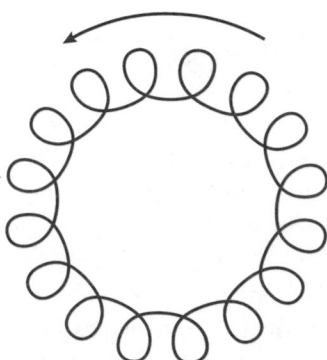

Figure 6.5. The circling motions of the dancers on the dance floor.

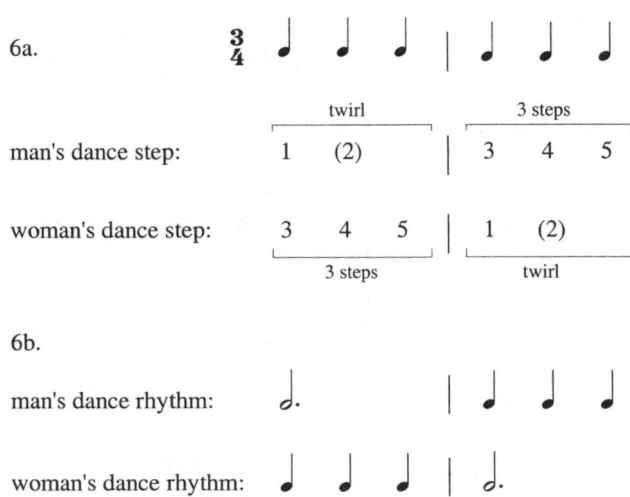

Figure 6.6. The two-bar step pattern of the *Valse à trois temps*.

[On the first beat,] the gentlemen sets off with the left foot. . . .
[On the second beat,] [h]e slides the right foot, slightly crossed,
behind the left. . . . [and] [a]fterwards, he turns upon his two feet,
on the toes.[72]

Although it appears that the dancer performs the twirl in two
steps, actually only one true step is involved. Once the dancer steps
on the left foot, the body weight remains on that foot for the
remainder of the measure. It serves as the pivot for the turn. That
is why in Figure 6.6a I enclose the second step of the twirl in
parentheses and in Figure 6.6b I notate the twirl with a dotted half
note.[73]

### CIRCLES

The *Valse à trois temps* is a dance of circles: small clockwise circles
embedded within larger counterclockwise circles.[74] Viewers on the
perimeter of the dance space were entertained to a whirling spectacle of couples "eternally turning in dizzying circles along a wider
circumferential path, self contained and oblivious planets."[75] As a
bodily motion, a circle involves a relatively even movement around
a fixed point that ends at its starting point. According to the composer and theorist Adolph Bernard Marx (1795–1866), waltz composers must "at the very least . . . bring into prominence this basic
motive of motion. . . . Each measure, or better, each two-measure

(Killian takes one of the women for a partner, the others follow, Bohemian Waltz.)

(Most of the dancers waltz into the Inn.)

Example 6.2. The waltz from Weber's opera *Freischütz*, act 1, scene 3.

segment, must correspond to the dance motive, marking . . . the swinging turn of the dance."[76]

As an example of what he considers a "genuine waltz motive," Marx cites the waltz from act 1, scene 3, of Carl Maria von Weber's *Der Freischütz* (first performance: Berlin, 18 June 1821), which is provided in Example 6.2. The Warsaw premiere of *Freischütz*, which Chopin eagerly awaited, took place on 4 July 1826. By that time, however, Chopin was most likely already familiar with much of the music; dance arrangements began to appear in Warsaw as early as 1822, and the *Freischütz* waltz was a particular favorite.

Marx explains the relation between Weber's waltz and the dance:

[Weber's] rustic dance satisfies itself with the pure unaltered raw material, the motive of three steps, without forming clearer musical segments for the complete movement of twice three steps, which befits a more complete and nobler conception of the dance.[77]

As can be seen, the basic motive of Weber's waltz is a melodic arch. In its circular design, a melodic arch is particularly apt as a musical vision of the rotating dancers: its beginning and ending points are the same, or nearly the same, and its pitches move at a relatively even rate around a fixed axis. After the um-pah-pah accompaniment, melodic arches are perhaps the next most important characteristic of waltzes, especially Chopin's waltzes. It was most likely this feature that prompted Lord Byron to take aim at the waltz and describe it as "a damned see-saw up and down sort of tune."[78] Certainly Weber's little waltz fits this description.

The arching motive used in the introduction to Chopin's posthumously published Waltz in E Minor, given in Example 6.3, opens with what Marx would surely call a genuine waltz motive. As shown in Example 6.4, the first complete measure is a tonal inversion of Weber's motive. In the music that follows Chopin injects this motive into the flesh and bones of the work. By the term *motive* I do not mean to imply a similarity relation based on a specific voice-leading technique or of characteristic scale-degrees but rather a basic shape or contour with a well-defined beginning, middle, and end.

The waltz proper begins in measure 9. Instead of using a more standard um-pah-pah accompaniment where the second and third beats are identical, the left hand registrally peaks on the second beat and then arpeggiates back down to the beginning of the next measure. Returning to the introduction, the downbeats of the first three measures imply an apparent ascending stepwise line D♯–E F♯–G A♯–B. The downbeats of the arching bass line in measures 9 through 14 present a varied repetition of this same line, thereby underscoring the relationship between the bass line and the dance motive of the introduction. The dance motive of the introduction is also used in the melody. The opening upward sweep of the first half of the arching motive reappears in slightly varied form as the basis of the melody in measures 10 and 11.

A new melody begins in measure 25, as shown in Example 6.5. Here Chopin incorporates the arching motive into a sequence of

KK IVa Nr. 15

Example 6.3. Chopin's Waltz in E Minor, KK 1213–14, mm. 1–16.

figurated 7–6 suspensions. In the eight-bar melody that follows (mm. 33–40) Chopin expands the dance motive into a "more complete and nobler" two-bar statement, while at the same time preserving the voice-leading organization of the previous eight-bar phrase (although without the suspensions). The expanded motive now perfectly matches the complete rotation of the dancers. Turn-

Weber's dance motive

DM:        I

Chopin's dance motive

em:        i

Example 6.4. A comparison of Weber's waltz motive with the waltz motive from Chopin's Waltz in E Minor, KK 1213–14.

ing our attention to the left hand, in measures 25–32 the arching bass line is rhythmically contracted to fit within the measure, thereby corresponding in duration to the melody's one-bar arches. In measures 33–40, the arch of the bass line is expanded back to its original duration. Although it is expanded in relation to measures 25–32, it does not match the durational expansion of the melody's arch: for every one arch of the melody, the bass completes two of its own.

The basic shape of the dance motive—an arch, typically ascending—is also present at the level of the eight-bar phrase. Musical climaxes in Western European art music typically occur toward the end of a musical segment, be that a phrase, a section, or the entire work.[79] The climax is usually achieved, in part, through an ascent to a registral high point. The opening eight-bar phrase from the first movement of Beethoven's Piano Sonata in F Minor op. 2 no. 1 is often used as a paradigmatic example of this type of organization. Example 6.6 presents an illustration from a well-known work by Chopin.[80] What we find in Chopin's waltzes, to a degree unknown in his other genres, are phrases organized as large arches in which the registral high point occurs roughly midway through the phrase. Returning to the E-minor waltz, the overall contour of the eight-bar phrase beginning in measure 9 is organized as a large arch. Although there is no single high point, the upward ascent of the first four measures, which is propelled by the varied fragment of the introduction's dance motive, is balanced by the downward sweeping gestures of the second four-bar segment.

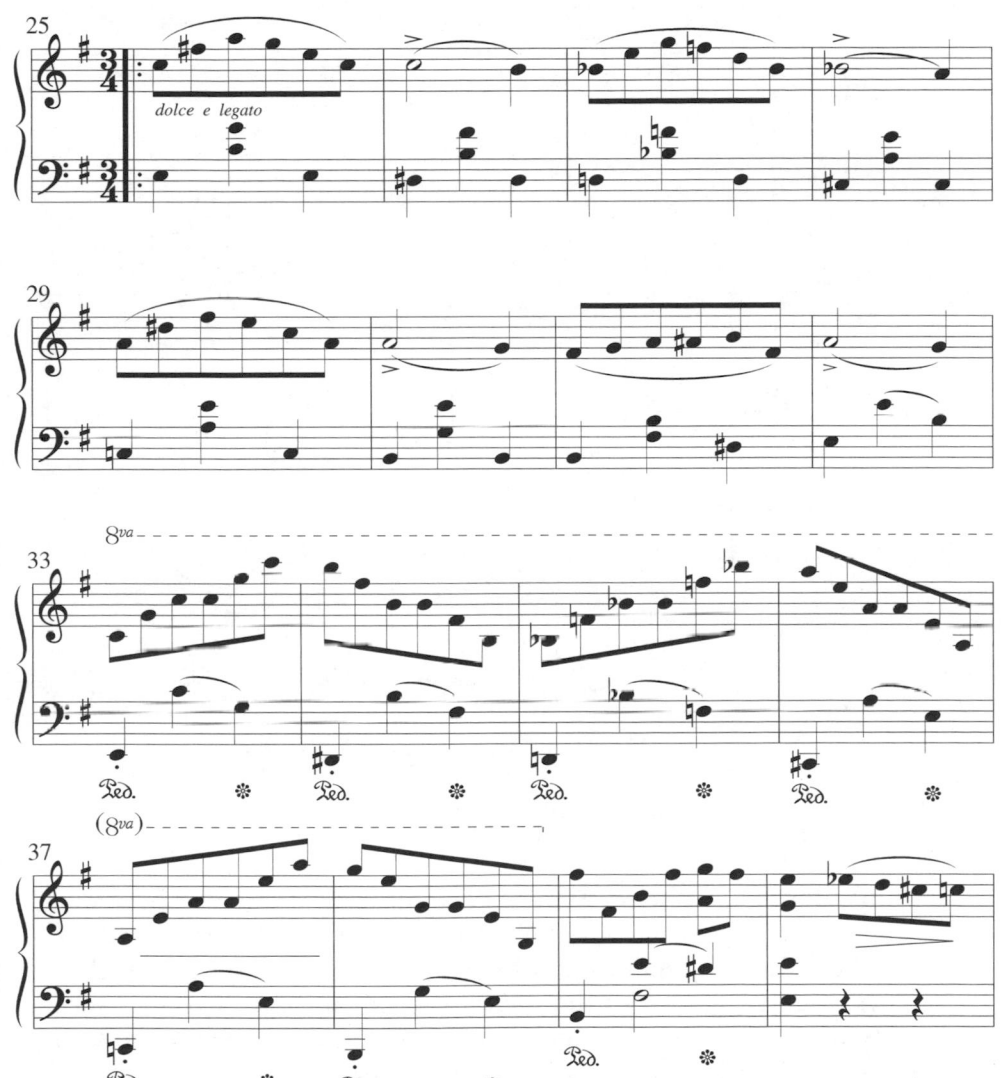

Example 6.5. Chopin's Waltz in E Minor, KK 1213–14, mm. 25–40.

Underneath, the step-wise ascent of the bass provides continuity across the 4 + 4 melodic division and places its registral climax more conventionally toward the end of the phrase.

The eight-bar phrase beginning in measure 57, given in Example 6.7, is also organized as a large balanced arch. Here there is a clear registral high point at the end of the first four-bar segment. The second four-bar segment provides a graceful descent to

* = structural highpoint

Example 6.6. Chopin's Prelude in A Major op. 28 no. 7.

the end of the phrase. Similar balanced arches can also be found in op. 18, op. 34 no. 3, op. 42, op. 64 no. 1, op. 64 no. 3, and op. 70 no. 3. It is significant, although perhaps not surprising, that, with the exceptions of the E-minor waltz and op. 70 no. 3, such expansions of the dance motive only occur in the waltzes he chose to publish, which were conceived on a larger scale than the waltzes he chose not to publish. In fact, Chopin's E-minor waltz shares many characteristics with his published waltzes: it is brilliant in style and Chopin has reworked the end of the last section of the ABA form in order to provide global closure. As is shown in Example 6.8, the A section returns in measure 97. The second statement of the opening eight-bar phrase, which begins in measure 105, is expanded from eight measures to a length of fifteen measures.[81] A crisis point is reached in measure 108 where, in place of a tonic chord, which had occurred on every prior appearance of this theme, Chopin substitutes a fully diminished seventh chord.[82]

Example 6.7. Chopin's Waltz in E Minor, KK 1213–14, mm. 57–72.

After the crisis point Chopin launches into an expanded cadential progression in which the dance motive spirals out of control into another fully diminished seventh chord in measure 113. Against a rising bass line, the melody falls to a perfect authentic cadence. The phrase expansion not only increases musical tension but also allows the final cadential measure of the phrase, measure 119, to

Example 6.8. Chopin's Waltz in E Minor, KK 1213–14, mm. 97–131.

arrive on a metrically strong measure, all of which increases the sense of closure. Except for this waltz, metrically accented cadences and crisis points are only found in Chopin's published waltzes.[83]

In the E-minor waltz the dance motive is used in varied forms, in different parts of the texture, and at different temporal levels.[84] The most condensed form of a melodic arch is a neighboring motion.[85] Despite its narrow range and apparent simplicity, neighboring motions are a potent source and generator of musical content on many levels of tonal structure. They are also a signal feature of Chopin's waltzes. Returning to Example 6.3, the successive rising statements of the introduction's one-bar dance motive are fused together by lower-neighbor notes on the downbeats of each measure. In measures 9–10, $\hat{5}$ is elaborated with a lower-neighbor motion, just as it was in measure 3. In the following measure, a complex of neighbor notes revolving around B delays the fragmented return of the dance motive. More specifically the B is prolonged by a double neighbor-note figure in which the upper neighbor, C♯, on the downbeat of measure 11, is itself elaborated with its own upper neighbor.

The opening of Chopin's Waltz in A Minor op. 34 no. 2 is

given in Example 6.9. Stephen Heller (1811–1885), a pianist and Chopin's friend, reports that when he told Chopin that he liked the A-minor waltz best out of all Chopin's waltzes, Chopin replied: "I am glad you do; it is also my favourite."[86] With its minor mode, slow tempo, prominent use of the low register, and smooth serpentine melodies, it is one of his most introspective and languid waltzes, a *Valse mélancolique.*[87] It also is a sophisticated study in neighbor notes.

The opening sixteen-bar parallel period (8 + 8) is comprised almost solely of neighboring figures. As shown in Example 6.10, during the first four measures the texture breathes in and out with steadily undulating one-bar neighbor motions. Furthermore, each note of the low-tenor melody is itself elaborated with its own neighboring motion, thereby creating circles within circles. In measure 5 the neighboring motion accelerates into a trill. The increase of energy generated by the trill, together with the culminating D♯ chromatic lower neighbor, catapults the melody temporarily into a higher register where it circumscribes $\hat{2}$ with upper and lower neighbors.

The next section, measures 17–36, is also organized as a parallel period. Its consequent phrase, though, is expanded from eight to twelve measures. As Example 6.11 illustrates, there are remarkable parallelisms between the opening two periods. The contents of both are largely generated by neighbor notes, and, more specifically, the twice-repeated neighbor motion $\hat{5}$–$\hat{6}$–$\hat{5}$ plays a prominent role in both.

The antecedent phrase beginning in measure 17 issues from an E, but it is two octaves higher than the opening melody. This high E initiates a middle-ground neighboring motion that is partially concealed by three register transfers. In measure 20 the F is transferred down one octave where it is held over as a suspension, which resolves on the third beat of measure 21. In measure 22, F is regained in the soprano voice but is immediately transferred to the bass voice through voice exchange, which places the neighboring F back in its original register (see measures 1–3). Also noteworthy are the alto's neighboring motions in measures 17–20, which prolong $\hat{1}$ through a double-neighbor motion, A–G♯–B–A. Chopin further elaborates this neighbor complex by providing the opening A and the penultimate B with their own upper neighbors, which resolve into suspension figures.

In the consequent, Chopin unleashes a cascade of figurations

# GRANDE VALSE BRILLANTE

à Madame la Baronne C. d'Ivry

Opus 34 Nr. 2

Example 6.9. Chopin's Waltz in A Minor op. 34 no. 2, mm. 1–36.

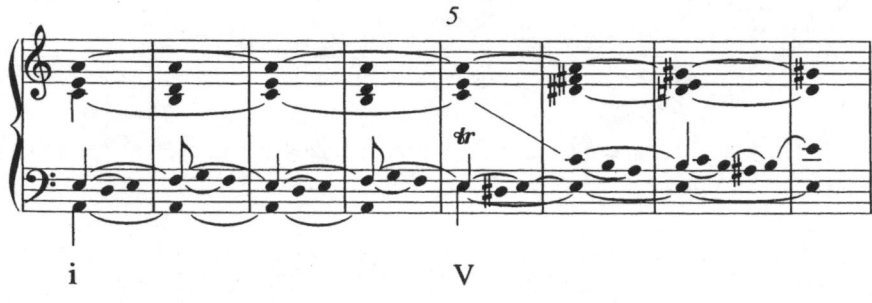

Example 6.10. Voice-leading sketch of Chopin's Waltz in A Minor op. 34 no. 2, mm. 1–16.

that both elaborate and expand the neighboring motions of the antecedent phrase. The phrase expansion occurs in two parts. The voice exchange between F and D that begins in measure 30 is extended by one measure through the insertion of a second-inversion passing chord in measure 31. The expanded voice exchange transfers the F from the soprano voice to the bass voice where it resolves to E, just as it did in the antecedent. Under the E in measure 33, however, there now appears a G♯ (itself a lower neighbor to the A of measure 25). The unstable inversion of the V⁷, together with a varied and transposed restatement of measures 29–32, propel the music forward to a perfect authentic cadence in measure 36. It is important to note that the phrase expansion does not disrupt the two-bar hypermeter but rather results in a symmetrical 4 + 4 group. The music is thus entirely danceable.

Perhaps the most well-known waltzes in which neighbor notes take root in the musical terrain are the Waltz in F Major op. 34 no. 3 and the Waltz in D♭ Major op. 64 no. 1. Example 6.12 provides the opening to op. 34 no. 3. After an eight-bar "call to the dance floor," measure 9 begins a stepwise ascent to the beginning

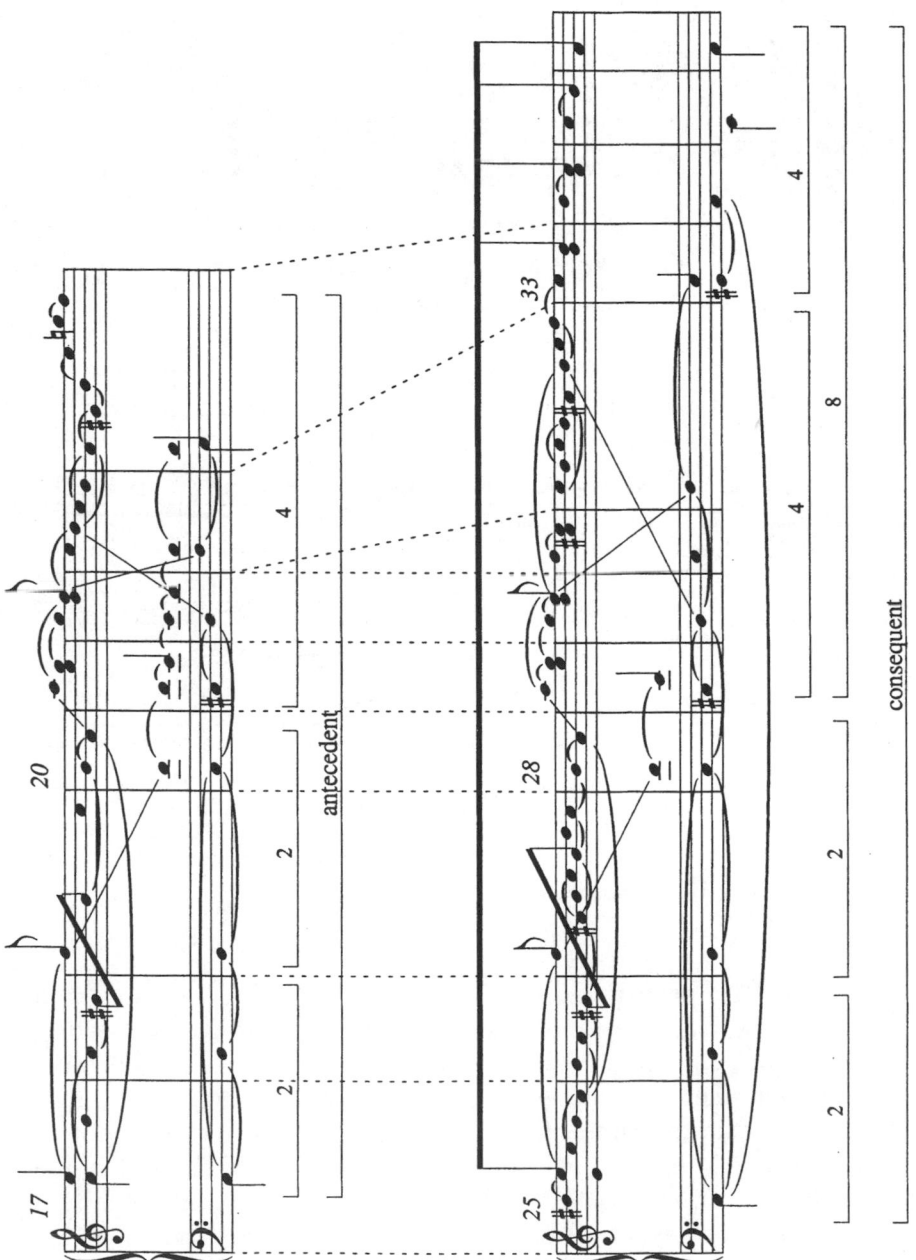

Example 6.11. Voice-leading sketch of Chopin's *Waltz in A Minor* op. 34 no. 2, mm. 17–36.

# GRANDE VALSE BRILLANTE

à Mademoiselle A. d'Eichtal

Example 6.12. Chopin's Waltz in F Major op. 34 no. 3, mm. 1–20.

of the waltz proper (m. 17). The ascent, which accelerates as it
nears its goal, is elaborated with incomplete double-neighbor figures. The only pitch in the ascent not to receive a neighbor-note
embellishment is $\hat{3}$, the goal and climax of the introduction. And
in the music that immediately follows, Chopin is careful not to
exceed the A. Instead, by means of a neighboring $^6_4$ chord, Chopin
leaves it to an inner voice of the accompaniment to provide the A
with its own upper neighbor, B♭. The melodic motion $\hat{3}$–$\hat{4}$–$\hat{3}$
(A–B♭–A), here buried within the texture, eventually emerges in this
waltz as an important structural motive.

The opening of Chopin's waltz in D♭ major op. 64 no. 1 is

Example 6.13. Chopin's Waltz in Db Major op. 64 no. 1, mm. 1–20.

provided in Example 6.13. The waltz begins with a whirlwind of neighboring figures, both complete and incomplete, rotating around Ab, $\hat{5}$. As shown in Example 6.14, the neighboring motion is $\hat{5}$–$\hat{6}$–$\hat{5}$, which accelerates in measures 3ff. (The neighboring-tone $\hat{6}$ is also embellished with its own incomplete neighbor, C.) The culminating arrival of the Bb on the downbeat of measure 9, an octave higher, creates a larger-level neighboring motion unifying

Example 6.14. Voice-leading sketch of Chopin's Waltz in D♭ Major op. 64 no. 1, mm. 1–12.

the entire passage. Also note that the entire phrase is a modified balanced arch. A heightening of energy and register in the first half of the phrase, which is augmented with a four-bar prefix, is balanced with a twice-repeated two-bar descent and decrescendo in the second half. And, finally, the accompaniment spins out arches on two durational levels. First the um-pah-pah creates a quarter-note pattern of low–high–high–low, and, second, the bass notes on the downbeats create a dotted half-note durational pattern of low–high–low. Frederick Niecks, an early biographer of Chopin, reports that the spinning motions of George Sand's dog trying to catch its tail served as the creative inspiration of this work.[88] Although the story is doubtful, the image of a perpetually circling object is apt.

### "LIFT OFF"

For dancers, the most active part of the two-bar rotation, in terms of motion and energy exerted, comes on beats 1 and 4. Going into beats 1 and 4 dancers rise from a sink, that is, they move from the heel to the toe, and then remain on the toe until the end of the measure. Also, the dancers' steps on beats 1 and 4 use the largest stride covering the most distance and thus require the fastest leg motion in order not to lose time with the music. And, finally, whoever is twirling needs to create enough momentum to continue the twirl into the second and third beats.

Accordingly, Marx advises the composer musically to mark the beginning of the measure with a

melody that springs energetically away from the first note. . . . In [Weber's] piece, auxiliary tones are placed before the purely chordal ones in order to bring out the beginning of the [dancer's] first step; every other melodic, harmonic, or rhythmic accentuation serves the same end.[89]

Marx translates physical motion into musical motion through the use of dissonance as found in auxiliary tones—what we would normally call appoggiaturas. As a musical entity, appoggiaturas provide a sense of motion in that they require resolution, a need to "move" to another more stable pitch. In contrast to the short eighth-note appoggiaturas found in Weber's waltz and in the introduction to Chopin's Waltz in E Minor (KK 1213–14), Chopin most often uses appoggiaturas of a dotted quarter note or half-note duration. The longer duration results in a musical correspondence between the appoggiatura and the three-beat twirl, which requires of the dancer only one true step.

As mentioned previously, the three-beat twirl is first performed by the man in the first measure and then echoed by the woman in the second measure of the six-beat rotation. Interestingly, Chopin most often uses the longer appoggiatura for the second measure of a six-beat rotation, thereby drawing attention to the woman's twirl. It is my opinion that this correspondence is not fortuitous but rather is a direct result of Chopin's firsthand knowledge of the dance as danced. Or, put another way, Chopin, in many of his waltzes, turns his gaze on the waltzing woman.

Example 6.15 provides an illustration. The waltz begins with a short introduction, organized in two four-bar segments. In the first segment, a *sonnerie* calls the dancers to the dance floor; the second segment announces the principal rhythmic motive of the work, the motive of the female dancer. A stepwise ascent leads to a half-note dissonant C♯ on the downbeat of measure 6. Although a dissonant neighbor rather than an appoggiatura, the effect is still the same— it requires resolution (movement) to the consonant B. In performance, the unstressed resolution of the dissonance provides a sense of relaxation and repose. Similarly, in the dance this is where the movement of the twirl comes to an end and where the dancer relaxes into a sink in preparation for the rise to the toes in the following measure. In measures 7–8 Chopin twice repeats the second measure of the motive, thereby creating waves of pulsating neighboring motions that suggest the twirling motions of both dancers. Neighboring figures are a prominent feature throughout this waltz.

The waltz proper begins in measure 9. The section of the waltz

# WALZER

Tempo di Valse

KK IVa Nr. 12

Example 6.15. Chopin's Waltz in E Major, KK 1207–08, mm. 1–24.

provided in the example is organized as a parallel period (8 + 8). At the head of each phrase appears the motive of the female dancer in its purest form, which is followed by varied repetitions of the motive. The woman's initial three steps are perfectly matched by three quarter notes and her twirl by a two-beat appoggiatura, which resolves on the last beat of the measure.

There is, in fact, a general tendency in Chopin's waltzes to highlight, through a variety of means, the measure of the woman's twirl. In measures 5–6, for example, the crescendo, melodic contour, dynamic accents, and the rhythmic acceleration leading to an agogic accent all serve to accentuate the beginning of the second measure. I know of no other composer of waltz music during this period that does this to the degree that Chopin does. It is interesting to note that, by highlighting the woman's twirl, Chopin provides a musical lift to the movement that carries with it the most risk. For it is at this point, while turning on a tight axis, that the woman would experience the greatest sense of spinning and, with it, a dangerous and, according to some, potentially lethal combination of euphoria and vertigo. The possibility of a woman losing control of her mind and bodily functions seems to have held a special fascination for male critics of the waltz. Writing in 1836, Donald Walker observes:

> Vertigo is one of the great inconveniences of the waltz; and the character of this dance, its rapid turnings, the clasping of the dancers, their excited contact, and the too quick and too long continued succession of lively and agreeable emotions, produce sometimes, in women of a very irritable constitution, syncopes, spasms and other accidents which should induce them to renounce it.[90]

From a cautionary, rather than critical, stance, the dancing master Cellarius has advice for the gentleman:

> Take care never to relinquish his lady until he feels that she has entirely recovered herself. The effect of the rotatory motion, even after stopping, is sometimes so great that he would risk his partner's losing her equilibrium by detaching himself from her too suddenly.[91]

In addition to auxiliary tones, Chopin commonly uses another device to provide a "lift" to the first beat of a measure: grace notes,

Example 6.16. Chopin's Waltz in B Minor op. 69 no. 2, mm. 31–40.

and particularly leaping grace notes. Chopin's Waltz in E Minor, shown in Example 6.3, illustrates the effective use of leaping grace notes to energize the first beat. Beginning in measure 13, which initiates the second part of an arching phrase, dissonant leaping sevenths accentuate the first beats of the measures. Notice also that the pitch to which the notes leap is an accented passing tone, what Marx would call an auxiliary note.[92] Leaping grace notes are also used in measures 57–72, which are shown in Example 6.7.

1 + 3

One of the more unusual ways that Chopin emphasizes the measure of the woman's twirl is by segmenting a four-bar melody asymmetrically into two parts: 1 + 3.[93] Because the three-bar segment is longer in duration than the one-bar segment, it is more strongly accentuated in the listener's mind. The second half of the introduction (measures 5–8) of Chopin's E major waltz, shown in Example 6.15, exhibits this grouping proportion. Another example of this technique can be found in Chopin's Waltz in B Minor op. 69 no. 2, shown in Example 6.16. The pickup into measure 33 begins a contrasting section. While the melody retains the same rhythmic pattern throughout (dotted quarter followed by three eighth notes), the voice-leading organization suggests a grouping division between the first and second measures. As the voice-

Example 6.17. Voice-leading sketch of Chopin's Waltz in B Minor op. 69 no. 2, mm. 32–40.

leading sketch in Example 6.17 illustrates, the arpeggiation from the A up to the F♯, which is embellished by an appoggiatura, brings the melody into a new register. The F♯ then initiates a descending third progression. Below the upper voice, the A continues as a common tone until measure 40 where it moves to an A♯, the leading tone of B minor.[94] The beginning of measure 34, the measure of the woman's twirl, is also highlighted by the crescendo/decrescendo markings, which, in combination with the registral high point, mark the downbeat of the second measure as the structural highpoint of the phrase.

The opening of Chopin's waltz, op. 70 no. 1, shown in Example 6.18, provides another example in which the voice leading is very similar to the waltz previously discussed. The asymmetrical grouping is more clearly established in this example by the initiation of

Example 6.18. Chopin's Waltz in G♭ Major op. 70 no. 1, mm. 1–4.

Example 6.19. Chopin's Waltz in G♭ Major op. 70 no. 1, mm. 33–37.

a different motivic design in measure 2, which is then repeated in measures 3 and 4. Notice also in this passage the profusion of neighboring motions. The opening melody of the B section, as shown in Example 6.19, also exhibits a 1 + 3 melodic organization.

It is important to note that the musical characteristics that I have cited as corollaries to the waltz as danced are not exclusive to the waltz: they can be found in other dances and non-dance genres.[95] In fact, the only essential characteristic feature of a waltz, if it is to be perceived unambiguously as a waltz, is a perpetual um-pah-pah accompaniment. As composers have proven many times, often with dreadful results, any tune, in any meter and any style, can be retooled as a waltz.[96] What is significant in Chopin's waltzes is (1) the high degree in which these characteristics occur in comparison with other genres; (2) their appropriateness as musical corollaries for the physical motions contained in the dance; and (3) their prominence in the opening sections of Chopin's waltzes, where it is most important to establish the genre of the work. When these secondary characteristics (melodic arches, neighboring motions, appoggiaturas, and grace notes) are used in combination with the um-pah-pah accompaniment, they serve to refine and amplify an artistic vision of the waltz.

### CHOPIN'S UNPUBLISHED WALTZES

As we saw with Liszt (p. 121), it was a common tactic for early commentators of Chopin's music to interpret his waltzes within the context of the ballroom. In a review of Chopin's op. 34 waltzes, Robert Schumann, an early champion of Chopin's music, makes this connection:

His three waltzes [op. 34] will delight above all—so different in type are they from the ordinary ones, and of a kind as could occur only to Chopin—perhaps he was inspired to new creations while he gazed, great artist that he is, among the dancers whom he has just roused by playing. So throbbing a life flows in them that they seem to have been actually improvised in the ball-room.[97]

In a somewhat similar vein I have argued that Chopin's waltzes are, on one level, based on the physical motions of the dance and, on another, are an artistic portrait, an idealized vision, of the dance. As an artistic vision, it is conceivable that Chopin, at times, turned his gaze on the dancing woman. Certainly, in the public reception of the waltz, it was the woman who attracted the most attention. Contemporary literary descriptions and criticisms, written almost entirely by men, are unswerving in their focus on what could, should, and would happen to a woman who dared to waltz. Perhaps the most famous literary portrait of the waltz is in Gustave Flaubert's novel, *Sentimental Education* (1869). It was largely his vivid description of beautiful waltzing women that scandalized the public and resulted in his book's temporary banning by the French government.

A waltz was striking up. At this the women sitting on the sofas along the walls all rose to their feet, one by one, with great alacrity, and their skirts and shawls and head-dresses all began to swirl around. They swirled past Frédéric so closely that he could see the tiny beads on their foreheads, and as this giddy spinning motion quickened and fell into a rhythm, he was gripped by a kind of intoxication and all these equally dazzling women gyrating in front of his eyes, each with her own special fascination, brought other thoughts surging into his mind.[98]

It follows that the music of the waltz also had strong feminine associations. Composers of waltz music could choose musically to accentuate and develop the idea of femininity or choose to develop another realm, such as virtuosity, humor, or melancholy. I have already suggested that, through a variety of means, in many of his waltzes Chopin strategically highlights both the measure of the woman's twirl as he musically captures its dynamic energy. As a working hypothesis I propose that since the man and the woman do not perform the same steps simultaneously, it is entirely possible

| woman's dance rhythm | |
| man's dance rhythm | |
| alternating twirls | |

Figure 6.7. Rhythmic representation of gender in Chopin's waltzes.

for a composer to focus on the rhythmic pattern of one or the other and thereby musically portray gender. The diagram presented in Figure 6.7 refines this hypothesis. The rhythms above the dotted lines correspond to the basic dance rhythms. Given below the dotted lines are common variants found in Chopin's waltzes.

A close examination of Chopin's waltzes reveals that the woman's rhythmic pattern is not a prominent feature of the waltzes Chopin chose to publish. It appears only in op. 18, and there it is in a formally subordinate section (mm. 165–80). Of the ten waltzes he withheld from publication, however, it appears prominently in all of them except two. One of these two, the Waltz in A♭ Major, KK 1209–11, is in a category by itself—more of a *Ländler* than a waltz. The other is the enigmatic A-minor waltz, KK 1238–39, which Chopin composed toward the end of his life. This evidence suggests that the majority of Chopin's unpublished waltzes are unified in their coded depiction of femininity.

Two of Chopin's unpublished waltzes were inspired by women he loved (or at least was deeply infatuated with): the Waltz in A♭ Major op. 69 no. 1 and the Waltz in D♭ Major op. 70 no. 3.

Example 6.20. Chopin's Waltz in A♭ Major op. 69 no. 1, mm. 1–16.

Op. 69 no. 1, the opening of which is shown in Example 6.20, was written in Dresden in the fall of 1835 during his courtship with Maria Wodzińska. Maria's younger sister, writing many years later, recalls that, during one evening of music making, Maria requested Chopin to improvise a waltz for her. On the day of his departure he presented her with an autograph of the waltz as a souvenir of their time together. Maria, in a letter written shortly after his departure, recalls to Chopin that the waltz "was the last thing we received and heard played by you."[99]

To a greater degree than any other waltz Chopin composed, this dance overflows with the rhythmic motive of the twirling female dancer. While Chopin artfully varies the faster rhythm of the first measure of the woman's dance figure, the twirl rhythm of the second measure is repeated like a mantra throughout the opening section (mm. 1–32). In sharp contrast, the B section (mm. 65–112), shown in Example 6.21, explores the rhythm of the male dancer, and perhaps of Chopin himself.

Note that a contrast in rhythm is evident not only between the two sections but also in the affective quality of the musical motion. A description that uses gendered metaphors commonly found in nineteenth-century musical criticism might describe the B section as masculine because of its more vigorous leaps, its energetic off-beat accents, and the self-assertive and goal-oriented drive of the ascending sequence in measures 81–88 that pushes toward a loud climax, a climax that, by halting the musical flow, demands attention. The A section, on the other hand, is more tender and lyrical in expression, more attention is given to the intricate detail of the musical surface,[100] and the descending chromatic bass controls and regulates the movement of the spontaneously ornamented melody.[101] The depiction of gender in this waltz thereby assumes a form-generative role in a ternary ABA form.

In a letter written on 3 October 1829 to his close friend, Tytus Woyciechowski, Chopin confides that both his Waltz in D♭ Major and the slow movement from his F Minor Piano Concerto op. 21 were inspired by his feelings toward the young and beautiful singer Konstancja Gładkowska, Chopin's "ideal." With regard to the waltz, Chopin tells his friend: "Pay attention to the passage marked with an X; nobody, except you, knows of this."[102] Although we cannot know for certain where Chopin placed his X since the manuscript is lost, the most striking moment in the piece occurs at the opening of the B section, which is pictured in Example 6.22. The entire waltz, in a ternary ABA form, is a duet, the only waltz Chopin conceived as such. In the opening A section, the soprano and alto move together in constant eighth-note motion. The tenor voice takes over in the opening B section, supported by the soprano in parallel sixths. Except for the opening G♭, a functional bass is absent. Chopin instructs Woyciechowski that the low voice "should dominate as far as the high E♭ of the violin in the fifth measure

Example 6.21. Chopin's Waltz in A♭ Major op. 69 no. 1, mm. 65–75.

Example 6.22. Chopin's Waltz in D♭ Major op. 70 no. 3, mm. 29–48.

[m. 37]."[103] Over all measures 33–41 is a large balanced arch initiated by the rising tenor melody, which is answered by the descending soprano voice (accompanied by a more clearly descending tenor).

In the two-bar motive that opens the passage, Chopin uses several techniques commonly found in his waltzes, all of which bring emphasis to the beginning of the second measure: the crescendo marking, the dynamic and agogic accents, the asymmetrical

Example 6.23. The opening of the last movement of Chopin's
Concerto in F Minor op. 21.

grouping organization 1 + 3, and, finally, the rhythm of the waltzing woman.

Interestingly, the motive of the female dancer, and perhaps of
Konstancja, appears as the principal motive of the third movement
of the F Minor Concerto op. 21, the opening of which is shown
in Example 6.23. Example 6.24 provides a rhythmic simplification
of the concerto motive and the waltz motive. As mentioned above,
both were conceived during the same period, the fall of 1829. By
3 October 1829 Chopin had completed the waltz and the slow
movement of the concerto. Chopin apparently had difficulty completing the last movement. On October 20 he tells Woyciechowski

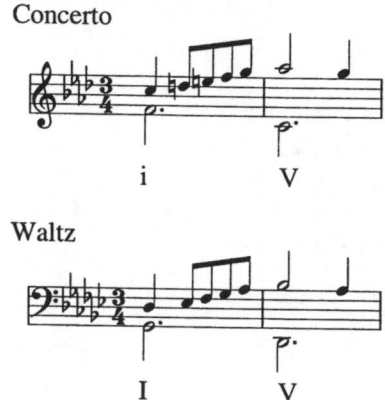

Example 6.24. Rhythmic simplification of the principal motives from the last movement of the Concerto in F Minor op. 21 and the trio from the Waltz in D♭ Major op. 70 no. 3.

that he is "not quite satisfied" with the last movement, and by mid-November it was still not finished.[104] The concerto premiered on 17 March 1830.

It is beyond the scope of this essay to develop this notion fully, but I believe the controlling genre of the last movement of the F Minor Piano Concerto to be a waltz rather than a mazurka, as has been commonly suggested.[105] In fact, in the opening section, where it is most important to reference the controlling genre, there is little to suggest the presence of a mazurka.[106] There are no dotted rhythms, no triple figures, no drones, no accents on the second or third beats (instead downbeats are emphasized), raised $\hat{4}$ does not play a prominent role, and the melodic motion is predominately stepwise with few melodic leaps within the melodic segments. Perhaps the most compelling evidence, aside from the motivic parallelism with the D♭ Major Waltz, is the piano accompaniment. It is a modified um-pah-pah in which the second and third beats arpeggiate the one-bar harmonic rhythm. Within Chopin's titled dance music, this type of um-pah-pah accompaniment only occurs in waltzes; moreover, it is most prominent in two waltzes written within the same time period (KK 1207–8 and KK 1213–14). Chopin creates two-bar arches in the accompaniment by using downward arpeggiations on the second and third beats in the first measure and upward arpeggiations in the following measure; the bass line follows this pattern of arpeggiations. The opening four-bar phrase is a balanced arch against which the cellos play a simplified inversion of the piano's arch. And in measures 5–8 the rhythm of the twirling female dancer twice appears in the soloist's left hand.

Lastly, in arranging themes from the concerto into a collection of mazurkas and waltzes (published by Brzezina, April 1830), Chopin's friend and classmate from the Warsaw Conservatory, Antoni Orłowski, set the opening theme of the last movement as a waltz rather than a mazurka. On three separate occasions Chopin makes reference in letters to Orłowski's arrangements; in none does he say Orłowski got the genre wrong.[107]

## Conclusions

The central goal of this essay is to demonstrate how knowledge of the waltz as danced can open up new modes of interpretation. The nineteenth century witnessed a virtual explosion of popular dance music that was fueled by the insatiable needs of the middle-class consumer. One outcome of this robust market was that composers could make a decent living solely on the composition of popular music. As popular music making became more isolated from high-art music, it increasingly developed its own musical language and supported its own composers. As Jim Samson observes, one of the great achievements of Chopin was his unmatched ability to move fluently between these two levels of music making.[108] Much attention has been given to Chopin's achievements as a composer of art music, so much, in fact, that his dance music tends to be viewed solely through the lens of the autonomous artwork, completely separated from any bodily association. Although such approaches are valuable inasmuch as they reveal inner artistic beauty and compositional craft, they overlook an entire domain of musical associations and influences based on social dance practices of Chopin's time. This article has attempted to place Chopin's waltz music back within the bustle of this once vital and ubiquitous domain, a domain that has gradually receded from our collective consciousness as the dance practices on which his waltzes were based fell from common use.

In her bucolic novel, *Les Maîtres Sonneurs* [*The Master Pipers*], George Sand, after describing how difficult it is to dance to the tunes of a musical oaf, reports the effects of a musician who truly understands the nature of the dance: "He gave us the finest dances in the world . . . so attractive and easy to dance to that we seemed to fly through the air."[109] I would suggest that Chopin was such a musician as Sand describes, and that when listening, performing, and studying his waltzes, mazurkas, and polonaises, one should keep the dancers in mind.

NOTES

I thank the American Council of Learned Societies for a fellowship that enabled me to work on this project uninterrupted for one year.

1. A notable exception is Sevin Yaraman's excellent dissertation, "The Waltz: A Musical Interpretation through the Steps" (Ph.D. diss., City University of New York, 1998); a chapter of this work explores Chopin's waltz music in relation to the choreography of the waltz.

2. Barbara Milewski, "Chopin's Mazurkas and the Myth of the Folk," *19th-Century Music* 23, no. 2 (1999): 113–35.

3. Halina Goldberg, "Musical Life in Warsaw during Chopin's Youth, 1810–1830" (Ph.D. diss., City University of New York, 1997), 3–4.

4. Łukasz Gołębiowski, *Opisanie historyczno-statystyczne miasta Warszawy* (Warszawa: Wyd. Artstyczne i Filmowe, 1979 [1827]) and *Gry i zabawy różnych stanów* (Warszawa: Wyd. Artstyczne i Filmowe, 1983 [1831]).

5. Gołębiowski, *Opisanie*, 222.

6. Ibid.

7. Ibid.

8. Ibid., 221.

9. Ibid., 223.

10. *Kurier warszawski*, no. 1 (1 January 1830): 2. I am indebted to Krzysztof Komarnicki for the translations.

11. Attendance reports in Warsaw's newspapers indicate that during carnival the National Theater routinely accommodated fifteen hundred to two thousand dancers (Museum Historyczne Warszawy, *Bibliografia Warszawy: Wydawnictwa ciągłe, 1795–1863* [Wrocław: Zakład Nardowy Imienia Ossolińskich—Wydawnictwo, 1992], 1324).

12. Gołębiowski, *Opisanie*, 225.

13. Ibid., 222.

14. Goldberg, "Musical Life," v.

15. Concerning Chopin's musical education, see ibid., 48–79.

16. In 1827 approximately 72 percent of Warsaw's population was Roman Catholic. Reported in *Przewodnik warszawski 1827* (Warszawa: Glücksberg, 1827), 46.

17. *Kurier warszawski*, no. 12 (13 January 1830): 53.

18. Jan Ciepliński, *A History of Polish Ballet, 1518–1945*, ed. and trans. Anna Ema Lesiecka (London: Veritas Foundation Publication Center, 1983), 27; Janina Pudełek, "Poland: Theatrical Dance," in *International Encyclopedia of Dance*, ed. Selma Jeanne Cohen (New York: Oxford University Press, 1998), 215.

19. Pudełek, "Poland," 215.

20. *Kurier warszawski*, no. 29 (3 February 1823): 20.

21. Ciepliński, *Polish Ballet*, 33. Warsaw's connection to French culture was particularly strong during the Napoleonic wars.

22. The ballet *Wesele krakowskie* (*Cracow Wedding*), which premiered in Warsaw in 1823, was the first Polish ballet based on traditional national dances (Pudełek, "Poland," 216). For a discussion of the introduction of folk dance in Polish opera, see Barbara Milewski, "Chopin's Mazurkas," 113–35.

23. In his treatise, *Fashionable Dancing* (London: Vizetelly, 1840), 8–11, Henri Cellarius was one of the first to articulate in a publication the division between theatrical and ballroom dancing techniques and the need for specialized instruction in one or the other.

24. *Przewodnik warszawski 1829* (Warszawa: Glücksberg, 1829), 47.

25. Those dancing masters and the dates of their notices are Ludwik Thiery [*sic*] (September 5), Jacób Zielińsky [*sic*] (September 15), F. Kunicki (October 5), Piotr Tomasini (October 12), Franciszek Domagalski (October 15), Jan Zurkowski [*sic*] (October 17), and Karol Göbel (October 26).

26. *Kurier warszawski*, no. 1 (1 January 1830): 2.

27. For a discussion of dance instruction in Warsaw's school curricula, see Antoni Magier, *Estetyka miasta stołecznego Warszawy* (Wrocław: Wydawnicto Ossolińskich, 1963), 58–60. For information on dance instruction in Warsaw's military academies, see Gołębiowski, *Gry i zabawy*, 327, 333; Seweryn Bukar, *Pamiętniki* (Warszawa: Biblioteka Dzieł Wyborowych, 1913), 65–66; Mieczysława Miterzanka, *Działalność pedagogiczna Adama Ks. Czartoryskiego* (Warszawa: Naukowe Towarzystwo Pedagogiczne, 1931), 33; Julian Ursyn Niemcewicz, *Pamiętniki czasów moich*, 2 vols. (Warszawa: Państwowy Instytut Wydawniczy, 1957), 1:57; and R. Ćwięka-Skrzyniarz, *The Great Polish Walking Dance* (Irvington, N.J.: R. Ćwięka, 1983), 65–66.

28. Quoted in Ćwięka-Skrzyniarz, *The Great Polish Walking Dance*, 66.

29. Quoted in Ćwięka-Skrzyniarz, *The Elegant Polish Running-Sliding Dance* (Irvington, N.J., 1984), 30.

30. See Goldberg, "Musical Life," 92–102; and Wojciech Tomaszewski, *Warszawskie edytorstwo muzyczne w latach 1772–1865* (Warszawa, 1992), 167–70.

31. Quoted in Goldberg, "Musical Life," 264.

32. Fryderyk Chopin, *Correspondance de Frédéric Chopin, l'Aube 1816–1831*, ed. Bronislas Sydow, Suzanne and Denise Chainaye, and Irène Sydow, 3 vols. (Paris: Richard-Masse, 1954–60), 2:235.

33. Richard Smith, *Notes Made during a Tour in Denmark, Holstein, Mecklenburg-Schwerin* (London: C. & J. Rivington, 1827), 148–49. Travel writers of the opening part of the nineteenth century constantly compared the Poles to the French in their dress, manners, and fondness for amusements. See, for example, John Lloyd Stephens, *Incidents of Travel in Greece, Turkey, Russia, and Poland* (New York: Harper & Bros., 1838), 213; and A. B. Granville, *St. Petersburgh: A Journal of Travels to and from That Capital; Through Flanders, the Rhenich Provinces, Prussia, Russia, Poland, etc.* (London: H. Colburn, 1828), 542, 569–70. For an extended discussion on French influence in Warsaw's society, see Jerzy Jedlicki, *A Suburb of Europe: Nineteenth-Century Polish Approaches to Western Civilization* (1988; English edition, New York: Central European University Press, 1999), 3–50.

34. To avoid vertigo partners dancing the waltz would normally fix their gaze on each other.

35. The first newspaper advertisement for Kurpiński's Polonez appears on 19 February 1829 in *Kurier warszawski*.

36. As Gołębiowski observed, social dance was an "innate and indispensable need of the people" (*Gry i zabawy*, 304).

37. *Przewodnik warszawski 1827*, 46.

38. Concerning the early development of the waltz, see Elizabeth Aldrich,

Sandra Noll Hammond, and Armand Russell, *The Extraordinary Dance Book T.B. 1826: An Anonymous Manuscript in Facsimile* (Stuyvesant, N.Y.: Pendragon, 2000), 19–24.

39. Kazimierz Wójcicki, *Społeczność Warszawy w początkach naszego stulecia* (Warszawa: Gebethner i Wolff, 1877), 155.

40. Quoted in Andrew Lamb's article "Waltz," in *New Grove 2*, ed. Stanley Sadie and John Tyrrel, 29 vols. (London: Grove, 2001), 27:73.

41. Princess Louise of Prussia, *Forty-Five Years of My Life (1770–1815)*, trans. A. R. Allinson (New York: McBride, Nast, 1912), 111–12.

42. Ibid., 112.

43. Ibid., 155.

44. Tomaszewski, *Warszawskie edytorstwo muzyczne*, 167.

45. Józef Damse, *Milion walców czyli Sposób układania miliony walców dla tych nawet, którzy muzyki nie znaja* (Warszawa: A. Brzezina, 1829). Such compositional manuals for the dilettante in which pieces were composed using simple formulas or by games of chance involving dice, spinning tops, and random number selection were not uncommon and belong to the eighteenth-century tradition of *ars combinatoria*. See Leonard Ratner, *"Ars Combinatoria:* Chance and Choice in Eighteenth-Century Music," in *Studies in Eighteenth-Century Music: A Tribute to Karl Geiringer on His Seventieth Birthday* (New York: Oxford University Press, 1970), 343–63.

46. *Kurier warszawski*, no. 3 (3 January 1830): 10.

47. Ibid., 12.

48. Ibid., no. 5 (5 January 1830): 19.

49. Ibid., no. 6 (7 January 1830): 10.

50. Ibid., no. 51 (22 February 1830): 255.

51. Milewski, "Myth of the Folk," 134–35.

52. Andrzej Edward Koźmian, *Wspomnienia* (Poznań: Nakł. Mieczysława Leitgabra, 1867), 72–73. For a discussion of Chopin's connection to these salons, see also Goldberg, "Musical Life," 273, 309–22.

53. Chopin relates the account in a letter to his family written 26 August 1825; for an English translation of this letter, see Adam Zamoyski, *Chopin: A New Biography* (New York: Doubleday, 1980), 26–27.

54. Reported by Kazimierz W. Wójcicki, *Cmentarz powązkowski w Warszawie*, 3 vols. (Warszawa: Gebethner i Wolff, 1855), 1:18.

55. Chopin, *Correspondance de Frédéric Chopin*, 1:141–42.

56. Ibid. (22 December 1830), 1:235.

57. See Krystyna Kobylańska, *Chopin in His Own Land*, trans. Claire Grece-Dabrowska and Mary Filippi (Kraków: Polish Music Publications, 1955), 231.

58. Kazimierz W. Wójcicki, *Pamiętniki dziecka Warszawy i inne wspomnienia warszawskie*, cited in Zamoyski, *Chopin: A New Biography*, 64.

59. Mieczysław Tomaszewski, *Fryderyk Chopin: A Diary in Images* (Warszawa: Arkady, 1990), 228.

60. Chopin, *Correspondance de Frédéric Chopin*, 1:44.

61. Ibid. (June 1826), 1:57–58.

62. Chopin describes Rembieliński's technique in a letter dated 30 October 1825 (Chopin, *Correspondance de Frédéric Chopin*, 1:42). Previously that year Rembieliński had returned from an extended stay in Paris, where he studied piano and composition (Albert Sowiński, *Les Musiciens Polonais et Slaves: Dictionnaire Biographique*, reprint of the first French edition, 1857 [New York: Da Capo, 1971], 476).

63. Chopin uses the same "rhythmic dissonance" in the opening section (mm. 9–40) of his Waltz in A♭ Major op. 42. Concerning the concept of rhythmic

dissonance, see Harald Krebs's excellent book, *Fantasy Pieces: Metrical Dissonance in the Music of Robert Schumann* (New York: Oxford University Press, 1999).

64. Note that the second waltz is by itself in a da capo layout.

65. I discuss Chopin's use of auxiliary progressions in "Auxiliary Progressions as a Source of Conflict between Tonal Structure and Phrase Structure," *Music Theory Spectrum* 18, no. 1 (1996): 51–76.

66. Moritz Karasowski, *Frederic Chopin: His Life and Letters*, trans. Emily Hill (1879; Westport, Conn.: Greenwood, 1970), 29–30. For other sources, see Pierre Azoury, *Chopin through His Contemporaries* (Westport, Conn.: Greenwood, 1999), 10.

67. Quoted in Tad Szulc, *Chopin in Paris* (New York: Scribner, 1998), 262.

68. Franz Liszt, *Frederic Chopin*, trans. Edward N. Waters (London: Free Press of Glencoe, 1963 [1851]), 136–37. More of a memorial than biography, this book was the result of a collaboration between Liszt and Princess Caroline Sayn-Wittgenstein, his Polish-born lover. Later in the article I discuss Schumann's interpretation of Chopin's waltzes.

69. Jim Samson, *Chopin* (New York: Schirmer, 1996), 43.

70. Elizabeth Aldrich, *From the Ballroom to Hell* (Evanston, Ill.: Northwestern University Press, 1991), 19–21.

71. A two-bar step pattern is also a defining feature of the minuet (most ballroom dances have step patterns no longer than one bar). Thus for both the minuet and the waltz to be "danceable," dancers needed to hear and respond to a clear and consistent two-bar hypermeter. The term *hypermeter* refers to metrical levels at force above the notated meter in which measures are heard in patterns of strong and weak beats.

72. Henri Cellarius, *Fashionable Dancing*, illustrated by Paul Gavarni (London: Vizetelly, c. 1840), 30.

73. Many historical reconstructions of dances from the seventeenth and eighteenth centuries are available today. Unfortunately nineteenth-century social dancing has not received the same attention. Perhaps the most accurate videos to date are those available in the on-line dance collection of the Library of Congress, which has been organized and annotated by the dance historian Elizabeth Aldrich. http://rs6.loc.gov/ammem/dihtml/dihome.html, accessed 16 May 2003.

74. The German word *waltz* is derived from the verb *walzen*, which translates as "to turn," "to revolve," or "to wander." *Waltzen* is related to the Latin verb *volvere* meaning to turn or rotate.

75. Wye Jamison Allanbrook, *Rhythmic Gesture in Mozart* (Chicago: University of Chicago Press, 1983), 65. The appropriation of astronomic metaphors (e.g., orbits, spheres, planets) in describing the motion of dancers of the waltz is common in the literature of the waltz, and Johann Wolfgang von Goethe was perhaps the first to use such terms. In a scene from *Die Leiden des jungen Werther* (1774) the characters Werther and Lotte "took to waltzing and circled round each other like the spheres" (quoted in Lamb, "Waltz," 72).

76. Adolph Bernard Marx, *Die Lehre von der musikalischen Komposition*, 2 vols. (Leipzig: Breitkopf & Härtel, 1837–38), 2:55. Although many dancing masters were able violinists or keyboard players, very few had the musical training to describe, in any meaningful way, what makes a good dance tune. Nor was it their primary concern. As Sevin Yaraman points out in her dissertation, the most detailed account on how to compose danceable waltz music comes from the German composer, theorist, and critic Adolph Bernard Marx (*The Waltz*, 31–32). In the section that follows I use Marx as a guide in locating points of correspondence between the music and the dance.

77. Marx, *Die Lehre*, 55.

78. Lord George Gordon Byron, "The Waltz: An Apostrophic Hymn" (London: S. Gosnell, 1813).

79. Concerning structural highpoints in music, see Kofi Agawu, "The Structural Highpoint as Determinant of Form in Nineteenth Century Music" (Ph.D. diss., Stanford University, 1982); and Zohar Eitan, *Highpoints: A Study of Melodic Peaks* (Philadelphia: University of Pennsylvania Press, 1997).

80. In this brief prelude Chopin employs the waltz as a musical topic.

81. The Arabic numbers between the staves indicate the hypermeter.

82. Crisis points, characterized by tonal disjunction and by a sudden halt of the accompaniment, are a common feature of Viennese waltzes; they draw attention to closure and also back to the performer, where in Vienna the phenomenon of "pop superstar" had fully emerged with Joseph Lanner and Johann Strauss (Sr.).

83. For crisis points in Chopin's published waltzes, see op. 18, measure 233, and op. 34 no. 3, measures 159–60.

84. At the largest level the entire waltz is organized in a circular form, ABA, and the A and B sections themselves are in rounded binary form. Viennese waltzes, on the other hand, are typically organized in a medley format: an introduction followed by a succession of five waltzes and concluded with a coda.

85. Yaraman also identifies neighboring motion as an important feature of nineteenth-century waltz music (*Waltz*, 49–54).

86. See Frederick Niecks, *Frederick Chopin as a Man and Musician*, 2 vols., 3rd ed. (London: Novello, 1902), 2:249.

87. According to Chopin's student, Wilhelm von Lenz, Chopin referred to this waltz as a *Valse mélancolique*. *Die Grossen Pianoforte-Virtuosen unserer Zeit aus persönlicher Bekanntschaft* (Berlin: B. Behr, 1872), 37.

88. Niecks, *Chopin*, 2:142.

89. Marx, *Die Lehre*, 55–56

90. Quoted in Aldrich, *Ballroom to Hell*, 154–55.

91. Cellarius, *Dancing*, 44–45. And drop they did, although not always just from dizziness. At the beginning of the 1830 carnival season, the *Kurier warszawski* (no. 3 [3 January 1830]) published a story about a mother whose beautiful and talented daughters, aged fifteen, seventeen, and eighteen, all died within a month of one another. Cause of death: "too much dancing" (9). More likely they died from respiratory illness, which was a leading cause of death in urban centers. Respiratory illnesses were aggravated by the conditions in dance halls, which were typically dusty, smoky, overheated, crowded, and poorly ventilated.

92. The use of grace notes is a prominent feature of Viennese waltzes and particularly those of Johann Strauss (Sr.) and Joseph Lanner. Chopin only began using leaping grace notes in his waltzes in 1830, beginning with the E minor waltz. It is possible that Chopin's exposure to Viennese waltz music during his trip to Vienna in 1829 served as inspiration for the incorporation of grace notes in his E minor waltz.

93. In some instances the first segment overlaps with the beginning of the second, resulting in the proportion 2 + 3. In such cases I still use the label 1 + 3.

94. In this phrase Chopin cleverly plays an enharmonic pun. The phrase begins with B♭ as flat $\hat{6}$ of D major but ends with A♯ as $\hat{7}$ of B minor. The shift to the diatonic collection of B minor is prepared in measure 37 where Chopin uses B♮ rather than B♭. Also notice how Chopin tonally dovetails the phrase ending in measure 32 with the phrase beginning with the pick up into measure 33. The V/III, which begins the new phrase, functions as a passing chord, connecting the tonic B minor chord of measure 32 to the D major chord in measure 34. In

measure 37 the V/III functions as a neighboring chord to the mediant. The grouping boundaries between the phrase structure and the tonal structure are thus in conflict with each other.

95. For example, melodic arches are also a characteristic feature of Chopin's mazurkas, as are um-pah-pah accompaniments. In fact, at times it is difficult to distinguish between the two genres. This potential ambiguity is reflected in the title and music of a dance published in Warsaw in the 1820s, "Mazurka—though not really a mazurka—but a waltz." Cited in Edwin Kornel Stadnicki, *Walc fortepianowy w Polsce w latach 1800–1830* (Warszawa: Polskie Wydawnictwo Muzyczne, 1962), 70, 124–26.

96. Across Europe and the United States popular tunes from the stage were routinely arranged and published as ballroom dance music. In Warsaw, for example, arias from Rossini's opera, *Barber of Seville*, were extremely popular as dance music (Stadnicki, *Walc,* 154).

97. Robert Schumann, *On Music and Musicians,* ed. Konrad Wolff, trans. Paul Rosenfeld (New York: Dennis Dobson, 1952 [1946]), 139.

98. Gustave Flaubert, *Sentimental Education,* trans. Douglas Parmée (Oxford: Oxford University Press, 1989), 131–32.

99. Chopin, *Correspondance de Frédéric Chopin,* 2:151.

100. In his article, "Harmony at the Tea Table: Gender and Ideology in the Piano Nocturne," Jeffery Kallberg discusses the gendered associations in musical finery in the genre of the nocturne (in *Chopin at the Boundaries: Sex, History, and Musical Genre* [Cambridge, Mass.: Harvard University Press, 1996], 30–61).

101. Notice that against the small ornamental neighbor motions of the melody, the repeating bass line composes out a large double-neighbor motion around 5̂.

102. Chopin, *Correspondance de Frédéric Chopin,* 1:132.

103. Ibid.

104. Ibid., 135.

105. For example, John Rink identifies the opening theme as a folk-inspired mazur melody (*Chopin: The Piano Concertos* [Cambridge: Cambridge University Press, 1997], 58–59).

106. See Chopin's concert piece, *Rondo à la mazur* op. 5 for a clear presentation of the genre of the mazurka.

107. The dates of the letters are 27 March 1830, 10 April 1830, and 17 April 1830.

108. Jim Samson, *The Music of Chopin* (Oxford: Oxford University Press, 1985), 127.

109. George Sand, *The Master Pipers,* trans. Rosemary Lloyd (Oxford: Oxford University Press, 1994), 75.

# 7

# *Chopiniana* and Music's Contextual Allusions

MARIANNE KIELIAN-GILBERT

Representational art as well as nonrepresentational art is inadequately comprehended in an analysis which deals only with content, character and narrative. The development of structuralist and semiotic modes of analysis has demonstrated that meaning is constructed at a variety of levels. The ideology of the novel is contained in the literary devices and stylistic aspects of the text as well as in the story.[1]
Cultural identity is not necessarily synonymous with somatic identity. Yet neither is somatic identity any more "real" or essential than a social one simply because it is anchored in the body.[2]

## *Prelude*

The words *I love you* can have an ordinary or extraordinary effect according to the manner in which they are spoken and the emotional and physical conditions of their articulation. A depth of feeling registers and resonates in the physical body of the speaker, and sound reaches the listener who "hears" the "grain" of that voice in that particular context, discerning, creating, and interpreting its meaning and significance. This hearing is a hearing of the body, of the psychic in the material. It is an answer, an antidote, to the apparent arbitrariness and conventionality of signs. Listeners engage with the intersensory, crossmodal, and material dimensions of sound in context: in connecting the physical, emotional, and material, they ground the psychic motivations of signs. Content thus embodies and resonates context: the material aspects of sound are dynamic and temporally contingent. This enables an exchange such that the speaker and the one spoken to, the lover and the beloved, are mutually constituted. The registering of meaning is an outcome of the quality of presence and the validity of the sounds, and those aspects are not localized in the speaker, listener, context, or sounds alone.

### CHOPINIANA I

Rose Subotnik has written about the character and implications of Chopin's "individuality" of style.[3] For contemporary listeners, Chopin's recognizable musical personality grows out of several aspects of his music: it is mainly instrumental music without voice or text; it requires few social resources because it is primarily confined to a single instrument found in the home; and its function is more that of aesthetic self-presentation rather than of fulfilling particular social functions (in this regard Subotnik notes that the funeral march from the B♭ Minor Sonata is a notable exception):

> We hear a work by Chopin and our first impression which remains throughout the piece as a kind of grounding principle is that we are hearing a piece by Chopin. . . . I think it is fair to say that no composer has ever exceeded the extent to which Chopin infused the listening experience with his own identity, and that very few have matched it.[4]

Such recognitions shift attention to "the reality of the contingent," and by this Subotnik means the concrete and the individual linked to "our knowledge of (and reaction to) the particular context in which [the music] originated."[5] The music of this composer, its sensuous and cultural particularity, is not that of a "self-evident intelligibility" or structure but of "a particular individual in a particular cultural situation."[6]

Yet our perceptions of Chopin's music (and music generally) are also continually nuanced and reshaped in and by specific lived *material* contexts. Sonic expressions in different *physical* (material) and *historical* contexts can interact with, and effect and change, the musical terms of our perceptions. The idea that different material contexts both suggest the kinds of musical structures and temporal qualities to characterize music experience and historicize others offers one way to construe the significance and subjective meanings of music. This essay explores settings of Chopin's music in audiovisual media in the twentieth century—ballet, film, and television—and the role and significance of different material contexts for particular characterizations of his music. The examples show that certain values are still in circulation in the twentieth and twenty-first centuries, referencing receptions and influences of historically specific times and places.

## Chopin's "Hands"

In 1900 James Huneker wrote in his book on Chopin (see the image in Figure 7.1a):

> Chopin's elastic hand, small, thin, with lightly articulated fingers, was capable of stretching tenths with ease. . . . His wrist was very supple. Stephen Heller said that "it was a wonderful sight to see Chopin's small hands expand and cover a third of the keyboard. It was like the opening of the mouth of a serpent about to swallow a rabbit whole." . . . Each one of his ten fingers was a delicately differentiated voice, and these ten voices could sing at times like the morning stars.[7]

The "alternate" hand (Figure 7.1b), though not specifically Chopin's, transforms the performative material aesthetic of Chopin's hand. As a political-social emblem of the 1995 Thirteenth International Chopin Competition, it projects a force that links Chopin's physical (and musical) body with the Solidarity Union's transformation of political power and national identity in Poland. I say "performative" because both these images situate, render, or "perform"—if you will—configurations of temporal, qualitative, and spatial values that link experientially in different ways. How do the performative values of the second image change or shift with the specific awareness that, in that same year, 1995, Lech Wałęsa lost the presidential election to a former Communist, Aleksander Kwaśniewski, a loss that marked the end of Wałęsa's political career even as the period of Poland's reclaiming its homeland continued?

The *material contexts* of music embody and shape its different values and weightings, its structures and orientations. These contexts also interact with, effect, and change our perceptions of music. Extending the work of Adorno as well as music scholars such as James Buhler, Lawrence Kramer, Susan McClary, Rose Subotnik,

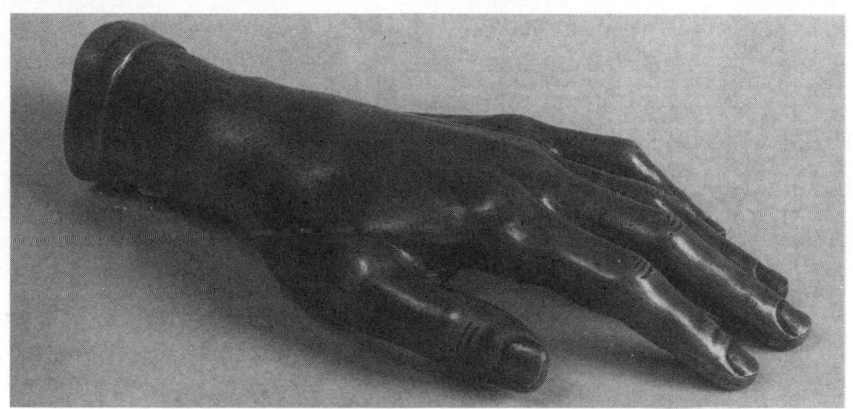

Figure 7.1. Both the bronze cast of Chopin's left hand (after J.-B. A. Clesinger) (above) and the poster of the Thirteenth F. Chopin International Piano Competition in 1995 by Roslaw Szaybo (below) are found in the collections of the Frederick Chopin Museum at the Frederick Chopin Society in Warsaw. Copyright by the Frederick Chopin Museum. Used by permission. All rights reserved.

and Alastair Williams,[8] by "materiality" I mean the historical and aesthetic context that includes (weaves together, connects) the specifics of a medium (painting, music, dance) and its related material artifacts and social formations. "Materiality" is that connection of music—its specific qualities and temporalities, its sonic substance and structure—with the iconography and social formations of particular *physical* and *historical* contexts. This claim is one of the main issues of this essay, namely, that different physical/experiential contexts and their sonic expressions—the material *Chopiniana*—interact with and effect our perceptions (the musical terms) of Chopin's relationships and structures. Given that music is always situated in a social-material context(s), why do some pieces seem to meld so seamlessly with certain contexts or stand apart from and resist others? What are the roles of alternate contexts for one's perceptions and characterizations of music?

The term *Chopiniana* in the title of this essay is emblematic of the materiality and layering of the historical-experiential contexts situating music. *Chopiniana* was the title of Glazunov's orchestral setting of four Chopin piano pieces, later choreographed by Fokine in a slightly different combination, and subsequently renamed *Les Sylphides* for the 1909 Paris ballet production performed by Diaghilev's Ballets Russes. These and other "Chopiniana" connect music with its physical experiential contexts; they situate its layers of historical reference, its contextual allusions.

### CHOPINIANA II

In 1893 Alexander Glazunov, an ardent admirer of Chopin, orchestrated four of Chopin's piano pieces in his *Suite for Grand Orchestra* op. 46, adding the subtitle *Chopiniana* to the collection. Rimsky-Korsakov conducted the first performance that same year. Some fifteen years later, the young St. Petersburg dancer and choreographer Michel Fokine encountered a piano arrangement of Glazunov's *Chopiniana* in a music store and was inspired to transform the suite into a ballet, with Glazunov's help. The ballet *Chopiniana* (subtitled *A Suite of Dances and Scenes*) premiered at Petersburg's Maryinsky Theater on 7 February 1907. Fokine gave each dance a programmatic theme based on aspects of Chopin's life and on Polish ballroom and character dances.[9] The dancers dressed in "rich" Polish costumes, and Fokine described the program of the Mazurka op. 50 no. 3 (to be followed by the Waltz op. 64, no. 2) as follows:

The next tableau, to the music of the Mazurka, depicted a wedding in a Polish village. An unfortunate young girl is being married to an elderly man whom she does not love. In the course of the general dancing, her beloved finds his way to her. As a result of his passionate pleas, she throws the wedding ring at the unwanted suitor and flees with her beloved. . . . This scene was followed by the Waltz.[10]

Fokine set a second *Chopiniana*, 8 March 1908, as a purely classical (white) ballet, orchestrated by Maurice Keller.[11] This second orchestrated version set different Chopin pieces but retained Glazunov's setting of the C♯ Minor Waltz op. 64 no. 2 of the first series (transposed to D minor).[12] According to Cyril Beaumont, "this production was an answer to those critics who asserted that Fokine wished to destroy the traditional ballet."[13] A year later Serge Diaghilev retitled *Chopiniana* as *Les Sylphides* for the Paris production of 2 June 1909 performed by his Ballets Russes with orchestrations by Glazunov, Stravinsky, and Taneyev and the set design by Benois. The new title further linked *Chopiniana* with the first romantic ballet, *La Sylphide* (1830), and the legacy of the visionary Romantic ballerina Marie Taglioni—graceful, ethereal, and chaste. Romantic traditions also figured strikingly in Fokine's *Chopiniana/Les Sylphides*.

## Chopiniana/Les Sylphides, *Waltz in C♯ Minor op. 64 no. 2*

Describing the *pas de deux* of this waltz in the ballet, Fokine wrote in his *Memoirs of a Ballet Master:*

> Here I should like to point out the failure of many audiences, dancers, and even those who compose dances, to notice that the same *movement* [my emphasis] can convey a totally different impression depending on whether a dancer is descending or rising on her toes on a certain musical beat. In the first instance, when she is on the downbeat of the measure or part of the measure, she expresses self-assurance; in the second instance, while rising into the air or on her toes, she is expressing lightness, airiness, the ethereal quality of a fantastic being [for my emphasis, the reader can replace the word *movement* with *music* in this citation].[14]

Fokine choreographed the waltz in *Les Sylphides* at a considerably slower tempo in comparison with the *Tempo giusto* of Chopin's Waltz op. 64 no. 2 (Example 7.1). He described the unique features of his choreography as follows:

> The choreography [of the Waltz] differed from all other *pas de deux* in its total absence of spectacular feats. There was not a single *entrechat*, turn in the air, or pirouette. There was a slow turn of the ballerina holding her partner's hand, but this could not be classified as a pirouette because the movement was not confined to the turn but was used for a change of position and grouping. . . . I simply could not conceive of any spectacular stunts to the accompaniment of the poetic, lyrical Waltz of Chopin.[15]

The movement of the dancers extends like a thread through his choreographic combinations; in analogous fashion the slower tempo highlights the seamless quality and continuity of the descending stepwise line in the melody of the opening section of the Waltz (D minor, mm. 1–32: F–E–D–C♯–C–B♭–A–[repeat]–E–D–C–B♭–A–F–E–D). The slower tempo and qualitative aspects of Glazunov's orchestral setting and Fokine's choreography configure a set of musical, visual, and kinesthetic effects that are inseparable from the Romantic cult of the ballerina, a tradition that embodies the mystique of femininity in transcendent form:

> The effect of these floating white clouds against the cold atmosphere of the scene reminds one of snowflakes whirled hither and thither by the wind in the moonlight of a winter's eve. At other times they resemble clouds of mist, the surf on a breaking wave, and perhaps best of all a little band of winter fairies at play beneath the waning moon in the shadow of a frosted glade. All the dances breathe an intense sadness.[16]

As Lynn Garafola notes, "this kingdom of the ideal belonged to the ballerina as did the larger domain of subjectivity—poetry, loss, grief, beauty, desire, eroticism."[17]

Notably, however, the formal premiere of *Les Sylphides* on 4 June 1909 also included the premiere of Fokine's *Cléopâtra* set to the music of Arensky, Taneyev, Rimsky-Korsakov, Glinka, and Glazunov. *Cléopâtra* was based on Fokine's 1908 ballet *Egyptian Nights* [*Une Nuit d' Egypte*]. *Cléopâtra*, with its theme of voluptuous sadism, opened a path to the emerging and modernist cult of the male

# VALSE

à Madame la Baronne Nathaniel de Rothschild

Opus 64 Nr. 2

Example 7.1. Chopin, Waltz in C# Minor op. 64 no. 2, mm. 1–32

*ballerino* in the Ballets Russes. At this time Diaghilev (and Fokine) began to eschew the idea of a "chivalric ideal of masculinity" linked with the ballerina in favor of the physique, prowess, and sexual availability of the ballerino (a homoeroticized male *danseur*) that he initially feminized as an object of desire and ultimately transformed as a hero.[18] Fokine's 1909 balletic setting of Chopin's Waltz in *Les Sylphides* thus also illumines (or stands in relation to) an alternate constellation and collision of values, even as it is also configured and reflected by them.

Jim Samson and others have written about the different ways that nineteenth-century receptions construed Chopin's music: for the French, Chopin's music was a vehicle of intimate communication. They highlighted the notion of expression in his music. The Germans elevated Chopin's music as an icon of the classical canon in such a way as to downplay its national character and origins. The Russians regarded his music as an artistic vehicle for fusing modernism and nationalism to further a cultural and political identity. For the Poles, the sense of national identity extended from Chopin's treatment of the genres of polonaise and mazurka rather than the nocturne. (They understood the nocturne more from the perspectives of literary narrative and epic forms than from those of the salon.) The English, affirming the ascendancy of the middle class, tended to regard Chopin's music in the contexts of feminine values and domestic music making.

These orientations create structural/perceptual orientations that configure varying senses of place (location, qualitative states, and sites of action) and the means of negotiating these contrasts of alternate states and conditions in Chopin's music. The audiovisual examples that follow show that many of these different values, that is, their contextual allusions, are still in circulation in the twentieth and twenty-first centuries. References of time and place and particular material conditions suggest, and resonate with, particular perceptions of music-structural relationships and orientations (and vice versa).

## Alternate Orientations and Allusions

It is my contention that Chopin's music, in particular, accentuates the relationship and drawing together of *alternate* or *contrasting* musical, physical, emotional, and social contexts. In his music, this kind of accentuation—a–b–a, statement–contrast–return on different levels—provides one basis for its continuing resonance in contemporary experience. Perceiving Chopin's music is to experience and grapple with contrasting or conflicting sets of presentational values, and different temporal and structural orientations. Alternate (non-simultaneous) orientations help to link varying material-interpretive situations and often embody different temporal perceptions. For example, according to Jean-Jacques Eigeldinger, the op. 28 Preludes exploit "the principle of alternation":

> between the cycle of fifths ascending through the sharp side and that descending through the flat side; between major and minor; between diatonic and chromatic; between opposing tempi and characters, sizes and lengths, rhythms and metres; between two oscillating harmonies; between ascending and descending melodic lines; between high and low, left hand and right hand, continuity and discontinuity in the passage from one piece to another; between single and dual thematic bases. *Not* that these oscillations are systematic: in taking these parameters singly or in groups one discovers no more than *partial* structures.[19]

Sensing alternating, non-simultaneous orientations calls to mind the perceptual situation of the rabbit-duck or the young woman/old woman figures. The different orientations (for example, as old versus young woman) are mutually exclusive, but the "composite" figure or "effect" includes the structural orientations and aspects that make possible the flip in perspective from one figure to another. Each view depends on a different axis of orientation.[20] Figure 7.2 shows an example derived from a lithograph design by Georges Braque (1882–1963), in which, according to Rudolf Arnheim,

> The shape of the profile line changes entirely, depending on which face it is seen to belong to. What was empty becomes full; what was active, passive. . . . the objects create the illusion of being materially present, only to change without notice into something completely different but equally convincing.[21]

These kinds of contextual allusions are embodied to some extent in all interpretive-experiential situations such that the act of selecting or characterizing the determinate aspects of one set of meanings may disturb or highlight an alternate set of values. Such allusions are distinct from vagueness, a situation that does not illicit attention, discernment, or specificity. They present a special kind

Figure 7.2. (left) From Rudolf Arnheim, *Art and Visual Perception: A Psychology of the Creative Eye.* © 1954 The Regents of the University of California. Used by permission.
  (right) *Woman before a Window with Pencil and Paper, and a Musical Instrument* by Georges Braque (after 1915) (lithograph, 10½ × 14 in.). © Geoffrey Clements/CORBIS

of ambiguity in the ways that they mediate categories by referencing different contexts. The categorization of gender, for example, suggests that binary distinctions (though never irrelevant) are continually nuanced, reshaped, or counterpointed in experienced material contexts. This shaping implies the consideration of contrastive (non-simultaneous or alternating) possibilities of particular relational orientations, that is, the alternate orientations to some extent are mutually implicated, though not necessarily equally weighted.

The contextualizing of the values and movements of music requires the experiential understanding of the possibility of relational contrasts—the kind registered, for example, by the two images of Chopin's hands. Perceiving this kind of "relational dynamics" (possibilities, range of contrasts) is to experience the forces at work in shaping experience and interpretation. The different orientations need not be projected solely in terms of logical contrasts or binary oppositions. Lawrence Kramer notes that acuity of experience also involves sensitivity to, or becoming haunted by, what is excluded or characterized elsewhere. For example, he characterizes Chopin's Prelude in A Minor op. 28 no. 2 as a "study in reversal or, more precisely, as a study in dialectic, conceived of in nineteenth-century terms as a series of dynamic oppositions that lead to reversals of meaning or value."[22]

## *Chopin's Prelude in A Major op. 28 no. 7*

The 1995 Independent Television Service (ITS) series, *The United States of Poetry*,[23] presents a theatrical rendition of sonnet and prelude—Elizabeth Barrett Browning's sonnet "How Do I Love Thee," with its fourteen lines, each of ten syllables, and Fryderyk Chopin's A Major Prelude op. 28 no. 7 with its waltz-like four-bar antecedent-consequent phrase pairings (see Example 7.2).[24] Barrett's sonnet, from her *Sonnets from the Portuguese*, was written from 1845 to 1850, a time marked by her first meeting Robert Browning in 1845 and their subsequent marriage in 1846 ("Portuguese" was Robert Browning's pet name for Elizabeth). Chopin composed his Prelude no. 7 as early as 1836. It appeared in the collection of Preludes in 1839, but, unlike the others of the set, it underwent virtually no revision. The ITS presentation of music and poem, particularly to the extent that we are familiar with them, projects their respective aesthetic stylizations of "waltz" and Victorian love in a theatrical setting that calls attention to their juxtaposition as well as their affiliations.

The theatrical context is a subtle parody. Lypsinka (performance artist John Epperson) mouths the words of the poem and, as a stylishly dressed woman, strolls down a parkway on the arm of a gentleman to the gaze of another male spectator. The overdubbing of the voice; the slightly delayed (and stylized) lip-synching of the poem; the play and performance of gender (display of camp?); the coordination of the raised foot with the mention of death; the wondering of whose voice, whose body inhabits the visual frame, and from whence that voice comes; the sense of irony and parody between the filmic and dramatic/performative context; the theater of Lypsinka's mouthing the lines as voiced by Jayne Mansfield in her 1964 rendition of the poem; the theatrical and gender-bending presence of Lypsinka; the diegetic/non-diegetic (inside/outside the world of the narrative) position of the music—these and other contrasts create a space of allusion and illusion, a play of irony, an oscillation between surface and background, extending the bounds of historical texts and performances into the present.

Chopin's music resists poetic and theatrical appropriation, as does Browning's poetry, even as one internalizes the other. Both the irony and the seriousness of the setting undo the notion of music–poetic–theatrical orientations as fixed or immobile yet at the same time play on the apparent shadow of their fixity.

Example 7.2. (*opposite page, top*). Chopin, Prelude in A Major op. 28 no. 7. (*opposite page, bottom*) Chopin, Prelude in A Major op. 28 no. 7, counterpoint of scale-degree patterns X($\hat{5}$–$\hat{3}$–$\hat{4}$–$\hat{2}$) and Y($\hat{2}$–$\hat{4}$–$\hat{3}$–$\hat{5}$). (*below*) Elizabeth Barrett Browning, "How Do I Love Thee," *Sonnets from the Portuguese*, XLIII.

How do I love thee? Let me count the ways.
I love thee to the depth and breadth and height
My soul can reach, when feeling out of sight
For the ends of Being and ideal Grace.
I love thee to the level of everyday's
Most quiet need, by sun and candle-light.
I love thee freely, as men strive for Right;
I love thee purely, as they turn from Praise.
I love thee with the passion put to use
In my old griefs, and with my childhood's faith.
I love thee with a love I seemed to lose
With my lost saints,—I love thee with the breath,
Smiles, tears, of all my life!—and, if God choose.
I shall but love thee better after death.[25]

From a music-structural perspective Rose Subotnik hears eight two-bar phrases in harmonically linked *antecedent-consequent pairs*. Alternately Brian Hyer argues for the integrity of the Prelude as "fragment," its "radical terseness" in part as the product of hearing the two long eight-bar phrases (with two cadences), both as *antecedents*.[26] My analysis in Example 7.2 shows the stratified and contrapuntal settings of melodic scale-degree patterns of the upper parts (see the upper stave of the sketch in Example 7.2) in contrast and in relation to harmonic-tonal progression and cadence (see the lower stave of the sketch). The perceptible counterpoint of repeated melodic patterns nuances both two-bar and eight-bar phrase pairings: pattern X, scale-degree pattern $\hat{5}$–$\hat{3}$–$\hat{4}$–$\hat{2}$ [E–C♯–D–B] in measures 1–2 and 4–6, and overlapping pattern Y, a reversal of X, scale-degree pattern $\hat{2}$–$\hat{4}$–$\hat{3}$–$\hat{5}$ [B–D–C♯–E] in measures 6–8 and 13–16. This alternate hearing—focusing on the counterpoint of scale-degree patterns in particular tonal fields—is one way to render or hear the gestural patterning of the Prelude as deliberately static, yet pliant. It lends technical insight in support of perceptions of a stylized waltz with a certain (ironic?) aesthetic distance of bearing, tone, inflection, and genre. Interestingly the static aesthetic quality of the Prelude also imbues the sense of harmonic progression. Scale-degree $\hat{2}$ undergoes a progressively denser textural setting (as an "outsider" note over an E pedal in m. 1, as a B minor triad over an E pedal in m. 5, and as a B minor tonal area linked with V in mm. 12–16).

Though this analysis emerged from my response to experiencing the Prelude in a particular contemporary (1996) performative context, that reading can also work in interesting ways in other contexts (e.g., the Prelude as static [aesthetic] surface is highlighted in *Les Sylphides* but without the ironic effect).[27]

Do these alternate contexts or frames of mind open up a space of definition through defamiliarization, through complementation, through the discharge of "third meanings"? If a listener had read Rose Subotnik's more than one-hundred-page interpretive meditation on the A Major Prelude in her *Deconstructive Variations* (1996), would perceptions of the surplus chord (the $^{V}7/ii$ of m. 12) and its coincidence with the conclusion of a $4 \times 4$ textual grouping of the Barrett Browning poem (on the word *Praise* of line 8) confirm the contingency, or accidental nature of the correspondence, or result in further interpretive reverberations on her reading of social-cultural narratives?[28] Alternate interpretations can sharpen, or show the pressures against, one's perceptions and interpretations of music.

These performances, contextual allusions, and combinations are, or can be experienced as, markedly *serious*, extending beyond the notion of appropriation. The term *appropriation* captures (or highlights) the distinctness and "lack" of interaction of contexts—or the sense in which one context seemingly takes control of or uses another. In contrast, the orientations of the term *reception* are interactive and draw attention to different kinds of relationship between music(s), artistic and social-cultural contexts, and listening communities. The terms of music structure mesh with the effects of specific materially conditioned listening practices. Music's different contexts of reception can thus call up alternate orientations toward or allusions to particular music-structural readings. The orientations are not "simultaneous," and in this sense they *require* different structural readings. Moreover, accounts of syntactic and semantic meanings are not separate from social-cultural stories; indeed, they shape and are the products of such narratives.

Films often draw on Chopin's music to point up a contrast or dissonant relationship in narrative "lived" contexts, producing and being produced by forces of identity and cultural representation. The contextual contrast can link with particular musical contrasts that, in turn, nuance the contextual settings. Chopin's music can call up familiar situations (the piano lesson), the connections of music to body language, or the human-relational situations of ac-

tual or imagined performance. It can draw attention to the psychic
consonance or dissonance of relational behaviors, particularly with
regard to the tensions and disjunctions of alternate temporal conditions (early vs. later memories, foreshadowings or premonitions,
psychic transformations, and the like). Transforming the tangible
timbral and acoustical aspects of the music in particular ways may
also emphasize these aspects.

Several instances of *Chopiniana* in different cinematic and narrative contexts are summarized in Figure 7.3.[29] It is no accident
that Chopin's music works as a site or process of negotiation in
networks of cultural representation and identity. When his music
articulates a "place," mood, memory, utopian possibility, or "cognitive dissonance," perceptions of (historical) stylization and aesthetic distance may come to the fore. As it articulates processes of
negotiation or "action," its "narrative" emerges, often through an
alternation and embedding of (a–b–a) contrasts. These aspects of
place or process or both facilitate a particular kind of interaction
between and within contexts.[30] Different material settings may
highlight different music-structural or perceptual orientations.

In the 1995 film *Welcome to the Dollhouse* Chopin's Waltz in Ab
op. 69 no. 1 is heard offscreen played on an out-of-tune piano,
providing the setting for a daguerreotype (historical) photo of the
teenager, Dawn, and her family; it returns for the credits at the
end, setting Chopin's music as a frame for distant/dissonant memories—here, of "seventh-grade" experience, the brutality of a bully
and the awkwardness and missteps of growing up.[31] *Five Easy Pieces*
(1970) features an onscreen performance of Chopin's F Minor Fantasy by a misfit protagonist on an out-of-tune piano in the back of
a pickup truck during a Los Angeles traffic jam to the amazement
and irritation of other motorists.[32]

Two films enact-embed interpersonal (relational) aspects of
performing Chopin's music. In Ingmar Bergman's *Autumn Sonata*
(1978) the growing tension between mother and daughter—as a
child, the daughter was abandoned by her famous concert pianist
mother—builds from an encounter in which the daughter's search-
ing performance of Chopin's Prelude in A Minor op. 28 no. 2 is
met with the mother's dismissal of the daughter's interpretation
(and thus of her "voice").[33] The mother responds with a performance that is meant to show the "correct" and "artistic" way that
the music should be played. Although the mother judges her own
performance as superior, the cinematic context underscores the

Figure 7.3. Chopin's music in cinema (selected examples). References are drawn from the Internet Movie Database, (IMDb), http://us.imdb.com/Name?Chopin, +Fr%E9d%E9ric, accessed 16 May 2003.

---

*The Picture of Dorian Gray (1945), directed by Albert Lewin*
Story: Oscar Wilde novel. "If the picture (a portrait of Dorian Gray) can change, and I can always be as I am now, I'd give my soul for that." This obsession of Dorian Gray's with youth leads to the consequences of eternal youth and Dorian's grieving for the return of his soul. When he dies, his body switches appearances with the image in the painting.
Music: Chopin, Prelude in D Minor op. 28 no. 24 (Dorian's leitmotiv)

*Five Easy Pieces (1970), directed by Bob Rafelson*
Story: Robert Dupea is a misfit creative/musical personality. At one point during a traffic jam, Robert jumps aboard a truck with a piano in the back and begins playing the Chopin Fantasy on the out-of-tune piano.
Music: The Five "Easy" Pieces" are Chopin, Fantasy in F Minor; Bach, Chromatic Fantasy and Fugue; Mozart, Eb Major Concerto; Chopin, Prelude in E Minor op. 28 no. 4; and, finally, Mozart, Fantasy in D Minor.

*Autumn Sonata (Höstsonaten) (1978), directed by Ingmar Bergman*
Story: Visiting her daughter, Eva, at her home for the first time in seven years, famous pianist Charlotte is surprised to find her other (mentally handicapped) daughter, Helena, there. Eva had taken Helena out of the institution where their mother had put her. The tension between mother and daughter Eva builds up slowly, until a nightly conversation releases all that they have wanted to tell each other in a shattering confrontation.
Music: Chopin, Prelude in A Minor op. 28 no. 2: played twice, first with the daughter Eva's performance and then with the mother's "correct" performance.

*Getting It Right (1989), directed by Randal Kleiser*
Story: Gavin, shy and thirty-one years old, still lives with his parents. Three women are interested in him: the "madwoman" Lady Minerva Munday lives in a basement, the "whore" Joan is an oversexed millionairess, married to a Greek architect. But he prefers his "ugly duckling" assistant at the barbershop.
Music: Chopin, selection from *"Les Sylphides."* Performed by the Sofia Philharmonic Orchestra. Gavin teaches "art" (e.g., Degas's painting of ballet dancers) to his assistant as "Chopin's" music plays in the background.

*Tombstone (1993), directed by George P. Cosmatos*
Story: Wyatt Earp's story.
Music: Chopin, Nocturne in E Minor op. 72 no. 1. Doc Holliday (Val Kilmer) plays an out-of-tune piano in a saloon: there is a contrast of class [classical (F. Chopin) vs. American (S. Foster) music].

*Scent of Green Papaya (Mui du du xanh) (1993), directed by Anh Hung Tran*
Story: The life and the sexual awakening of a servant girl (later, the servant of a Vietnamese composer) who grows into a mesmerizing woman.
Music: Chopin, Preludes op. 28 no. 23 in F Major, and no. 24 in D Minor. Fiancée of composer (F Major Prelude) realizes that the servant girl is the object of the composer's love/desire and feels jealousy, anger, and loss (D Minor Prelude).

*The Net (1995), directed by Irwin Winkler*
Story: A software analyst, Angela Bennett, is accidentally drawn into a dangerous conspiracy. Next on the hit list, assassins delete her official identity—her
driver's license, credit cards, and bank accounts.
Music: Chopin, Nocturne in B Major op. 32 no. 1. In institutional care, the
mother, an Alzheimer's patient, plays a Chopin piece and cannot remember
how it continues; daughter (Sandra Bullock) helps her, and together they are
able to play it.

*Welcome to the Dollhouse (1995), directed by Todd Solondz*
Story: Life in the seventh-grade-from-hell for eleven-year-old Dawn Weiner
("Wienerdog"), who deals with the brutality of the school bully and her class-
mates, and the awkwardness of growing up.
Music: Chopin, Waltz in A♭ op. 69 no. 1. Performed by Eugeniya Berman. Accompanies a picture of the "family" at the beginning of the film, played on
an out-of-tune piano (returns in flashbacks at the end).

*The Truman Show (1998), directed by Peter Weir*
Story: An insurance salesman/adjuster (Jim Carrey) discovers that his entire life
is actually a TV show.
Music: Chopin, Piano Concerto No. 1 in E Minor op. 11. Second Movement:
"Romance—Larghetto." Performed by Arthur B. Rubinstein; Stanislaw Skro-
waczewski, conductor. Courtesy of BMG Classics/RCA Victor. Accompanies
scene in which "Sylvia" tries to tell him his life is not "real."

---

contingent and meaningful interactions of physical body, emotional
character, and music.

The 1995 film *The Net* features a performance, also interacted
between mother and daughter, of a portion of a Chopin nocturne.[34]
Both characters lead isolated lives: the mother is an institutionalized Alzheimer patient, and the daughter a computer recluse. The
mother plays the Chopin piece, stops and hesitates, not remembering how it continues. The daughter responds: the emotional
contact between them occurs on a nonverbal level as they negotiate
the music as a duet, each playing with one hand—the daughter,
the melody; the mother, the left-hand harmonic setting.

The other films of Figure 7.3 show similar themes at work:
situations of "cognitive dissonance" present Chopin's music at the
extreme end (as aesthetic stance), that is, in contrast to a "contemporary" situation (*Getting it Right*, 1989; *Tombstone*, 1993; *The Truman Show*, 1998); or the film-music combinations express contrasts,
or an alternation of contrasting states (a–b–a, etc.), within the narrative setting (*Picture of Dorian Gray*, 1945; *Scent of Green Papaya*,
1993).

# Tabu: A Story of the South Seas *(1931)*

F. W. Murnau, the famous director of the Weimar Cinema, came to Hollywood in 1925; his final film was *Tabu*, an independent production filmed in the South Seas in 1929 with the documentary filmmaker, Robert Flaherty.[35] The film blended ethnographic documentary and expressionist drama: the setting is an island in Bora Bora lagoon; a young pearl fisherman, Matahi, and the girl, Reri, fall in love. Reri is chosen by the gods to be the holy maid, and, by that act, she becomes "tabu" (taboo) for all men. Reri and Matahi try to run away from the taboo, but in a "civilized" (economic) society they fare no better. The elder haunts Reri's dreams, and she responds. As Matahi tries to follow her, the forces of the taboo prevail and, exhausted from swimming, he drowns in the sea.

In the scene involving Chopin's Nocturne in F Minor op. 55 no. 1, Reri realizes that, to save Matahi, she must leave him and return to the elder.[36] According to Janet Bergstrom, Murnau's films, both in Germany and America, were noted for their pictorial beauty: "Extreme pictorial loveliness of an almost abstract nature is juxtaposed with a lack of virility; their proximity is enough to inspire fear."[37] Bergstrom links this juxtaposition with "Weimar cinema's tendency to abstraction [that] allowed for modes of viewing more commonly associated with the fine arts" thereby casting "a kind of aesthetic veil over images of feminized male figures as well as one-dimensional female characters."[38] Murnau's choice of Chopin's Nocturne in F Minor op. 55 no. 1 for the final scenes as offscreen and "orchestral" music links an "orientalized," "exotic" ethnographic context with cultural perceptions of feminine values of the nocturne.[39] Isolated, static shots create a perceptual and temporal context that emphasizes an aesthetic mode of viewing that is more associated with painting. This mode of apprehension links the distanced and detached stance of the viewer as spectator and consumer with an aesthetic and abject loveliness of the music and visual images.

# Ashes and Diamonds *(1958)*

The powerful 1958 film *Ashes and Diamonds* [*Popiół i diament*], directed by Andrzej Wajda, is the last film of his trilogy depicting the experiences of Poles during World War II and the turmoil, tensions, and hopes of a new Poland in the aftermath of the German occupation.[40] Maciek, the protagonist, is a young Polish

Example 7.3. Chopin, Polonaise in A Major op. 40 no. 1 ("Military"), mm. 1–8.

resistance fighter. For the "right cause" he assassinates another Pole on the last day of the war and begins to question his life and purpose—a conflict of idealism and instinct. Although not seen directly, the presence of the Soviet Red Army is felt as an underlying force: the senselessness of Poles fighting Poles ushers in a Poland subjected to Communist domination.

The end of the film interweaves scenes of the shooting and meaningless death of the young Maciek with scenes of a group of people (the characters of the film) at the end of a party. The guests march aimlessly to an out-of-tune performance of Chopin's Polonaise in A Major op. 40 no. 1 "Military" (Example 7.3), performed by an exhausted wind band and its conductor. In Wajda's cinematic treatment, the scene of the party with its Chopin polonaise both precedes the death scene and alternates with it. Chopin's polonaise,

Example 7.4. Michał Kleofas Ogiński, Polonaise in A Minor, 1794
"Pożegnanie ojczyzny" ["Farewell to the Fatherland"], mm. 1–8.

out-of-tune, with its weary band of performers and the dispirited marching of the guests, conveys the psychic dissonance of displaced peoples and its own temporal displacement in a directionless and confused postwar society. Notably the dissonance of the heroic character of the A Major Polonaise in this context is made more poignant by the juxtaposition of an offscreen, but in-tune, performance by a string orchestra of the Polonaise in A Minor of Michał Kleofas Ogiński, a Polish composer who lived a generation before Chopin, 1765–1833. Ogiński's polonaise is titled "Pożegnanie ojczyzny" ["Farewell to the Fatherland"] (Example 7.4).[41] This polonaise is part of the collective memory of the Polish nation and thus impacts this setting of Chopin's polonaise, conveying a sense of promise unrealized. The musical, visual, and historical juxtapositions express the sense of loss in a context in which death is both awkward and meaningless.

The out-of-tune performance of the Chopin polonaise by the wind band is a material manifestation of the social-psychic "tuning" of that piece in that context. Its actually being out-of-tune is a material aspect of and emblem for the different ways that music "tunes" and is "tuned" to the contexts of its production and reception. Like performances, such "tunings" convey the contingencies of specific music-structural orientations and material contexts.

## Face/Off *(1997)*

Chopin's D♭ Prelude op. 28 no. 15 registers unspoken premonitions when heard as offscreen music in the 1997 movie *Face/Off*, a movie about reversal and alternate identities.[42] Pursuing FBI agent (Sean Archer played by John Travolta) and terrorist (Castor Troy played by Nicolas Cage) have switched physical bodies. The terrorist (Castor Troy now played by Travolta) impersonates the FBI agent (Sean Archer now played by Cage) in a dinner scene with Archer's wife. The scene is rendered by offscreen music, the D♭ major-mode music of the nocturne-like initial section of the Prelude no. 15. This candlelight dinner leads to the (offscreen) seduction of the wife, portended by the (offscreen) D♭ minor-mode music of the Prelude's funeral-like middle section, and thus to the further entanglement of the evil Castor Troy in Sean Archer's life. The terrorist has dinner at home with "his" wife (D♭ major section) and her unseen subsequent seduction (D♭/C♯ minor section) is emblematic of the further entanglement of the fateful force of Castor Troy in Sean Archer's life. We see Archer behind bars—a supposed criminal—at the end of the scene.

How it is that, in this context, the Prelude's major and minor mode musics offer the seeds that portend or foreshadow the subsequent turn of fate, in this case the terrorist's subsequent seduction of the wife?

Chopin's D♭ Major Prelude (Example 7.5) is a musical study in tensions between the tonal-harmonic forces of prolongation and the transformations of melodic repetition. The Prelude creates the effects of a temporal oscillation of musical spans by the alternation of repeated I–V–(I) patterns, such that their grouping or the "return" of tonic is held in abeyance. The outcome is the alternate groupings of the harmonically distinct functions of tonic and dominant.[43]

In explanation of this idea, consider the analogy to two different groupings found in an oscillating, alternating series

abababababababababababab

such that both "ab" and "ba" orientations are possible and operating at "different musical times" (Figure 7.4). The music analogue is the temporal ambiguity of prolongationally distinct (con-

Example 7.5. Chopin, Prelude in D♭ Major op. 28 no. 15, mm. 1–57.

tradictory) functions and spans of tonic or dominant influence. We are aware of these conflicting orientations in an "alternating," non-simultaneous fashion (related to the visual problems of the alternate orientations of the woman faces: see Figure 7.2). The alternate groupings of tonic and dominant pairs infuse the Prelude, especially upon hearing repetitions of the same music. In classical practice the tonic (as the deeper, or initial, prolongational function) usually governs and groups the succession of harmonies (Figure 7.4 and Example 7.6a). The sketch of example 7.6b suggests the implications of hearing the second harmonic function (V) as conditioning and/or nuancing the first (I) (Figure 7.4 and Example 7.6b). In other words, the harmonic function of the dominant conditions, nuances, and even reconstitutes the tonic notes (in $^6_4$ configurations) in different temporal frames.

Figure 7.4. Alternating series and alternate combinations

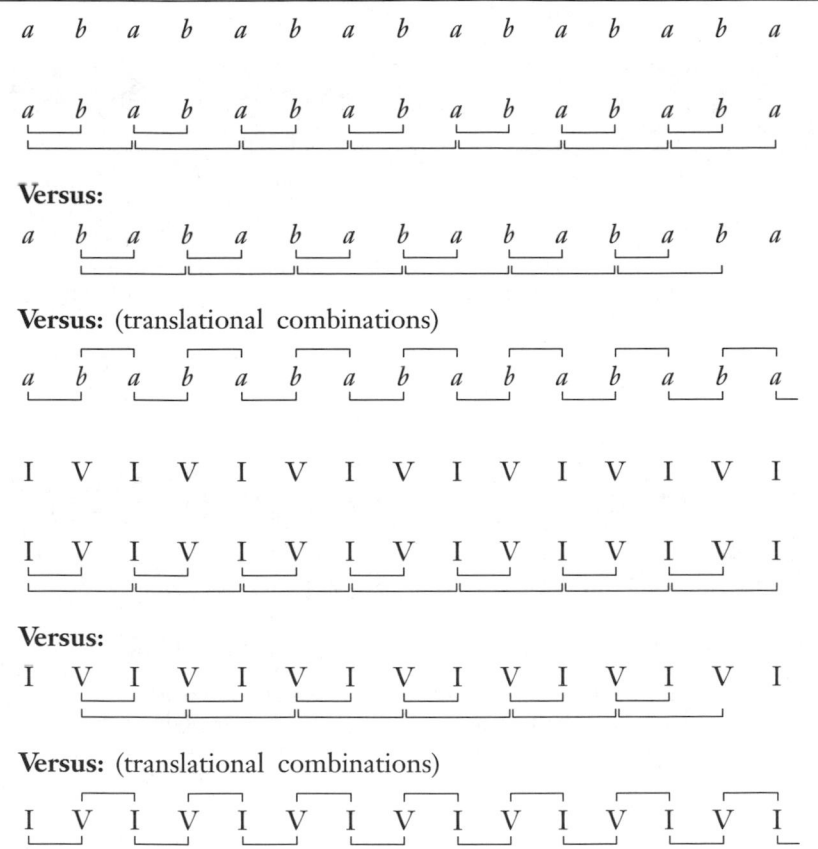

For example, the readings (see Examples 7.6a and 7.6b) show, respectively, the tonic or dominant implications—the six-four sonority implying either a dominant six-four or a tonic function over the course of the opening phrase. In Example 7.6a, tonic orientations implicate a hearing of the melodic g♭² as a neighbor to an extended f²; in Example 7.6b, dominant orientations suggest hearing g♭² as initiating a third span to e♭² at the end of the melody within which the f² works as a consonant passing tone in an extension of dominant harmony. These orientations project the double neighbor figure F–E♭–G♭–F in distinct temporal distributions and, significantly, each figure applies to harmonically conflicting (nonsimultaneous) temporal groupings of the music. This temporal overlapping or redistribution of distinct I or V harmonies continues throughout the Prelude.

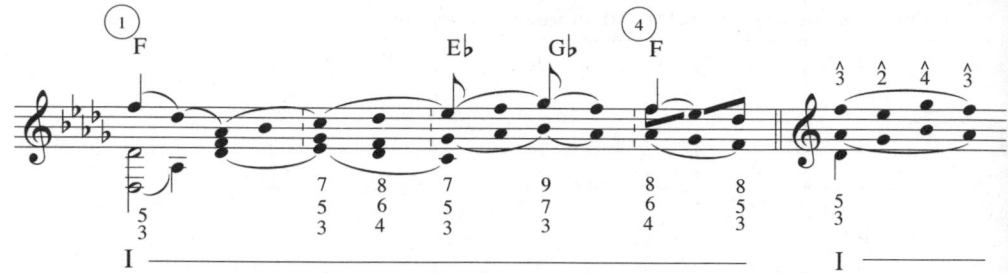

Example 7.6a. Chopin, Prelude in D♭ Major op. 28 no. 15, "Tonic" implications of the phrase, mm. 1–4; melody g♭² as neighbor to an extended f². [F–E♭–G♭–F]

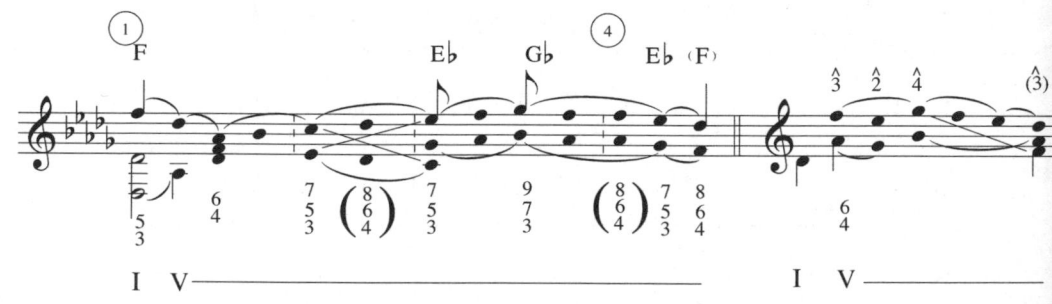

Example 7.6b. Chopin, Prelude in D♭ Major op. 28 no. 15, "Dominant" implications of the phrase, mm. 1–4; melody g♭² as initiating a third span to e♭². [F–E♭–G♭–E♭–(F)](n.b. the repeated a♭³ calls the functional status of tonic into question on beat 3, and specifically in m.2.)

A similar mix of tonal scale-degree orientations is played out over the entire expanse of the texturally contrasting minor-mode and funeral-like B section (Examples 7.7a, 7.7b, and 7.7c). The groupings present the C♯-minor harmony alternately, as a ⁵₃ extension of tonic function (C♯/D♭ minor) (Example 7.7b) or as a ⁶₄ extension of dominant function (G♯ minor) (Example 7.7c). Similarly, the scale-degree orientations and priority surrounding C♯/D♭ (as tonic) and G♯/A♭ (as dominant) are reversed from the temporal and scale-degree orientations that were projected in the first section. Although the identity of tonic and dominant is not in question, their accompanying functions are in temporal flux or oscillation throughout the *entirety* of the B section, continuing, relating, and transforming the temporal processes of the nocturne-like A section within the funeral-march B section, interrelating nocturne and funeral march. These occur in relation to the alternate groupings of double neighbor figures, C♯–B♯–D♯–C♯—implying tonic function,

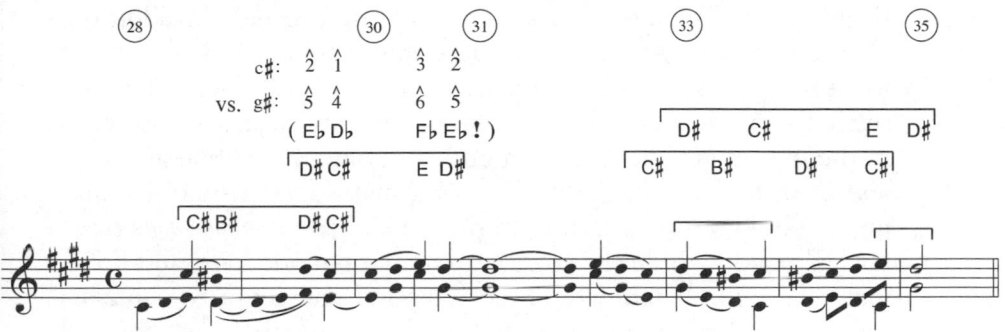

Example 7.7a. Chopin, Prelude in D♭ Major op. 28 no. 15, double-neighbor pattern, mm. 28–35: C♯–B♯–D♯–C♯ (C♯ as "tonic" function) and D♯–C♯–E–D♯ (C♯ as "six-four" articulation of "dominant" function).

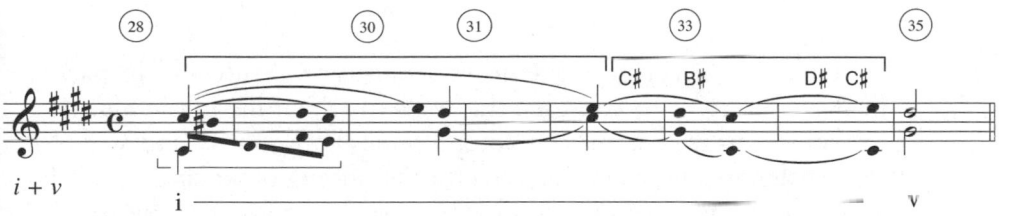

Example 7.7b. Chopin, Prelude in D♭ Major op. 28 no. 15, double-neighbor mm. 28–35. C♯ as articulation of "tonic" function.

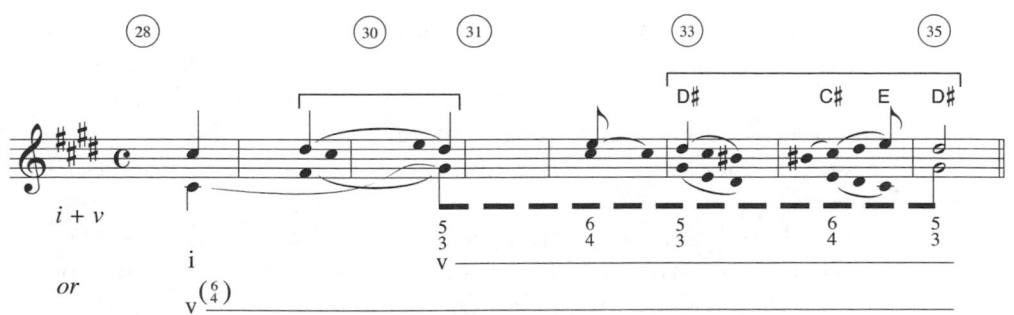

Example 7.7c. Chopin, Prelude in D♭ Major op. 28 no. 15, double-neighbor pattern mm. 28–44. C♯ as "six-four" articulation of "dominant" function.

and D♯–C♯–E–D♯—implying dominant function (see Example 7.7a and Examples 7.7b and 7.7c, respectively).

The temporal oscillation of functional orientations makes possible the continuation of aspects of the nocturne-like A section of the Prelude in its funeral-like B section—a reading that also resonates with the plot and characters of the movie.[44] In addition, alternate embeddings of major versus minor tonal areas offer a way to hear the B section as a musical "turning inside out" of the A section—that is, in B, an exchange of sonority relationships heard in the A section. The A section embeds *minor-mode* tonal areas (A♭ and B♭ minor) within the context of a major-mode tonic (D♭ major).[45] The B section (starting in m. 28) embeds a *major-mode* tonal area (E major) within the context of a minor-mode tonic and dominant (C♯ and G♯ minor). These temporal and sonority contrasts help to transform and interrelate aspects of the initial nocturne and subsequent funeral march. Though the analysis resonates in this particular cinematic context, these interpretations of Chopin's "temporal" strategies also inform a particular understanding of his harmonic-tonal innovations.

\* \* \*

One way of construing Chopin's musical individuality in particular contexts is to consider the ways in which his music allows or requires us to redefine the "dichotomies" of sonority and structure or design and structure. This means, among other things, calling attention to the intimate link between structure and the temporal process and character of music—its materiality and experiential contexts—and to Chopin's particular "temporalization" of a depth of harmonic-tonal relationships. In this "temporalization" the character of temporal-musical engagement of and in Chopin's music is such that opposites are allowed to alternate, to oscillate, to resonate, and thus to come into contact.[46] The aspect of reconciliation is never quite achieved, thus rendering a sense of nostalgia, morbidity of obsession, or promise of visionary reconciliation.

As Leo Treitler has noted, however, evidence for the "cultural currency" of particular themes or interpretations should not be mistaken as evidence of a belief (historical or otherwise) that those themes reside in or constitute the music.[47] Programmatic interpretations in the nineteenth-century, as Eigeldinger, Kallberg, Samson, and others have argued, were often more indicative of a way of guiding listeners to the ineffable temporal experience of music through a kind of metaphorical transfer than of an intention to locate or fix the "truth" or meaning of the subject matter. Thus, although Chopin himself used "images . . . when teaching to make his intentions understood," he himself eschewed the use of programmatic titles.[48]

---

*"Oliver Cromwell"* [Chopin, Polonaise no.6 op. 53 in A♭, mm. 1–80]

[*Spoken*]
And Cromwell sent Colonel Pride
to purge the House of Commons of
the Presbyterian Royalists, leaving
behind only the rump Parliament . . .

Which appointed a High Court at
Westminster Hall to indict Charles I for . . . tyranny
OOOHHH!
Charles was sentenced to Death
Even though he refused to accept
That the court had . . . jurisdiction
SAY GOOD-BYE TO HIS HEAD.

Poor King Charles laid his head on the block
JANUARY 1649
Down came the axe, and . . .

In the Silence that followed, the
only sound that could be heard was
a solitary giggle, from . . .
[*Spoken*]
Oliver Cromwell, Lord Protector of England
*OLE*
Born in 1599 and died in 1658
SEPTEMBER
Then he smashed
IRELAND
Set up the Commonwealth
AND MORE
He crushed the Scots at Worcester
And beat the Dutch at sea
In 1653 and then
He dissolved the rump Parliament
And with Lambert's consent
Wrote the instrument of Government
Under which Oliver was Protector at last
The end.

---

Perhaps a better or different way to frame the relationships of material context and musical structure might be to ask: in what ways might different material contexts suggest the *kinds* of musical structures and the *kinds* of temporal qualities *to begin to account for or characterize* in experiencing Chopin's music (recognizing the dialectical relationship between musical organization and the contexts of reception)? The terms of musical structure (or the temporal orientations of music) are not fixed or unchanged despite their position in, or encounter with, different social-cultural landscapes, yet they are not completely determined by those contexts either. Neither are they exempt from their own set of receptions. They in turn can shed light on a range of cultural landscapes, as shown by the final two examples.

Monty Python "sings" Chopin's Polonaise in A♭ Major op. 53 in their narration of "Oliver Cromwell" (see the textual excerpt in Figure 7.5).[49] They perform this text to the rhythms and contours of Chopin's "refrain" (Example 7.8). The combination of text and musical profile is not simply a parody (debasement, misappropriation) of Chopin's Polonaise but a carnivalesque, "in-your-face" vocal lampoon that offers a *musical* perspective on the fragility and impermanence of predications and expressions of power. As alluded to in the epigraphs of this essay, the terms of culture infuse the structural and material dimensions of a piece and its performance.

The various interconnections between music and particular material-social settings may have an *analogue* in the ways that music can internalize and reference other musics. Compositions can include other music in direct quotation, stylistic evocation or assimilation, thematic and intertextual reference, and juxtaposition. These kinds of inclusions also vary in the degree or the relationship of their "reception" ("appropriation") and integration in the broader compositional context.

## George Crumb, "Dream Images (Love–Death Music)"

George Crumb's "Dream Images (Love–Death Music)" no. 11 of his *Makrokosmos*, vol. 1 (Example 7.9), features a passage, which Crumb has quoted and identified on the score, from Chopin's *Fantaisie-Impromptu* in C♯ Minor op. 66, namely, the opening of its contrasting D♭-major "B" section. "Dream Images" is fashioned in the manner of a musical mosaic that unfolds in a gesture-pause pattern. Cut-in, like film montage technique, the references to

Example 7.8. Chopin, Polonaise in A♭ Major op. 53, "refrain," mm. 65–73.

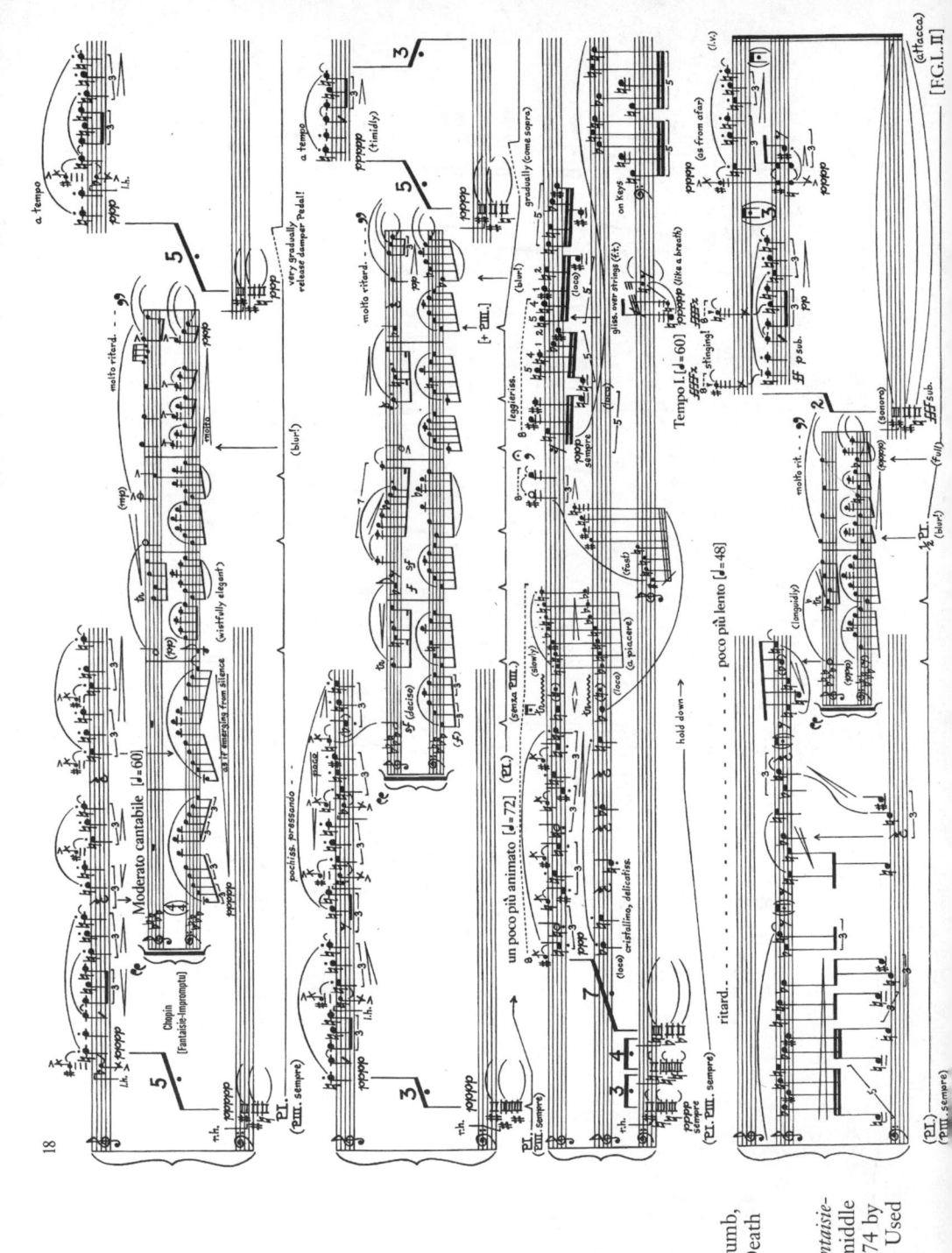

18

Example 7.9. George Crumb, "Dream Images (Love-Death Music)," no. 11 of *Makrokosmos*, vol. 1—quotation of Chopin's *Fantaisie-Impromptu in C# minor* (middle section: Db major). © 1974 by C.F. Peters Corporation. Used by permission. All rights reserved.

Chopin's *Fantaisie-Impromptu* are intertextual and symbolic, drawing Chopin's music from an outside context. Yet these references also engage in a kind of musical commentary that the composer intends to be integrated into and part of the work, not functioning in isolation as a "special effect."[50] This integration is particularly evident in the subtle ways that Crumb offsets and relates his own musical language to that of Chopin's. In related fashion, music finds its way into social-cultural contexts that range from the familiar and predictable to the alien and indifferent.

The terms and relations of music-structural analysis do not function in isolation. Sensitivity to the materialities of music—its sound and music-structural temporalities—has significant potential to impact and be impacted by stories and, by extension, contexts of many sorts, not simply those of music-structural narratives. Performing music on historical instruments, performing transcriptions of music with alternate instrumental forces, or vocalizing or moving to an instrumental part are just a few of many ways to engage with music in different mediums. Similarly, music "materializes" as it is embodied in particular historical, social-cultural, performative, and sonic-structural material/media.

Particular contexts shape our music perceptions and descriptions by drawing out different values of that music. Observations may be persuasive or have validity from particular perspectives; alternately, music may present *many* values, and particular contexts or interpretations may respond to *some* of those values and not to others.[51] Thus it is helpful to examine which values play a role in our perceptions.

Music's meaning and significance arise from the materiality of lived experience in connection and interaction with things in past experience. Processes of apprehending the new or re-experiencing the old are intimately connected. Music receptions do not simply embody an unbroken continuum or accumulation of previous receptions; they are not undifferentiated possibilities, equally suitable for any situation. Rather, receptions present points of pressure or contextual allusions that define, stand apart from, and link contemporary and historical contexts and meanings. In Chopin's case these "Chopiniana" bring his legacy into our time, and, in turn, they are a part of a multitude of ways that we engage and create that legacy. Separately, in combination, and in interaction, "Chopiniana" speak of the ways that we engage sounds and materialize music.

NOTES

1. Janet Wolff, "The Ideology of Autonomous Art," in *Music and Society: The Politics of Composition, Performance, and Reception,* ed. Richard Leppert and Susan McClary (New York: Cambridge University Press, 1987), 11.

2. Ann Cooper Albright, *Choreographing Difference: The Body and Identity in Contemporary Dance* (Hanover, N.H.: Wesleyan University Press, 1997), 12.

3. Rose R. Subotnik, *Developing Variations: Style and Ideology in Western Music* (Minneapolis: University of Minnesota Press, 1991), 148–55.

4. Ibid., 151.

5. Ibid.

6. Ibid., 152.

7. James Huneker, *Chopin: The Man and His Music,* with a new introduction, footnotes, and index by Herbert Weinstock (New York: Dover, 1966 [1900]), 55–56.

8. James Buhler, "Informal Music Analysis: A Critique of Formalism, Semiology, and Narratology as Discourses on Music" (Ph.D. diss., University of Pennsylvania, 1996); Lawrence Kramer, *Music as Cultural Practice, 1800–1900* (Berkeley: University of California Press, 1900); Susan McClary, *Feminine Endings and Conventional Wisdom: The Content of Musical Form* (Berkeley: University of California Press, 2000); Rose Subotnik, *Developing Variations;* also *Deconstructive Variations: Music and Reason in Western Society* (Minneapolis: University of Minnesota Press, 1996); and Alastair Williams, "Torn Halves: Structure and Subjectivity in Analysis," *Music Analysis* 17, no. 3 (1998): 281–293.

9. Cyril W. Beaumont, *Michel Fokine and His Ballets* (New York: Dance Horizons, 1981), 102.

10. Michel Fokine, *Memoirs of a Ballet Master* (Boston: Little, Brown, 1961), 103.

11. Fokine wrote that *Les Sylphides* "contains no plot whatsoever. It was the first abstract ballet" (ibid., 131). Today the ballet is danced in white and staged without plot; it has aspects of both mood and abstract ballet.

12. See *Chopiniana* (1907) / *Les Sylphides* (1909), music by Fryderyk Chopin; choreography by Michel Fokine; orchestrated by A. Glazunov (and Maurice Keller). American Ballet Theatre at the Met [videorecording]. National Video Corporation, directed for television by Brian Large (New York: Thorn EMI/HBO Video, 1984). In Fokine's first series of dances of 1907, each dance had a programmatic theme. The first set included orchestrations of Chopin's Polonaise op. 40 no. 1; Nocturne op. 15 no. 1; Mazurka op. 50 no. 5; Waltz op. 64 no. 2 (added by Fokine and Glazunov); and Tarantella op. 43. Pavlova, in the long white tutu of *La Sylphide,* and Oboukhoff danced the Waltz. The second orchestrated version of 1908 consisted of Chopin's Nocturne op. 32 no. 2; Valse op. 70 no. 1; Mazurka op. 67 no. 3; another Mazurka op. 33 no. 2; the A Major Prelude op. 28 no. 7; the Waltz from the first version op. 64 no. 2; and a final Valse op. 18 no. 1, presented by the entire company. Pavlova, Karsavina, Baldina, and Nijinsky were the soloists of the 1909 performance. See Fokine, *Memoirs;* and Beaumont, *Michel Fokine,* 39–40.

13. Beaumont, *Michel Fokine,* 40.

14. Fokine, *Memoirs,* 101.

15. Ibid.

16. Beaumont, *Michel Fokine,* 50–51. A critic from *Le Journal* (2 June 1909) wrote: "You cannot conceive anything more ethereal, more seraphic, and more voluptuous than the evolution of all those fragile forms of those 'happy shades' in the emerald-green reflections of the moonlight. . . . It is difficult to think of

Chopin's music in connection with a ballet, but in this particular case, which suggests a dream, a hallucination, the choice is defensible and almost legitimate" (cited in Beaumont, *Michel Fokine*, 51).

17. Lynn Garafola, "Reconfiguring the Sexes," in *The Ballets Russes and Its World*, ed. Lynn Garafola and Nancy Van Norman Baer (New Haven, Conn.: Yale University Press, 1999), 247.

18. See Garafola, "Reconfiguring the Sexes." Jeffrey Kallberg has attributed the contrasting social functions of Chopin's nocturne in his day and ours to complex interconnections of issues of gender, musical genre, and reception. See his *Chopin at the Boundaries: Sex, History, and Musical Genre* (Cambridge, Mass.: Harvard University Press, 1996). Also see Parakilas's essay in this volume.

19. Jean-Jacques Eigeldinger, "Twenty-four Preludes, Op. 28: Genre, Structure, Significance," in *Chopin Studies*, ed. Jim Samson and John Rink (Cambridge: Cambridge University Press, 1988), 180.

20. The ears and neck of the young woman in one view are alternately the eyes and mouth of the old woman in the other view (other aspects remain the same for both figures, e.g., the coat and scarf). See Henry Gleitman, *Psychology* (New York: Norton, 1981), 252.

21. Rudolf Arnheim, *Art and Visual Perception: A Psychology of the Creative Eye*, rev. ed. (Berkeley: University of California Press, 1974 [1954]), 226–27. Image (Figure 7.2a) is on page 226, Figure 159.

22. Lawrence Kramer, *Music as Cultural Practice, 1800–1900* (Berkeley: University of California Press, 1990), 73.

23. *The United States of Poetry* (videorecording). Washington Square Films; Independent Television Service; producer/creators, Joshua Blumand, Bob Holman; director, Mark Pellington; director of photography, Thomas Krueger San Francisco?: KQED Video, c. 1996. Fryderyk Chopin, Preludes op. 28 no. 7, and Elizabeth Barrett Browning, "How Do I Love Thee," Sonnet XLIII from *Sonnets from the Portuguese*. Lypsinka (John Epperson, performance artist) mouths the lines of Elizabeth Barrett Browning as voiced by actress Jayne Mansfield (1964). Also see the book based on the ITV production: *The United States of Poetry*, compiled by Joshua Blum, Bob Holman, and Mark Pellington (1996). Notably both poem and prelude are recorded rather than directly performed.

24. According to Chopin scholar Jean-Jacques Eigeldinger, though Chopin took a conservative position on metaphorical images suggested by his music, there were a number of occasions—some that he likely participated in—where his peers performed certain of his preludes with poetry or provided programmatic descriptions (see Eigeldinger, "Twenty-four Preludes," esp. 179).

Goldberg's essay in this collection presents some possible instances of such performances involving Chopin himself. The most specific is Januszkiewicz's report that Chopin improvised as Niemcewicz narrated historical scenes to children. Fontana's account of Chopin's improvisation "from open book" to Wincenty Pol's new poems does not make it clear whether Chopin's improvisation was purely instrumental or if the poems were sung or recited. Shortly after Chopin's death, settings of his works to what was known as melodeclamation became very fashionable (the larger tradition for works with descriptive text was already established, going back as far as Marin Marais's *Tableau de l'opération de la taille*, though it is not always clear in which instances actual declamation was intended). The earliest such publications of Chopin's works were to poems by Kornel Ujejski. They first appeared in 1858 and were so popular that Ujejski went on to provide numerous other poems for Chopin's (and Beethoven's) works. Their popularity is attested to by subsequent re-editions of Chopin's pieces with Ujejski's poems to be recited in Polish, German, French, and English well into the twentieth century. Ujejski's poetic setting of the A Major Prelude, entitled "Wniebowzięcie (Ascension-Dream—Himmelfahrtstraum)," was particularly popular. This fashionable trend attracted numerous imitators: some of them set already existing poetry (the works of Włodzimierz Wolski received many such settings, especially his "Fryderyk Szopen. Fantazja" of 1850); others, like Bolesław Szczęsny Herbaczewski, created new texts. A bibliography compiled for the anthology of poems about Chopin provides the most complete source for these works. See Edmund Suszkiewicz, *Wiersze o Chopinie* (Kraków: Polskie Wydawnictwo Muzyczne, 1968). Thanks to Halina Goldberg for this information.

25. Elizabeth Barrett Browning, *The Complete Works of Elizabeth Barrett Browning*, ed. Charlotte Porter and Helen A. Clarke, vol. 3 (New York: Thomas Y. Crowell, 1900; reprint, AMS Press, 1973), 248.

26. Subotnik, *Deconstructive Variations*, 144. Eigeldinger argues against this position ("Twenty-four Preludes," 178–79): "The Preludes do not in any sense belong to the esthetic of the fragment" (178).

27. Against the backdrop of a static tableau, the music of this prelude in *Les Sylphides* occurs three times: the first is "introductory"; the second focuses on the solo ballerina; and for the third, the ballerina positions her movements in relation to each of the different groups of the cours de ballet.

28. Grouping of lines of the poem: 4 (1 + 3), 4 (2 + 2), 6 (2 + 3 + 1). The music of the Prelude concludes before the performance of the poem is finished.

29. These are ordered by date. See Internet Movie Database, (IMDb), http://us.imdb.com/Name?Chopin,+Fr%E9d%E9ric, accessed 16 May 2003. As of this writing, the database lists 135 instances of Chopin's music in cinema from 1931 to 2002, ranging from F. W. Murnau's 1931 film *Tabu: A Story of the South Seas* to Peter Weir's 1998 film *The Truman Show* and Roman Polanski's *The Pianist* (2002). Compare to 254 entries for Beethoven, 340 for Mozart, 67 for Schumann, and 154 for Schubert.

30. Chopin's Prelude in E Minor is a prominent example in Carl Schachter's essay "The Triad as Place and Action," *Music Theory Spectrum* 17, no. 2 (fall 1995): 149–69, in which he applies ideas of "place" and "action" to tonal processes of presentation and elaboration. In the Chopin example, functions of place and action interact with aspects of music design (genre, lament, two-part continuous binary design) and motive.

31. *Welcome to the Dollhouse* (videorecording). A Suburban Pictures production. Culver City, Calif.: Columbia TriStar Home Video, 1996 (film released in 1995). Producer/writer/director, Todd Solondz.

32. *Five Easy Pieces* (videorecording). Five Easy Pieces Productions, directed by Bob Rafelson; produced by Bob Rafelson and Richard Wechsler; screenplay by Adrien Joyce. Burbank, Calif.: RCA/Columbia Pictures, 1988 (film released in 1970).

33. *Autumn Sonata* (*Höstsonaten*) (videorecording). Produced by Persona Film. Chicago, Ill.: Home Vision, 199–? Ingmar Bergman, director and writer. In Swedish with English subtitles. Originally released in 1978 as a motion picture, Janus Films presentation.

34. *The Net* (videorecording). Culver City, Calif.: Columbia Tristar Home Video, 1995. Directed by Irwin Winkler; written by John Brancato and Michael Ferris.

35. *Tabu: A Story of the South Seas* (videorecording). Told by F. W. Murnau and R. J. Flaherty; directed by F. W. Murnau; a Paramount release. New York: Milestone Film and Video, 198–? Silent film with music and English captions (originally released as a motion picture in 1931).

36. Subsequent pieces featured in the scene are Chopin's Prelude op. 28 no. 2 in A Minor, and Robert Schumann's "Chopin" from *Carnaval* op. 9; all three orchestral settings are in the tradition of classic Hollywood cinema.

37. Janet Bergstrom, "Sexuality at a Loss: The Films of F. W. Murnau," in *The Female Body in Western Culture: Contemporary Perspectives,* ed. Susan R. Suleiman (Cambridge, Mass.: Harvard University Press, 1986), 246.

38. Ibid.

39. See also Jeffrey Kallberg's study of the nocturne in his *Chopin at the Boundaries.*

40. *Popiół i diament* [*Ashes and Diamonds*] (videorecording), produced by Film Polski; directed by Andrzej Wajda. Los Angeles, Calif.: Embassy Home Entertainment, 1986. Screenplay, Andrzej Wajda and Jerzy Andrzejewski (from the novel of the same name by Jerzy Andrzejewski). The films of the trilogy are *A Generation* (1954), *Kanał* (1957), and *Ashes and Diamonds* (1958).

41. My thanks to Halina Goldberg for identifying this excerpt. The Ogiński polonaise, unlike that of Chopin, would likely not be known to American audiences. Ogiński participated in the Kościuszko Uprising of 1794, an event of profound significance for the Polish people. His "Pożegnanie ojczyzny" ["Farewell to the Fatherland"] became one of the most widely known polonaises of the day. According to Stephen Downes, "it was pieces such as this that the poet Adam Mickiewicz must have been remembering when he wrote an impassioned description of a polonaise at the end of his epic poem 'Pan Tadeusz' (1834)." See *New Groves II* http://www.grovemusic.com, accessed 10 March 2003, s.v. "Polonaise" (Stephen Downes). Ogiński's piece shown in Example 4 is the original keyboard version—the setting in the film is for a string orchestra.

42. *Face/Off* (videorecording). Produced by David Permut, Barry Osborne, Terence Chang, and Christopher Godsick; written by Mike Webb and Michael Colleary; directed by John Woo. Hollywood, Calif.: Paramount Pictures, 1997. Story: "In order to catch him, he must become him." Music: Chopin, Prelude in D♭ op. 28 no. 15. Performed by Irina Zaritzkaya. Courtesy of Naxos of America by arrangement with Source/Q.

43. For a detailed discussion of the theoretical orientations underlying these observations, see my article, "Interpreting Schenkerian Prolongation: Harmonic Oscillation and Prolongational and Translational Parallelism," *Music Analysis,* vol. 22 (2003).

44. For Frederick Niecks, the B section evoked "the image of a monastery with monks processing in a funeral march." See Jim Samson, *The Music of Chopin* (Oxford: Clarendon, 1994 [1985]), 143. Niecks's book is *Chopin as a Man and a Musician,* 2 vols. (London, 1988 [1973]).

45. Jim Samson characterizes this contrasting "b" section within the opening A section as typically more periodic, sequentially structured, and deriving generally from a stanzaic type, rather than an aria type of melodic writing (as found in the opening "a" of the three-part A section). See Jim Samson, *Chopin* (New York: Oxford University Press, 1996), 169–172.

46. In Chopin's *Fantaisie-Impromptu* (op. posth. 66, c. 1834), the outer sections articulate fiery and circular C♯-minor figurations in contrast to the inner sections that present a "transcendental" D♭-major melodic line that articulates harmonic and melodic oscillations of A♭ and B♭. In the coda the D♭-major melody returns in rhythmic augmentation, now in the bass as a left-hand melody. The orientation of the melody as a "harmonic" bass now underpins the figurative right hand, and both suggests and suspends the sense of reconciliation between their previous respective identities as figuration and melodic line. Also see note 50, below.

47. Leo Treitler, "History and Archetypes," *Perspectives of New Music* 35, no. 2 (1997): 9.

48. Eigeldinger, "Twenty-four Preludes," 179.

49. "Monty Python . . . Sings." Virgin Records [Capitol Records] V2–86253, 1989. [Kay-Gee-Bee Music Ltd., 1989: 0777 7 8625322.]. The text is set against measures 1–80 of the Polonaise; this excerpt begins at measure 47, @2'18"; the text accompanying the refrain (m. 65ff.) begins with line 4, "Oliver Cromwell, Lord Protector . . . ," of the second part of the text shown in Figure 7.5.

50. Originally Crumb had intended to work with a composition by Sergei Rachmaninoff—the eighteenth variation of the *Rhapsody on a Theme of Paganini* for piano and orchestra—in the same key of Db, but the copyright permission proved to be complicated, so he turned to the Chopin work. See Peter Henderson, "Musical Quotation in George Crumb's Oeuvre" (DMA Document, piano performance, Indiana University, 1999), 37. Also see note 46, above.

51. Also see my "On Rebecca Clarke's Sonata for Viola and Piano: Feminine Spaces and Metaphors of Reading," in *Audible Traces: Gender, Identity, and Music,* ed. Elaine Barkin and Lydia Hamessley (Zurich: Carciofoli, 1999), 71–114.

# Part III

Gender, Genre, Genius

# 8

## "Nuit plus belle qu'un beau jour": Poetry, Song, and the Voice in the Piano Nocturne

### JAMES PARAKILAS

Chopin's conception of musical genres attracts attention not only because he favored generic titles for his compositions but also because, in many cases, he wrote what have become the defining examples of the genre. Of course, to say that he wrote the defining examples of the ballade or the mazurka or the nocturne is to beg the question of what they define. The nocturne has proven a particularly difficult case—and therefore a rich subject for consideration—because it is not easily defined either through internal investigation (looking for common qualities in all the Chopin nocturnes) or through external investigation (holding those works up against whatever can be considered to have been Chopin's models).

From internal investigation, all that has emerged as definitive is that the Chopin nocturnes are generally lyrical in style—often elaborately lyrical but sometimes very plainly so. Otherwise there does not seem to be a defining nocturne form or nocturne character or nocturne texture, and, above all, there is no defining nocturne rhythm. A defining rhythm might be expected in particular because Chopin generally seems to have associated each genre he employed with a particular rhythmic nature, not only when working in dance genres where a defining rhythm was a given but even when it was not, as in the ballade or the impromptu. In the case of his nocturnes, however, the opposite seems to be true. In their rhythmic nature they are distinguished more by overlap with other genres than by distinctiveness from them: we often hear the rhythm of a barcarole or lullaby, sometimes of a march, occasionally of a hymn, at least once of a mazurka,[1] and so on. And—to reach now from the internal realm to the external—the same can be said of Chopin's great predecessors in the genre, the nocturnes of John Field.

In this dilemma we can be grateful for the wisdom of Jeffrey Kallberg, whose reflections on the question of genre in a Chopin nocturne led him to suggest that we think of genre less as "classification" than as "communication" between composer and audience.[2] What, then, might the title *Nocturne* have communicated to Chopin's potential customers? Would it inspire poetic or dramatic associations of the word *nocturnal* or musical associations with earlier piano pieces of the same title (like Field's) or thoughts of vocal music that bore the same generic designation? It is hard to know, and if we want to follow up the associations with vocal music, there is a further difficulty. When critics have sought the stylistic roots of the piano nocturne in vocal music, they have turned almost invariably to the richly embellished vocal lines of early-nineteenth-century Italian opera (in the case of Chopin, the example of Bellini is most frequently cited).[3] But Field and Chopin are unlikely to have chosen the title *Nocturne* to draw their public's thoughts toward operatic models since that designation was seldom given to operatic numbers in their day, whereas it was used endlessly in a homelier species of vocal music.[4]

Today it takes some sorting to discover just which homely vocal species Chopin's customers would have thought of when they saw the name *Nocturne*. In the German-speaking lands the term *nocturne* or *notturno* had long been used as an alternative to *serenade*, referring to songs imagined as being sung by a man at night under the window of the woman he was courting, though often in practice they were part-songs for male voices.[5] When piano nocturnes came along, German musicians pronounced them to be derived from that vocal genre. Carl Czerny, for instance, wrote in 1839:

The *Notturno* for the Pianoforte is really an imitation of those vocal pieces which are termed *Serenades*, and the peculiar object of such works—that of being performed by night, before the dwelling of an esteemed individual—must always exercise an influence upon its character.[6]

Ever since Czerny's day, this linkage to the male vocal genre of the serenade has been central to definitions of the piano nocturne in German-language studies and music dictionaries, and it recently provided Kallberg with evidence for his case that the piano nocturne as a genre should be understood as a male construction of the sensibility of a woman being serenaded by a male suitor.[7]

Meanwhile, however, there was another, fairly distinct species of vocal nocturne, established by the very beginning of the nineteenth century and flourishing throughout Chopin's life. The creation of Italian composers, the most important being Felice Blangini (1781–1841), who spent his entire career in Paris, it was taken up by French composers such as Auguste Panséron (1796–1859) and Antoine Romagnesi (1781–1850). These composers were extremely popular in their day as singers, teachers of singing, and composers of vocal music—comic operas as well as salon vocal music. Their nocturnes became fixtures of the Paris salon. At the same time, they became symbols of the Paris salon throughout Europe, since they were published, with their French texts, in many other musical centers (in Warsaw, for instance, by the time Chopin was eight years old).[8] If we think of a generic title as a device of communication between composers and audiences, then surely the two primary composers of piano nocturnes would have counted on the title *Nocturne* to evoke the Parisian vocal nocturne far more readily than its German cousin, since John Field was living and publishing his nocturnes in St. Petersburg—a city where the upper classes were French in language and culture—and Fryderyk Chopin wrote and published most of his nocturnes in Paris itself. Nevertheless, even scholars who have noticed the existence of the Parisian vocal nocturne repertory have not until now investigated that repertory as a source of inspiration for the piano nocturne. The present study (along with a recently published study by Jeffrey Kallberg)[9] is designed to remedy that neglect; it is motivated by the belief that the vocal nocturne, because it was a shared point of reference between composers and audiences of the piano nocturne, can help us resolve some of the issues that make the piano nocturne so elusive a genre to define.

In generic terms the Parisian vocal nocturne was almost invariably a duet, with piano accompaniment. The nocturne of Chopin's generation seems to have been the duet variant of the solo romance. In fact, nocturnes were frequently published in collections that also included romances, as well as chansonnettes and other genres, and the principal distinction between the nocturnes and the other genres is clearly that the works in the other genres are solos whereas the nocturnes, as a rule, are for two voices, and never fewer than two. Indeed, that seems to be the sole distinction the different titles convey: the texts of romances usually have nocturnal settings, just as those of nocturnes do, whereas the texts of nocturnes are generally about romantic love, just as those of romances are.

These vocal duets called for a woman to be at least one of the singers; that is, nocturnes were written for two sopranos, or soprano and tenor, or less frequently some other combination. In other words, the Parisian nocturne was by no means cast for serenading men. And that vocal casting fits with the typically top-dominated textures of the piano nocturne. It cannot be claimed that the nocturnes of Field or Chopin or other early-nineteenth-century composers always imitate a vocal duet, but they almost always suggest a soprano voice, and somewhere along the way—especially in Chopin's nocturnes—there is usually some suggestion of a second voice, most frequently another woman's voice.[10] In fact, one of the wonders of the Chopin nocturnes is his infinite inventiveness in playing on the idea of a duet in close harmony.

It may seem that, in the singing of love poetry, a performance by two sopranos signifies something very different from a performance by a soprano and a tenor. But even though the performance may be given by two singers, the poetry they sing does not on the whole embody two distinct roles; on the contrary, the two singers intone a single poetic text, representing a single persona, or "voice." Sometimes that persona is of unspecified gender, as is the beloved being addressed. Occasionally it is a female persona, speaking to or about a male lover. More often the persona is male. But that does not stop the composer from setting the poem to be sung by two sopranos, or one soprano and one tenor. An example is Auguste Panséron's nocturne, "La nuit s'est endormie" (Example 8.1). The text of this nocturne takes us into a couple's bed after

Example 8.1. Auguste Panséron, "La nuit s'est endormie" (words by Bétourné), from Panséron, *Dix Romances et Cinq Nocturnes à deux voix* (Paris: Launer Girod, n.d.), mm. 1–26.

they have spent the night together. We presume that the speaker is male because he addresses his lover in words that identify her as female: "Quittons-nous, mon amie" [Let us take leave of each other, my beloved]. Later he also addresses her as "Belle d'amour." But the music is to be sung by two sopranos. So, what is going on?

We should hardly expect any exact correspondence between the singer and the song: singers have always appropriated songs that apparently belong to the opposite sex, and audiences have always accepted that.[11] In the early nineteenth century, in particular, audiences were quite accustomed to hearing at the opera the sort of gender bending that we find in "La nuit s'est endormie": the roles of male lovers might be sung by castrati or by women, so that in either case the audience would be treated to love duets sung by two high voices. Presumably this effect provided the frisson of displaying a relationship that was transgressive but at the same time safe: the sight and sound of two women singing rapturously together was permitted, in effect, because they were representing, say, Romeo and Juliet, just as that particular Romeo and Juliet were permitted to express themselves in more explicitly sexual music than a male Romeo and female Juliet might be, precisely because they were not a man and woman singing together. A love duet sung by two women owed its effect not simply to the idea of gender bending but also to the sound they produced. Two high voices endlessly and closely entwining with each other could provide the most exquisitely sexual pleasure because they exquisitely embodied the union of two people, regardless of their relative sexual identities, as a sound. And what is astonishing about the piano nocturne—especially Chopin's—is how it manages to convey the sexually exciting sound of those two intertwining high voices without using voices at all. A passage from Chopin's E♭ Nocturne op. 55 no. 2, a duet filled with mutual incitements and responsive sighs, illustrates just one side of this art (Example 8.2).

What light can the Parisian vocal nocturne shed on the issue raised earlier about the piano nocturne as a genre that has no distinctive rhythmic character but rather borrows the rhythmic characters of other genres? As it happens, the vocal nocturne does the very same thing; in fact, it borrows pretty much the same set of rhythmic characters from other genres. But vocal nocturnes do have texts, and we can explore those texts in an effort to make sense of the rhythmic variety of their music. The key to under-

Example 8.2. Chopin, Nocturne in E♭ Major op. 55 no. 2, mm. 47–55.

standing this variety, I believe, is that though nocturne texts are almost all love poems they elaborate different poetic conceits, and it is from those conceits that the musical settings derive their different rhythmic characters. It may seem strange for a duet about love to be in march rhythm, for instance, but take a nocturne by Felice Blangini in which the text tells us about the fleetingness of love through an image of lightning:

Come fugace lampo disparve in un momento . . .
[As a fleeting stroke of lightning disappears in a moment . . . ]

Blangini uses the rhythm of a march with offbeat accents to capture the forcefulness and abruptness of that lightning—and, by extension, of love (Example 8.3). Such effects make it possible to understand how Chopin nocturnes that open with march-like bass lines (for example, the Nocturnes op. 37 no. 1, op. 48 no. 1, op. 55 no. 1, and op. 62 no. 2) might have convinced listeners—if we imagine listeners steeped in the vocal nocturne repertory—that they were songs of love rendered on the piano.

Quite a number of nocturnes employ the religious mode, their texts playing shamelessly on the idea of religion as a cover for sexuality, conflating in the process two apparently opposed images of nighttime—as a time for prayerful devotion and as a time for lovemaking. Antoine Romagnesi set a "Prayer to Saint Germaine" that calls on the saint to pray for all the lovers in Paris:

Show yourself favorable to our loves!
Only good hearts are made for passion.[12]

Another nocturne by Romagnesi, "Gentille nonette," is a man's appeal to a gentle young nun, who prays every day by herself, to intercede with God for a poor sinner, apparently himself. In the first verse the tone of his address to her—"speak to the Lord, speak to Him, my dear, of the poor sinner"—already suggests that the young nun is the object of his desire at the same time that she is expected to be the means of saving his soul from that desire. This ambiguity is even more explicit in the third and final verse as he conflates her saintliness with her attractiveness, her intercessions with lovemaking:

Votre bouche pure
Et votre ferveur

Example 8.3. Felice Blangini, "Come fugace lampo," from Blangini,
*Eight Italian Notturnos for Two Voices* opp. 21 and 22 (London:
Birchall, n.d.), mm. 1–5.

Des maux qu'il endure
Guériront son cœur.

[Your pure mouth
And your fervor
Will cure his heart
Of the pains it endures.]

It is this poetic blurring of chaste prayer with sexual passion that
explains how a nocturne could be a love song—in this case for
soprano and tenor—set in the style of a hymn. It may also explain
why the hymn-like music of this nocturne takes such lurid turns
to the minor mode as the man calls on the nun to speak to the

Lord "of the poor sinner," repeating the phrase "the poor sinner" three times (see Example 8.4).

Here, too, the exploration of poetic texts in the vocal nocturne lends some rationale to what otherwise seems like the intrusion of an alien genre into the piano nocturne. There are several hymn passages in the Chopin nocturnes (op. 15 no. 3, mm. 89ff.; op. 37 no. 1, mm. 41ff.; op. 48 no. 1, mm. 25ff.), and each of them intrudes on music of a more lyrical and passionate nature—music that seems more appropriate for a love song. The piano nocturne, lacking a text, evidently needs an episodic construction to express contradictions of tone; thus while Romagnesi plays religion against sexual passion by introducing lurid modulations within a duet that is entirely hymn-like in texture, Chopin characteristically plays one against the other by embedding a hymn passage that is itself entirely calm—perhaps as a reminder of religious possibilities or memories—within a song of passion (Example 8.5).

Like the devotional hymn, the lullaby is a genre representing an innocent nocturnal activity that can cover for a more passionate one. In Panséron's nocturne, "Protège notre amour," for instance, the lover speaks of nightfall as the time when everyone heads off to sleep—the fisherman makes it home, the bird finds its nest (Example 8.6). The gentle rocking of the music confirms the lullaby as the prevailing conceit of the piece. But for the lover himself and his beloved, the night has another function: to protect their love from view. It is that protecting darkness, after all, that allows him to say "ô nuit plus belle qu'un beau jour"—a line that occurs in so many vocal nocturnes that it could be called the slogan of the genre. It is no coincidence that a version of that line also occurs in the most famous French operatic duet of love sung by two women:

> Belle nuit, ô nuit d'amour,
> Souris à nos ivresses.
> Nuit plus douce que le jour,
> O belle nuit d'amour.
>
> [Lovely night, O night of love,
> Smile down upon our raptures.
> Night more lovely than the day,
> O lovely night of love.]

Clearly Offenbach's Barcarole is a nocturne, though he does not call it that.

Example 8.4. Antoine Romagnesi, "Gentille nonette" (words by Boucher Deperthes), from Romagnesi, *Collection des romances, chansonnettes et nocturnes*, vol. 3 (Paris: chez l'Auteur, n.d.).

Example 8.5. Chopin, Nocturne in G Minor op. 37 no. 1, mm. 61–72.

Similarly many vocal nocturnes are barcaroles by rhythmic character, as are many piano nocturnes, Chopin's among them. Antoine Romagnesi's "Pensers du soir," for instance, a nocturne for soprano and tenor or two sopranos, is a barcarole in its wavelike bass and its melodic rhythm of quarter-eighth, quarter-eighth—but it is also a lullaby, to judge by the line "Je me berçai d'un riant avenir" [I lulled myself with a smiling future]. The opening of this nocturne, marked by incessant repetition of its extremely simple opening phrase, fits the description given above of the vocal nocturne as a homely species of vocal music (see Example 8.7). But the ending of the song takes an unexpected turn to the operatic: the singers treat us to a joint roulade (see Example 8.8). This

Example 8.6. Auguste Panséron, "Protège notre amour" (words by
Emile Barateau), from Panséron, *Dix Romances et Cinq Nocturnes*,
mm. 1–14.

phrase casts a new light on the question of how Chopin's piano
nocturnes, or for that matter Field's, could so often be operatic in
style—that is, of a grandly embellished lyricism—and yet be named
for the vocal nocturne. The answer may be that the vocal nocturne
was not a genre that entirely shunned the splendors of operatic
singing. It may have been a salon genre, but the greatest singers
of the Paris operatic stage also sang at Paris salons, and the composers of vocal nocturnes were also composers of operas. What is
more, the apparent simplicity of sentiment and modesty of style
that made the vocal nocturnes of Blangini and Panséron and Rom-

Example 8.7. Antoine Romagnesi, "Pensers du soir" (words by Leduc), from Romagnesi, *Collection des romances, chansonnettes et nocturnes*, vol. 3, mm. 1–16.

Example 8.8. Romagnesi, "Pensers du soir," mm. 34–36.

Example 8.9. Chopin, Nocturne in G Major op. 37 no. 2, mm. 1–10.

agnesi accessible and appealing to huge numbers of amateur performers should not make us forget that, to nineteenth-century
artists, simplicity was an affectation. The composers of vocal nocturnes were ready to ask their singers—whether amateurs at a family gathering or opera stars—to remove the mask of simplicity at
a moment's notice for a ravishing roulade, just as they were ready
to use the image of a praying nun to convey the lustfulness of a
self-styled sinner.

The vocal nocturne, in other words, turns out to be no easier
a genre to define than the piano nocturne. But its ambiguities are
nevertheless helpful in making sense of those of the piano nocturne. Consider one final example of duet texture in a Chopin
nocturne (Example 8.9). Here a duet passage—this time a sweetly
harmonious love duet instead of a passionate one—is for once the
opening and principal theme of a piano nocturne rather than an
intensifying development. This nocturne, beginning as it does, re-
minds us more forcefully than any other Chopin nocturne that the
principal model of the piano nocturne was a genre of vocal duets.
When we think of the florid lyricism of the Chopin nocturnes,
then, should we think exclusively of embellished solo lines and not
at all of embellished duet lines such as these? Furthermore, does
this passage remind us of the opera house or of the salon? Do we
connect its sweet harmoniousness with one source and its restless
modulation with another? And now that we have peeked at some
specimens of the vocal nocturne, why would we expect to be able
to make such a distinction?

NOTES

1. The significance of the mazurka rhythm in Chopin's G Minor Nocturne
op. 15 no. 3 is examined by Jeffrey Kallberg in "The Rhetoric of Genre: Chopin's
Nocturne in G Minor," reprinted in his *Chopin at the Boundaries: Sex, History, and
Musical Genre* (Cambridge, Mass.: Harvard University Press, 1996), 3–29.

2. Ibid., esp. 3–11.

3. Nicholas Temperley gives a representative, though judicious, assessment
of the Italian operatic model: "The similarity of Chopin's nocturnes to Bellini's
cavatinas (such as 'Casta diva' from *Norma*) has often been noticed, though there
is little evidence of direct influence in either direction. The influence of Rossini's
and Weber's operatic melodies is apparent" ("Fryderyk Chopin," in *The New
Grove Early Romantic Masters 1* [New York: Norton, 1985], 43). Will Crutchfield
has recently moved the discussion of Chopin's operatic models from the written

notes of composers such as Bellini to the improvised embellishments of the singers Chopin heard performing Italian opera (*New York Times*, 20 June 1999, Arts section, 21–22).

4. Nonetheless, music dictionary writers of the time (Castil-Blaze and Lichtenthal, in particular) did maintain that an operatic type of *nocturne*, a number of nocturnal character or setting, was to be found in operas from as early as 1791; see Christoph von Blumröder, "Notturno/Nocturne" (1982), in Hans Heinrich Eggebrecht, ed., *Handwörterbuch der musikalischen Terminologie* (Wiesbaden: Franz Steiner), 6.

5. See ibid., esp. 4–5.

6. Carl Czerny, *School of Practical Composition; or, Complete Treatise on the Composition of All Kinds of Music*, Op. 600, trans. John Bishop, 3 vols. (London: Robert Cocks, 1848; reprint, New York: DaCapo, 1979), 1:97.

7. See Wolfgang Krueger, *Das Nachtstück: Ein Beitrag zur Entwicklung des einsätzigen Pianofortestückes im 19. Jahrhundert* (Munich: Emil Katzbichler, 1971); and von Blumröder, "Notturno/Nocturne"; Kallberg, "The Harmony of the Tea Table: Gender and Ideology in the Piano Nocturne," reprinted in his *Chopin at the Boundaries*, esp. 45–47.

8. A Nocturne for two treble voices, to the words "Quand le sommeil," composed by "B . . . (Felix)" [presumably Felice Blangini] as published by Klukowski in Warsaw in 1818, is reproduced in Wojciech Tomaszewski, *Bibliografia warszawskich druków musycznych 1801–1850* (Warszawa: Biblioteka Narodowa, 1992), 338. I thank Halina Goldberg for pointing out this publication to me.

9. Kallberg's study, " 'Voice' and the Nocturne," appears in Bruce Brubaker and Jane Gottlieb, eds., *Pianist, Scholar, Connoisseur: Essays in Honor of Jacob Lateiner* (Stuyvesant, N.Y.: Pendragon, 2000), 1–46. The two studies were prepared independently of each other.

10. Suggestions of a second voice are more rare and slighter in Field's earliest nocturnes (several of which, in any case, were originally published as *romances* rather than *nocturnes*), but in the later ones (as, for example, the eleventh, in E♭, of 1833) he sometimes develops a second "voice" at length, in either the tenor or mezzo-soprano range.

11. See Mark W. Booth, *The Experience of Songs* (New Haven, Conn.: Yale University Press, 1981), 14–17.

12. "A nos amours montrez vous favorable! / Les bons cœurs seuls sont faits pour s'enflammer" (Antoine Romagnesi, "Prière à Ste. Germaine" [words by Simonnin], in Romagnesi, *Etrennes lyriques: recueil composé de romances, nocturnes, contredanses, walses et galops* [Paris: chez l'Auteur, n.d.]).

# 9

## Gender and Genius in Postrevolutionary France: Sand and Chopin

### WHITNEY WALTON

Let us begin with two caricatures produced in France in the 1840s and published in the popular satirical journal *Le Charivari* (to which Chopin subscribed, incidentally).[1] The first is by Honoré Daumier, and it is part of a series he created in 1844 entitled "Les Bas-bleus," or "The Bluestockings." Here, an extremely thin, even scrawny bluestocking dressed in her underclothes preens before a mirror. "It's strange how this mirror flattens my figure and slims my chest," she says to herself. "But what do I care? Mme de Staël and M de Buffon have declared that genius has no sex" (Figure 9.1). In this caricature the figure's silly pretension suggests that her talent as an intellectual is highly doubtful, but equally questionable is her femininity, for she is portrayed as notoriously lacking in even the most basic of feminine attributes—breasts and hips, to say nothing of beauty or even attractiveness. All of Daumier's representations of women in the Bluestocking series contribute to a stereotype of the intellectual woman, a stereotype that was reinforced in textual caricatures also written during the July Monarchy (1830–48). Characteristics of the bluestocking are sometimes contradic-

Figure 9.1. Honoré Daumier. *C'est singulier comme ce miroir m'applatit la taille . . .* (1844). From *Le Charivari*, 30 January 1844. Washington, D.C., Library of Congress, Rare Books. Photo Library of Congress.

tory, but she is commonly ugly, unfeminine, sexually promiscuous, neglectful of household, wifely, and child-rearing responsibilities, and ridiculously proud of her presumed artistic genius. The caricatures indicate that women with intellectual pretensions are bourgeois, and that they have violated bourgeois ideals of femininity—beauty, submissiveness, devotion to husband, home, and children, and cultivation only of social graces rather than of the intellect or of professional skills.[2]

Just two years earlier another caricature also invoked the saying "genius has no sex" but this time in a portrayal of a particular individual rather than a generic stereotype. In 1842 *Le Charivari* published a caricature by Alcide Lorentz of the successful writer George Sand that represents her dressed in men's clothes and standing in a cloud of smoke, apparently generated from the cigar she holds in her left hand. Beneath her right elbow and her right hand, which holds a quill pen, are titles of some of her novels (*Indiana* and *Valentine*) but also political statements that Sand never made, calling for a chamber of female deputies and a chamber of mothers. A few lines of verse at the bottom of the illustration read, "If the Georges [*sic*] Sand of this portrait leaves you a little perplexed, it is because genius is abstract and is, as we know, unsexed" (Figure 9.2). While this caption might refer to Sand's cross-dressing as "perplexing" and as suggesting an ambiguous sexuality, it also seems to deride Sand's literary accomplishment through association with "extreme" feminist political stances. Sand's feminine body very clearly defies the attempt at masculinization through cross-dressing: the vest stretches tightly across her breasts, and the trousers strain at her crotch from the breadth of her hips. So the quip about genius and sex seems to focus more on questioning Sand's genius rather than her sex.

Both these caricatures highlight the problematic of gender and genius in postrevolutionary France, specifically the difficulty of imagining a genius as a woman. In this essay I explore this problematic by charting the development of the meanings of the term *genius* in the late eighteenth and early nineteenth centuries in France. I then consider the gendered complexities of genius in relation to George Sand and Fryderyk Chopin, who were intimate for nearly nine years, from 1838 to 1847. Both Sand and Chopin were considered geniuses by many in their time, and both were represented as having characteristics of the opposite sex. However, I contend that there was an asymmetry in the respective genderings

Figure 9.2. A. Lorentz. *Miroir drolatique* (1842). From *Le Charivari*, 5 August 1842. Washington, D.C., Library of Congress, Rare Books. Photo Library of Congress.

of their genius. In making the case that genius was more problematic for Sand than for Chopin, I present examples of critics' ambivalence toward Sand as a genius, and I analyze how Sand dealt with the negative implications of genius in relation to women. I argue that Sand's "solution" to the problem of the female genius was the pursuit of an ideal of justice and equality. For Sand, in a reformed society and polity women would be able to exercise genius free of the constraints and prejudices that hindered them in Sand's own time.

Several scholars have studied the evolution in the West of the term *genius* from antiquity to the present, and they discern a decisive change in its meaning during the Enlightenment. From being a universal quality possessed by all men in varying quantities, genius became a unique faculty that blessed only a few, according to the ideas of eighteenth-century thinkers. Characteristic features of genius in this rendering are inspiration, creative imagination, spontaneity, feeling, and originality. An unresolved problem, however, for several *philosophes*, was the role of reason in genius. Did a man of genius produce something of greatness in a moment of emotional frenzy, beyond the laws of reason and bordering on madness? Or was the genius guided by an innate understanding of natural laws and rationality that his work embodied in a new form? Diderot theorized a compromise position between these two possibilities by asserting that both imagination and reason were necessarily part of genius, and that the work of genius was produced in stages of the two experiences. "It is when great sorrow has passed, when extreme sensibility is moderated, . . . when the soul is calm . . . that memory unites with imagination, the one to recover, the other to exaggerate the sweetness of a past moment; that one possesses oneself and speaks well."[3] Although some *philosophes* were unwilling to abandon completely the idea that reason was a part of genius, it was, paradoxically, during this period of the celebration of reason that the idea of genius as fundamentally irrational emerged.[4]

Most eighteenth-century theorists of genius assumed that genius was a strictly masculine attribute; that is, both in terms of feeling and reason women were deemed inferior to men, which implied that they lacked the capacity for genius. Rousseau maintained that women were incapable of genius because they lacked the depths of emotion necessary for generating works of genius.[5] Moreover, eighteenth-century scientists proclaimed that women were less intelligent than men, based on (erroneous) renderings of the male and female human skeleton that represented the female head as smaller and the female pelvis as larger than those of the male.[6]

Yet what to do, then, with Madame de Staël (1766–1817) whose brilliant conversation and stunning literary works led many, including herself, to consider her a genius? What was a female genius? How was a woman a genius? Staël's own life, but especially the character of Corinne, the female genius she created in her book of the same name (1807), reveals the difficulties of this figuration. Corinne is a renowned artist and scholar who is publicly celebrated in Rome, much to the amazement of an English visitor, Oswald, who notes that he had often seen men carried in triumph by the people, "but this was the first time that he witnessed such honors given to a woman, a woman famed only by the gift of genius."[7] She captivates audiences with her brilliance as a performer, extemporaneously reciting speeches or singing poems of her own, spontaneous creation that also reflect her profound erudition and intelligence. Among her admirers is Oswald, whom she comes to love but who eventually leaves her to marry a more conventionally feminine woman, a domestic creature who is neither a genius nor a public figure. Having lost Oswald, Corinne stops performing and dies. Genius and femininity thus appear incompatible or mutually exclusive in a woman. Or is Staël suggesting something quite different: that men have constructed gender and genius in a way to render the female genius an impossibility?[8]

Recall that the first caricature invokes Staël, along with the naturalist Georges-Louis Leclerc, comte de Buffon, as authorities for the position that "genius has no sex." My limited research has failed to reveal a direct quote from either Staël or Buffon to this effect, but it is likely that the saying is a variation on a statement by the seventeenth-century thinker François Poullain de la Barre who wrote, in 1673, "L'esprit n'a point de sexe" [The mind has no sex]. Giorgio Tonelli explains that the French word *esprit* has several meanings, including mind or wit, and that in certain eighteenth-century usages "*esprit* is a synonym of *génie*."[9] The nineteenth-century caricaturists may have substituted *génie* for *esprit* with the understanding that the words were synonymous. Moreover, both Staël and Buffon had, in very different ways, and unlike many other Enlightenment thinkers, posited equality between women and men in terms of intellectual and creative abili-

ties.[10] Let us turn now to Sand and Chopin, and to the meanings
and usages of genius in their time.

George Sand (1804–1876) started her writing career in the revolutionary year of 1830. At that time she arranged with her husband to live apart from him in Paris for part of the year, and she
determined to earn her living as an author. Her self-imposed education to this end included cross-dressing. Sand maintained that
she needed to wear men's clothes because they were cheaper and
more durable than women's attire, and because they allowed her
to experience more of life than was possible for a respectable,
middle-class lady. According to Sand, only by frequenting art museums, the theater, political clubs, and the Paris streets in the guise
of a young man could she gain the worldly knowledge necessary
for her to become an artist.[11] The first book she published under
the name of G. Sand was *Indiana* in 1832, and this was both a
critical and popular success. Shortly thereafter the author signed
herself George Sand, creating a new identity for herself, and, in
her own words, wedding herself to the literary profession: the
pseudonym "was a contract, a new marriage, between the poor
apprentice poet that I was and the humble muse who had consoled
me in my hardships."[12] From then on Sand was a professional
writer, producing scores of novels, short stories, plays, essays, and
political pieces (to say nothing of a massive correspondence) until
her death in 1876.[13]

Both Sand and Chopin were professionally well known and
established when they met in Paris in 1838 and subsequently em-
barked on an intimate relationship that lasted until 1847. Much
has been written and speculated about this relationship, notably
regarding perceived gender role reversals. Some have noted Sand's
"masculine" role in pursuing the younger and physically frail Chopin, her "dominance" over him owing to her energy and strength
of character, the "heartless" manner of her ending of the relationship, and the "fatal" effect of all this on the musician who died
only two years after the rupture.[14] While the "truth" about Sand
and Chopin as a couple will doubtless continue to entice and elude,
some scholars have analyzed different representations of the two
to better understand the cultural and social history of the middle
decades of the nineteenth century.[15] This approach also bears on
the issue of genius during that time—for part of Sand's masculine
image derives from the attribution of genius, as does Chopin's effeminacy. To be sure Sand did, in fact, dress in men's clothes,

smoke little cigars, live an independent life, and succeed in literature—all practices that violated feminine norms of behavior in her time. And Chopin was, in fact, usually in poor health, thin, weak, and careful about his dress and interior decoration—all characteristics associated with femininity rather than masculinity.[16] Still, I wish to focus on representations of gender specifically in its relation to genius.

Gender ambiguity or confusion was not unique to Sand and Chopin, for it was also evident in the culture and even politics that surrounded them. The offbeat socialist sect known as the Saint-Simonians both challenged and reinforced gender differences in their various efforts to transform society in the 1830s. The basis for their utopia was the celebration of so-called feminine and masculine characteristics as equally valuable and necessary in individuals, and for social harmony and prosperity. For their pains, however, Saint-Simonians confronted lawsuits and engendered public ridicule, and female Saint-Simonians especially were frequent objects of derision.[17] Further, the 1830s and 1840s were notable for the visibility of women writers as well as male authors. New technologies, a growing urban middle class, and an increase in literacy contributed to a boom in the publishing of books, periodicals, and newspapers. Although literature and journalism were male-dominated fields, female as well as male authors succeeded in getting their work in print as publishers sought to meet an almost insatiable demand for stories, articles, and books. Indeed, it was the visibility and success of women writers that led to the stereotype of the bluestocking, represented by Daumier's and Lorentz's caricatures.[18] In both cases—the Saint-Simonians and the women writers—boundaries between masculine and feminine were blurred, yet reactions against this blurring targeted women more than men.[19] A similar development was linked with genius.

The attributes of genius in postrevolutionary France were in some ways feminine, in that they included spontaneity and natural propensity: "talent, natural inclination, aptitude for something," according to an 1835 dictionary definition. Yet this same definition suggests the exclusive masculinity of genius: "It refers particularly to this quality of superior minds that renders them capable of creating, inventing, accomplishing extraordinary things, and so forth; and, in this sense, it is often used absolutely. *He is a man of genius. That man has genius.*"[20] Christine Battersby asserts that while male geniuses could partake of certain feminine qualities associated with genius, women artists in the Romantic era could not: "A woman who created was faced with a double bind; either to surrender her sexuality (becoming not *masculine* but a surrogate *male*), or to be *feminine* and *female*, and hence to fail to count as a genius."[21] According to the research of Jeffrey Kallberg, the case of Chopin supports Battersby's contention.

Kallberg has catalogued many descriptions of Chopin's performances in France that describe him in feminine or androgynous terms—angel, sylph, elf, Ariel, delicate, fabulous, impressionable, virginal, and so on.[22] Such appellations blurred Chopin's sexual identity, but they did not necessarily challenge Chopin's capacity for genius, for these terms also were part of the 1835 definition of genius: "having to do with fairies, gnomes, sylphs, genies, etc."[23] Indeed, effeminacy distinguished some men from the conventionally masculine and therefore brought them closer to a divine or otherworldly source of genius.[24] Liszt's assessment of Chopin includes numerous feminine attributes, for example, "The frailness of his heart and constitution forced upon him the feminine martyrdom of tortures never admitted, and weighted his destiny with certain features of feminine fate." Yet he also claimed that Chopin's focusing of his feeble energy on small piano pieces as opposed to larger, classical genres was, in fact, his genius, and not a limitation.[25] Sand also described Chopin's genius in similarly varied ways. Suggestive of feminine qualities are the following statements: "The genius of Chopin is the most profoundly feelingful that has ever existed," and "He did not need massive means to express his genius." But Sand also cast Chopin's genius as masterful and original, and in keeping with the greatest of (male and masculine) musicians: "The whole world will know that a genius as vast, as complete, as knowing as that of the greatest masters whom he had assimilated contained an individuality even more exquisite than Sebastian Bach's, even more powerful than Beethoven's, even more dramatic than Weber's."[26] Sand also recognized the agonizing revisions that accompanied Chopin's brilliant inspirations. "His creativity was spontaneous, miraculous. . . . But then would begin the most heartbreaking labor I have ever witnessed. It was a series of efforts, indecision, and impatience to recapture certain details of the theme he had heard."[27] Ultimately Sand allowed Chopin's uniqueness as a genius: "His genius is the most original and the most individual that exists."[28]

Thus for his close friend and fellow musician, Liszt, and for his longtime companion, Sand, Chopin's genius partook of some feminine characteristics but without detracting from his identity as a man of genius. Even Kallberg's collection of feminine and androgynous metaphors for Chopin and his work imply tolerance, if not acceptance, of androgyny in a man of genius, at least in the first half of the nineteenth century. By contrast, sexual confusion and androgyny in representations of Sand and her work rendered her a considerably more dangerous figure than when linked with Chopin. This is clear in the many reviews of Sand's writings.

Reviews of her first two works identified Sand as an author of great talent who brilliantly conveyed contemporary conditions. An anonymous reviewer of *Indiana* considered it "among the best novels of our time."[29] A reviewer of *Valentine* asserted that Sand's portrayals of aristocratic and bourgeois habits were "drawn with the impartiality of a superior talent."[30] By the 1840s it was common for critics to refer to Sand as a genius, though critical analyses of Sand's works were by no means uniformly positive. Some reviewers questioned the morality of Sand's plots and characters, and others took issue with the social criticism and radical political stances she put forward in her fiction.[31] Several were flummoxed by the difficulty of a creative talent, perhaps even a genius, in the form of a woman. In many cases descriptions of Sand's work as virile or firm and comparable to that of a man were complimentary. Yet such masculine attributions often explicitly connoted monstrosity.

In 1844 an article on French women writers of the time appeared in one of the most widely read weeklies of the nineteenth century, *L'Illustration*. The anonymous author begins by questioning the view, represented in the caricatures of bluestockings, that an intellectual woman is either a monstrosity or an impossibility. He (more likely than she) takes seriously the adage that genius has no sex:

> Ah, good God! Who would think to dishonor genius because it is incarnated in a woman? Genius is an all-powerful force that imposes itself on all, whatever the organ that it chooses; genius has no more sex than the sun. Who would dream of hardening oneself against grace, sensibility, poetic emotion because they would speak their natural language, that of woman? No one.[32]

This author concedes that women can be geniuses, yet he also makes a distinction between conventional women and women who write. After describing the "typical" woman as a devoted wife, mother, and homemaker, he then asserts that, for himself, "a woman of letters is never worth as much as a woman." Moreover, when he acknowledges the genius of Sand and places her indisputably at the forefront of all contemporary women writers, he avoids presenting her as a female genius. He describes her thus: "neither a man or a woman, but simply, in our view, one of the beautiful literary geniuses to have shone upon the world."[33]

Also problematizing Sand's sex, the famous critic Jules Janin poses these questions regarding Sand: "Who is he or who is she? Man or woman, angel or demon, paradox or truth?"[34] In comparison with other women writers Sand stood out as superior, according to one reviewer, yet, he opined, this quality clearly was at the expense of her femininity. Commenting on a collection of stories by different female authors, this reviewer writes: "After George Sand, this woman who, unfortunately and fortunately, has more mind than heart, one could very well say: *Quo est homo!*—then, shyly and in their natural appeal, come young women poets."[35] Another writer asserted that Sand was not a woman because she created female characters that were unfeminine. He said of these characters: "Among so many beautiful, passionate intelligent young women who will pass and pass again before your eyes, carefully outfitted by genius, have you encountered a mother, a companion, a daughter, even a lover? No!" Later in the article the author refers to Sand as "this sexless soul" [*cette âme sans sexe*] and exhorts women readers not to consider her a member of their sex. He writes himself into the position of having to classify Sand, since he denies that she is a woman: "As for us, since we must admit that George Sand is either a man or a monstrosity in the moral order, we had decided for the former, out of respect for a great talent, and out of the sympathy that leads us to the most beautiful and the most honest half of the human species."[36] Thus it still seems impossible for a woman, or at least for Sand, to be a genius and to remain a woman.

Was this a problem for Sand alone, because of her cross-dressing and her masculine pseudonym? Or because Sand was unique among women writers in her high level of success, earning more money for her serialized stories than Balzac, though not as much as Victor Hugo or Paul de Kock? Or because these factors combined to generate a distinctive image of Sand as threatening to the existing social and gender order because of her independence, freedom, and literary authority?[37] These are all likely explanations. Yet another explanation is that the content of Sand's works, notably her social criticism and political advocacy, became more pointed and also more transgressive. It was bad enough, in the view of numerous, mostly male writers, that Sand made a successful career in literature for herself, but her presumption to address philosophical and political issues in print challenged the laws that excluded women from civic responsibility.

Sand's first two novels, *Indiana* and *Valentine*, were passionate denunciations of contemporary marriage practices and laws that condoned male tyranny at the expense of mutual love and respect between spouses, and that prohibited divorce. Although they both were serious social critiques, they were focused on women's civil status rather than their civic exclusion. Yet even with her third novel, *Lélia* (1833), the form and content sparked controversy.[38] Characters in this book represented the struggle of the spirit to overcome hypocrisy, despair, and degeneracy, and Sand subjected the Catholic Church to serious questioning as the lives of her characters played out. This and other novels led Mme Simon-Viennot, the editor of a woman's periodical, to denounce Sand for her "implacable maledictions . . . against the ideas of her century and the institutions of her homeland." Simon-Viennot counseled her readers to avoid Sand, asserting her wish "to encourage the complete repudiation of all the works by this writer." In her view, Sand's genius was utterly debased by her misguided, even immoral attacks on social conditions and established institutions: "genius becomes depraved and destroys itself each time that it is nourished by sources of error and evil passions."[39]

Then, in the mid-1830s Sand became a staunch advocate of socialist republicanism, and many of her works of the 1840s made heroes out of working-class idealists and activists. Sand's novels of this period were open in their celebration of working-class dignity and honor, and in their promotion of eradicating class hierarchies, transforming an unjust society into a loving community, and even eliminating private property. Criticism of Sand's writing and of her person became even more virulent. In 1844 the literary critic Lerminier compared Sand to two women writers who were "the honor of French *esprit*," Madame de Sévigné and Madame de Staël. According to this article, these two authors, unlike Sand, had retained their femininity, the former through the centrality of her love for her daughter, and the latter because she loved her father and admired superior men. Lerminier asserted that, "for a moment, ten

years ago, after the stunning debut of Mme Sand, one had the
magnificent hope that these two illustrious women of whom we
speak might have had a rival." But Sand failed to live up to this
promise, according to Lerminier, because she became too imitative,
referring to the political ideas Sand "borrowed" from radicals and
socialists. "With the vigorous and supple talent that is her gift,
Mme Sand could correct herself, transform herself again. But for
this it is necessary that she retake her freedom, that she think for
herself, and not via others."[40] Similarly, in 1847, another critic indicated that Sand's initial enthusiasm and seriousness of purpose
had foundered on her adoption of unstated philosophical ideas. He
even questioned the sincerity of Sand's ideals by implying that she
had sold her name to political publications for mere profit, though
he stopped short of an outright accusation.[41]

Many in postrevolutionary France acknowledged Sand as a genius, but still had difficulty reconciling this gift with her sex. Mme
Simon-Viennot refused even to consider Sand as a *woman* writer:
"we have abstained from judging G. Sand, in this article, under the
point of view of the sex that he has literally abdicated."[42] Sand was
well aware of the negative connotations attached to women who
wrote, and she rejected for herself the appellations that would cast
her in the bluestocking mold. "Never call me a woman author
[*femme auteur*]!" she wrote to a friend in 1832. And in 1834 she
asserted in another personal letter, "I know that I am tainted with
the label of woman of letters [*femme de lettres*]."[43] Sand preferred
to think of herself as an artist or a poet, figures that could more
easily accommodate the "feminine" characteristics of genius like
inspiration, imagination, emotion, and spontaneity, if not originality. Further, Sand's autobiography, written from 1847 to 1853
(when Sand was in her forties), emphasizes her feminine qualities
as much as her professional accomplishments. The autobiography
was an opportunity for Sand to represent herself publicly in her
own terms, a means of countering others' public representations
of her in book reviews, essays, and caricatures.[44] But Sand did more
than simply defend herself against negative criticism. In her work
she sought to change readers' views about many things, including
women artists and women of genius.

Sand was deeply concerned with the creative process and artistic production, and numerous stories she wrote focused on various types of artists—singers, painters, producers of mosaics, stage
performers, and, especially after she met Chopin, musicians. To

my knowledge Sand never created a character that was a writer. And to my knowledge Sand never claimed for herself the label of genius. Perhaps writing connoted intellectual endeavor and rationality, whereas artistic production partook of the characteristics of genius; after all, it was feminine aspiration to intellectual greatness that served as the target of satirists of the bluestocking. And Sand, along with her contemporaries, had the greatest difficulty in accepting equality of intellect and reason in women and men. By contrast, artistic performances by women in music and on the stage did not similarly connote masculinity or monstrosity. As Sand wrote in 1836, up to that time, only in singing, dance, and the painting of miniatures "could women presume to a rank equal to men in the practice of art." She hoped, nonetheless, for a better future for the deployment of women's talents: "A time will come, perhaps, when the areas of science, the arts, and philosophy will be open to the two sexes."[45]

For Sand, art and political engagement toward an ideal future were inseparable. Indeed she, like other Romantic artists, viewed art as a means of social transformation. For example, Sand questioned the value of the French Academy, that forty-member body of "immortals" that presumed to honor and preserve the best in French literature, when the majority of the French population was illiterate and hungry. Sand imagines herself a literary genius, elected into the Academy, and finds that the two conditions are incompatible. "Why, I say to myself, were I to have genius, I would thereby also have goodness, commiseration, devotion to humanity, the abnegation of all personality." A true genius in Sand's imaginings would address herself or himself to the poor and the poor in spirit. This genius would raise questions about the meaning of genius—was it merely individual or did it refer to the quality of an entire nation? The Academy, according to Sand, is anachronistic. It can no longer claim to judge works impartially strictly on the basis of literary merit, because true works of art must necessarily contain philosophical or personal points of view: "There is no more literature if the mind is forbidden from struggle and if taste presumes to proscribe the freedom to contest." Sand believes that she lives in a progressive era and that progress entails the challenging of old ideas and free expression of the new. "The gifts of intelligence are the more or less spontaneous products of a culture itself that no one can regulate, and traditions shatter like glass at the point where genius begins."[46] In other words, it is not for serious

artists, and especially not for women, to aspire to enter the Academy, but rather to address their talents to the social and philosophical issues of the day.

How is a female genius to be? In her writings Sand created
female artists who struggled with their creative endeavors and with
their femininity in the form of family attachments and social responsibilities. In Sand's longest work, *Consuelo*, written during the
early years of her relationship with Chopin and during her close
friendship with the singer Pauline Viardot, the main character is a
gifted singer who works diligently and overcomes numerous obstacles to develop her musical genius. Consuelo survives tests of
her strength, courage, and faith finally to triumph on the stage at
the courts of both Maria-Theresa of Austria and Frederick II of
Prussia. Ultimately, however, she ceases to sing and devotes herself
to her husband's quest for spiritual renewal and social change,
though music is an essential part of her family's collective mission.[47]
Consuelo's renouncement of her artistic genius in favor of social
reform and spiritual regeneration does not necessarily reflect Sand's
acceptance of the impossibility of the female genius. Rather, Sand
suggests in *Consuelo* and in many other works that only in a new
world of community, justice, and equality will a female genius be
imaginable and possible.

Thus, in her life and work, Sand articulated a new definition
of genius, one that would include social responsibility as well as
creative effort, women as well as men. Having become the standard
and model of a woman genius, Sand was well positioned to try to
manipulate her own image. Yet she would not succeed. In the latter
half of the nineteenth century, and particularly after Sand's death,
no other woman genius with as much influence as Sand followed
her. Sand herself was pilloried in vehement terms, along with other
women writers, and her works were ignored for several decades.[48]
According to Kallberg, Chopin suffered a similar fate, though not
as extreme; by the late-nineteenth century biographers and critics
attributed more than effeminacy to Chopin, by using language that
associated him with hermaphroditism and sodomy. Moreover critics disparaged so-called effeminate music, including the nocturne,
a genre Chopin had made very popular in his day.[49] Apparently,
though, in hindsight, the gender ambiguity surrounding genius in
postrevolutionary France benefited both Sand and especially Chopin. Chopin was not rendered deviant by the feminine character-

istics associated with his genius. And, as Victoria Thompson has argued, the period of the July Monarchy was one of sexual and gender fluidity that accompanied social upheaval and the process of stabilizing social order. This process would end, however, in the 1850s and 1860s when "sexuality and gender were increasingly organized into rigidly defined categories."[50] Clearly Sand became monstrous in public representations because of the masculinity associated with genius, yet she was, nonetheless, deemed a genius. I maintain that her politics and social criticism contributed greatly to her monstrous image. But it was precisely her politics, and her idealism for a better society, that also allowed her to respond to this negative image with a hopeful alternative for feminine genius.

NOTES

1. Letter from Sand to Marie de Rozières from Nohant, 21 July 1842. Sand requests little cigars for herself, and that Rozières renew Chopin's subscriptions to two newspapers: "Chopin asks that you renew for three months his subscriptions to [*Le Journal des*] *Debats* and *Le Charivari* that expire at the end of this [month]" (George Sand, *Correspondance*, ed. Georges Lubin, 26 vols. [Paris: Garnier, 1969], 5:728).

2. Jules Janin, "Le Bas-bleu," in *Les Français peints par eux-mêmes: Encyclopédie morale du dix-neuvième siècle*, 9 vols. (Paris: L. Curmer, 1842), 5:201–31; C. Feuillide, "Les Bas-bleus. Fragment," *L'Europe littéraire* 69 (9 August 1833): 4; Frédéric Soulié, *Physiologie du bas-bleu* (Paris: Aubert, 1841). For analyses of such representations of women writers, see Janis Bergman-Carton, *The Woman of Ideas in French Art, 1830–1848* (New Haven, Conn.: Yale University Press, 1995); Kirsten Powell and Elizabeth C. Childs, eds., *Femmes d'esprit: Women in Daumier's Caricature* (Hanover, N.H.: University Press of New England, 1990); Christine Planté, *La Petite Sœur de Balzac: Essai sur la femme auteur* (Paris: Seuil, 1989); Whitney Walton, *Eve's Proud Descendants: Four Women Writers and Republican Politics in Nineteenth-Century France* (Stanford, Calif.: Stanford University Press, 2000), chap. 4.

3. Denis Diderot, "Paradoxe sur le comédien," in *Œuvres complètes de Diderot*, ed. Jules Assézat and Maurice Tourneux, 20 vols. (Paris: Garnier, 1875–77), 8:386; quoted in Kineret S. Jaffe, "The Concept of Genius: Its Changing Role in Eighteenth-Century French Aesthetics," *Journal of the History of Ideas* 41 (1980): 596.

4. Kineret, "The Concept of Genius," 579–99; Giorgio Tonelli, Rudolf Wittkower, and Edward Lowinsky, entries on "Genius," in *Dictionary of the History of Ideas*, ed. Philip Wiener, 5 vols. (New York: Scribner, 1973), 2:293–326.

5. Christine Battersby, *Gender and Genius: Towards a Feminist Aesthetics* (Bloomington: Indiana University Press, 1989), 36.

6. Londa Schiebinger, *The Mind Has No Sex? Women in the Origins of Modern Science* (Cambridge, Mass.: Harvard University Press, 1989), chaps. 7–8.

7. Madame de Staël, *Corinne, ou l'Italie*, 2 vols. (Paris: Editions des Femmes, 1979), 1:46.

8. For a brilliant analysis of literary and lived representations of genius, see Bonnie G. Smith, "History and Genius: The Narcotic, Erotic, and Baroque Life of Germaine de Staël," *French Historical Studies* 19 (fall 1996): 1059–81.

9. Tonelli, "Genius from the Renaissance to 1770," 294.

10. Smith, "History and Genius"; Schiebinger, *The Mind Has No Sex?* 158.

11. George Sand, *Story of My Life: The Autobiography of George Sand*, a group translation, ed. Thelma Jurgrau (Albany: State University of New York Press, 1991), 892–93, 903.

12. Sand, *Story of My Life*, 908. Numerous motivations were behind Sand's and other women writers' adoption of masculine pseudonyms. A masculine name might help them get unbiased reviews from critics who considered writing an inappropriate activity for women and generally expected little of serious art in writings by women. Married women, like Sand and Marie d'Agoult (1805–1876), did not wish to implicate their husbands in their writing by using their married names. Further, pseudonyms were part of some women writers' creation of a new, public identity, chosen consciously by the women themselves and not assumed by law and social convention, as were their married names (Walton, *Eve's Proud Descendants*, 81). Sand's decision to drop the *s* from the French masculine name *Georges* suggests her preference for androgyny rather than masculinity (Isabelle Hoog Naginski, *George Sand: Writing for Her Life* [New Brunswick, N.J.: Rutgers University Press, 1991], 3).

13. This summary biography of Sand does not begin to convey the richness and complexity of her life. Such information and interpretations are readily available elsewhere; biographies of Sand are numerous and highly varied in their viewpoints. A comprehensive biography of Sand that emphasizes her humaneness and humanitarianism is Wladimir Karénine [Varvara Dmitriëvna Komarova], *George Sand: Sa Vie et ses œuvres, 1804–1876*, 2nd ed., 4 vols. (Paris: Librairie Paul Ollendorff, 1899; Plon, 1912–1926). Studying Sand out of interest in her influence on famous men is André Maurois, *Lélia: The Life of George Sand*, trans. Gerard Hopkins (New York: Harper and Brothers, 1953). During the 1970s several biographies of Sand appeared either claiming her for feminism, for example, Tamara Hovey, *A Mind of Her Own: A Life of the Writer George Sand* (New York: Harper and Row, 1977), and Renée Winegarten, *The Double Life of George Sand: Woman and Writer—A Critical Biography* (New York: Basic Books, 1978), or removing her from feminism, for example, Ruth Jordan, *George Sand: A Biographical Portrait* (New York: Taplinger, 1976), and Curtis Cate, *George Sand* (Boston: Houghton Mifflin, 1975). Interest in Sand persists, as evidenced in Belinda Jack, *George Sand: A Woman's Life Writ Large* (New York: Knopf, 2000). See also Walton, *Eve's Proud Descendants*. This is by no means a complete list of Sand biographies.

14. Franz Liszt, *Frédéric Chopin*, trans. Edward N. Waters (New York: Vienna House, 1963 [1852]), chap. 7; Frederick Niecks, *Frederick Chopin as a Man and Musician*, 2 vols. (New York: Cooper Square, 1973 [1902]), 1:xiv, chap. 19; 2:9–13, 202–3; James Huneker, *Chopin: The Man and His Music* (New York: Charles Scribner's, 1923 [1900]), 46–52, 55, 60–61. Less condemning of Sand for her behavior, masculine or otherwise, are Marie-Paule Rambeau, *Chopin dans la vie et l'œuvre de George Sand* (Paris: Les Belles Lettres, 1985); Sylvie Delaigue-Moins, *Chopin chez George Sand à Nohant* (Chateauroux: Les Amis de Nohant, 1986); and William G. Atwood, *The Lioness and the Little One: The Liaison of George Sand and Frédéric Chopin* (New York: Columbia University Press, 1980).

15. Isabelle de Courtivron, "Weak Men and Fatal Women: The Sand Image," in *Homosexualities and French Literature: Cultural Contexts/Critical Texts*, ed. George Stambolian and Elaine Marks (Ithaca, N.Y.: Cornell University Press, 1979), 210–27. See also Naomi Schor, *George Sand and Idealism* (New York: Columbia University Press, 1993), 180–83.

16. *Chopin's Letters*, ed. Henryk Opieński, trans. E. L. Voynich (New York: Knopf, 1931). See also references above regarding the Sand/Chopin relationship.

17. Henry-René d'Allemagne, *Les Saint-Simoniens, 1827–1837* (Paris: Gründ, 1930); Claire Goldberg Moses and Leslie Wahl Rabine, *Feminism, Socialism, and French Romanticism* (Bloomington: Indiana University Press, 1993); Kari Weil, "A Woman's Place in the Utopian Home: The 'New Paris' and the Saint-Simoniennes," in *Home and Its Dislocations in Nineteenth-Century France*, ed. Suzanne Nash (Albany: State University of New York Press, 1993), 231–46; Michèle Riot-Sarcey, *La Démocratie à l'épreuve des femmes: Trois figures critiques du pouvoir, 1830–1848* (Paris: Albin Michel, 1994).

18. Claude Bellanger et al., *Histoire générale de la presse française*, Vol. 2: *De 1815 à 1871* (Paris: Presses universitaires de France, 1969), 109–43; Martyn Lyons, *Le Triomphe du livre: Une Histoire sociologique de la lecture dans la France du XIXe siècle* (Paris: Editions du cercle de la librairie, 1987); James Smith Allen, *Popular French Romanticism: Authors, Reading, and Books in the Nineteenth Century* (Syracuse, N.Y.: Syracuse University Press, 1981); Planté, *La Petite Sœur de Balzac*, 43–44.

19. See also Victoria Thompson, "Creating Boundaries: Homosexuality and the Changing Social Order in France, 1830–1870," in *Homosexuality in Modern France*, ed. Jeffrey Merrick and Bryant T. Ragan, Jr. (New York: Oxford University Press, 1996), 102–27.

20. *Dictionnaire de L'Académie française* (1835), 1:831. This reference comes from The ARTFL Project, University of Chicago. Project for American and French Research on the Treasury of the French Language. Dictionnaires d'autrefois. http://duras.uchicago.edu/cgi-bin/quick_look.new.sh?word=genie, accessed 20 June 2001.

21. Battersby, *Gender and Genius*, 36. See also Marcia J. Citron, *Gender and the Musical Canon* (New York: Cambridge University Press, 1993), esp. chaps. 2 and 5.

22. Jeffrey Kallberg, "Small Fairy Voices: Sex, History, and Meaning in Chopin," in *Chopin at the Boundaries: Sex, History, and Musical Genre* (Cambridge, Mass.: Harvard University Press, 1996), 62–86.

23. *Dictionnaire de L'Académie française* (1835), 1:831.

24. Andrew Elfenbein, *Romantic Genius: The Prehistory of a Homosexual Role* (New York: Columbia University Press, 1999), 30–34.

25. Liszt, *Frédéric Chopin*, 107–8, 31–33.

26. Sand, *Story of My Life*, 1092.

27. Ibid., 1108.

28. George Sand, *Impressions et souvenirs* (Paris: Levy, 1873), 81.

29. Anonymous, review of "*Indiana*, par G. Sand," *La France littéraire* 2 (June 1832): 676.

30. Anonymous, "Album," *Revue de Paris* 44 (December 1832): 198. Reviews in *Journal des débats politiques et littéraires* and *Figaro* were equally enthusiastic. See also Annarosa Poli, "George Sand devant la critique, 1831–1833," in *George Sand*, ed. Simone Vierne (Paris: Editions CDU et Sedes Réunis, 1983), 95–100.

31. Several truly nasty accounts of Sand were published as books or in journals, asserting that Sand's works were dangerous to society, that her children would be punished for her sins, and that "evil is often a woman." See Anonymous,

"Galérie de portraits. 4. Lélia," *Revue critique* 4 (March 1840): 2–3; Theobald Walsh, Cte., *George Sand* (Paris: Hivert, 1837); and Ahasverus, "Profils républicains. George Sand," *La Mode* 19 (November 1848): 979–88. See also Mme Simon-Viennot, "Célébrités contemporaines. Influence de Georges [*sic*] Sand," *Journal des mères et des jeunes filles* 1 (August 1844): 200–11; and Jules Janin, "Mme George Sand," in *Les Femmes célèbres contemporaines françaises* (Paris: Le Bailly, 1843), 439–55.

Although women were not commonly literary critics, two of Sand's fellow writers were less hesitant than other reviewers to name Sand a genius with positive connotations. Delphine Gay de Girardin implied that Sand was a woman of genius [*une femme de génie*] in an article that associates Sand with Byron and Luther in beneficial rebellion against society or the church. She also credits Sand with being a great poet and thus expressing in her work the conditions of existence around her. A poet "cannot change his thought; his thought . . . he does not choose, he produces it, it is the fruit of his heart" (Delphine Gay de Girardin, "Lettres parisiennes, 24 May 1837," in *Œuvres complètes de Madame Emile de Girardin née Delphine Gay*, 6 vols. [Paris: Plon, 1860], 4:100). In a letter to Sainte-Beuve, Hortense Allart criticizes Sand's rustic novels for catering too much to the popular classes, yet she still considers Sand to be a writer of genius: "Some of her works . . . *André, Horace, Isidore*, are they not masterpieces of morality and of sentiment? With this manner of genius which attains all the summits, opens the immensity and takes us along with her?" Allart goes on to complain that in these times when political men are weak and ineffectual, "isn't it good to be able to praise here a complete merit . . . and when *political genius* is lacking, to have in full a *poetic genius*" (Letter of 13 February 1850, in Hortense Allart, *Nouvelles lettres à Sainte-Beuve [1832–1864]*, ed. Lorin A. Uffenbeck [Geneva: Droz, 1965], 91).

32. Anonymous, "Femmes de lettres françaises contemporaines," *L'Illustration* 69, no. 3 (22 June 1844): 264.

33. The original reads: "un ecrivain qui . . . n'est ni un homme ni une femme, mais tout simplement, à notre sens, un des beaux génies littéraires qui aient lui sur le monde" (ibid., 266).

34. Janin, "Mme George Sand," 439.

35. "Feuilleton du journal des débats du 29 novembre. Variétés: *Les Heures du soir, Livre des Femmes*," *Journal des débats politiques et littéraires* (29 November 1833): 2.

36. Ahasverus, "Profils républicains. George Sand," 981–82.

37. Lyons, *Le Triomphe du livre*, 58; Allen, *Popular French Romanticism*; Courtivron, "Weak Men and Fatal Women."

38. Anonymous, "Galerie de Portraits."

39. Simon-Viennot, "Célébrités contemporaines," 201, 203.

40. Lerminier, "Poètes et romanciers contemporains. Second phase. I. Mme Sand," *Revue des Deux Mondes* 6, no. 14, new series (1844): 84–117.

41. Saint-René Taillandier, "Simples Essais d'histoire littéraire. La littérature et les écrivains en France depuis dix ans," *Revue des Deux Mondes*, series 2, vol. 18, no. 2 (1847): 961–96.

42. Simon-Viennot, "Célébrités contemporaines," 210.

43. Letter to Charles Meure, 27 January 1832, and letter to Alfred Tattet, 22 March 1834, in Sand, *Correspondance*, 2:16, 546–47.

44. Walton, *Eve's Proud Descendants*, chap. 4.

45. George Sand, "Souvenirs de Madame Merlin," in George Sand, *Questions d'art et de littérature*, ed. Henriette Bessis and Janis Glasgow (Paris: des femmes, 1991), 83.

46. George Sand, "Réception de Sainte-Beuve" and "Pourquoi des femmes à l'académie?" in Sand, *Questions d'art et de littérature*, 147–60, 257–69.

47. George Sand, *Consuelo. La Comtesse de Rudolstadt*, 3 vols. (Grenoble: Les Editions de l'Aurore, 1991). For an extended analysis of *Consuelo*, and a fascinating examination of music in Sand's work generally, see David A. Powell, *While the Music Lasts: The Representation of Music in the Works of George Sand* (Lewisburg, Pa.: Bucknell University Press, 2001), esp. 121 and chap. 6.

48. Jules Barbey d'Aurévilly, *Les Bas-bleus* (Geneva: Slatkine Reprints, 1968 [1878]); Sainte-Beuve, "Sur George Sand," in *Mes Poisons* (Meaux: Plon, 1965), 109–12; Schor, *George Sand and Idealism;* Jo Burr Margadant, "Introduction: Constructing Selves in Historical Perspective," in *The New Biography: Performing Femininity in Nineteenth-Century France*, ed. Jo Burr Margardant (Berkeley: University of California Press, 2000), 20–21.

49. Kallberg, "The Harmony of the Tea Table: Gender and Ideology in the Piano Nocturne," in *Chopin at the Boundaries*, 30–61.

50. Thompson, "Creating Boundaries," 103.

# *Part IV*

Chopin Appropriated

# 10

# Chopin's Reception as Reflected in Nineteenth-Century Polish Periodicals: General Remarks

ZOFIA CHECHLIŃSKA

The reception of musical works is conditioned by a variety of factors, and very often it differs among various audiences even during the same time period. My essay will consider the reception of Chopin's music as reflected in Polish periodicals, and thus the reception of his music among critics, people involved with music more or less professionally, whose views were particularly important since they could influence and form public opinion. The period I investigate is the second half of the nineteenth century; the decades directly after the composer's death, when his work was already a closed chapter. The main question I wish to answer is this: to what extent was the reception of Chopin's work in Poland different than among other European audiences, and to what extent was it similar?

After Poland's loss of independence, the emphasis on national distinctiveness and the assertion of national identity became extraordinarily important. Herder's theories, and the concept of national art that resulted from them, were typical of much of Romantic music, but they found particularly fertile ground in Poland.

Music was, after all, one of the few areas in which national individuality could be revealed and emphasized. The idea of national
music dominated Polish musical culture of the time, and the degree
to which music was saturated with Polish elements became a main
criterion for evaluating it. Those Polish elements were initially
conceived in a relatively simple way: there was either a Polish
theme in those works with texts, or at least titles suggesting a Polish theme, and in a purely musical structure the idiom of the
metro-rhythm of Polish dances or the incorporation of Polish melodies. (For a more detailed examination of these criteria and
Herderian contexts for the reception of Chopin, see Maja Trochimczyk's extensive essay in this volume.) Chopin grew up in this
kind of atmosphere—charged with the patriotic obligation to create music with national color—and, like other Polish composers of
the time, he used Polish melodies and the rhythms of Polish dances
already in the works from his Warsaw period (the finale of the two
concertos, Fantaisie op. 13, *Rondo à la Krakowiak*, not to mention
the mazurkas and polonaises). This, combined with the superior
artistic level of his works compared to those by other Polish composers, was the main reason that, after the Warsaw concerts in
which Chopin had performed his large works, the critics univer-
sally proclaimed him as Poland's national composer. Thus appeared
one of the main features that would be later generally attributed
to Chopin's music. At the same time Polish music critics hailed his
originality, lyricism, and distinctive emotionalism, which were also
central to the general reception of Chopin's music in Europe.

After Chopin's departure from Poland, the popularity of his
works in his homeland was, at least initially, very limited.[1] In the
1830s Chopin's compositions were almost completely absent from
concert programs; at the end of the 1830s and in the 1840s they
began to appear more frequently, and by the 1850s Chopin was
already the composer whose works turned up most frequently on
concert programs, at least in Warsaw.[2] That did not mean frequent
performances, since the total number of concerts held at the time
was rather small. It is also clear that in the 1840s Chopin's works
were performed in salons and private homes, but it is uncertain
how widespread these performances were.[3] On the other hand, the
press reported about Chopin constantly: about his life, contacts,
and especially his compositional successes, his numerous achievements, and general international artistic status. It was widely
known that Chopin was Polish and that he had become one of the

most highly regarded European composers. A nation that not only had lost its independence but had also undergone the defeat of the November Uprising of 1830, which had been oppressed and subject to numerous setbacks, began to treat Chopin as its ambassador. He was a personification of the Polish spirit, a symbol of Polishness and Poland, which, in spite of its political defeats, had won recognition in the world. Chopin gradually became a symbol of national might, and a cult developed around him even before knowledge of his works was firmly grounded. This attitude toward Chopin dominated his reception in the second half of the nineteenth century.

The first articles devoted exclusively to Chopin's work appeared in Poland in the 1840s. (Halina Goldberg refers to several of these in her essay in this volume.) In 1849, in connection with Chopin's death, several articles discussing the composer's output appeared, the most important being the broad, fifty-page study by Józef Sikorski, one of the most prominent Polish music critics of the nineteenth century.[4] From then on, articles about Chopin's work appeared with increasing frequency. Chopin became a point of reference in the description of various music topics. It can thus be generally asserted that in the second half of the nineteenth century Polish writing was filled with more or less developed opinions about Chopin.

The feature of Chopin's music that all authors refer to is its national character. The reception of Chopin's music in national terms was actually not limited merely to Polish writers alone. Schumann in his writings attributed a Polish idiom to all Chopin's works, discerning it also in the etudes, and he generally identified the individual features of the composer's style with his national idiom. Evaluation of this national orientation was not always positive outside Poland.[5] The negative attitudes of German critics are widely known, particular those of Rellstab. Johann Schucht, the author of the first German biography of Chopin, also considered the national character of his music to be a weakness.[6] In Poland, however, the national quality in Chopin's music was considered its great value, and Polish traits were perceived not only where they were demonstrably articulated, as in dance rhythms or the few quotations from the Polish songs, but rather in Chopin's output as a whole.

Józef Sikorski, cited above, belonged to that group of authors who in that period formulated their thoughts somewhat more carefully: he claimed that the national character of art does not depend on the use of folk melodies but on capturing the real spirit of national music.[7] However, he also commented on the expression of this spirit in musical structures which, to a greater or lesser degree, were stylizations of dance rhythms, and in melodic expression typical of specific songs or Polish music in general. Sikorski detected such melodic expression "typical of our music" in, for example, the march from the Fantaisie op. 49 (see Halina Goldberg's essay in this volume).[8] Whether or not those analogies were defensible, it should be emphasized that Sikorski attempted to justify his view about the national character of Chopin's music by stressing the composer's musical resources. Since he could not always find justification for this in Chopin's music, Sikorski was one of the few to assert that Chopin's music was not always Polish. For example, according to Sikorski, in the Ballade in F Major Chopin creates a legend "a threatening legend, not like ours, but like the German one."[9] The lack of national element did not detract, however, according to Sikorski, from the value of Chopin's art.

In contrast to Sikorski, other authors saw the national character in Chopin's entire output. "Every note of his bears a national stamp," wrote Antoni Woykowski in his 1849 article.[10] The national character of Chopin's music is not only about capturing "the real spirit of Polish national music" as Sikorski claimed, but capturing and expressing the spirit of the nation in general. In addition to emphasizing the self-evident Polish musical elements (mainly in Chopin's Mazurkas and Polonaises), some writers went beyond purely musical structures to find confirmation for their assertions in the composer's allegedly purely Polish psyche, which found expression in his music. In other words, the purely expressive side of the music was supposed to be proof of its Polishness. The following are just a few of the formulations illustrating the national identification with Chopin's music at the time: "Chopin thought and felt just like the Polish nation"; "Chopin expresses the sentiments of the nation"; "The sad tone of Chopin's music, its spirit of longing and sorrow makes him so intelligible for us . . . since he expresses the longing, sadness and sorrow of our spirit"; and, finally, "Chopin's music is a harp, on which the nation plays all its pain."[11] European criticism typically associated the categories of sadness, longing, and pain with Chopin's own illness or private experiences. By contrast, in Poland the categories of sadness, longing, and pain were applied to the situation of the country, where the people had been deprived of their own state, enduring the successive defeats of unsuccessful uprisings. Whereas Sikorski and many foreign commentators saw Chopin as expressing himself in his art, in the view of later critics he was articulating the sentiments of the nation. Thus his music not only had an artistic function, but it also became something of a national standard or symbol. This kind of reception was intensified by the fall of the next uprising in 1864.

The dominant stereotypes and philosophical concepts of the era also influenced the reception of Chopin's work. The Polish character of Chopin's music was related to a specific extra-historical individuality and identity of the nation, which that music supposedly expressed. Kleczyński, one of the leading music critics in Warsaw in the second half of the nineteenth century, wrote in 1879 that the French are witty, elegant, lively, and joyful, whereas the Poles are melancholy, sad, and very emotional but also courageous, gallant, and full of humor. And it was precisely these Polish traits that Chopin's works supposedly expressed. Kleczyński himself admitted that this is difficult to prove, but, as he wrote, it is "so typical."[12]

The Polish environment and the conditions in which Chopin grew up supposedly influenced his psyche and likewise found immediate reflection in his works, which some writers treated as illustrations of landscapes from Kujawy and Mazowsze, the regions of Poland where the young Chopin most often spent his vacations. This theme appears as early as the mid-nineteenth century in the writings of Szulc, but it is revealed most emphatically in the writings of Noskowski, a composer whose own works often had program-illustrative features and were connected with images of nature. "Chopin picked his melodies from our fields and forests" he wrote; "his [Chopin's] first master was our environment"; "Chopin's melodies are the poetification of the landscapes upon which the master gazed in the years of his youth, they are their reflection"; "In many of the Mazurkas we can sense the color and light of the landscape which the master saw with the eyes of his soul"; "The Mazurka in B♭ Minor op. 24 no. 4 brings before our eyes the beginning of autumn when the leaves on the trees begin to turn red, the plains grow gray and the fields become empty"; "The Mazurka in C♯ Minor op. 41 no. 1 reveals a gloomy view of the earth covered with snow, the clouds above it, as well as the expression of longing for spring and green meadows."[13] These environmental topics were common in the nineteenth-century critical reception of Chopin and later took on a more specific ideological angle under the influence of Hippolyte Taine's philosophical theories (which are discussed at great length in Maja Trochimczyk's essay in this volume, and include an examination of the changing contexts of the environmental tropes in the reception of Chopin).

The reception of Chopin's works as reproductions of the environment was sometimes evoked by the knowledge of the circumstances in which the particular works were created. Thus, for example, the Preludes, for Noskowski, are not simply purely Polish; they are the reproduction of the Mediterranean climate, since it is known that they were composed on Majorca (or at least were finished there). Legends emanating from the circle of Chopin's friends were also the source for certain interpretations of various works, for example, the Prelude in B Minor no. 6, or in D♭ Major no. 15, about which George Sand herself created legends.[14]

In the second half of the nineteenth century programmatic readings of Chopin's works were rather common. It is noteworthy that this kind of reception of Chopin's music did not exist at all in Polish criticism of the first half of the century. This, perhaps, was because of Chopin's well-known dislike of every kind of programmatic interpretation of music. Most probably, however, it was owing to the general changes in the attitude toward music under way at the time. The increasingly frequent linkage of music with a specific program by composers themselves in a certain sense familiarized the listeners with the reception of music in precisely such terms. Therefore listeners began to find programs even in works in which the composer offered no indication of their existence. As Kleczyński wrote: "The newest music often can be clarified only from the point of view of its program."[15] Program interpretations again served to underscore the national character of Chopin's works. This was especially applicable to the Polonaises, the Mazurkas, and the Ballades. The Mazurkas, as mentioned above, were associated with typical Polish landscapes and scenes from country life. The Polonaises were understood as the image of the nation's chivalrous past (Szulc, Kleczyński). In the Trio of the Polonaise in F♯ Minor op. 44, Kleczyński heard the "echo of distant battles and gunshots";[16] in the Polonaise in A♭ Major op. 53, he heard "an excellent apotheosis of the past,"[17] painting simultaneously a picture of a rich old Polish castle and, in it, a dancing pair dressed in traditional national costumes—a picture, as he himself said, that resembled a poem by the great Polish Romantic poet Mickiewicz.

The *ostinato* octaves of the same Polonaise were interpreted as "the trampling horses or something else."[18] An obvious implication is made here: that although the music refers to specific extra-musical phenomena, it is not always possible to decipher these phenomena in an unequivocal way.

In turn, it was believed that the Ballades were based on programs taken from literary prototypes. Here, the Polish readings repeated interpretive legends already established in the larger European tradition. For example, according to a tradition apparently born in the circle of Chopin's intimate associates, the Ballade in A♭ Major was supposedly the story of Loreley.[19] Noskowski accepts this interpretation and asserts that "the Ballade in A♭ Major contains general human features and its background is not Polish."[20] It is worth recalling, as mentioned above, that Sikorski, probably also under the traditional influence of the alleged program, had similarly described the Ballade as "a threatening legend, not like ours, but like the German one." And, further, Noskowski wrote: "Support for this conviction [that Loreley is the theme of the Ballade] is found in the entire development of the Ballade, its intensifying anxiety, its increasingly quick figuration in the left hand, the extraordinary return to the gloomy key of C♯ minor, and at last the final fortissimo, expressing a kind of triumphant cry of a witch after casting an unfortunate victim into the deadly depths of the sea."[21] Kleczyński associates, probably by mistake, the theme of the Ballade in A♭ Major not with Loreley but with Mickiewicz's ballade "Świtezianka," which traditionally is associated with the Ballade in F Major.[22] In this way, depending on the author's beliefs about a supposed program underlying the work, the work could be interpreted as Polish or non-Polish. Thus these interpretive legends, typically products of the Romantic imagination of individuals from Chopin's intimate circle, continued to exert influence on the reception of his work.

Generally the categories in which Chopin was received in Poland did not differ fundamentally from those in which he was received at the time in Europe as a whole. Yet the interpretation of those traits attributed to his works was often completely different: pejorative connotations underwent transformation to the positive. For example, Polish critics opposed the description of Chopin's music as being effeminate, a charge made primarily by German critics, insisting instead that it was characterized by "feminine tenderness," which carried positive implications. Polish critics also spoke emphatically against the descriptions of Chopin's music as being unhealthy. Kleczyński wrote outright that the artist's psychological or physical problems have no direct impact on the expression of his works.

> It is an immense . . . exaggeration to look for traces of Chopin's nervous breakdown in his Preludes . . . since, during their composition, he experienced . . . the joy that creating brought to him, which made him indifferent to temporal life and poured into his soul the blessing of immortality. . . . Chopin . . . while alive, did not reveal to the world what lay in his heart. Likewise, there is nothing in his work that would offend his dignity.[23]

Only two of Chopin's works, and then by only one critic, Kleczyński, were ever described in nineteenth-century Poland as unhealthy: The *Polonaise-Fantaisie* op. 61 and the Prelude in A Minor; the latter work, in any case, does not possess, as he claimed, "aesthetic beauty."[24] Such an evaluation should not be surprising in the 1870s, when the innovative qualities of these works were not understood in Europe in general. Polish critics definitely opposed the tendency to place Chopin in the categories of sentimentality and mawkishness, seeing in his works an enormous depth of expression and an extraordinarily powerful emotionalism.

The atmosphere of veneration surrounding Chopin prevented writers from negative critical evaluation of his oeuvre. In Poland, just as in the rest of Europe at the time, it was mainly the composer's earlier works that were performed in concert: compositions for piano and orchestra, as well as the remaining works from the late 1820s and 1830s. Later works, including the sonatas, appeared only sporadically in concert programs. While the earlier works met with the most enthusiastic reception not only among audiences but also among critics, the later pieces, too difficult for audiences at the time, were considered to be weaker. This evaluation was seen as evidence of the composer's declining creative powers as his illness progressed. Here are a few examples: "The last two nocturnes [op. 62] bear within themselves the traits of that forced, truly painful creativity with which Chopin composed at the close of his life";[25] "We like the last ballade less. It obviously comes from the period in which creating was more difficult for Chopin and complicated combination sometimes had to substitute for simplicity";[26] "Chopin was less a genius in the classic forms, whose examples include the three sonatas, the trio, and the cello sonata. . . . Fashioning these works was sometimes too heavy and complicated."[27] (On a similarly troubled reception in the United States of Chopin's late, more complicated works, including opp. 52, 54, 58, and 62, see Sandra P. Rosenblum's essay in this volume.) The Polish critics, however, were not unanimous in their views: Szulc thought very highly of the Nocturnes op. 62 and, on the basis of this evaluation, asserted that Chopin retained complete creative vigor to the very end. Woykowski, as early as 1849, found great praise for Chopin's Sonata in B Minor,[28] as did a host of other critics somewhat later. The critical appraisals cited here are among the most severe found in the Polish press. In comparison with the charges European critics made, particularly English and German critics,[29] the fundamental acceptance of Chopin on the part of Polish critics is apparent.

Polish critiques did not limit themselves to the questions related to national character and its expression in Chopin's work. They contain a wide variety of remarks regarding compositional resources, sometimes surprising in their accuracy and currency. Sikorski's remarks are distinctive in this regard. As early as 1849 he pointed out the significance of piano texture in Chopin (although he did not use this expression); its innovative character and influence on the quality of sound; the connection between Chopin's fingering and the desired sound effect; and Chopin's typical broad chord voicings.[30] Sikorski also called attention to the significance of chromaticism in general and, in particular, to its significance for the color of Chopin's music, and pointed to cross-rhythms and rhythmic disruptions as typical features of Chopin's style. Musical ideas, although frequently restated within a piece, were almost never repeated in quite the same manner, thus creating a sense of variety. On the subject of fragmented forms, which musicology noticed only recently, Sikorski commented: "It seems that there was no beginning whatsoever, and that what we are hearing is already the continuing part of the ideas existing in the artist's mind. Sometimes there is no end either."[31] Sikorski noticed the evolution of Chopin's style, simultaneously detecting the unity of his style but, above all, stressing his innovations. And in words that sound almost prophetic, Sikorski wrote: "We may not like certain things in Chopin's works because we simply do not understand them yet, but there will come a time when they will be understood and appreciated."[32]

The views of Kleczyński, particularly regarding the manner in which Chopin's works are performed, are similarly astounding for their modernity. They exhort simplicity, the avoidance of any pathos and exaggeration in playing, but, above all, the steadiness of rhythm. (For similar opinions found in the American press, see Sandra P. Rosenblum's essay in this volume.) In Kleczyński's words, "sustained inspiration [ought to be] the anchor of rhythm and symmetry,"[33] an idea that was completely new at the time when the universal manner of performing Chopin entailed complete rhythmic freedom.

Polish critics also opposed the widespread view of the formal insufficiency of Chopin's works, stressing their formal perfection. As early as 1849 Woykowski wrote that Chopin's greatness is in the breaking of earlier rules and the creation of new ideas with the aid of new forms.[34] The recognition and acceptance of Chopin's innovations in certain areas are especially surprising when we consider how conservative and resistant to change Polish composers and music critics were in the second half of the nineteenth century. At the same time, these critics could not fathom the consequences Chopin's achievements might have for the later development of music, and they did not display the same broadmindedness toward other composers breaking the received rules of composition. Thus, although certain innovative elements of Chopin's work were appreciated, their significance was not understood at all.

The reception of Chopin in Polish music publications undoubtedly had many features in common with his reception in the rest of Europe at the time. Those features mainly belong to the categories in which Chopin was received: lyricism, emotionalism, nationalism, poetry, and originality. The reception in Poland was influenced by the same range of factors that influenced his reception in Europe as a whole, including literature, chiefly Schumann's writings and Liszt's biography of Chopin (as discussed in Irena Poniatowska's essay, which follows), the aesthetic and philosophical ideas dominant at the time, as well as the details of the composer's life and various legends created in the circles of Chopin's intimates. Nevertheless different traditions and political conditions, and the fact that Chopin was a Pole, determined many of the differences in his reception. First and foremost, the attitude toward Chopin had an emotional character in Poland. Perhaps it was precisely that emotional character that enabled Polish critics to distinguish in his works the innovative traits which West European critics for a long time would consider insufficiencies.

NOTES

1. In 1849, in an article published in Poznań, right after Chopin's death, Antoni Woykowski wrote: "Here in Poland Chopin's works are generally neither familiar nor widespread" ("Fryderyk Chopin," *Gazeta polska*, no. 258 [1849]). He probably had in mind the Poznań community, and possibly not as much Chopin's presence in concert repertoires as in music at home and in salons, since Woykowski adds later: "We thus prefer Herz and Hunten, whom mediocre artists easily play and everyone understands them." In the same Poznań environment, Marceli Antoni Szulc, who later wrote Chopin's first Polish biography, wrote a bit earlier: "there is hardly a mention [of Chopin's works] anywhere to be found" (*Tygodnik literacki*, no. 10 [1842]: 42). Nevertheless, in the same year, the same author, discussing new editions of Chopin's works, wrote about one of the Mazurkas: "we shall not describe it more fully here as everyone more or less knows Chopin's mazurkas" (*Tygodnik literacki*, no. 11 [1842]: 83). These sorts of contradictory opinions make it difficult to construct a uniform picture.

2. Zofia Chechlińska, "Chopin's Reception in Nineteenth-Century Poland," in *The Cambridge Companion to Chopin*, ed. Jim Samson (Cambridge: Cambridge University Press, 1992), 211.

3. All the German editions of Chopin's works were brought to Poland immediately after their publication and spread quickly. Yet the number of copies is not known, nor is it known if the purchasers seriously used them. Thus it is difficult on this basis to conclude how widely known Chopin's music was.

4. Józef Sikorski, "Wspomnienie Chopina," in *Biblioteka warszawska*, vol. 4 (1848).

5. For instance, one of the Swedish critics described Chopin as "a somewhat uncouth, careless, and half-savage Pole" (Tore Uppström, *Pianister i Sverige* [Stockholm: Nordiska Musikförlaget, 1973], 212).

6. Johann Schucht, *Friedrich Chopin und seine Werke* (Leipzig: C. F. Kahnt, 1879).

7. Józef Sikorski, "Pieśni ludu polskiego przez Oskara Kolberga," *Gazeta codzienna*, no. 219 (1856).

8. Józef Sikorski, "O muzyce," in *Biblioteka warszawska*, vol. 2 (1842).

9. Sikorski, "Wspomnienie Chopina," 254.

10. Woykowski, "Fryderyk Chopin."

11. Józef Kenig, "Z powodu wydania pośmiertnych dzieł Chopina," *Gazeta warszawska*, no. 121 (1856).

12. Jan Kleczyński, *O wykonywaniu dzieł Chopina* (Kraków: Polskie Wydawnictwo Muzyczne, 1959 [1879; 1882]), 36.

13. Zygmunt Noskowski, *Istota utworów Chopina* (Warszawa, 1902); quotation from the edition *Kompozytorzy polscy o Chopinie* (Kraków: Polskie Wydawnictwo Muzyczne, 1960), 81–82.

14. George Sand, *Histoire de ma vie* (Paris: V. Lecou, 1854); a condensation of this book was published in *Biblioteka warszawska*, and fragments of it were contained in Marceli Antoni Szulc, *Fryderyk Chopin i utwory jego muzyczne* (Poznań: Żupański, 1873), and thus the legends George Sand transmitted about the origins of some works were well known in Poland.

15. Jan Kleczyński, *Chopin w celniejszych utworach swoich*, new and rev. ed. (Kraków: Polskie Wydawnictwo Muzyczne, 1960), 124–25.

16. Ibid., 123.

17. Ibid.

18. Ibid., 124.

19. Zdzisław Jachimecki claims that the tradition of this program originated in the circle of Chopin's intimates (*Chopin* [Kraków: Drukarnia Narodowa, 1949]).

20. Noskowski, *Istota utworow Chopina*, 89–90.

21. Ibid.

22. Kleczyński's interpretations are to be repeated later by Huneker in *Chopin: The Man and his Music* (New York: Scribner, 1900).

23. Kleczyński, *O wykonywaniu dzieł Chopina*, 33–34.

24. Ibid., 34.

25. Kleczyński, "Fryderyk Chopin," *Tygodnik ilustrowany,* no. 7 (1870): 33.

26. Ibid.

27. Kleczyński, "Fryderyk Chopin," *Tygodnik ilustrowany*, no. 108 (1870): 43.

28. Woykowski, "Fryderyk Chopin."

29. See Derek Carew, "Victorian Attitudes to Chopin," in *The Cambridge Companion to Chopin*.

30. Sikorski, "Wspomnienie Chopina."

31. Ibid., 552.

32. Ibid.

33. Kleczyński, *O wykonywaniu utworów Chopina*, 100.

34. Woykowski, "Fryderyk Chopin."

# 11

## The Polish Reception of Chopin's Biography by Franz Liszt

### IRENA PONIATOWSKA

Franz Liszt's book *Frédéric Chopin*, published in 1852, in Paris, by Escudier, was the first monograph devoted to the life and works of the Polish composer.[1] Already in its original form as a series of lengthy articles, which appeared in *La France musicale*, 5 February–17 August 1851, the study elicited strong reactions from Chopin's most intimate circles. During the hundred years following the book's publication, Polish musicians and writers on music provided an array of responses, ranging from enthusiastic praises of Liszt's true friendship and his understanding of the Polish composer's musical soul; to complaints about the exalted tone of the book and its disregard for factual accountability; to the disbelief that the first, and for many years the only, extensive study of Chopin was not penned by a Pole, preferably one of the composer's close friends.[2]

Chopin's most devoted friends—Wojciech Grzymała and Julian Fontana—were the ones most capable of writing his biography. Indeed, such were their intentions, but their plans were never carried out. We learn about Fontana's project from his correspondence with Chopin's childhood acquaintance, Stanisław Egbert

Koźmian, who encouraged him to write a study of Chopin. Initially, on 7 July 1850, Fontana wrote from Saratoga Springs:

> How should one write about Chopin? Either volumes, or nothing. How can one complete, in just a few lines, a description of such an extraordinary character, so extraordinary works, limitless in their wealth of innovations and ideas. And to write it for audiences who—as you say yourself—are completely indifferent and incapable of elevating themselves to a trifle higher level from the one at which not even Chopin's foot can be seen. This is what you scribbled to me! Nonetheless, I will try. Though you will never believe how the local air keeps one away from work.[3]

The following year Fontana again had honest intentions to begin work. In the letter dated 18 May 1851, he assured Koźmian:

> I hope—though I do not yet make a formal pledge—that finally, calmed down by the quiet, peace, and country air, I will get to writing about Chopin. Not for *Gazeta* or *Goniec*, but for *Przegląd*, because I believe that when it comes to a subject so important for Poland and art; so rich and at the same time so mysterious, a few lines or pages will not suffice.[4]

Therefore he wanted to publish a longer essay. He further explained that being in possession of "a pile of letters" from Chopin, especially from Majorca and Paris (written to America), he believed that organizing them and selecting the appropriate quotations would prove to be a Herculean task.

During this period Franz Liszt's articles on Chopin began to appear in *France musicale*. After the eleventh installment of Liszt's study, Fontana wrote to Koźmian, in the above-quoted letter:

> Some points are very well taken, some are entirely false, proving how little did he [Liszt] know him [Chopin]. More significantly, there are these philosophical–artistic–humanitarian debates that completely diverge from the objective, so that in one of the articles, in five columns, there is not a single mention of Chopin, not even to make a connection—only at the very end, as if he just remembered the title, he once quotes the name à propos the debate; as if to quiet his conscience. However, he always speaks of him as the brightest star of the nineteenth century; always bows down in devout reverence. On this point at least we agree, even though I must tell you that I have no intention of entering into any kind of polemics with Liszt.[5]

Although Liszt was writing his study of Chopin, Fontana did not yet abandon this topic. In a letter dated 6 June 1851, however, the question of Fontana's promised essay on Chopin returns in a different light:

> As for the article about Chopin, to tell you the truth, I regret that I made the half-promise, which you call a pledge of timely delivery. I have thought about it quite a bit, but now I see myself in great predicament. Liszt is signing his piece and his name carries authority. If I venture to criticize and evaluate [Chopin], every reader will feel the right to ask: who are you? And even if I sign, he will say "*connais pas*." Also, I would have as much to say about the man, as about the art. His tact, combined with unusual sense of humor, hid from the world what was not a secret to me, who knew him for almost thirty years. If I remove the curtain and show him not quite the way public opinion wants him, they will say that I am motivated by jealousy or self-interest. Anyway, how do you show an intimate side of a man, without providing the reader with a proof? Thus, when I sign my name, I may be placing myself in a negative light, and when I remove myself, I withhold seriousness and accountability of the whole thing. Think about this and write back as soon as possible. Thus far, I only dug up his letters from my bundle. . . . I got fifty-eight, of which eight or ten are cards containing a few lines each.[6]

Fontana continued that Chopin's letters from Palma and La Châtre contain allusions to living people and therefore he would have to withhold much information. The sense of responsibility, concerns about the difficult task, and fears of judgment by contemporaries, who might not have liked the image of Chopin Fontana presented, caused him to abandon plans of Chopin's biography and concentrate on the posthumous edition of his works. This motif of faltering—fear of showing Chopin's real personality, his weaknesses and faults—returns in Chopin literature, for instance, after the publication of Ferdynand Hoesick's historic monograph.[7] In a review written at that time, the father of Polish musicology, Adolf Chybiński, commented: "Chopin's life explains nothing about his art; on the contrary, Chopin's art will reveal to us more pages of his internal life—that is the actual life," and he added, with exaggeration, "we escape from Chopin, the man, into the more fragrant interior of his art."[8] The need for a myth demanded that Chopin's faults be hidden, so that nothing tarnishes the idealized image.

Fontana's reflections in his letter to Koźmian constitute the first, unofficial review of Liszt's study of Chopin by a Polish musician (and Chopin's closest friend). Subsequent comments, although not penned by a Pole, were written to Chopin's sister, Ludwika Jędrzejewicz. The author is Chopin's student and friend, Jane W. Stirling. In a letter dated 5 March 1852, she writes to Ludwika:

> You will be very displeased with the recent publication [Liszt's book]. A very reliable person evaluated it using a well-known expression: "he spit on the plate to spoil others' appetite"—he wrote it so that nobody else would want to write. . . . As for the beautiful and inventive philosophy of piano playing that transformed it into a new instrument, there is not even a word about it, which amazes me to no end. Did he not understand it? Maybe he intentionally kept silent about it. Using his penmanship, which in my view is often sophisticated (even though it has been said that he cannot write in French), he could have expressed many beautiful thoughts. Instead, as a pianist, for reasons I do not understand, he left out astonishing truths that can be achieved by a Genius, but, as C[hopin] said, that are not his [Liszt's] invention. He is vain and petty, because he thinks of himself only.[9]

Jane's evaluation is emotional, filled with aversion for Liszt. One must say, though, that it is in accord with the attitude of the Chopin family toward Liszt. In an 1841 letter to his father, Chopin, hurt by Liszt's review of his concert (*Gazette musicale*, 2 May 1841), expressed his resentment. Disagreements between the two artists began even earlier, and, soon after, all contacts between them came to an end.[10]

Perhaps Jane Stirling and Ludwika Jędrzejewicz exchanged some comments on Liszt while Ludwika was in Paris before and after Chopin's death, and this permitted Stirling to attack Liszt in such an overt manner in the letter to Ludwika. It is regrettable that there is no record of the visit Liszt paid Chopin's family in Warsaw, during his 1843 concert tour. Did they simply exchange the expected pleasantries? It is unfortunate that apparently no recollections or documents relating to this subject exist.

Jane Stirling had her own ideas about a biography of Chopin. In the above-quoted letter she informed Ludwika that she had suggested to a friend, Wojciech Grzymała, that together they go through Chopin's letters and immediately take notice of all false information that needs to be addressed in relation to Liszt's book. She believed that Grzymała should be the one to write Chopin's biography, based on his correspondence as well as the personal recollections of his friends and students. This idea occurred to Grzymała himself shortly after Chopin's funeral; in a letter to the financier August Léo (8 November 1849) he writes of his intentions to publish Chopin's *Opera Omnia*, preceded by a biographical sketch.[11] From Jane Stirling's letter to Ludwika (Paris, 18 June 1852) we learn that Grzymała started his work and was sharing his progress with her. "He is doing all the work alone—and we know that it comes from the bottom of his heart—and the French text will require minor amendments," wrote Stirling.[12] Further, in a letter written from Scotland (17 October 1852) she explained that Grzymała's work would benefit from an intermission, so that he could return to it with a more critical outlook, capable of greater objectivity. "This project has been abandoned for such a long time that a few more months will make no difference. I believe they could be a blessing! After all that Liszt said, he [Grzymała] feels he cannot remain silent."[13] Stirling had some objections regarding Grzymała's writing abilities, especially in French; Grzymała, on the other hand, was concerned that Jane Stirling would want to actively participate in the creation of the biography.

Did Liszt indeed hinder the creation of a Polish study of Chopin's émigré years? The answer is not straightforward. Liszt carried out an aesthetic evaluation of the Chopin phenomenon that neither Grzymała nor Fontana could achieve. It was expected that they would provide a factual biography, quoting letters and the recollections of friends; that they would portray the greatness of Chopin's personality and perhaps include the flaws Fontana mentioned. They were overwhelmed by the responsibility and had need of temporal distance. Jane Stirling conceived of a biography free of the errors Liszt had committed, but she probably also did not wish to expose any of Chopin's weaknesses so as to avoid destroying his image of a "genius." Liszt's essay was therefore the first book on Chopin characterized by a typically Romantic overgrowth of expression over content, though even Liszt wanted to verify some facts at the source.

Before he began the book, Liszt wrote a letter to Ludwika Jędrzejewicz (Pilzen, 14 November 1849) containing a kind of questionnaire with twelve questions. Some were simple questions: date and place of birth, manifestations of musical talent in early childhood, school and circle of friends, why Chopin left the Polish Kingdom, which Polish families did he contact in Paris, and so forth. Other questions referred to Chopin's relationship with George Sand and the feasibility of drawing an analogy between their relationship and her novel, *Lucrezia Floriani*, specifically the relationship of the heroine and the prince. Liszt also asked about the possibility that Sand's ultra-democratic ideas might have influenced Chopin, and he inquired into the reasons for their breakup. Finally, he was curious about Chopin's final trip to London, the year Chopin developed "chest disease," and his behavior during his last days. He asked, among other inquiries, whether it was true that Chopin, before his death, had asked to be dressed as if for a performance. Ludwika never responded to Liszt's letter: the attitude the Chopins had toward Liszt was already determined; in any case, some of the questions touched on very sensitive issues. Ludwika passed the questionnaire on to Jane Stirling, who in turn sent Ludwika a copy of her response to Liszt. The Chopin family kept copies of both, the questions and the answers, but only a copy of the questions is still extant (The Fryderyk Chopin Society, M/328). Fortunately Mieczysław Karłowicz published the entire text, both questions and Stirling's answers, in French and Polish.[14]

With regard to the first two questions, Jane Stirling suggested that Liszt communicate with Chopin's mother. She wrote with great pride about his extraordinary patriotism and his response to the November Uprising; about the Parisian circles of Polish aristocracy (Hôtel Lambert); and about the friends who remained with Chopin until his death. Chopin's relationship with George Sand, however, was a subject she considered too private to discuss. She added that it was Solange, not her mother, Mme Sand, who was at Chopin's side when he died. Stirling also explained that Chopin accepted death like a true Catholic, and any rumors about his last moments should be considered impertinent. Jane Stirling's position is clear from her response. She was primarily interested in defending Chopin's honor from Liszt's nosiness; she had no intention, however, of collaborating with him in any analysis of Chopin's personal traits and actions.

It appears that Liszt did not gain much from the response to his questionnaire. In his text, he emphasized, among other issues, Chopin's dislike for public performances—in accord with Jane Stirling—both of them explaining it as a desire to maintain freedom of expression and as a manifestation of Chopin's sensitivity. Nonetheless, to this day Liszt is held responsible for not verifying his information. Chopin's biographer, Antoni Marceli Szulc, believed that Grzymała was to blame for providing Liszt with faulty information about Prince Radziwiłł, who allegedly provided for Chopin's education. According to Szulc, Liszt sought Grzymała's advice on many particulars of Chopin's biography.[15] Julian Fontana, Jan Kleczyński, and Maurycy Karasowski also disputed what they considered false information regarding Prince Radziwiłł's financial assistance to Chopin.[16] In contrast, Gastone Belotti—although he knew about the questionnaire Liszt sent to Ludwika—criticized him for not verifying the biographical data by consulting with Chopin's closest friends, meaning Grzymała, Fontana, Stirling, and Chopin's family.[17] In Belotti's view, Liszt had written the book in order to eliminate any threat that the memory of Chopin might have posed to Liszt.[18]

Even the basic question of Chopin's birth date currently remains unresolved. Liszt must have collected other facts and dates in a haphazard manner, without much attention to documentation. It appears that Liszt was more concerned with the narrative than with concrete facts, perhaps because it is the narrative that explores the deeper psychological layers that determine the actions of the protagonists. This may have been why he was interested in allusions, real or imaginary, to the plot of George Sand's novel, *Lucrezia Floriani*, in which he obstinately searched for the cause of their breakup. Perhaps he also wished to introduce some theatricality and sensationalism into the image of Chopin that he presented in the book.

The responses in the Polish press to the 1852 publication of Liszt's *Frédéric Chopin* were somewhat enigmatic and delayed—one must recall that at the time there was no specialized musical journal in Poland. *Ruch muzyczny*, appearing during the years 1857–63, contained some references to the book. The earliest published remark, which appeared in an 1858 communiqué from Lublin, complains that instead of Poles writing about Chopin, it is done by foreigners, for example, Liszt, who is using his "fiery pen."[19] In an article entitled "The Most Recent Revolution in European Music," the author stresses that if Chopin were German or French many books about him would have already been written. "Neither the so-called biography that Liszt wrote nor the numerous minor articles that appeared after his death in various European journals will suffice as the biography the world deserves."[20] In a later issue of *Ruch muzyczny*, in "Some Pronouncement about Chopin," the anonymous author makes a more substantial comment about Liszt's book. The article refers to the French edition and the later German publication included in Liszt's *Gesammelte Schriften* (Kassel, 1856), as explained in the editorial note. The author writes:

> Liszt's innovative monograph is a fitting monument to Chopin. Its value is in the magnificent writing style, not in appearing at the right moment (shortly after Chopin's death). One can read in it the curiosity of a kindred spirit, full of love; the wonderful charm of a mature, developed genius, who with great dignity rolls back the mysterious curtain, behind which one can see the man's heart. [He] permits us to deduce the sources of his most exquisite ideas but does not fatigue the reader with gloomy philosophical discourses. One phase of his [Chopin's] artistic life, however, is still not clear. To explain Chopin's premature demise, the biographer tells us that Chopin was not able to endure the separation from George Sand, but he says nothing about this amorous crisis.[21]

The editor intended to fill this lacuna with his own ideas and hypothesis.

The longest response to the first edition of Liszt's book is the article "A Few Words about Chopin" in the journal *Księga świata*. In the note referring to the title of this unsigned article the editor comments that Liszt

> presents himself in this book as a talented and passionate writer. Although he spent little time among us, he was able to penetrate the spirit of Polish music, and, although a foreigner, he very accurately characterized the polonaise and the mazur. Also of interest are the details of his life and the last moments before the death of our Chopin, to whom Liszt was attached through friendship and admiration. [The editor disregarded Princess Wittgenstein's participation in the writing of this book and in providing the characterization of Polish dances and customs.][22]

The entire text is a kind of summary of Liszt's *Frédéric Chopin*. This is apparent in both the organization and the content of the article. Liszt's views are readily recognizable, and several direct quotations of his opinions and expressions are included.[23] But with regard to the Chopin–Sand question the editor kept silent about any allusions to the novel *Lucrezia Floriani*.

Such were the earliest official responses to the original edition of Liszt's book. However, before the first translation was published, the first Polish monograph of Chopin appeared: *Fryderyk Szopen i utwory jego muzyczne* by Marceli Antoni Szulc (Poznań, 1873).[24] In the introduction to his book, Szulc expressed a regret that Fontana did not fulfill his task of writing Chopin's biography. The only work on Chopin in the original French and German is out of print, and there is no Polish translation. In Szulc's view, Liszt's style is pompous and exaggerated, and although the many digressions in the book may be of some benefit to foreigners, he feels they are useless to Polish readers. Nevertheless Szulc finds in this work the "charm of a mature genius," someone who has rolled back the curtain to unveil the mystery of creation (compare this wording to the 1859 *Ruch muzyczny* article above).[25] He himself borrows from Liszt regarding the questions of Chopin's predilection for piano compositions (88–89), his preference for performing in the salon rather than the concert hall (99), allusions to the novel *Lucrezia Floriani* (136–37), and the characterization of Chopin's personality (148).

Felicyan Faleński's Polish translation of Liszt's book was published in Warsaw in 1873, and in the same year the first reviews appeared. The opinions about the book reflect two aesthetic trends, or modes of thought, in the nineteenth century. One—the Romantic trend—was manifested in the uncritical, completely admiring attitude toward Liszt's text, replete with praise for the amazing friendship between the two great artists. In this manner the unknown author of a review in *Tygodnik illustrowany*, pleased that one can now place Liszt's oeuvre beside the Polish works of Józef Sikorski, Maurycy Karasowski, and Jan Kleczyński (Szulc's monograph is not mentioned) writes:

> This is neither a dry biography of Chopin nor an erudite discourse on his works, but rather a living recollection about a friend by a friend, full of honest affection, warmed by sincerity, and richly adorned by blossoms of poetry. The language is luscious, which is typical of Mr. Faleński's prose. . . . Beautiful publication.[26]

Another unknown writer in *Kronika rodzinna* compares the two artists to unearthly beings:

> Two gods standing on their suns stand in front of their reader as the judge and the judged, the admired and the admiring. One of them was proud to have been born in Warsaw and to have made

the goal of his life the advancement of Polish folk rhythm to an ideal; the other—who recently, on the fiftieth anniversary of his professional career, was inundated with signs of adoration—with pride acknowledges the friendship and guidance of the first one and equals him in his kindness for his native land. In Liszt's book, breathing the aroma of poetry and love, there is a lot of spiritual pleasure, but also much edification for the reader.[27]

The second—positivist—trend is represented by the 1874 review in *Bluszcz*, written by one of the most important critics of the time, Jan Kleczyński (see the discussion of Kleczyński's other writings on Chopin in the essays in this volume by Zofia Chechlińska (essay 10) and Maja Trochimczyk (essay 12).[28] Kleczyński exposes Liszt's factual errors and the translator's sloppiness. At first he raises the matter of the support for Chopin's education allegedly provided by Prince Radziwiłł, a story repeated without any corroboration by other writers after Liszt. "Liszt quotes this fact with so much self-confidence that he even puts in charge of the funds one Antoni Kożuchowski," writes Kleczyński, when, in truth, this fact "is entirely false."[29] He also accuses Liszt of unnecessarily elaborating the scene of Chopin's death. It is not true that Chopin fainted when Delfina Potocka was singing: Chopin had asked Delfina to sing because he wanted his sister, Ludwika, to hear her voice. It is equally untrue that Chopin kissed Gutman's hand before dying. "In daring to correct these details," adds Kleczyński, "I believe that I do not destroy the charm that pleasingly adorns our new *wieszcz*, but does one need to invent poetry where the truth is beautiful enough?" Kleczyński also discusses the question of Chopin's birth date. He accepts 1810 but demands that the precise date of 1 March 1810 must be given, as specified by the family. He criticizes Fétis for giving the date as 2 March 1809.

Many of Kleczyński's corrections pertain to the translation. For instance, Faleński translates "*indubitables*" as "doubtful" instead of "doubtless" (44); writes "emissaries" instead of "poets" (which in Polish could constitute a typographical error); changes the phrase "*il jouait de longues heures chez lui*" to "relentless playing at night," although night is not mentioned in the text; and, on page 37, "the author [translator] adds, from his own inspiration, a comment about a section from Mickiewicz's *Forefathers' Eve*, which does not exist in the original."

Kleczyński points out another statement in Liszt's book, perhaps the most important one, regarding the substance of Chopin's music as Chopin himself defined it. On pages 66–68 Liszt relates how one time, in Chopin's salon, in Liszt's presence, a certain lady ventured to ask Chopin why his music

> forces itself into one's heart? Why in its happiest (!) sections it is languishing and yearning? In a word, in her profane courage, she wished to penetrate to the core of the enigmatic essence of his genius; demanded that he expose himself completely. Chopin, who never liked to reveal himself, was in a particular mood that day, and, feeling that he was in the company of kindred spirits, he wanted to share his confession. He said then that in his opinion the secret key to his spirit is the word *żal* [sorrow, longing, regret] unsuitable for translation. He repeated the word several times as if he wanted to be satiated, permeated by its sound. Indeed, having read this fascinating fragment, where Liszt succeeded in capturing such an uncommon moment of the genius's confession, we also must admire the aptness of Chopin's view of himself, and how fitting the word was, which, being a pure linguistic root, contains many varied shadings and, through its meaning, exposes diverse landscapes. Therefore I believe that it is the translator's gravest error to have used the word *żałość*, which, being one of the forms derived from the root *żal*, does not have so many meanings, and could not be used by Chopin as the key to his spiritual treasure.

Kleczyński's point is crucial. Chopin's purported confession, disseminated through Liszt, remains a recurrent component in descriptions of the expressive character of his music. The word *żal* appears in many monographs on Chopin and, to this day, is very much alive in French writings on Chopin's music.

The translation of Liszt's book had further repercussions in Polish studies of Chopin. Maurycy Karasowski referred to it in a very direct manner in his book, *Fryderyk Chopin: Życie-listy-dzieła* (published in Polish in 1882, and in German five years earlier). Karasowski also scolded Liszt for Prince Radziwiłł's alleged financing of Chopin and his characterization of Chopin as a youth.[30] According to Karasowski, Chopin was not a faint young man with "a sad countenance of a woman," but was full of life and joy, though he was of slight physique. However, he used the stories about Chopin parodying Liszt, about Liszt substituting for the missing pedals in Chopin's piano, and how Chopin did not like to respond to invitations.[31] Most extensively he quoted Liszt on the subject of *ad libitum* playing, and in reference to Chopin's preference for piano compositions, which Liszt compared to the unique canvas of the Italian masters, the poetry of Béranger, or the sonnets of Petrarca.[32] Following the publication of Karasowski's work in Germany, the celebrated writer, poet, and critic Józef Ignacy Kraszewski commented on what he learned about Liszt's accuracy:

> Even Liszt, who based his brochure on a personal acquaintance with Chopin and gathered accounts of him, composed his brochure *con brio*, like a fantasy for the piano: he knew nothing of the life and the past of the artist. Indeed, a more suited title for the brochure would be *Fantaisie brillante*, as they were called in the times of Herz and Czerny.[33]

Another author, Aleksander Arct, based his pocket format book on Karasowski and Liszt.[34] In it, all the quotations from Liszt are scrupulously marked. The following fragment illustrates the manner in which Arct parodies Liszt's views on Chopin's cyclic forms—the sonatas and the concerti. He prefaces Liszt by saying:

> When entering the domain of Classicism, which required stricter forms, his thought would lose its typical freedom of inspiration; the fantasy, exploding with verve, would wrestle with the restrictive bonds of form. For this reason the sonatas, though they have an important place among his works, do not present us with a complete and exact impression of his creative talent.[35]

And he quotes Liszt further regarding the claim that Chopin found it difficult to contain these frail, irresolute ideas within the rigid, inflexible restrictions: "he was not able to force into them his liquefied, hazy indeterminacy, which, diluting the most characteristic outlines of forms, envelops them as if with a gust of air."[36] He admits, however, that an uncommon dignity characterizes the style of Chopin's sonatas and that some fragments are amazing in their "solemnity." Arct's book testifies to the influence Liszt's study had on Polish studies of Chopin, particularly in reference to his oeuvre. Only later in the twentieth century, through musicological research and analysis, have these opinions about Chopin's cyclic forms (also his ballads, Polonaise-Fantasy, et al.) changed.

When Breitkopf & Härtel in Leipzig planned a new enlarged edition of Liszt's book, Liszt wrote to Princess Wittgenstein (1 January 1876) that in 1849 he did not understand the intimate beauty of Chopin's last works, but now he appreciates their noble inspiration and artistic proportions.[37] But this had no noticeable effect on Liszt's new presentation of Chopin's oeuvre. In the *Kurier poznański*, the reviewer (possibly Stanisław Egbert Koźmian, discussed above) wrote:

> The new, very splendid edition of Liszt's biography of Chopin just came out. It is a peculiar book: the glittering and pompous style, the audacious language—he constantly creates new words—the abundance of superlatives and excess of fantasy, straying from the subject to ever new pastures of the flippant imagination. Sometimes it is difficult to find the scattered details about Chopin's life and character in this deluge of words. His description of [Chopin's] death is in accord with the letter of Father Jełowiecki, who, with such Christian simplicity, depicted the last moments of the immortal artist. Liszt's new edition contains many particulars that were absent earlier. He devoted, for instance, a much longer passage to Countess Delfina Potocka, who, with her enchanted singing, eased Chopin's last agony.[38]

Beyond that, the Polish press barely announced the edition. A review in *Echo muzyczne, teatralne i artystyczne* gave the following summary:

> There are no important . . . facts in the new edition, just a few remarks and not on every subject (for instance, the report that Chopin was educated at Prince Radziwiłł's expense—so disagreeable for the family, and essentially false—remained in this edition). It is understandable, though, that the book is full of poetry and enthusiasm, and makes for a captivating reading.[39]

The above examination of nineteenth-century sources demonstrates that there were two sides to the nineteenth-century reception of Franz Liszt's book, *Frédéric Chopin*, and its Polish translation. The official course of this reception, found in commentaries and reviews, is dominated by a tone of admiration for this work and for the friendship between Liszt and Chopin, in spite of small criticisms regarding Liszt's accuracy. This mood is captured in Szulc's statement: "The closeness between Liszt and Chopin recalls the ideal friendship of which we do not have many instances."[40] The other, far less enthusiastic facet of the reception is private, hidden in correspondence and the attitudes of Chopin's family—

only the publication of letters and later research allowed at least partial access to it.

How did the reception of Liszt's study of Chopin change in the next century? The reactions to the new translation of Liszt's book (1924) seem to be a continuation of the attitudes of the previous century.[41] The musicologist, Adolf Chybiński, who wrote the preface to the new edition, believed that this translation was important and necessary because

> Liszt's study of Chopin and Wagner's of Beethoven are the most classical examples of literature . . . having pluses and minuses, but always interesting as an artistic-literary (not scholarly) interpretation of the spiritual aspect of the masters' oeuvre, and as psychological testimonials for the authors, who were also and foremost great composers and virtuosos.[42]

Chybiński praised Liszt's language for its literary imagination, "charming phraseology," which "directly influences the lay reader though its dramatic or emotional color and dynamics." He also noted the insightfulness of Liszt's judgments about the national character of Chopin's music. This was a trait not easily understood by foreigners, including Liszt, which is why—according to Chybiński—he was forced to use depictive presentations for certain elements of the national style.[43] Overall, Chybiński characterized the book as "Dichtung und Wahrheit" (poetry and truth). It is difficult to comprehend, however, on what grounds Chybiński based his opinion regarding the relationship between Chopin and Liszt. He writes that Liszt, in his study of Chopin, "provided proof and a monument to his adoration and friendship for the great artist, although he well knew that complete reciprocity and friendship on Chopin's part would never have been possible."[44] The contacts between Liszt and Chopin require further investigation, but it appears that Chybiński's conclusion resulted from his conviction about Chopin's greatness and his introverted, nostalgic nature, rather than on any factual knowledge. After all, in the beginning, the friendship between them was undisturbed, and it was only later that Chopin developed resentment toward Liszt. Moreover, Chopin had maintained deep ties with other foreign musicians and composers, for instance, Auguste Franchomme.

The review of the same edition of the book by the famous writer and columnist Jarosław Iwaszkiewicz[45] contained the important idea that Chopin's contemporaries did not understand him.

Not only Liszt but other critics and musicians in the second half of the nineteenth century believed that Chopin did not comprehend the rules of large forms, specifically that his sonatas lacked internal cohesion and that the Polonaise-Fantasy and other forms were incomprehensible. Iwaszkiewicz thought that Chopin's departures from an accepted formal ideal could only be understood by succeeding generations, that "only time can reveal the complete beauty and achievement of these new inspirations in their new garments."[46] Iwaszkiewicz was most astonished, however, by Liszt's account of the artistic aura that surrounded the Polish Romantics. What we find irritating in Liszt's exalted descriptions of Polish customs and dances thrilled Iwaszkiewicz. Whereas we regard Liszt's poetic exaggeration with skepticism, Iwaszkiewicz was entertained by the images of the Romantic atmosphere of life, yet under the surface he perceived the depth of emotion that the reticent Chopin experienced. Although at first he characterizes Liszt's text as outdated, he finds it full of meanings. In his rich, evocative language, Iwaszkiewicz thus represents Liszt's vision of Poland as seen through the prism of the Ukrainian home of Princess Karolina (Liszt's companion, Carolyne von Sayn-Wittgenstein) in Woronince:

> The unrivaled pages containing descriptions of Poland—Poland as it was imagined in the West, as Liszt himself saw it from the Woronince salons of Princess Karolina, and possibly as Balzac saw it in Wierzchownia [the Ukrainian residence of Balzac's great love, Countess Hańska]. These scattered anecdotes, the references to diverse people, to diverse Polish homes—especially to Polish women, for whom Liszt's enthusiasm glows with the most fervent flame—constitute priceless contributions, brilliantly illuminating the surface of the Romantic life: the surface that this life wanted to bestow on posterity, that was sketched in letters, memoirs, recollections. . . . There is something in this book from the atmosphere of Woronince, where for months the enamored Liszt collected the frail Ukrainian grain heads for the parvenu princess, born in the modest Braniłów residence; from where he traveled by the discerningly matched four- or six-horse, *bałaguły*-style [traditional, colorful, eastern Polish] hitch to the Berdyczów market; where he got drunk in a company (what company!) and danced the mazur—at which time, judging from the description of the mazur in his book, the good pianist must have seen double.
>
> When one recognizes how full of convention is Liszt's fervent and passionate writing . . . , when one considers that, be-

tween the lines of a book on Chopin, Liszt rambles on about himself—all the more tragic is the expression of Chopin's eternal silence, his aversion for the slightest confession, the slightest divulgence of his inner self. We are touched by what Liszt tells us: how frequently Chopin escaped into the company of children and women, "as less demanding"—and, his heartfelt relationships notwithstanding, he always remained a stranger in the artistic circles of Paris. Until the end of his life he would show the note in his passport with a smile: "in transit through Paris."[47]

We have, however, a diametrically opposed review of the 1824 translation that Bronisława Wójcik-Keuprulian wrote. In her review she concentrated exclusively on the quality of the translation, claiming that if the edition is to fulfill its mission, it must be fundamentally correct.First she explained that it was not a translation of Liszt's original but a direct translation from the 1880 German text by La Mara (Marie Lipsius), who freely paraphrased Liszt's study, cutting, adding, transposing individual segments, and so on. The title page did not indicate the source, nor was it mentioned in Chybiński's introduction. Marja Pomian, the Polish translator, consulted the French original in some places, which Wójcik-Keuprulian considered the reverse of what she should have done: she should have used the French original as a basis of her translation, and referred to the German source only to verify incomprehensible expressions. One may not, according to Wójcik-Keuprulian, arbitrarily disseminate false biographical details, which the translator left without commentary, only noting that Liszt includes "details that no one should have trouble correcting." Among the vast number of factual, grammatical, stylistic, and other errors—which suggest, in the reviewer's opinion, an acute lack of familiarity with Chopin's works as well as a lack of general philological and humanistic competence—most disturbing are the blatant errors pertaining to purely musical matters. Wójcik-Keuprulian provides a long list of these and other errors to show that the translation is worthless, the printing sloppy, and the paper cheap—all of which leave a dismal impression.[48]

These two attitudes—a painstaking, academic scrutiny of the translation (Wójcik-Keuprulian) and a purely aesthetic reception of Liszt's study (Iwaszkiewicz)—complement each other, but they do not constitute a cohesive bridge between literary criticism and scholarly analysis.

After World War II a new translation of Liszt's work was completed. Naturally the translator did not return to La Mara's version but turned to Liszt's 1852 original. The book was published in 1961 (on the sesquicentennial of Chopin's birth); it was translated by Maria Traczewska and edited by Jerzy Popiel, and it included brief commentaries about Liszt's erroneous biographical information. Although Jadwiga Podolska (the daughter of Hoesick, the author of the first monumental monograph devoted to Chopin) wrote in a review of this new edition that the book is "poetic, of yesteryear, exactly what a book about Chopin should be," the criteria of evaluation have completely changed.[49] Liszt's study has acquired historical value: it has become *signum temporis*, a document of a Romantic emotional response to the art of a great artist by another creator: a kind of musical reception.[50] Perhaps this is why we are interested in, even astounded by, this book, but the requirements of the modern writing style and the contemporary response to art are different than they were in the time of Liszt and Chopin.

NOTES

1. This essay intentionally sidesteps the complex question of the extent to which Liszt's companion, Princess Carolyne von Sayn-Wittgenstein, was involved with this book. Elsewhere a vast body of scholarship attempts to disentangle the existing evidence; see Emile Haraszti, "Franz Liszt: Author Despite Himself," *Musical Quarterly* 33 (1947): 490–516; Maria Eckhardt, "New Documents on Liszt as Author," *New Hungarian Quarterly* 95 (1984): 181–94; Alan Walker, "The Scribe of Weimar," in *Franz Liszt: The Weimar Years* (New York: Knopf, 1989), 368–96; and Charles Suttoni, "Liszt the Writer," in *Liszt and the Arts: A Collection of Papers Presented at a Liszt Centennial Celebration Sponsored by the Heyman Center for the Humanities, Columbia University* (New York: The Center, 1996), 64–73.

2. However, several biographical notes and larger articles appeared in Polish periodicals during his lifetime and shortly after his death.

3. "Wybór listów Juliana Fontany do Stanisława Egberta Koźmiana z lat 1844–1868," edited from manuscripts by Józef Fijałek, in *Rocznik Biblioteki Polskiej Akademii Nauk w Krakowie* 3 (1957): 187–268.

4. Ibid., 222.

5. Ibid., 223.

6. Ibid., 225.

7. Ferdinand Hoesick, *Chopin, życie i twórczość* (Warszawa: Hoesick, 1911).

8. Adolf Chybiński, "Chopiniana," *Museion*, no. 4 (1912): 116–17.

9. Hanna Wrólewska-Straus, "Listy Jane Wilhelmine Stirling do Ludwiki Jędrzejewiczowej," *Rocznik chopinowski* 12 (1980): 140.

10. I have partially addressed the relationship between Chopin and Liszt in the essay "Chopin-Liszt: Uwagi o środkach wirtuozowskich i wzajemnych rela-

cjach obu arystów," in *Historia i interpretacja muzyki. Z badań nad muzyką od XVII do XIX wieku*, 2nd ed. (Kraków: Musica Iagellonica, 1995), 117–44.

11. Gastone Belotti, "Okoliczności powstania pierwszej monografii o Chopinie," *Rocznik chopinowski* 7 (1965–68): 43 n. 57.

12. Wróblewska-Straus, "Listy Jane Wilhelmine Stirling," 149.

13. Ibid., 160.

14. Mieczysław Karłowicz, *Nie wydane dotąd pamiątki po Chopinie* (Warszawa: Fiszer, 1904), 351–67.

15. Marceli Antoni Szulc, *Fryderyk Chopin i utwory jego muzyczne: Przyczynek do życiorysu i oceny kompozycji artysty* (Poznań: Żupański, 1873; new ed., Kraków: Polskie Wydawnictwo Muzyczne, 1986), 278.

16. Julian Fontana, foreword to the *Posthumous Edition of Chopin's Works* (Paris: Schlesinger, 1855–59); Jan Kleczyński, "Ruch muzyczny" section, *Bluszcz*, no. 2 (1874): 14–15; Maurycy Karasowski, *Fryderyk Chopin. Życie-Listy-Dzieło* (Warszawa: Gebethner i Wolff, 1882), 62–63. Also, in an earlier German edition, *Friedrich Chopin, sein Leben, seine Werke und Briefe* (Dresden: Ries, 1877).

17. Belotti, "Okoliczności powstania pierwszej monografii o Chopinie," 9.

18. Ibid., 29.

19. *Ruch muzyczny*, no. 40 (1858): 317.

20. Ibid., no. 19 (1859): 164.

21. Ibid., no. 24 (1859): 205.

22. "Słów kilka o Szopenie," *Księga świata*, no. 2 (1858): 69–76.

23. The parallels between the article in *Księga świata* and Liszt's book are the following: (1) the defense of Chopin's choice to devote himself to piano music, staying away from symphonies, oratorios, or operas; (2) the praise for Chopin's harmonic language and the "ideal beauty" in Chopin's compositions; (3) the negative assessment of classical forms, such as Chopin's concertos and sonatas (here he directly quotes Liszt's expression that "there is more will than inspiration" in the concertos); (4) the variety of expression in Chopin's works but with a tone of *żal* [longing] present; (5) the characterization of the mazurkas and the polonaises; (6) the description of Chopin's spiritual traits (sense of honor, personal charm, sense of humor); (7) the description of a soiree at the Chaussée d'Antin salon of Chopin, when he improvised in the presence of musicians and poets; and (8) the depiction of Chopin's last moments.

24. Szulc began work on this book in 1869, intending to complete it in time for the anniversary of Chopin's death. It was not finished, however, until 1872, at which time he offered it to three publishers: B&B in Berlin, Żupański in Poznań, and Leitgeber in Poznań. Ultimately Żupański bought the rights for five years, and the book appeared in 1873, denounced by the Prussian censor for emphasizing Chopin's Polishness and the national qualities of his music. The editor demanded changes, but the author did not yield, even five years later when Żupański again sent the book to be censored.

25. See Szulc, *Fryderyk Szopen i utwory jego muzyczne*, 26–27.

26. *Tygodnik illustrowany*, no. 313 (1873), "Nowości wydawnicze" section, 322–23.

27. *Kronika rodzinna*, no. 24 (1873), "Silva rerum" section, 389.

28. Jan Kleczyński (1837–1895) was one of the most important Polish writers on music of the second half of the nineteenth century (he wrote some seventeen hundred reviews), as well as a pianist, a teacher, and a composer. A number of his writings were devoted to Chopin and his music, including discussions of interpretation and the earliest writings about his teaching methods. Kleczyński also edited a twelve-volume edition of Chopin's works (Warszawa, 1882).

29. Kleczyński, "Ruch muzyczny" section, 14–15.

30. Karasowski, *Fryderyk Chopin*, 1:62–63, and 1:125–26, respectively.

31. Ibid., 2:150–51, and 2:213, respectively.

32. Ibid., 2:224–25, and 2:230–31, respectively.

33. Józef Ignacy Kraszewski, *Bluszcz*, no. 12 (1877): 89–90.

34. Aleks[ander] A[rct], ed., *Fryderyk Chopin. Jego życie i dzieła podług Karasowskiego, Liszta i innych* (Warszawa: A. Arct, 1901).

35. Ibid., 47–48.

36. Ibid.

37. A larger excerpt of the letter is cited in Poniatowska, "Chopin-Liszt," 123 n. 5.

38. [Stanisław Egbert Koźmian and Konstancja Morawska], *I z bliska i z daleka. Poczet stu felietonów umieszczonych w "Kurierze poznańskim" od października 1878 do września 1880, w skróceniu* (Poznań: Żupański, 1881), 41.

39. "Najnowsze biografie Chopina," *Echo muzyczne, teatralne i artystyczne*, no. 1 (1881): 6. The persistent error regarding Prince Radziwiłł's alleged support of Chopin is maintained to this day. Irena and Maria Poniatowska, the authors of the introduction to the new edition of Liszt's original, 1852 text (Paris: Liana Levi, 1990), commented on the inaccurate biographical data. However, the editor removed the correction pertaining to the prince's alleged assistance.

40. Szulc, *Fryderyk Szopen i utwory jego muzyczne*, 94. Karasowski is more critical and stresses that for some unknown reason the two artists parted ways (*Fryderyk Chopin*, 2:156).

41. Translated by Marja Pomian, from La Mara's German version (Lwów: Altenberg, 1924).

42. Ibid., 3–4.

43. Ibid., 4–5.

44. Ibid., 5.

45. Jarosław Iwaszkiewicz (1894–1980), a towering figure in Polish twentieth-century culture, was a poet, writer, dramatist, translator, and essayist. He had particularly strong connections with music, having studied the piano at the Kiev Conservatory and having tried his hand at composition. Karol Szymanowski (who was his distant relative) and several other prominent composers of the Young Poland movement used his librettos and poems in dramatic works and songs. Music inspired his own literary works through themes and formal structures modeled after musical forms and genres. He also wrote three studies about Szymanowski (*Spotkania z Szymanowskim*, 1947; *Karol Szymanowski a literatura*, 1963; and *Harnasie Karola Szymanowskiego*, 1964), a play (*Lato w Nohaut [A Summer in Nohaut]*), as well as monographs devoted to Bach (1951) and Chopin (1938; new ed., 1976).

46. Jarosław Iwaszkiewicz, "Liszt o Chopinie," *Wiadomości literackie*, no. 23 (1924): 4.

47. Ibid.

48. Bronisława Wójcik-Keuprulian, "Przekłady z literatury muzycznej—Franciszek Liszt Chopin. tłumaczyła Marja Pomian. Z przedmową Prof. Dr. Chybińskiego. Lwów, 1924. Ksiegarnia H. Altenberga . . . ," *Przegląd warszawski*, no. 37 (1924): 107–8.

49. Jadwiga Podolska, "Liszt a Chopin," *Poradnik muzyczny*, no. 12 (1961): 4–6.

50. I write more on this subject in "Frühe Monographien über F. Chopins Werk. Ein Beitrag zur Rezeption der Musik im 19. Jahrhundert," *Chopin Studies* 4 (1994): 93–108.

# 12

## Chopin and the "Polish Race": On National Ideologies and the Chopin Reception

MAJA TROCHIMCZYK

### Introduction

In a monumental study of Chopin's life, work, and reception, Mieczysław Tomaszewski describes the issues of patriotism and national spirit as predominating in the Polish interpretations of Chopin's music throughout the nineteenth century.[1] A similar conclusion ends Zofia Chechlińska's essay on the topic of the Polish reception of Chopin.[2] Indeed, the focus of Chopin's followers and devotees in the nineteenth and early twentieth centuries rested on his usefulness for their causes, not on a full understanding of his musical achievements. Thus Fryderyk Chopin held an elevated position in the national pantheon as a poet-prophet [*wieszcz*] whose musical statements equaled in significance the poetic proclamations of Adam Mickiewicz, expressing the true spirit of the nation.[3] Jan Kleczyński (1837–1895), Zygmunt Noskowski (1846–1909), Władysław Żeleński (1837–1921), Stanisław Przybyszewski (1868–1927), Jarosław Zieliński (1847–1922), Ignacy Jan Paderewski (1860–1941), Stanisław Niewiadomski (1859–1936), and Karol Szymanowski (1882–1937) were preoccupied with demonstrating the ways that identified Chopin and his oeuvre as truly and fully Polish.[4] Their essays contributed to a Polish tradition of constructing Chopin's identity, a tradition that evolved through distinct stages of Polonizing the composer, based on shifting definitions of the essence of nationality.[5]

In this essay I trace the evolution of nationalist views of Chopin's musical and personal Polishness, views of an increasingly all-embracing nature, connected to the Romantic idea of the "Polish spirit" (primarily expressed in Chopin's music) and to the notion of the "Polish race" (exemplified by Chopin himself). The conceptual background for this evolution is provided by ideas put forward by such European writers on nationhood and the arts as the German Romantic philosopher and critic Johann Gottfried Herder (1744–1803), whose well-known idea of the "spirit of the people," the *Volksgeist*, influenced the texts of Kleczyński, Noskowski, and Żeleński; and the French philosopher and historian of social-Darwinist orientation Hippolyte Taine (1828–1893), whose theories of artistic expressions of the nation-race had an impact on the writings of Przybyszewski, Niewiadomski, Zieliński, Paderewski, and Szymanowski. The gradual replacement of the older German notion of the "national spirit" (Herder) with the more modern notion of the "national race and milieu" (Taine) is evident in the argumentation used in texts about Chopin's place in Polish musical culture until the outbreak of World War II.

## Defining National Traits

In the process of depicting Chopin as Poland's paradigmatic national composer, his followers expressed their beliefs about national messages that Chopin supposedly conveyed in his music. Initially their definitions of national identity, inspired by Herder's notion of the *Volksgeist*, envisioned it as a spiritual phenomenon, centered on the experiences and productions of the *Volk* [folk], that is, the inhabitants of the countryside enjoying spontaneously creative lives in a close connection to nature, the pristine and enchanting fields and meadows of Poland. In this interpretative tradition, Chopin's music was not valued in and of itself; instead, the quality of his music was measured in terms of its closeness to the Polish folk song and to the Polish landscape. The writings about Chopin, however, feature a wider variety of arguments while explaining the

Table 12.1. Selected Criteria for Defining the Polish Identity of Composers

*A. Biographic Criteria (personal identity, background, and choices, defined by self and others)*

1. "name"—Polish forms of the first and last name
2. "family-of-origin"—Polish family background, typically patrilineal and at times connected to the notion of the "Polish race"
3. "psychosomatic identity"—being the embodiment of Polish traits in the whole person, body and spirit (given, not self-defined)
4. "emotional and patriotic identity"—having a "Polish heart" and displaying a deep attachment to Poland (chosen, self-defined)
5. "official identity"—with a Polish national identity and citizenship
6. "native language"—using Polish as the native language
7. "community"—engaged in the Polish community, through the place of residence, membership in organizations, and charitable activities for Polish causes

*B. Musical Criteria (traits chosen by the composers or ascribed to their works by others)*

1. "language"—the use of Polish texts and titles in works
2. "genre"—the use of Polish genres, for example, the mazurka or polonaise
3. "quotation"—citing from Polish folk music, national songs, or anthems
4. "style"—the presence of various melodic and rhythmic elements definable as "Polish," especially originating from Polish dances
5. "content"—Polish subjects in explicit (defined by the composer) or implicit forms, the latter "heard" by reviewers; themes borrowed from Poland's history, mythology, literature, religion and customs, climate and geography, and so on
6. "spiritual content"—expressions of the "Polish spirit" in general terms or in the form of a predominant character trait ascribed to the whole nation, such as "sorrow" [*żal*], or "arrhythmia"
7. "music community"—Polish performance and programming contexts, for example, festivals of Polish music, concerts for Polish causes; the music being understood by Poles alone

composer's Polish identity and his significance for Polish culture. It will be informative to briefly review the main criteria, or markers, for ethnic/national identity that recur in Polish writings addressing the national identity of Chopin and other composers, and it might be relevant to our discussion as well (see Table 12.1).

Both categories of this list include issues over which composers have a degree of control by consciously choosing to be Polish and to compose Polish music filled with national traits. Simultaneously the list of biographic criteria includes characteristics that pre-date the composers' birth and pre-define their identity as Poles in ways transcending the intentions of the composers' themselves. Furthermore, the composers' lives and music may be depicted as far more Polish than those originally intended, especially when viewed from a posthumous perspective of "late grandchildren"[6] who have the freedom of interpreting the composers' biographical background and achievements without taking into account their wishes. This openness to fanciful and arbitrary interpretations characterizes particularly the criteria of family-of-origin, psychosomatic identity, and community in the area of biography, and the criteria of style, community, content, and spiritual content in the domain of music.

The essays about Chopin have provided partial and contradictory answers to the following questions: Was Chopin a Polish composer? Was Chopin a purely Polish composer, without a trace of French identity? Was Chopin's music entirely Polish and, if so, why? What Polish traits did Chopin capture and express? What is the definition of being Polish in music? Numerous thematic threads have been intertwined in these texts that could be given the collective subtitle "How Polish Was Chopin?" On the basis of scattered references in Chopin's letters we might note that the composer's self-definition during his years in Paris was as an exiled Pole.[7] Moreover, Chopin seemed to believe that there were emotional and personality traits that were distinctly national, pointing to the essential character differences separating a Slav from a Scandinavian or a Spaniard.[8] Yet Chopin's personal beliefs in this matter were immaterial for the authors of texts about him, texts that straddle the areas of music aesthetics, music biography, and national ideology. These narratives follow a twisted path through the list of criteria: the issue of Polonizing Chopin's name came to the forefront of discussions in the 1930s (though it was initiated at the end of the nineteenth century; see the comments on Niewiadomski's essays), whereas the awareness of the presence of a vaguely defined "Polish spirit" in Chopin's music permeated the literature of this subject from its inception (see my comments about the writings of Przybyszewski, Noskowski, and Paderewski, and Zofia Chechlińska's essay in this collection). Relying on the criteria described above to provide a general framework for conceptualizing the Polishness of Chopin's music, I will follow a roughly chronological trajectory. This approach allows me to highlight the appearance of significant concepts and interpretations, in particular, the charged notion of the "Polish race."

## The Rise and Fall of the "Polish Race"

The tendency to circumscribe the national identity to common genetic origin and shared personality traits and to define art as an expression of such narrowly described features increased in the Western world toward the end of the nineteenth century. Europeans and Americans habitually described spiritual essences of their nations in terms of their shared genetic heritage. Such descriptions permeate the aesthetic writings of Hyppolyte Taine which greatly influenced generations of Polish music critics and historians.[9] The concept of race itself was developed much earlier in Germany (by Johan Blumenbach, 1752–1840) and France (by Joseph Arthur de Gobineau, 1816–1862).[10] From its inception, it served to provide arguments about the supposed inequality of the world's peoples and the superiority of Europeans, or, in particular, the French or the Germans. Different genealogies were compiled for various national races, and their hierarchies reflected the nationalistic and political views of the writers.[11]

The term *Polish race* referred to people of inherited Polish ethnicity, that is, those who were born to Polish parents, who, in turn, were children of Polish parents, and so on. The chain of origin extended back in time indefinitely to the nation's mythical birth from several Slavonic tribes who "dwelt from time immemorial" on the vast plain "between the Baltic sea and the Carpathian mountains."[12] One could be Polish only when sharing the Polish genes; this heritage was thought to engender common psychological and spiritual traits of the Polish nation. These racial definitions of Polishness were found in self-definitions proclaimed in Poland and abroad, as well as in descriptions offered by outsiders.[13] Jakob Riis saw "the thrifty Polish race" (1890) among impoverished emigrants to America; James W. Gerard mused about the great future of "the splendid Polish race" in its own, independent country (1918).[14]

A fascinating genealogy of the "Slavic or Slavonic race" precedes an account of musical achievements of the "Polish race" in a 1902 essay by the émigré composer and pianist Jarosław Zieliński (1847–1922).[15] The Slavic race includes Poles, Czechs, Lithuanians, Ruthenians, Servians, Croatians, Carinthians, Illyrians, and Vends, but it excludes the "Muscovites," who claim to be Great Russians but—according to Zieliński—are in fact a Tartar race. In this narrative the Slavs' history unfolds as a struggle against their neighbors in the south—Byzantine—and in the west—Germanic. The Germans, in addition to frequent military confrontations, crowded Poland as craftsmen, merchants, and teachers, thus having the opportunity to wreak havoc with national identity by prejudicing "their pupils against the Polish language."[16] The theory that Poland had two enemies, Russians and Germans, stemming from the historical fact of Poland's partition by Russia, Prussia, and Austria at the end of the eighteenth century, is given here a racial justification. Similarly to Zieliński, Charles Phillips (1923) rhapsodized about the perennial "racial competition"—based on the principle of the "survival of the fittest"—between the races of the German (i.e., Teuton, who was "steady, powerful, ponderous, self-righteous, self-satisfied, and static") and the Pole ("dynamic, flexible, un-self-satisfied, self-critical, idealistic, and tenacious of his ideal").[17]

The notion of the "Polish race" appeared in various Polish-American writings; for instance, in the amended 1914 Charter of a paramilitary youth association, the Polish Falcons of America, whose main objective was "to regenerate the Polish race in body and spirit and create of the immigrant a National asset, for the purpose of exerting every possible influence towards attaining political independence of the fatherland."[18] While the unabashed patriotism of the Polish Falcons seems praiseworthy, their goal of renewing and unifying the nation through strengthening its youth resembles the objectives of totalitarian organizations in various (actual or imagined) political systems, from Plato's Republic to Nazi Germany. In this context it is important to note that the concept of the "Polish race" met its demise at the outset of World War II, when the hard-won sovereignty of Poland was again under attack from Germany seeking to expand its territories. On 22 August 1939, a week before the invasion of Poland and the beginning of World War II, Hitler addressed his military commanders ordering them "to kill without pity or mercy all men, women, and children of Polish race or language."[19] Therefore the term acquired a genocidal connotation that rendered the notion of the "Polish race" unacceptable, banishing it from respectable nation-building discourse.

Before it disappeared, though, the "Polish race" played an increasingly prominent role in constructing the Polish identity of Chopin and his music. In 1923 Charles Phillips ended his list of positive characteristics of the "dynamic and idealistic" Pole with the statement "Chopin is an example."[20] Let us begin the examination of this topic with a review of national traits associated with Chopin's music.

## The Musical Evocations of Polish History
## and Landscape

The quest for Polish subjects in Chopin's solo piano works (Musical Criterion 5: content) is a recurring topos in nineteenth-century responses to his music. Romantic writers provided fantastic descriptions of historical subjects hidden in purely instrumental compositions. For instance, Marceli Antoni Szulc envisioned the Polonaise op. 53 in A♭ Major as an image of a national procession of hetmans and voivodas, colorfully costumed in the precious garb of Polish seventeenth-century noblemen (see also Kleczyński's interpretation of this piece in Zofia Chechlińska's essay in this volume).[21] Writing in this vein, Stanisław Tarnowski (1837–1871) sought a connection between Chopin's compositions and Polish poetry. Not surprisingly he found a direct patriotic inspiration in numerous pieces, including the Preludes op. 24, many Mazurkas, and the Funeral March from the Sonata in B♭ Minor. Tarnowski saw the latter work as a "funereal conduct of the whole nation watching its own funeral."[22]

A similar patriotic vision is captured on a late nineteenth-century postcard depicting the pianist Ignacy Jan Paderewski—a foremost Chopin interpreter of his time (Figure 12.1). Here a solemn procession of Polish kings and noblemen arises above bluish light emanating from the keyboard; Paderewski's outstretched hands and intensely focused face indicate that these great heroes of the past have been brought to life by his music. This image reveals the role that music played in the cultivation of Polish culture and identity after Poland's loss of sovereignty. The postcard also illustrates a statement from Ignacy Jan Paderewski's famous speech of 1910 that Chopin's compositions truly contain "the spirit of the land of his fathers, the spirit of his nation."[23] Paderewski thus described a ghost-filled scene evoked by Chopin's music: "Finally . . . spectres fulfill their shadowy rights. What ghost was that? Whose spirit there went past? Was this Żółkiewski? Or Czarniecki's noble shade?"[24]

While the Polish character of Polish dance genres, such as mazurkas and polonaises, could not be doubted (Musical Criterion 2: genre), these works themselves have been taken to a second level of Polishness by being read as programmatic representations of the Polish landscape and village scenes (Musical Criterion 5: content).

Figure 12.1. Anonymous postcard. *Paderewski: Improvisation.*
Kraków: Wydawnictwo Salonu Malarzy Polskich, ca. 1900.
Paderewski Memorabilia Collection. Polish Music Center,
University of Southern California, Los Angeles. Used by
permission.

Fifty years after the composer's death, Zygmunt Noskowski took
for granted a thesis that "Chopin's melodies are poetic transformations of the sights that the master absorbed in his youth. . . .
From many a mazurka one can guess the color and light filling a
landscape that the master saw with the eyes of his soul while writing his beautiful poem."[25] Noskowski proceeded to associate particular images with individual mazurkas, impromptus, sonatas, and
ballades. The Impromptu in F♯ Major was assigned the most elaborate program. Noskowski interpreted this work as an extended
"Sunday-in-a-village" scene, replete with "the voices of church
bells calling to the service" over summer fields "covered with newly
ripened wheat, gently swaying under a slight breeze."[26] The com-
mentator concluded: "Nature in its entirety is praying in this moment . . . and the holiday sentiment pervades everything." Thus, in
Noskowski's nationalistic/religious interpretation of Chopin's piano
compositions, a pastoral idyll arises from the music that perfectly
captures the serenity of a people united with their land. The music
is important—and Polish—because it portrays the landscape of Poland and the religious moods associated with it.

The language of description used by Polish composers and music critics in the nineteenth and early twentieth centuries often employs figures of speech equating the folk song with field flowers. The trope that Chopin's folk-inspired music is, as it were, permeated with "the fragrances of delicate flowers of Polish meadows" first appears in Józef Sikorski's article of 1849.[27] Sikorski discussed the national traits of Chopin's music (seen in the use of genre, style, and quotation; Musical Criteria 2–4) and his inspiration from Polish folk songs. For Sikorski, these songs were elevated, charming, and simple, while remaining as fleeting and ineffable as the "fragrance of a violet." This synaesthetic reference articulates a widespread belief that folk music belonged to the utopia of cultivated nature, the idyllic and serene "national garden of Eden."[28] Similarly Cyprian Kamil Norwid (1821–1883), characterized Chopin ("a Varsovian by birth, a Pole by heart, and a citizen of the world by talent") as someone who "knew how to gather field flowers, without shaking off even a slightest drop of dew, or a smallest speck of dust from them."[29]

Norwid's reference to the folk song as "field flowers" articulates the connection between the beauty of the Polish countryside and the music its inhabitants created. The association of Chopin with the lost paradise of the native country recurred in an essay by Józef Ignacy Kraszewski (1812–1887) where Chopin himself (not just his music, but the whole person) became a "phenomenon, as it were, straight from our fields and meadows, those of old, those that blessed our evenings with a marvelous fragrance of the breath of our beloved soil."[30] Zygmunt Noskowski also penned a noteworthy passage equating the folk song with field flowers and describing Chopin as someone who "brought a breeze of fresh air" to the "atmosphere of exotic fragrances" of the Romantic salon.[31] The freshness and originality of Chopin's music stemmed from his closeness to Nature, "his first mistress [whose] brilliance and beauty entranced him and left their traces deep in the soul."[32] To find inspiration in folk music, like painting landscapes outdoors, was to choose the natural over the artificial.[33]

Folk art as nature might be an environmental trope, rather than a national one, but in the Polish context it has strong nationalistic overtones. Through the nineteenth century the Poles comprised a nation without sovereignty over its territory, a nation reduced to the status of an ethnic minority in three different countries. Since they lived under constant threat from the occupying nations and struggled to regain ownership and control of their land (the Prussians being particularly eager to remove Poles from their farms or Germanize them or both), their attachment to the ancestral land was an expression of their patriotism. These difficult circumstances engendered the myth-making process that transformed Chopin into "a singer of Polish fields and meadows," praised by Noskowski for the accuracy and authenticity of his musical landscape depictions.[34] The ecological nationalism of most "flower" references reveals a people's dependency on their Herder-sanctioned connection to the land they inhabit. In this style of nationalistic readings of Chopin's music, both the Polish folk song and Chopin's music based on it have a straightforward link to benevolent and nurturing Nature.

In other nationalistic interpretations, the same music may be seen as a vehicle for conveying the national spirit and expressing the traits of the nation's personality (Musical Criterion 6: spiritual content). Arguments used in this area increasingly take into account Chopin's personal characteristics and heritage (Biographic Criteria 2–4, pertaining to the composer's family of origin, psychosomatic identity, and emotional identity). Thus, through the nineteenth century, nationalistic writers gradually shift their attention from generalized and colorful rhapsodizing about the Polish content of Chopin's music (Musical Criteria 5 and 6) toward statements about his personal relationship to the "Polish race" and its musical manifestations. Let us first examine the varieties of musical expressions of the Polish spirit.

## *Chopin's Music and Traits of the Polish Spirit*

In an essay welcoming the publication of Chopin's posthumous works in 1856, Józef Kenig (1821–1900) lauded Chopin's music for contributing the distinct Polish voice to the "concert of the nations."[35] The composer himself was seen as the founder of the future national school of music and as a musician-poet who may be compared to "an Aeolian harp on which the nation plays, breathing all its sorrows, all its delights; at times [he is] the tool of Providence, suitable for moaning only."[36] The emphasis on sorrowful aspects of the Polish national spirit was politically motivated since it reflected the emotional response to the plight of the nation without a state. Over the course of the century the definitions of the Polish spirit connected to Chopin's music acquired an increasingly negative valence, shifting from the domain of nobility, energy, and spontaneity to the melancholy realms of sorrow, longing, and despair. The pivotal text in this regard was Chopin's biography by Franz Liszt, first published in 1852 (the Polish reception of Liszt's book is discussed in Irena Poniatowska's essay in this volume).[37] Liszt's book—filled with so many factual errors that, according to a comment by Józef Ignacy Kraszewski, its title should be changed to "Fantaisie brillante"—established the trope of *żal* or *żałość* [sorrow] as the principal characteristic permeating Chopin's personality, his music, and Polish identity in general.[38]

Despite the growing acceptance of Liszt's idea, the focus on the sorrowful aspects of Polish national identity was neither obvious nor universal. Kraszewski, for instance, considered the melancholy of Chopin's music as a reflection of his personal painful history, his lost battle with illness, his exile, his homesickness, and his longing. The nostalgia was Chopin's own, and it did not articulate any traits of the national spirit. In fact, according to Kraszewski, it did the opposite: its presence in the mazurkas destroyed the genre's identity by diffusing the national characteristics of a "noble strength and energy."[39] Similar to Kraszewski's view, Jan Kleczyński's definition of the "Polish type" (i.e., the exemplary personality of the nation) included an array of positive features: "warmth, zest, politeness, goodness, boisterousness, compassion, naturalness, generosity, elegance."[40] The writer claimed that these traits permeated Chopin's polonaises and mazurkas, thus connecting the "genre" and "spiritual content" criteria of Polish identity (Musical Criteria 2 and 6). In addition to this range of national features noted in reference to Chopin's works, Kleczyński speculated about the general Slavic traits of Chopin's musical personality, singling out *rzewność* [tenderness] as the main Slavic characteristic.

The melancholy spirit returned in other studies; for instance, Maurycy Karasowski's monograph of 1882 emphasized the saturation of Chopin's music with sorrow and nostalgia, which he described as prime features of Polish Romantic poetry.[41] In 1899 the composer Władysław Żeleński defined this sorrowful quality as *tęskna nuta* [a longing tone] and noticed its paucity among Chopin's predecessors.[42] To him, Chopin was the first to use folklore quotation and stylization (Musical Criteria 3 and 4) as well as find a true Polish character (Musical Criterion 6: spiritual content), because he was neither a foreigner nor a follower of alien inspirations, remaining instead a true, native son of the Polish soil (Biographic Criteria 2–4). Thus the purity of the national expression in Chopin's music is linked to the purity of Chopin's personal identity as a Pole—both inherited and consciously cultivated.

Zygmunt Noskowski concurred with his predecessors's view that Chopin's works revealed a "distinct mood, representative only of our people."[43] Citing Liszt as his inspiration, Noskowski proceeded to identify this national mood as *żal* [sorrow] and pointed out the purposeful and self-defined aspect of the expression of the Polish spirit in Chopin's music. The predominant sorrowful mood of Chopin's pieces—though different from pain, longing, pensiveness, or complaint—was an expression of emotional experiences that the composer cultivated and dwelled on. In this account the feeling of sorrow was a marker of national identity, differentiating true Poles from foreigners. In addition, Noskowski maintained that Chopin personally represented the suffering Polish nation: "his path of life, i.e., his mental and physical suffering, still amplified this sensitivity which necessarily had to be reflected in his works."[44]

Whereas the presence of sorrow, nostalgia, and melancholy in Chopin's music was seen in Poland as a manifestation of its purely Polish character, the same traits were construed abroad as expressions of a more general, human quality. It is interesting to note that these Polish (or Slavic) traits of melancholy and oversensitivity appear as defining features of the most Romantic among the "representative men" whom Hyppolyte Taine described in his *Philosophy of Art*.[45] Taine envisioned the modern man of the nineteenth century as being primarily melancholic and considered melancholy to be the main characteristic of the whole period. The "representative man" of the late nineteenth century was, according to Taine, "the melancholy insatiable Faust or Werther," who "entertains a horror of cheerful music" and who "will enjoy only the music of Chopin and the poetry of Lamartine or Heine."[46] According to Taine's theory, all the arts of a given time embody or portray the main characteristics of their period; sorrow—the emotion of the times—was also the hallmark of the Romantic arts in general.[47] Perhaps for this reason, sorrowful Poland, a nation languishing without sovereignty throughout the century, became such a cause célèbre in Romantic Europe: it was a paradigmatic national example of the main personality feature permeating the whole European culture.

## "Racial" Nationhood and Art according to Taine

Taine's thinking about the representative man of the times seems to diffuse the clarity of arguments presenting melancholy as an exclusively Polish or Slavic trait. In contrast, his ideas about inherited national character, based on the notion of ethnicity-as-race, have shaped the conceptual frameworks of art history and aesthetics.[48] His books were translated into many languages and repeatedly reprinted in Europe and North America during the period from 1870 to 1910; his theories also reached Poland.[49] Taine's philosophy emphasizes the primordial unity of ethnic groups, shaped by their genetic kinship, their natural environment, and their location in historical time. The culture of different nations, for example, ancient Greeks or seventeenth-century Dutchmen, was supposed to be predetermined by their inherent, genetic characteristics, historical milieu, and the climate and geographic features of their countries. The three interrelated sources of identity included racial background, natural environment, and cultural experiences accumulated over the centuries. Inspired by Darwin's theory of evolution, Taine proposed a kind of environmental determinism based on the notion of the essential character of a country, from which "spring an infinity of peculiarities, summing up the entire nature of the country, not only its physical outlines, what it is in itself, but again the intellectual, moral and physical qualities of its inhabitants, and of their works."[50]

For instance, the essential character of the Netherlands was that of "alluvial plains," and the abundance of agricultural produce made available by the rich soil resulted in the affluence of human life that found its most perfect expression in the paintings of Rubens.[51] Similarly ancient Greeks made art that possessed a certain quality because they were all "men of the same race, the same education, the same language . . . a remarkably handsome, intelligent race, viewing life in quite a new way."[52] In addition to these three general characteristics, defining the whole culture of a given nation, Taine discussed the factors that influence an individual artwork that should never be seen in isolation but always in its proper context. These factors formed three aggregates: the artist's own works, the ideas of his colleagues, and the context of the contemporaneous world.[53] This conceptual background surrounds each work of art with a unique aura and predetermines the artistic modes of expression. Simultaneously it needs to be purposefully addressed and presented. The main task of the artist, according to Taine, is to capture and portray the essential character of an object or country. In this activity, however, the artist is constrained by the particular manifestations of the national character. Therefore "the social medium, that is to say, the general state of mind and manners, determines the species of works of art in suffering only those which are in harmony with it, and in suppressing other species, through a series of obstacles interposed, and a series of attacks renewed, at every step of their development."[54]

Taine's speculations about the origins of aesthetic traits of a national art in that nation's racial heritage and geographic-climactic conditions were not questioned by Polish writers who embraced his holistic and simplistic explanations of national identity and extended his ideas into the domain of music. In the first half of the twentieth century Taine's racial terminology, so jarring today, was used without remorse or apology by Ignacy Jan Paderewski, Karol Szymanowski, Stanisław Niewiadomski, Piotr Rytel, and Mieczysław Gliński.[55] Szymanowski's search for "the deepest and most essential aspect of Polish soul, national soul, or the depth of the race" discussed in the closing segment of this chapter indicates an awareness of Taine's ideas of the essential character of a nation, based on inborn "racial" characteristics that distinguish one nation from another. The presence of racial terminology in musical studies from the first half of the twentieth century discussed in the remainder of this article highlights a disquieting connection of music aesthetics to the most extreme form of racial nationalism. While the intentions of Polish composers turning to race in their nationalist project could be described as noble, rather than criminal (as had been Hitler's), the results had harmful ramifications for the definitions of national identity and the acceptance of ethnic minorities within the Polish nation.

## Toward the All-Polish Chopin: Przybyszewski, Zieliński, and Paderewski

In the process of asserting Chopin's Polish identity at the beginning of the twentieth century, an awareness of his double cultural and personal background was replaced by a belief in his fully Polish origins. Two texts about Chopin, written by a fin de siècle writer

known for his charismatic personality, Stanisław Przybyszewski
(1868–1927), enable us to perceive this transformation with the
greatest clarity.

Przybyszewski's first study, *Chopin and Nietzsche* (1892), placed
the composer half-way between Polish and French cultures, emphasizing the presence of both heritages in his personality and musical output.[56] In this text Przybyszewski considered Chopin as an
exemplar of a Nietzschean super-hero and described the composer's personality as "a product of a crossing of two races and two
cultures—Slavic and Gallic."[57] According to Przybyszewski's interpretation of Chopin's psychosomatic and emotional identities (Biographic Criteria 3 and 4), the composer's Slavic features included
a delicacy of feeling, refinement, an inclination to alternate between the extremes of contrasting emotional states, melancholy,
and "a sublimated egotism" that reduces all experiences to a focus
on oneself. Gallic traits in Chopin's personality included certain
light-mindedness, seductiveness, and feminine characteristics, as
well as a joy of life and an emphasis on reason. Already in this text,
however, Przybyszewski gave priority to Chopin's Polish heritage
and claimed that the composer's personality revealed a predomi-
nance of a "Slavic inclination to morbidity."

In order to transform Chopin into an unambiguously national
composer his background had to be rewritten and the Latin element removed. Chopin's music could fully epitomize the Polish
nation if he were completely a part of it in his body and soul. This
transformation took place in Przybyszewski's second essay on the
subject, *Chopin and the Nation* (1910).[58] Here Przybyszewski returned to the theory of one predominant characteristic of the national spirit introduced by Taine and applied to Polish music by
Żeleński and Noskowski (Musical Criterion 6: spiritual content).
This tone, "the most primal unit in the makeup of the soul . . .
colors all the feelings, impressions, experiences, with all his characteristics."[59] In accordance with Taine's thesis about the three defining factors of national identity in art and the significance of
geographic milieu for the structuring of national traits, Przybyszewski maintained that the Polish soul was united with the native
landscape of Mazovia: "broad plains" filled with the "blossoming
rye" and the mournful sounds of "the wind wailing in the bare
steppe."[60] For the writer, the Polish spirit was suffused by "the tone
of insufferable despair" and "filled with curses and mutiny."[61] Since
there are no steppes in the densely populated Mazovia, Przyby-

szewski's description would have been more appropriate for the barren Russian landscape. Similarly the endless despair and darkness of Przybyszewski's typical Pole better suits the stereotypes of the nostalgic Russian soul, not the Polish one.[62] While emphasizing the melancholic morbidity of Chopin's personality (Biographic Criteria 3 and 4: psychosomatic and emotional identities), Przybyszewski describes a dire, soulful landscape that finds perfect expression in Chopin's music (Musical Criteria 5 and 6: content and spiritual content).

The transformation of Chopin into an "all-Polish" composer and a national symbol required the Polonization of his whole family. This step was taken in a legend about Chopin's French forefathers as actually having been Polish, a legend introduced by Oskar Kolberg and reported by Marceli Szulc (1873), Maurycy Karasowski (1882), and Ferdinand Hoesick (1904),[63] as well as Jarosław Zieliński (1902).[64] Zieliński was commissioned by Ignacy Jan Paderewski to write an article, "The Poles in Music," for *The Century Library of Music*, edited by the Polish pianist. The "Chopin" section of Zieliński's study is dedicated in its entirety to proving that Chopin, indeed, was an all-Polish composer (Biographic Criterion 2: family-of-origin). Here, instead of summarizing the nature of Chopin's contribution to Polish music—the topic of entries on all the remaining composers—Zieliński cites a fictitious genealogy provided by Oskar Kolberg and meant to dispel any doubts that Chopin was a real Pole. According to this account, Chopin's French forefathers included the descendants of courtiers of the Polish king Stanisław Leszczyński, who left Poland after a reign of five years (1704–1709) and settled in the duchy of Lorraine, France. Apparently Leszczyński's courtiers included two "natives of Kalisz, Jean Kowalski and Nicholas Szop," who changed their names to "Ferrand and Chopin" and settled at Nancy in Lorraine.[65] Nicholas's son, Jean Jacques, married a widow, Desmarets (or Desmarais), and became a teacher; of their four children the youngest, Nicholas, moved back to Poland to become the father of Frédéric.

The patriarchal framework of this story is fascinating. For Zieliński (as well as Szulc and Karasowski, who cited this narrative before him), the Frenchness of Nicholas Chopin's mother did not matter at all in the patrilineal genealogy proving the composer's indisputable Polishness. To substantiate the claim of Chopin's undiluted Polish blood, it was sufficient to find a Polish male ancestor who had emigrated to France. While ignoring the French heritage of Chopin's grandmother, Zieliński was equally insensitive to the forms of the family's names (Biographic Criterion 1: name). He used French first names for all the members of the family and friends: Jean, Nicholas, Frédéric. Zieliński needed the legend about the Polish ancestry of Chopin's French forefathers to Polonize the composer whose music could then provide the stylistic archetypes of musical Polishness.[66]

In the article Zieliński described a set of musical characteristics that he defined as typically Polish, or "characteristic of the Slavonic type," and these included the common occurrence of "forbidden progressions of intervals, such as augmented seconds, diminished thirds, augmented fourths, diminished sevenths, minor ninths, etc."; harmony with "successions of chords presenting no logical contradiction, and yet at variance with established usage"; melodic features "exactly the reverse of that practised in other lands" and a general trait of "a freedom of form and variety of rhythm exclusively Slavonic and particularly Polish." The rationale for this creative freedom stemmed from personality characteristics; Zieliński claimed that "the temperament of the Slav does not tolerate oppression nor even constraint."[67] It would be impossible to locate a profusion of harmonic means listed by Zieliński in the national operas by Karol Kurpiński, Józef Elsner, or Stanisław Moniuszko.[68] In fact, of the Romantic composers, only Chopin fits the pattern of "freedom of form" and harmony filled with "forbidden progressions"—his unique approach to chromaticism and harmony has often been commented on, for instance, by Ludwik Bronarski and Maciej Gołąb.[69] Thus it appears that Zieliński derived his list of Polish musical characteristics from the oeuvre of one composer who—because of his French family background—was not even fully Polish. The fanciful Polish genealogy of Chopin's family was meant to solve that problem.

A focus on Chopin's whole oeuvre as a repository of the "Polish spirit" and on Chopin himself as an ideal Pole permeates texts by the pianist-composer Ignacy Jan Paderewski (1860–1941), especially his speech on the occasion of the one hundredth anniversary of Chopin's birth, given in 1910 during a festival in Lviv (then known as Lemberg) and published in English translation in 1911 as *Chopin: A Discourse*.[70] The speech articulates the existence of a strong link between the country, the "Polish race," and Chopin's art. Paderewski envisions Chopin's music as a true expression of the Polish spirit (Musical Criterion 6: spiritual content), claiming that in his works one may hear "the voice of every generation, the voice of a whole race, and the voice of the very earth which brought them forth" (13).This statement directly reflects the three criteria of musical identity that Taine provided: race, history, and milieu. Paderewski's text features other, well-known Romantic interpretative tropes, as it associates Chopin's music with the evocations of the heroic, mythical past and the images of Polish nobility (some of these associations have been mentioned earlier). Moreover, Chopin's music is supposedly filled with a pastoral imagery of the Polish fields, forests, and rivers; it depicts a peaceful landscape, sorrowful in the fall, joyous in the spring, a musical countryside that is permeated by the sounds of folk music and nature (Musical Criteria 3–5: quotation, style, content) (18–22). In contrast to Przybyszewski's preoccupation with bleak landscapes as signs of Polish despair and morbidity (and similar to Noskowski's idyllic vision), Paderewski portrays Chopin's works as evocations of Poland's idealized past, replete with festive celebrations and pastoral scenery.

The term *race* in reference to the national identity of common origin recurs frequently throughout the speech, even in the foreword by the translator, Laurence Alma Tadema, who refers to "the spirit of the Polish race." Paderewski talks about the "justifiable and conscious pride of race" and "our stricken race" when calling forth for the renewal of a national spirit and resistance to the denationalization efforts by Poland's enemies (8–9). He then conjures up a vivid image of the embattled white Polish eagle, threatened by black eagles of the Austrian Hapsburgs, the Prussians, and the Russian Romanovs. Thus he stirs the patriotic imagination of his listeners before turning to what should provide them with solace and a sense of identity: Chopin's music. Not only music, though: the national salvation was to come from the whole "radiant spirit" of Chopin, who "by a bloodless fight fought on the plains of peace, assured the victory of Polish thought" (8–9). In arguing for Chopin's significance as a national symbol, Paderewski echoes Taine's ideas of racial determinants of creativity, as he advances a thesis that all art, "in common with all that springs from the depths of the human soul and is the outcome of a union between reason and emotion, bears the inevitable stamp of race, the hall-mark of nationality." Each human generation, in each nation, creates new

forms and works of art that express the preoccupations of that
generation or period. Paderewski believes that in Chopin's music
Poland found its true and timeless voice:

> This music, tender and tempestuous, tranquil and passionate,
> heart-reaching, potent, overwhelming: this music which eludes
> metrical discipline, rejects the fetters of rhythmic rule, and re-
> fuses submission to the metronome as if it were the yoke of some
> hated government: this music bids us hear, know, and realise that
> our nation, our land, the whole of Poland, lives, feels, and moves,
> "in Tempo Rubato." (15–16)

Paderewski's claim about the Polishness of Chopin's music was
supported by detailed claims of a full congruence between the "national spirit" and the stylistic and spiritual properties of Chopin's
music (Musical Criterion 6: spiritual content). He also used an argument based on Musical Criterion 7 (performance context): Chopin's music is all-Polish because his Polish listener understands it
as such, "he understands all, feels all, because it is all his, all Polish"
(17). A Polish listener hears in Chopin's music "the voice of his
whole race," because Chopin himself, "by the grace of God, was
spokesman of the Polish race" (21). Nonetheless, for Paderewski,
"Polish" was not equivalent to "Catholic." In contrast to writers
who wished to inseparably connect the Polish spirit and imagery
of Chopin's music to Catholicism (see Noskowski above), Paderewski referred to a variety of Slavic, pagan deities evoked in Chopin's
works: "the wild frolics of demi-god and goddess" in the Scherzos,
the "deathless song" of the Queen of Love, Dziedzila, and the
thunderous voice of the mighty Perun in fast, dramatic movements.[71]

Similar to Zieliński who struggled to exclude the Russian
"Muscovite" from the Slavic family of nations, Paderewski contrasted the Chopin's Polish spirit ("his grace and charm, his wealth
of colour, of lights and shades") with the "somber and monotonous
although clever Russian muse" which reflected the "withering despair which blows towards us as a blast frost-laden, across steppes
immeasurable, boundless, hopeless."[72] It is interesting to note that,
for Paderewski's contemporary Przybyszewski, such boundless despair and steppes were the hallmarks of Chopin's Polish identity.
In constructing this image, Przybyszewski accepted the negative
German stereotyping of Poles-as-Slavs that Paderewski rejected.[73]

Paderewski's concept of the "Polish race" was not elucidated in any more detail in other texts.[74] Nonetheless, the scope of his ideas of Polish nationhood may be gleaned from his speeches given during a campaign for Poland's independence that he undertook during World War I, touring the United States with Chopin recitals and patriotic appeals.[75] The composer sought to re-create Poland as a great, multinational country, modeled upon the United States and called "The United States of Poland." The homeland that Paderewski wanted to resurrect would guarantee freedoms to all its inhabitants; his conception of Polish statehood was not based on racial exclusivity and hatred.[76] Yet the invocations to the Polish race and the mysterious, timeless national spirit that permeate Paderewski's Chopin lecture were absent from his speeches and appeals directed at non-Polish audiences in America. Thus it seems clear that only those preoccupied with ethnically exclusive definitions of Polish identity could accept the narrowly nationalist rhetoric of Chopin and the "Polish race."

The tone of narratives about Chopin's Polishness changed after the country regained its independence. The emphasis on the all-encompassing expression of sorrow disappeared and so did the focus on the musical evocations of the Polish land. Of prime importance in the new country were the independent spirit, heroism, creativity, and strength of character of its citizens. During the interwar period Stanisław Niewiadomski and Karol Szymanowski provided new interpretations of Chopin's relationship to the "Polish race." The review of their ideas will bring this study to the brink of World War II and the demise of the notion of the "Polish race" that created room for modern concepts of Polish identity and Chopin's relationship to it.

## Portrayals of Szopen and Nationalism in Independent Poland

After Poland was restored as a sovereign country in 1918, arguments drawn to prove the intensity of Chopin's Polishness continued to include the fusion of the psychological makeup of one individual, that is, Chopin himself, and that of a whole nation. Not surprisingly, the emphasis on the physicality of the connections of his music to the land somewhat diminished: the Polish countryside, now within borders of an independent Poland, did not need to be worshiped and idealized. Simultaneously sorrow ceased to remain a central feature after its main cause (i.e., grief over Poland's deprivation of statehood) was removed by the creation of an independent country.

Chopin's purported psychological characteristics became more complex and less unified. Charles Phillips welcomed the creation of *The New Poland* with a peon to the virtues of "the Pole himself . . . a puzzling mixture of human contradictions" best exemplified by the personality of Chopin who was "truly and typically Polish," with the coexistence of "the brilliance, the tragedy, the delicacy, the *tęsknota*" and the virtues of "a power of concentration, a capacity for tireless work, for infinite painstaking, for detail and sustained effort, unsurpassed in the history of any other artist."[77] Similar to Phillips (and his predecessors, Przybyszewski and Paderewski), Stanisław Niewiadomski described Polish character traits as being based on the "opposition of extremes," swinging back and forth between tragedy and optimism.[78] In a 1932 essay dedicated to the subject of "Chopin and Poland," Niewiadomski regarded Chopin's music as the sonorous embodiment of these national contradictions.

In another article ("Spelling Identity: Ch or Sz?") Niewiadomski took pains to argue away any suspicion of Chopin's non-Polishness, starting from the spelling of his name (Biographic Criterion 1: name).[79] Actually his article was a late contribution to a debate about "Szopen" and "Chopin" that erupted in the late nineteenth century. At that time the musical periodicals *Echo muzyczne* and *Kurier codzienny* published several polemical articles about the spelling of Chopin's name.[80] Niewiadomski joined the ranks of those in favor of its Polonization and claimed that foreigners were neither able to understand nor maintain any interest in Chopin's life and music: "For whom do we write and discuss Szopen? Who reads the monographs of Hoesick, Opieński, Jachimecki, and others—foreigners or locals [*swoi*]? This is why we should have preserved the Polish spelling. . . . Szopen's music is something as Polish as one can imagine."[81] While discussing the connection of the composer to his home country, Niewiadomski mentioned and dismissed some of the composer's Parisian friends in order to claim Chopin's whole person as belonging to Poland. Even the second half of his life was connected less to France, the country of his residence, than to Poland: Chopin was bound to his native land "through ties of love, longing, and duty."[82] Niewiadomski's survey of Chopin's abundant links to Poland concluded with a statement that, to the composer, "the past, the present, and the future of

Poland were not only sacred, but simply part of his flesh and blood." Therefore Chopin's compositions bear "profoundly prophetic and national features, in which almost every note repeats: 'Poland, Poland, Poland.' "[83]

Here the nationalistic fervor is unmistakable. It could seem innocuous if we did not examine its political context. Perhaps we might see Niewiadomski's whole-scale Polonization of Chopin in a different light when we learn that the composer-writer's relative, Eligiusz Niewiadomski, a fanatical right-wing painter and writer, murdered the first democratically elected president of Poland, Gabriel Narutowicz (1865–1922).[84] Narutowicz's 1922 election was supported by the votes of ethnic and religious minorities and was strongly opposed by Polish nationalist right-wing parties such as Roman Dmowski's *Endecja* (National Democrats, founded in 1897).[85] The National Democrats wanted to unify the narrowly defined Polish nation by drawing their criteria from personal ethnic heritage, especially by excluding Polish Jews; the Christian Democratic Party added Catholicism to this nationalistic equation. Dmowski's National-Democratic brand of "enlightened and progressive" (though markedly anti-Semitic) nationalism found ample support among the Polish intelligentsia. In this political option, only Catholics and Slavs could be patriotic Poles, and *God Save Poland* should become the national anthem.[86] However, as Norman Davies writes in *God's Playground*, nationalism was not limited to the right-wing National Democrats: "The political stance of the leading circles was unashamedly nationalist. Polishness became the touchstone of respectability. . . . The fires of Polish nationalism were fueled by the fact that the ethnic minorities were so large."[87] Therefore the nationalist fervor was partly based on the fear of Otherness; its expressions in music aesthetics do have a disquieting political dimension.

For right-wing groups, Chopin had to be completely Polonized in order to become a perfect representative of the "Polish race." The thicker the nexus of connections between the composer and his country, its landscape, folklore, people, and their national character, the more exclusive and racially oriented was the definition of Chopin's personal Polishness. At first seen just as a "singer of Polish fields and meadows" (Noskowski), Chopin was later transformed into a paragon of Polish ethnicity. Nationally inspired writers disregarded and marginalized his French heritage in order to claim—as Niewiadomski did in "Chopin and Poland"—that

Poland was enshrined in "Chopin's flesh and blood."[88] Those who wished to present the composer as a nationalist composer understood these terms literally.

Niewiadomski worked as a music critic for the newspaper *Rzeczpospolita*, published by the right-wing Christian Democratic Party [*Stronnictwo Chrześcijańsko-Narodowe*]. Nonetheless, his concern with defining Chopin as a true Pole and his attempts to describe the essence of the national spirit in music were not as radical as the chauvinistic pronouncements of his younger colleague, Piotr Rytel (1884–1970).[89] The latter, in his capacity as a music critic for the right-wing daily published by Dmowski's National Democrats, *Gazeta warszawska*, frequently denounced the harmful effects of Jewish–French–Russian modernism on the future of music, an art that—as he believed—should instead return to its roots in the German heritage. Rytel's musical xenophobia, while excluding Germans and Italians whom he approved of, extended to other musical traditions. His statements about the national spirit in Poland emphasized the need to be independent of foreign influences, especially those of Russian origin: "Polish music should be an expression of the collective Polish soul. Its liberation from the foreign chains will happen automatically, at a moment when the soul of the nation fully develops."[90] Both critics, Niewiadomski and Rytel, were of conservative musical tastes and engaged in vitriolic polemics with the progressive Karol Szymanowski. It might be surprising, therefore, that the strongest statements about Chopin's music and the "Polish race" came from the pen of the latter composer, who himself, as a radical modernist, was a frequent object of the critics' attacks. Conservative critics saw Szymanowski as a supposedly crucial element in the Polish expansion of the "international–Jewish–masonic–conspiracy."[91] In this context it may be regarded as a paradox that Szymanowski himself envisioned Chopin as an exemplar of the pure "Polish race" that he defined in opposition to the corrupt and cosmopolitan musical Jewishness.

## Szymanowski's Chopin and the "Polish Race"

In Karol Szymanowski's texts about music, the terms *rasa* [race] or *rasowy* [racial] appear twenty-eight times—according to the number of entries in the index in Kornel Michałowski's critical edition of Szymanowski's writings.[92] Usually the context is national and includes references to either Chopin or folk music or both. Even the music of Igor Stravinsky is seen through the lenses of race: according to Szymanowski, Stravinsky resembled Chopin in an effort to draw from music "racial features that have been accumulating through the genetic inheritance for generations."[93] In dealing with the Bartókian approach to using folk music as a source of material for modernist compositions, Szymanowski defined folk music as "supra-historical and the most direct expression of the spiritual properties of a race."[94] The composer concluded this essay about relationships between folklore and contemporary music with opinions about the inherent Polishness of all Chopin's music. Here, Szymanowski claims that these "racial" subtleties are "far easier to understand by us, Poles, than by foreigners. This perhaps explains why the Polishness of Chopin is not properly understood even by his greatest enthusiasts abroad."[95] This trope of Poles alone being able to properly understand Polish music (Musical Criterion 7: community belonging) is strongly articulated in the articles about Chopin by Paderewski and Niewiadomski.

In Szymanowski's first article published after his return to Poland in 1919, "Remarks Concerning the Contemporary Musical Opinion in Poland," Chopin becomes an essential Polish composer who created "great, Polish, national music" permeated with expressions of the "soul of the nation [*lud*], in its fathomless racial depth."[96] During World War I Szymanowski rejected his earlier lack of interest in national issues and musical patriotism; he started composing songs for the Polish troops and thinking about expressions of Polish identity in music. The turn to the figure of Fryderyk Chopin as a model was a natural choice.[97] In the important and often reprinted essay on Fryderyk Chopin (written in 1922 and first published in 1923) Szymanowski discusses the Polishness of Chopin as transcending the choice of the forms of the polonaise and mazurka or the representation of national events and personages: "As a Pole he did not aim to reflect the tragic events in the history of his nation but, instinctively, sought to express the supra-historical essence of his race which lies beyond national history."[98] In another Chopin-themed article of 1924, "Fryderyka Chopina mit o duszy polskiej" [Chopin's myth about the Polish soul] celebrating the seventy-fifth anniversary of Chopin's death, Szymanowski used even more florid and lofty language to express his views on Chopin's relationship to the Polish identity.[99] The text centers on a thesis that Chopin dealt in his music with "the power and profundity of the Polish Soul" and that his works bear the traits of an "unchangeable Polishness."[100] According to Szymanowski, Chopin found himself at the apex of national identity because "in tranquility and concentration he listened to the mysterious whisper reaching him from the profound and bottomless soul of the nation."[101] In the manuscript the "soul of the nation" was added later to replace the original expression, "the abyss of race" [otchłań rasy].[102] Therefore, for Szymanowski, these terms were synonymous. The replacement of the one by the other in 1924 does not mean that Szymanowski abandoned racial vocabulary in his later essays. The term *race* returns in 1930 in Szymanowski's lecture on Chopin where the composer's Polish identity is described as "joyous, proud, invincible," while his music, based on folk song, is a harmonious "expression of race."[103] Notice the absence of morbid melancholy in this description of uplifting national characteristics. In a 1930 essay, "Fryderyk Chopin and Contemporary Music," Szymanowski claimed that Chopin should serve as an excellent, unsurpassed model for creating the new musical style, a "faithful reflection of racial characteristics and distinguishing traits."[104] Other texts by Szymanowski include references to the "creative genius of our race" [le génie créateur de notre race], that is, the Polish nation (1931),[105] or the "racial properties of a given nation" (1930),[106] or the "racial features of other national groups" that have to be lifted to the highest spiritual level of musical values (1927).[107]

Thus references to racial traits and characteristics abound in Szymanowski's musical texts (including those in German and French) throughout his life; the majority of them appear in the context of defining Chopin as a national composer. A different aspect of the theory of Chopin's racial Polishness emerges from Szymanowski's self-definition as a Polish composer, triggered by a 1922 incident when his name appeared in a review of a new music concert held in New York. In this review, published in the *New York Tribune*, the influential critic Henry E. Krehbiel listed Szymanowski among Polish Jews who—along with Russians—were transforming the image of contemporary music.[108] This reassignment of his identity disturbed the composer, and he wrote a letter to the critic explaining his purely Polish heritage. This mistake, as well as later attacks by Polish radical nationalists of conservative musical tastes (Niewiadomski and Rytel cited above) equating Futurism and Modernism with Jewish influences in music, put Szymanowski on a path toward defining Chopin's Polish identity in terms of the "Polish race." According to Kornel Michałowski, first drafts of his earliest and most extensive text about Chopin were probably written during his stay in New York (two trips in 1921 and 1922).[109] At the same time Szymanowski worked on versions of "The Question of Jewry," which contained disturbingly anti-Semitic ideas.[110] The character of his unfinished essay can be gauged from the first sentence in the notebook: "If the Jews did not so mercilessly hate us, Aryans, and if they did not fill their lives to the brim with this hatred—they would probably die of disgust with themselves."[111] The earlier draft includes further speculations about "Pan-Semitic" and "Pan-Aryan" worlds that are irreconcilably separated and opposed, and a peculiar criticism of Mahler, whom Szymanowski construed as an exemplar of a melancholy, amoral musical Jewishness.[112] Finally, he defended modern music from charges of its close connection to Jewish composers by accusing them of lacking the true creative spirit: "Futurism is a purely Aryan invention. It is a manifestation of an Aryan genius—that always casts itself with courage into yet unexplored domains; [these domains are] later exploited in a more or less honorable fashion by the Semitic talent."[113] The vehemence of anti-Semitic sentiments in this essay is especially startling in the context of Szymanowski's life at the time: his travels to New York were organized and sponsored by his friends, pianist Artur Rubinstein and violinist Paweł Kochański, both Polish Jews. In other writings, diaries, and letters, Szymanowski praised the musical talents of both performers and enjoyed their company, yet he was able to condemn all their compatriots. Obviously, in a twisted manner, emblematic of those who embrace racial ideologies, he differentiated between the despised race and its individual members.

The simultaneous emergence of the incomplete and unpublished text of "The Question of Jewry" and the first in a series of essays on "Fryderyk Chopin" in which the concept of the "Polish race" plays an important role provides a proper—if disturbing—context for Szymanowski's ideas about Polish racial nationality.[114] His attitude toward Jews was both anti-Semitic (general, directed toward the whole race) and philo-Semitic (personal, directed toward eminent individuals). The negativity has been downplayed in scholarly interpretations of his views; for instance, Teresa Chylińska and Zofia Helman pointed out that references to Jews were much milder in Szymanowski's later texts.[115] In the 1930s the composer left his Viennese publisher, Universal Edition; at the same time he started to describe himself jokingly as being supported by "the international Jewish masonry."[116] By doing so he parodied his critics of a right-wing nationalistic orientation who used such arguments to attack this Modernist composer. With the rise of Nazi ideology, Szymanowski moved away from speculations about the "Polish race" and the concept of race-as-nation; in an essay about the future of music he ironically pointed out that even Beethoven was not of a "pure race."[117] Yet the depth of his earlier involvement with this subject should be noted as it reveals the pervasiveness of racial concepts of national identity in interwar Europe.

## Chopin beyond the Polish Spirit and Race

The range of arguments put forward in order to claim Chopin's music for Poland is simply astounding. The definitions based on musical criteria of genre, quotation, style, or content are well known and have been researched by numerous scholars. I gathered the most significant points in an introductory overview in order to reveal the antecedents of the racial concept of Polish identity applied to Chopin's music and person. With a French last name, French father, and a French city of residence for most of his adult life, Chopin's personal identity posed an obstacle for those who assumed that only someone born Polish could be Polish and create music fully expressing the "Polish spirit" or the "supra-historical essence of the race"—to borrow a phrase from Karol Szymanowski. Hence writers of a nationalist orientation engaged in efforts to rename Chopin as Szopen, to reclaim and rewrite his past by adding a Polish Szop to his French ancestors, and to suffuse his whole world and personality with the traits of the "Polish race."

The particular characteristics of the supposedly eternal national spirit changed according to the political and ideological needs of a time: from sorrow and melancholy (in late Romantic texts, e.g., by Noskowski), to *arrhythmia* and spontaneity of a nation that lives in *tempo rubato* (in Paderewski), to the "vitality, joy, and pride" (in Szymanowski). The elements that remained constant in the evolving definitions were Chopin himself and the Polish nation, into whose history he has been so inseparably inscribed. In the process, the concept of the "Polish race" was introduced and rejected. Composers and musicologists stopped discussing aesthetic issues in terms of genetically inherited racial features (Szymanowski) or "the voice of our race" (Paderewski). The cultural insecurity that had required the introduction of a Polish spelling of the composer's name or the affirmations that "the past, the present, and the future of Poland were not only sacred, but simply part of his flesh and blood" (Niewiadomski) was replaced by a fuller awareness of Chopin's lasting and indisputable presence in Polish culture. The nationalist speculations about the nature of the Polish spirit and Chopin's embodiment and expression of it have been abandoned for the sake of comprehensive historical and aesthetic studies of his involvement in, and influence on, Polish music.

The twin notions of the "Polish spirit" rooted in Herder's *Volksgeist*, and the "Polish race" shaped under the influence of Taine's philosophy belong among categories of nationalist discourse that have outlived their usefulness. I, like the philosopher of culture Julia Kristeva, "am among those who dread and reject the notion of *Volksgeist*, 'spirit of the people,' which stems from a line of thinkers that includes Herder and Hegel" and that results in the emergence of a repressive and exclusive nationalism ("a repressive force aimed at other peoples and extolling one's own")[118]—the source of murderous ethnic conflicts in the late twentieth century. Kristeva's misgivings about *Volksgeist*-nationalism provide a useful insight for the analysis of attempts to Polonize or nationalize Chopin. The questions of "how Polish was Chopin" and how useful his music could be for defining Polish racial identity stemming from common genetic heritage and national character traits reflect a tainted framework of nineteenth-century racial and nationalistic ideologies. Such issues are best supplanted by the question of "how great was Chopin" as an individual of a unique, complex background and talent.

### NOTES

1. See Mieczysław Tomaszewski, *Chopin: Człowiek, dzieło, rezonans* (Poznań: Podsiedlik, Raniowski i Spółka, 1998), 663.

2. Zofia Chechlińska, "Chopin Reception in Nineteenth-Century Poland," in Jim Samson, ed., *The Cambridge Companion to Chopin* (Cambridge: Cambridge University Press, 1992), 206–21, cited at 221. Also see Chechlińska's essay in this volume.

3. Maria Janion and Maria Żmigrodzka, "Fryderyk Chopin wśród bohaterów egzystencji polskiego romantyzmu," *Rocznik chopinowski* 19 (1987): 33–48. Halina Goldberg discusses this topic at length in her essay in this volume.

4. Szymanowski, Niewiadomski, Noskowski, and Żeleński were compos-

ers; Kleczyński, Paderewski, and Zieliński are most remembered as pianists, and Przybyszewski is a well-known literary figure. English translations of essays by Noskowski, Żeleński, Niewiadomski, and Szymanowski, in Maja Trochimczyk, ed., *After Chopin: Essays in Polish Music* (Los Angeles: Polish Music Center at the University of Southern California, 2000). Some of these essays appeared in Polish in *Kompozytorzy polscy o Chopinie. Antologia*, Mieczysław Tomaszewski, ed. (Kraków: Polskie Wydawnictwo Muzyczne, 1980). Certain issues and the views of some of these writers are discussed in Leszek Polony, *Polski kształt sporu o istotę muzyki* (Kraków: Akademia Muzyczna, 1991). An earlier version of part of the present study constituted the introduction to the *After Chopin* volume.

5. The issue of "constructing" national identity in music has attracted considerable scholarly attention. See Harry White and Michael Murphy, eds., *Musical Constructions of Nationalism: Essays on the History and Ideology of European Musical Culture, 1800–1945* (Cork: Cork University Press, 2001).

6. Cyprian Kamil Norwid's expression from the poem "Fortepian Szopena" (1865). Published with a French translation by Joseph Pérard (Warszawa: TiFC, 1980). French translation, Christophe Jezewski and Francois-Xavier Jaujard, *Le piano de Chopin* (Paris: Editions Richard-Masse, 1983).

7. See Chopin's letters to his friends in Bronisław Sydow, ed., *Korespondencja Fryderyka Chopina*, 2 vols. (Warszawa: Państwowy Instytut Wydawniczy, 1955). In a letter of 4 April 1848 written to Julian Fontana (from Paris to New York) Chopin refers to himself and his friends as the "Polish orphans" [*sieroty polskie*]. See Chopin, *Korespondencja*, 2:239. All translations are the author's unless otherwise specified.

8. In a letter from London to Wojciech Grzymała in Paris, dated 13 May 1848, Chopin discussed a home visit of the Swedish soprano Jenny Lind, with the following comment about the singer: "Such a different character as ours is different; we—have something Slavic, they—something Scandinavian in themselves; both [characters] are very different, but we are closer to each other than an Italian to a Spaniard" (Chopin, *Korespondencja*, 2:245). Chopin also discussed Lind's Scandinavian character in a long letter to his family in Warsaw, written from Edinburgh on 19 August 1848: "It is something quite different from others. It could be called the Scandinavian note [literally, *struna* ("string")]; it is an entirely different nature from the southern one, of, for instance, Pauline Viardot" (Chopin, *Korespondencja*, 2:267). In addition to discussing national personalities of Sweden and Spain, he frequently made negative comments about his "dishonest" Jewish publishers (e.g., writing from Nohant to Julian Fontana in Paris, 20 October 1941; in *Korespondencja*, 1:341), and the permanence of such national characteristics: "The Jews will always be Jews and the Germans—Germans [literally, *Szwaby*, a derogatory term]" (Chopin's letter from Marseille to Wojciech Grzymała in Paris [March 1839], in *Korespondencja*, 2:45).

9. Hyppolyte Taine, *Philosophie de l'art* (Paris: Bailliere, 1865). English translations, *The Philosophy of Art* (London: Williams and Norgate, 1867; New York: Holt and Williams, 1873). The latter is used here. Details of Taine's theory are discussed in a later portion of this essay.

10. For an introduction to the subject of race, see Les Back and John Solomos, eds., *Theories of Race and Racism: A Reader* (London: Routledge, 2000), in particular the essay by Slavoj Žižek, "Enjoy Your Nation as Yourself."

11. See Zygmunt Bauman, "Modernity, Racism, Extermination" and Sander L. Gilman, "Are Jews White?" in Back and Solomos, *Theories of Race*. See also Peter Ratcliffe, ed., *"Race," Ethnicity, and Nation: International Perspectives on Social Conflict* (London: UCL, 1994).

12. Expressions cited from a children's textbook issued by the Polish government for propaganda purposes abroad and edited by Joseph Statkowski, *Poland: History, Culture, Civilization*, 2nd ed. (Warszawa: Arct, 1935), 5.

13. See Antonina Kloskowska, "Nation, Race, and Ethnicity in Poland," in Ratcliffe, *"Race," Ethnicity, and Nation*.

14. Jacob Riis, *How the Other Half Lives* (New York: Scribner's, 1890); (Bartleby.com, 2000. www.bartleby.com/208/ [28 November 2002], chap. 12: "The Bohemians"); James W. Gerard, *Face to Face with Kaiserism* (New York: Doran, 1918), chap. 24.

15. Jarosław Zieliński, "The Poles in Music," in Ignacy Jan Paderewski, Fanny Morris Smith, and Bernard Boekelman, eds., *The Century Library of Music*, 20 vols. (New York: Century, 1902), 18:591–609. Jarosław Zieliński, or, as he was known in the United States, Jaroslaw de Zielinski (1847–1922), emigrated to the United States in 1864, participated in the secession war, and remained a Polish patriot while actively working in Michigan, New York, Alabama, and California as a music editor, teacher, and critic.

16. Ibid., 591.

17. Charles Phillips, *The New Poland* (London: Allen and Unwin, 1923), 35–36.

18. The Polish Falcons of America, "a fraternal benefit society and physical fitness organization," was founded in the United States at the end of the nineteenth century as an outgrowth of a Polish organization created in 1867, after the fall of the January Uprising. According to the organization's website http://www.polishfalcons.org/history.html (accessed 28 November 2002), its first lodge in the United States was organized by Felix L. Pietrowicz in 1887 in Chicago, Illinois. In Amendments to the Charter on 14 April 1914, the corporate name became "Polish Falcons Alliance of America," and its purposes were modified to include the "Polish race" rhetoric.

19. *Office of United States Chief of Council for Prosecution of Axis Criminality, Nazi Conspiracy, and Aggression* [Red series], 8 vols., 2 supplements (Washington, D.C., 1946–48), 7:752–54 (Document L-3). See also Winfried Baumgart, "Zur Ansprache Hitlers vor den Fiffirern der Wehrmacht am 22. August 1939," *Vierteljahrshefte fur Zeitgeschichte* 16 (1968): 120–49; 19 (1971): 294–304; and Kevork B. Bardakjian, *Hitler and the Armenian Genocide* (Cambridge, Mass.: Harvard University Press, 1985), 52–58.

20. Phillips, *The New Poland*, 36.

21. Marceli Antoni Szulc, *Fryderyk Chopin i utwory jego muzyczne: Przyczynek do życiorysu i oceny kompozycji artysty* (Poznań: Żupanski, 1873), 183–84; new ed., Kraków: Polskie Wydawnictwo Muzyczne, 1986).

22. Stanisław Tarnowski, *Chopin i Grottger: Dwa szkice* (Kraków: Księgarnia Spółki Wydawniczej Polskiej, 1892; reprinted in *Przegląd polski*, April 1971.

23. Ignacy Jan Paderewski, *O Szopenie; mowa wygłoszona na obchodzie Szopenowskim w Filharmonii dnia 23 października 1910* (Lwów: Nakładem Tow. Wydawniczego, 1911); English translation, Laurence Alma Tadema, *Chopin: A Discourse* (London: Adlington, 1911); reprinted in *Polish Music Journal* 4, no. 2 (2001). Expression cited at page 29 of the London edition.

24. Paderewski, *Chopin: A Discourse*, 22. Stefan Czarniecki (1599–1665) was a general in the Polish army who distinguished himself in wars defending the territorial integrity and sovereignty of Poland (against Sweden and Cossack insurgents). He is a symbol of a faithful, patriotic solider and is mentioned in the national anthem. Stanisław Żółkiewski (1547–1620), chancellor of Poland, was a

patriotic and dedicated army commander who fought against the Russians, Turks, and Cossacks.

25. Zygmunt Noskowski, *Istota utworów Chopina* (Warszawa: Saturnin Sikorski, 1902). The text is a lecture for the fiftieth anniversary of Chopin's death, given in 1899. English translation, Maja Trochimczyk and Anne Desler, "The Essence of Chopin's Works," in Trochimczyk, *After Chopin*, 23–46, cited at 34.

26. Ibid., 39.

27. Józef Sikorski (1813–1896), "Wspomnienie Chopina," *Biblioteka warszawska* 4 (1849): 510.

28. Leszek Polony, *Polski kształt sporu*, 140.

29. Cyprian Kamil Norwid (1821–1883), "Promethidion," in Marian Dobrosielski, ed., *Myśli o Polsce i Polakach* (Białystok: Krajowa Agencja Wydawnicza, 1983), 46.

30. Józef Ignacy Kraszewski, review of Maurycy Karasowski, *Friedrich Chopin—Sein Leben, seine Werke und Briefe* (Dresden 1877), *Bluszcz*, no. 12 (1877). Reprinted in Stefan Świerzewski, ed., *J. I. Kraszewski i polskie życie muzyczne XIX wieku* (Kraków: Polskie Wydawnictwo Muzyczne, 1963), 281–89, cited at 289.

31. Noskowski, *Istota utworów Chopina*, in Trochimczyk, *After Chopin*, 32.

32. Ibid., 33–34.

33. This became Béla Bartók's main thesis; for instance, see his 1928 essay, "The Folk Songs of Hungary," in Benjamin Suchoff, ed., *Béla Bartók Essays* (London: Faber and Faber, 1976), 338. Bartók's views on folk music include an idealization of "racially pure" Hungarian peasants; this topic is hotly debated in recent research, for example, David Cooper, "Béla Bartók and the Question of Race Purity in Music," in White and Murphy, *Musical Constructions of Nationalism*.

34. Noskowski, *Istota utworów Chopina*, in Trochimczyk, *After Chopin*, 33–34.

35. Józef Kenig, "Z powodu wydania pośmiertnych dzieł Chopina," *Gazeta Warszawska*, no. 121 (1856). Reprinted in Stefan Jarociński, ed., *Antologia polskiej krytyki muzycznej* (Kraków: Polskie Wydawnictwo Muzyczne, 1955), 131–37, cited at 132.

36. Ibid., 133.

37. Franz Liszt, *Frédéric Chopin* (Leipzig: Breitkoft & Härtel, 1852; Paris: M. Escrdier, 1852; reprint, New York: Vienna House, 1973 [this edition cited in notes]). English translation, Martha Walker Cook, *Life of Chopin* (Boston: Ditson, 1863); Polish translation, Felicjan Faleński, *Fr. Szopen* (Warszawa: Gebethner i Wolff, 1873).

38. Liszt, *Chopin*, 29.

39. Józef Ignacy Kraszewski, "Jeszcze o Apolinarym Kątskim," *Gazeta warszawska*, no. 118 (1857): 1–3; reprinted in Kraszewski, "Jeszcze o Apolinarym Kątskim," 169–77, cited at 176.

40. Jan Kleczyński, "O wykonywaniu utworów Chopina: odczytów dwie serie" (Warszawa: J. Sikorski, 1879); reprint, Kraków: Polskie Wydawnictwo Muzyczne, 1950; 2nd ed., 1960). Also reprinted in Mieczysław Tomaszewski, ed., *Kompozytorzy polscy o Chopinie. Antologia* (Kraków: Polskie Wydawnictwo Muzyczne, 1959), cited at 23 of this edition. For a more detailed discussion of Kleczyński's writings on Chopin, see Zofia Chechlińska's essay in this volume.

41. Maurycy Karasowski, *Fryderyk Chopin. Życie, listy, dzieła* (Warszawa: Gebethner i Wolff, 1882), 229. English translation, Emily Hill, *Frederic Chopin: His Life, Letters, and Works* (London: Reeves, 1906).

42. Władysław Żeleński's 1899 speech was published in *Echo muzyczne, teatralne, and artystyczne*, no. 837 (15 October 1899). English translation, Małgorzata

Szyszkowska and Brian Harlan, "On the 50th Anniversary of Chopin's Death," in Trochimczyk, *After Chopin*, 17–22, cited at 18.

43. Noskowski, *Istota utworów Chopina*, in Trochimczyk, *After Chopin*, 28–29.

44. Ibid., 29.

45. Taine, *Philosophy of Art*, 182.

46. Ibid., 112–13.

47. Ibid., 183.

48. Hyppolyte Taine has been an immensely influential historian and philosopher, one of the towering intellectual figures at the end of the nineteenth century. Reprints of his *Philosophie de l'art* by the Parisian publisher Hachette appeared in 1882, 1901, 1904, 1906, 1909, 1913, 1926, and 1948. (Reprint, Paris: Fayard, 1985).

49. For the Polish reception of his thought, see Henryk Markiewicz, "Les Avatars polonais de l'esthetique de Taine," in Jacques Gaucheron and Philippe Ozouf, eds., *Litteratures sans frontières: Mélanges offerts à Jean Perus* (Clermont-Ferrand: Adosa, 1991), 121–28.

50. Ibid., 70.

51. Taine, *Philosophy of Art*, 68.

52. Ibid., 119.

53. Ibid., 22–28.

54. Ibid., 116.

55. Zofia Helman discusses Szymanowski's connection to Taine in her study, "The Dilemma of Polish Music in the 20th Century: National Style or Universal Values," in Trochimczyk, *After Chopin*, 205–42.

56. Stanisław Przybyszewski, *Zur Psychologie des Individuums* (Berlin: Fontane, 1906 [1892]), vol. 1: *Chopin und Nietzsche*. See also Polony, *Polski kształt sporu*, 152.

57. Przybyszewski, *Chopin und Nietzsche*, 14–15.

58. Stanisław Przybyszewski, *Szopen a naród* (Kraków, Spółka nakładowa "Książka," c. 1910s). Przybyszewski's writings on Chopin have been examined by Leszek Polony, *Polski kształt sporu*, and Maciej Żurowski, "Chopin interpréte par Przybyszewski," in Joanna Zurowska, ed., *Frédéric Chopin et les lettres* (Warszawa: Centre de Civilisation Française, éditions de l'Université de Varsovie, 1991).

59. Przybyszewski, *Szopen a naród*, 25.

60. Ibid., 27–29.

61. Ibid., 32–35.

62. See the discussion of Western stereotypes of Russia in Richard Taruskin, *Defining Russia Musically: Historical and Hermeneutical Essays* (Princeton, N.J.: Princeton University Press, 1997).

63. Szulc, *Fryderyk Chopin i utwory jego muzyczne*; Karasowski, *Fryderyk Chopin. Życie, listy, dzieła*; Ferdinand Hoesick, *Chopin: Życie i twórczość*, vol. 1: *Warszawa 1810–1831* (Warszawa: Hoesick, 1904); reprint, Warszawa: Hoesick, 1910–11, 1927; and Kraków: Polskie Wydawnictwo Muzyczne, 1967). The Polish genealogy of Chopin is discussed on pages 24–25 of the 1967 edition.

64. Zieliński, "The Poles in Music," 606–07.

65. Ibid., 607.

66. French scholars soon set out to refute this thesis in a series of documentary articles published in 1912–27: A. Lévy, "L'Origine lorraine de Chopin," *Le Mercure de France* 100 (1912): 297–302; Abbé Evrard, "Origines lorraines de Chopin," *La Pays Lorrain* (1926); and *La Revue Pleyel*, nos. 42–43 (1927). After World War II Jean Kastener's archival research provided the Chopin family with a French genealogy going back to the seventeenth century (Jean Kastener, "La famille

loraine de Frédéric Chopin," *Le Pays Lorain*, no. 2 [1951]). Yet the issue remained controversial in Poland. See Józef Chomiński, *Chopin* (Kraków: Polskie Wydawnictwo Muzyczne, 1978), 19–22; and Janusz Szprot, ed., "Spór wokół Chopina," *Ruch muzyczny*, no. 18 (16–30 September 1973): 8–9.

67. Ibid., 592.

68. See Michael Murphy, "Moniuszko and Musical Nationalism in Poland," in White and Murphy, *Musical Constructions of Nationalism*.

69. Ludwik Bronarski, *Harmonika Chopina* (Warszawa: Towarzystwo Wydawnicze Muzyki Polskiej, 1935); Maciej Gołąb, *Chromatyka i tonalność w muzyce Chopina* (Kraków: Polskie Wydawnictwo Muzyczne, 1991); in German, *Chopins Harmonik: Chromatik in ihrer Beziehung zur Tonalität* (Cologne: Bela Verlag, 1995).

70. Paderewski, *Chopin: A Discourse.*

71. Dziedzila was a love goddess from the pre-Christian Slavic pantheon; Perun, also known as Svarog, was the main deity in the Slavic pantheon, associated with oak trees, lightning, fertility, and rain; see Paul M. Barford, *The Early Slavs: Culture and Society in Early Medieval Eastern Europe* (Ithaca, N.Y.: Cornell University Press, 2001).

72. Ibid., 27.

73. In a similar vein, Charles Phillips observes: "It is curious how readily the world has accepted all that this greatest of Polish artists produced as 'French' or as 'of the German school' . . . yet whenever the weaknesses or the frailties of his art or his flesh are mentioned, promptly labeling them 'Polish' " (Phillips, *The New Poland*, 36).

74. Another proof of Paderewski's opposition to narrowly nationalistic views may be seen in his musical oeuvre, for instance, in his only opera, *Manru* (1901). Its libretto, adapted from a novel by Ignacy Kraszewski by a Jewish writer, Alfred Nossig, presented the tragic consequences of ethnic intolerance and conflicts between Gypsies and Polish peasants. See Aleksandra Konieczna, "*Manru* Paderewskiego: Kilka uwag o stylu i dramaturgii," in Andrzej Sitarz and Wojciech Marchwica, eds., *Warsztat kompozytorski, wykonawstwo i koncepcje polityczne Ignacego Jana Paderewskiego* (Kraków: Musica Iagellonica, 1991), 134–48. English translation: Maja Trochimczyk, "Stylistic and Dramatic Features of Paderewski's *Manru*," *Polish Music Journal* 4, no. 2 (winter 2001).

75. See Małgorzata Perkowska, *Diariusz koncertowy Ignacego Jana Paderewskiego* (Kraków: Polskie Wydawnictwo Muzyczne, 1990). See also Ignacy Jan Paderewski, "Appeals for Polish Victims' Relief Fund," *Polish Music Journal* 4, no. 2 (winter 2001).

76. Paderewski's unfortunate brief political alliance with the anti-German and anti-Semitic Dmowski has unjustly tarred his political reputation: he shared the former stance with his future adversary but not the latter.

77. Phillips, *The New Poland*, 34, 36.

78. Stanisław Niewiadomski, "Fryderyk Szopen a Polska," in Mateusz Gliński, ed., *Szopen. Monografia zbiorowa* (Warszawa: Nakładem Miesięcznika Muzyka, 1932), 17–20. English translation: Małgorzata Szyszkowska and Brian Harlan, "Fryderyk Chopin and Poland," in Trochimczyk, *After Chopin*, 63–69.

79. "O pisowni nazwiska Chopina," *Echo muzyczne*, no. 23 (1 December 1879); "Problem pisowni nazwiska Chopin według *Kuriera codziennego* oraz zdaniem redakcji *Echa muzycznego*," *Echo muzyczne*, no. 20 (1880): 2–3. I thank Dr. Barbara Zakrzewska-Nikiporczyk for these references.

80. Attempts at Polonizing the French name of the composer dated back to Maurycy Mochnacki's mention of "Pan Szopę" in an 1830 report in *Kurier polski*. See Maurycy Mochnacki, *Kurier polski*, no. 97 (12 March 1830); reprinted

in Stefan Jarociński, ed., *Antologia polskiej krytyki muzycznej XIX i XX wieku* (Kraków: Polskie Wydawnictwo Muzyczne, 1955), 64–65. In an 1835 letter to Chopin, Maria Wodzińska noted the problem Chopin's name caused in defining his Polish nationality: "We do not cease to regret that you are not called Chopinski or that there are no other signs that you are a Pole, because—as it is—Frenchmen may argue with us for the honor of being your compatriots" (Letter from Dresden to Paris, September 1835; in Chopin, *Korespondencja*, 1:262–63).

81. Stanisław Niewiadomski, "Ch czy Sz?" in Mateusz Gliński, ed., *Szopen. Monografia zbiorowa* (Warszawa: Muzyka, 1932), 88–90. English translation: Małgorzata Szyszkowska and Brian Harlan, "Spelling Identity: Ch or Sz?" in Trochimczyk, *After Chopin*, 71–75, cited at 73.

82. Niewiadomski, "Chopin and Poland," 64.

83. Ibid., 67.

84. The assassination is described briefly in Norman Davies, *God's Playground: A History of Poland*, 2 vols. (New York: Columbia University Press, 1982), 2:71, 426. Eligiusz Niewiadomski (1869–1923) was a painter and writer; he published *Atlas do dziejów Polski według Lelewela i innych* (Warszawa: Wydawnictwo M. Arcta, 1907); and memoirs from prison, *Kartki z więzienia* (Poznań: Wielkopolska Księgarnia Nakł. K. Rzepeckiego, 1923). Maurycy Urstein wrote a short study of his insanity, *Eligjusz Niewiadomski w oświetleniu psychjatry* (Warszawa: Druk "Rola" J. Buriana, 1923).

85. Or *Chadecja* (Christian Democratic Movement, founded in 1902, and Christian Social Movement, founded in 1908; both united into the Christian Democratic Party after the restoration of independence).

86. It did not; the secular "Dąbrowski Mazurka" took this place only in 1926 thanks to the efforts of Marshall Józef Piłsudski. I discuss this issue in "Sacred/Secular Constructs of National Identity: A Convoluted History of Polish Anthems," in Trochimczyk, *After Chopin*, 263–94.

87. Davies, *God's Playground*, 2:404.

88. Niewiadomski, "Chopin and Poland," 67.

89. Piotr Rytel was a composer and pianist, and a student of Zygmunt Noskowski and Kazimierz Michałowski in Warsaw; he taught at the Warsaw Conservatory since 1911. His compositions included symphonic poems based on European literature (Byron, Dante), *Żelazowa Wola* for orchestra (1951) celebrating Chopin's birthplace, and cantatas to Polish poetry by Adam Mickiewicz and Juliusz Słowacki. Rytel was not the most radical racist and nationalist among Polish composers; this title should be awarded to Michał Kondracki (1902–1984), who was active as a music critic and writer on music, publishing in *Muzyka* and other journals.

90. Piotr Rytel, " 'Splendid isolation' P. K. Szymanowskiego," *Gazeta warszawska*, nos. 327 and 328 (30 November and 1 December 1922). Cited in Kornel Michałowski, ed., *Karol Szymanowski: Pisma*, vol. 1: *Pisma muzyczne* (Kraków: Polskie Wydawnictwo Muzyczne, 1984), 74.

91. These terms are sarcastic utterances describing Szymanowski's position in the music world and the tone of the attacks by his nationalistic enemies, from Michał Choromański's essay "Karol Szymanowski" (*Wiadomości literackie* 1932), reprinted in Szymanowski, *Pisma muzyczne*, 411, 423.

92. See also Leon Markiewicz, "Fryderyk Chopin w świetle wypowiedzi Karola Szymanowskiego," in *Karol Szymanowski o Chopinie, o własnej twórczości, o pedagogice* (Katowice: Akademia Muzyczna im. Karola Szymanowskiego, 1995), 5–19.

93. Karol Szymanowski, "Igor Strawinski," in Szymanowski, *Pisma muzyczne*,

48–55. The article, written in 1921, was not published; fragments were first printed in Teresa Chylińska, *Karol Szymanowski* (Kraków: Polskie Wydawnictwo Muzyczne, 1962), 114–15.

94. Karol Szymanowski, "Zagadnienie ludowości w stosunku do muzyki współczesnej," in Szymanowski, *Pisma muzyczne*, 168–75, cited at 168–69. First published in *Muzyka*, no. 10 (1925). English translation: Alistair Wightman, "The Ethnic Question in Relation to Contemporary Music," in Alistair Wightman, ed. *Szymanowski on Music: Selected Writings of Karol Szymanowski* (London: Toccata, 1999), 126–35.

95. Ibid., 173.

96. Karol Szymanowski, "Uwagi w sprawie współczesnej opinii muzycznej w Polsce," *Nowy przegląd literatury i sztuki*, no. 2 (July 1920). Reprinted in Szymanowski, *Pisma muzyczne*, 33–47, cited at 40. English translation: Alistair Wightman, "On Contemporary Musical Opinion in Poland," in *Szymanowski on Music*, 73–94.

97. Tomaszewski downplays the nationalistic aspects of Szymanowski's writings on Chopin and considers the emphasis on Chopin's originality in harmonic and formal experimentation, as well as his inventiveness in renewing the musical language, as Szymanowski's most important contribution to the Chopin reception. See Tomaszewski, *Chopin*, 780 and 682.

98. Karol Szymanowski, "Fryderyk Chopin," *Skamander* 3, no. 28 (1923): 22–27; nos. 29–30 (1923): 106–10), reprinted in Szymanowski, *Pisma muzyczne*, 89–102. Cited in the English translation by Maria Pilatowicz, in Trochimczyk, *After Chopin*, 47–62. Another English translation is Alistair Wightman, "Fryderyk Chopin," in Wightman, ed., *Szymanowski on Music*, 177–96.

99. Karol Szymanowski, "Fryderyka Chopina mit o duszy polskiej," *Muzyka*, no. 1 (1924): 3–5; reprinted in *Muzyka*, nos. 4–5 (1937), and in Szymanowski, *Pisma muzyczne*, 133–36 (source of subsequent citations). This article was originally a lecture given at the celebration of the seventy-fifth anniversary of Chopin's death at the Warsaw Philharmonic.

100. Szymanowski, "Fryderyka Chopina mit," 135, 134.

101. Ibid., 135.

102. Ibid. The negative connotations of "abyss" are even stronger in the original Polish *otchłań*, which means bottomless pit or gorge (as in hell).

103. Szymanowski, "Chopin" (lecture at Warsaw University, 1930), *Wiadomości literackie*, no. 48 (30 November 1930); reprinted in *Muzyka*, nos. 7–9 (1932): 7–12 (special Chopin issue), and in Szymanowski, *Pisma muzyczne*, 256–63, cited at 259 of this edition.

104. Karol Szymanowski, "Fryderyk Chopin i muzyka współczesna," *Biuletyn koncertowy Filharmonii Warszawskiej*, nos. 3–4 (17 and 24 October 1930); reprinted in Szymanowski, *Pisma muzyczne*, 296–301, cited at 300.

105. Szymanowski, "Frederic Chopin et la musique polonaise moderne," *La revue musicalem*, no. 121 (1931): 30–34. Polish translation: Jarosław Iwaszkiewicz, "Fryderyk Chopin a polska muzyki współczesna," in Stanisław Golachowski, *Karol Szymanowski o Fryderyku Chopinie* (Kraków: Polskie Wydawnictwo Muzyczne, 1949). Reprinted in Szymanowski, *Pisma muzyczne*, 314–17 (translation), 317–20 (original); cited at 320 of the latter.

106. Karol Szymanowski, "Wychowawcza rola kultury muzycznej w społeczeństwie," *Pamiętnik Warszawski*, no. 8 (November 1931): 57–89. Reprinted in Szymanowski, *Pisma muzyczne*, 264–92, cited at 283.

107. "Karol Szymanowski o nowej muzyce," interview for *Prager Presse* (in German) (3 May 1927); reprinted in Szymanowski, *Pisma muzyczne*, 377–78, cited

at 378 (Polish translation) and 381 (original German: "Rasseneigentümlichkeiten").

108. Henry E. Krehbiel, "New Composers Get Hearing as Slavic Invasion Continues. Songs by Lazare Saminsky. Cantata by Samuel Thewman. Presented at Town Hall by Society of Friends of Music," *New York Tribune* (6 February 1922). Reprinted in Karol Szymanowski, *Pisma*, vol. 2: *Pisma literackie*, ed. Teresa Chylińska (Kraków: Polskie Wydawnictwo Muzyczne, 1989), 230. Krehbiel wrote about the invasion of composers from Russia and the Polish Jewry, naming Poldowski (i.e., Irena Wieniawska, from the Polish-Jewish family of Wieniawski), Szymanowski, and Prokofiev. The account is based on Teresa Chylińska's introduction to Szymanowski's "Kwestia żydostwa," in Karol Szymanowski, *Pisma*, vol. 2: *Pisma literackie* (Kraków: Polskie Wydawnictwo Muzyczne, 1989), 226–230. Szymanowski's essay appears on pages 238–40 and is preceded by fragments on Judaism and Christianity, "Pansemityzm-Panaryjskość, and Gustav Mahler" (231–37).

109. Kornel Michałowski, introduction to Karol Szymanowski's essay "Fryderyk Chopin," in Szymanowski, *Pisma muzyczne*, 89.

110. Karol Szymanowski, "Kwestia żydostwa," in Szymanowski, *Pisma literackie*, 238–40. According to Chylińska's introduction to this essay, the earliest notes about readings on the "Jewish question" date back to 1918–19, a longer fragment was written after 1920, and the essay was completed in 1922 (Szymanowski, *Pisma literackie*, 227–28).

111. Szymanowski, notes for "Kwestia żydostwa," n.d., in Szymanowski, *Pisma literackie*, 231.

112. Szymanowski, "Sztuka Mahlera" (among his notes for "Kwestia żydostwa"), in Szymanowski, *Pisma literackie*, 235–36.

113. Szymanowski, notes for "Kwestia żydostwa," in Szymanowski, *Pisma literackie*, 237.

114. The term *race* is also used in reference to the "Negroes" described by Szymanowski in a 1922 interview as "a despised race and, indeed, consisting of an uncertain social material," yet being capable of creating great dance, music, and rhythm. While belittling the "Negroes," the composer simultaneously praised the "musical talents of the Anglo-Saxon race" ("Karol Szymanowski o muzyce współczesnej," reprinted in Szymanowski, *Pisma muzyczne*, 58–66, cited at 61.

115. Teresa Chylińska's introduction to Szymanowski, *Pisma literackie*; Zofia Helman, "The Dilemma of Polish Music in the 20th Century: National Style or Universal Values," in Trochimczyk, *After Chopin*, 205–41.

116. Szymanowski used this term in reference to himself in a conversation with Michał Choromański (*Wiadomości Literackie*, no. 44 [16 October 1932]: 1–2). Reprinted in Szymanowski, *Pisma muzyczne*, 411–26, cited at 423.

117. Karol Szymanowski, "L'Avenir de la culture," in *L'Avenir de la culture* (Paris: Institut International de Cooperation Intellectuelle, 1933), 188–95. Reprinted in Szymanowski, *Pisma muzyczne*, 335–42; Beethoven is discussed at 339 (French original: "race pure").

118. Julia Kristeva, "Open Letter to Harlem Desir," in *Nations without Nationalism*, trans. Leon S. Roudiez (New York: Columbia University Press, 1993), 53–54.

# 13

# "A composer known here but to few": Reception and Performance Styles of Chopin's Music in America, 1839–1900

### SANDRA P. ROSENBLUM

In October 1839, at a private party in New York City, a newly arrived German immigrant named Ludwig Rakemann played

> some nocturnes of a composer known here but to few—Chopin, a Pole. This author does not so much astonish by the velocity and apparent difficulty of his passages, as he entrances his auditors by the fire, the soul-stirring pathos of his compositions. He appears to expand the powers of the instrument by a masterly combination of melody and harmony—*singing* divinely.... [T]hese effusions of a master mind [were] given with an intensity of feeling and a power of expression which we have seldom heard equalled—never surpassed.[1]

The particular nocturnes that Rakemann played are not recorded in the *Evening Star*, which published that communication from a perceptive listener who recognized the originality of Chopin's musical and pianistic style. This first documented performance of Chopin's music in America was followed by Rakemann's public debut on October 16, when he played a "Notturno and Two Mazurkas."[2] Thus Chopin was introduced in America through genres valued especially for two outstanding attributes of his musical style: expressive, often melancholic lyricism and musical nationalism.

In Boston two weeks later Rakemann played "an exquisitely beautiful 'Nocturne Melancholique' " by Chopin, noted the *Evening Transcript.*[3] *The Musical Magazine* described the program as "probably the finest musical treat of the kind ever offered" in Boston. It was "the first illustration of the style [of the] modern pianoforte school" and of its "leaders, Thalberg, Henselt, and Chopin, [that] has ever been offered to the Boston public."[4] When John Sullivan Dwight reflected on Boston's musical season of 1839–40, Rakemann's concert was among the few events he remembered "with most pleasure." The compositions of the "new school of Piano Forte playing . . . are rich, brilliant, wild, astonishing." In the "Notturnes" of Chopin he found "sweet pathos."[5] But, thinking back in 1856, Dwight considered it "almost a sin to class a pure star of genius," like Chopin, "with lights that must prove so much more ephemeral."[6]

Two important premières took place in New York in 1846. In October Julian Fontana introduced Chopin's Fantasie op. 49 as his solo in a concert featuring the singer Madame Ablamowicz. In a long review the *Morning Courier* stated only that Fontana played "in a manner which showed him a worthy pupil of [Chopin]."[7] *The Albion* credited Fontana with "good execution and much expression; . . . all he does proves him to be a thorough musician."[8] There was not a word about that sublime Fantasie, so rich in references to diverse genres and Poland's tragedy.[9] (Regarding op. 49, see Halina Goldberg's essay in this volume.) Unfortunately, until later in the century, most concert reviews did not include discussion of the music itself, even when it was new; rather, reviews were mainly news accounts of the weather, the type of audience, the program, and the player's technique and expressive ability.[10] Any attention to piano music was usually an experiential response to its emotional qualities, with only rare and cursory mention of technical aspects such as form or harmony. Finally—and very discouraging to a researcher—piano concerts were reviewed only erratically.

In November 1846 Henry Timm and the New York Philharmonic premiered the second and third movements of Chopin's Concerto op. 11.[11] George Templeton Strong, an upper-class New York lawyer and musical sophisticate, wrote in his diary: "pretty thing and cleverly played."[12] Henry Cood Watson, a critic who had emigrated from London, observed in the *Evening Mirror*:

> Chopin, who is the greatest writer for the piano since Hummel, is almost unknown in our musical circles: it is greatly to be re-gretted—for as a composer . . . for the piano forte, he is undoubt-edly the greatest living master. . . . In his writings [the Romantic] school possesses a dignity and force which redeem it from . . . that sickening sentimentality which in general is its bane and defect. . . . The *andante* [of the Concerto] is remarkable for the wonderful sustainment of its lovely subject, and . . . the *finale* is replete with those peculiar beauties which form the charm of Chopin's style.[13]

Watson would have heard the new piano music before leaving London; thus his comments represent a seasoned viewpoint rather than a response to a first hearing, which is what many American writers would have offered. The lyrical, poetic slow movements and the piquant finales with dance-like rhythms were the favored movements of both Chopin's Concertos and were often singled out for comment when a complete concerto was played, which was also the case in Poland according to Zofia Chechlińska.[14] That is cer-tainly the impression of the audience reaction that Chopin con-veyed in his letter to Tytus Wojciechowski after the first public performance of op. 11 in Warsaw. "The first *Allegro* is accessible only to the few; there were some bravos, but I think only because they were puzzled . . . and had to pose as connoisseurs! The Adagio and Rondo had more effect; one heard some spontaneous shouts."[15]

Also in 1846 Dwight's review of Chopin's recently published Tarantelle contains the prescient comment that the piece modu-lates "perpetually by almost insensible chromatic changes, as is the way with Chopin always, who seems [to be] groping after the in-tervals of a more finely graduated scale." This was probably the first American recognition of Chopin's profound expansion of the prevailing harmonic language, an idea not widely appreciated until late in the century. Dwight also used the same review to present other impressions of Chopin and his music that became funda-mental to the American reception: he is an "inspired young Pole, the worshipper of freedom. . . . He is always himself and 'nothing else.' . . . [His] music floats around you and subdues your senses like clouds of incense, a mingling of most exquisite aromas."[16]

The content and style of these phrases have a familiar ring.

Indeed, in an earlier essay Dwight had quoted at length from Liszt's review of Chopin's concert of 26 April 1841, in which some of the same attitudes and metaphors are expressed.[17] There is also resonance in Dwight's writings from other European sources, including Schumann's review of the Sonata op. 35[18] and J. W. Davison's "Essay on the Works of Frederick Chopin," a *puff* for London publisher Wessel.[19] Thus Dwight was one of many American commentators whose views on Chopin were informed to some extent by previous European writing or training. His inferences to the feminine spirit of some of Chopin's more delicate works notwithstanding, Dwight repeatedly mentioned and expected performers to express the virile, vigorous side of Chopin, as when he described the Ballade op. 23 as "a composition of great power and breadth and depth of feeling, taxing the strength . . . of a player to the utmost, full of imagination and fire."[20] Discussion of supposedly masculine and feminine traits in Chopin's music became increasingly common in American writing.[21] After Edwin Klahre's all-Chopin program in New York in 1890 the *New York Times* remarked that "the young pianist . . . plays [Chopin] with intelligence, and does not emasculate him."[22]

There must have been enough private as well as public playing of Chopin's music in the 1840s so that five publishers in Boston and Philadelphia were willing to bet that carefully selected pieces would be commercial successes. As shown in Table 13.1, aside from the Berceuse and the popular Impromptu op. 29—the first section of which Dwight actually compared to a tarantella[23]—the pieces published even up to 1855 were related to genres already popular in a vernacular or utilitarian style for household use. Unsophisticated and technically easy marches, variation sets, and dances—of which the waltz was the most popular—were the mainstay of the repertoire for the majority of amateur players.[24] The publishers listed were betting that the name "Chopin" would attract some pianists to better quality and perhaps to bragging rights.

Chopin's Marche funèbre remained a favorite in multiple publications, transcriptions, and simplifications throughout the century.[25] Of all his works in the private, nineteenth-century collections of piano music that I have examined, the *Marche funèbre* appeared most frequently, followed by the Waltz op. 18.

In April 1852 Dwight founded his own influential *Journal of Music*. His purpose was to educate a public largely unsophisticated in matters of music to the best in "classical" music, by which he

Table 13.1. Works Published in the United States c. 1840–1855*

| [c. 1839–42] | Waltz in A♭ op. 34 no. 1 | Meignen | Philadelphia |
|---|---|---|---|
| [c. 1840] | Impromptu in A♭ op. 29 | Klemm and Bro. | Philadelphia |
| 184-? | "Chopin's Beautiful Mazurka" in B♭ op. 7 no. 1 | Geo. P. Reed | Boston |
| 184-? | Grande Valse Brillante in E♭ op. 18 | A. Fiot | Philadelphia |
| [1844] | Valse op. 34 no. 2 | O. Ditson | Boston |
| [1844–49] | "Esmeralda Polka"** | W. Dubois and A. Fiot | New York and Philadelphia |
| [1845] | Tarantelle | Ditson | Boston |
| [c. 1846] | Marche funèbre | Ditson | Boston |
| 1847 | Grand Valse Brilliante op. 18 | Ditson | Boston |
| [185-?] | Marche funèbre | Firth, Pond & Co. | New York |
| [185-?] | Marche funèbre | Beck & Lawton | Philadelphia |
| [1852] | Marche funèbre | Geo. P. Reed | Boston |
| 1853 | Mazurkas op. 7 | Geo. P. Reed & Co. | Boston |
| 1853 | Grand Waltz in E♭ op. 18 | Geo. P. Reed & Co. | Boston |
| 1853 | Waltz op. 64 no. 1 | Nathan Richardson's *Modern School for the Piano-forte* | Boston |
| 1854 | Marche funèbre (arr. as a duet) | Ditson | Boston |
| 1854 | Trois Valses op. 64 | Richardson's "Correct Editions" | Boston |
| 1854 | Deux Polonaises op. 26 | Richardson's "Correct Editions" | Boston |
| 1854 | Berceuse op. 57 | N. Richardson | Boston |
| 1854 | Trois Valses Brillantes op. 34 | Richardson | Boston |
| 1855 | Valse in A♭ op. 42 | Ditson | Boston |

*Sources for works published include music journals, catalogs, and early editions in libraries (some from private collections).
**False attribution!

meant music of the great composers.[26] From more than a decade of experience writing in a number of periodicals Dwight was already known for the high quality of his music criticism, to which his wide reading of European intellectual and musical writing had contributed. In 1847 the *New York Tribune* acknowledged that he was "one of the very best and most conscientious music critics in the country."[27] In a circular of February 1852, in which Dwight laid out a plan for his *Journal*, he included the following: "The *tone* to be impartial, independent, catholic, . . . aloof from musical cliques. . . . [It] would be an 'organ' of . . . the Musical *Movement* in our country, of the growing love of deep and genuine music, of the growing consciousness that music . . . is intimately connected with Man's truest life and destiny."[28] Among the European journals from which he selected articles to translate and reprint in his *Journal* were *La France musicale, Revue et gazette musicale, Musical World* (London), *Quarterly Musical Review, Allgemeine musikalische Zeitung, Niederrheinische Musik-Zeitung,* and many more. He also had an outstanding group of contributors from all the major American cities and some in Europe. After only six issues, a note in the Baltimore *Sun* acknowledged that the new journal was "gaining much credit for its ability and good taste in musical matters."[29] In November 1881 the editor of *Harper's New Monthly Magazine* was moved to write that "the oldest, ablest, and most independent of musical journals in the United States has just suspended publication . . . for want of adequate support,"[30] followed by a long encomium to Dwight's sagacious stewardship. Indeed, *Dwight's Journal* had become the most influential periodical of its kind in nineteenth-century America, providing intellectual leadership in musical matters, including the establishment of substantive music criticism.

Typical of his continuing interest in Chopin, Dwight immediately translated and printed nine lengthy segments from the biography of Chopin just published under Liszt's name.[31] For better or worse, that book remained an important source for much American writing about Chopin until the publication of Niecks's *Chopin* in 1888 and the writing of the independent-minded American Henry T. Finck in the last quarter of the century.[32]

In his third issue Dwight reviewed a concert by the Pole Wojciech Wołowski. "The set of Mazurkas by Chopin was of course good; but how strange the style, how headlong the time, how perplexing the expression, of that rendering of them!"[33] Part of Dwight's unease with the performance must have reflected the unusual accent patterns and rubato inherent in the Polish playing of mazurkas. Somewhat later, the recognition that these pieces demanded unfamiliar rhythmic practices, along with their relative lack of bravura, may have contributed to their infrequent public performance except by touring Slavic virtuosos. The mazurka's role of representing Chopin's Poland in concert was taken over by the polonaise.[34]

Chopin's music performed in Boston by two pianists from December 1852 through December 1853, as well as publishing activity, marks 1853 as a watershed year for his conquest of America. Alfred Jaëll, who had been Chopin's student in 1846,[35] played the entire Concerto op. 11 twice (giving it its Boston première), the Ballade op. 23 twice, along with a Waltz from op. 64, a polonaise, and the Marche funèbre twice.[36] Dwight found the Ballade "full of poetry and meaning."[37] My search for another early review of that work led me to newspapers of Providence, where Jaëll was expected to perform "the same program" two weeks later. However, for that smaller, presumably less sophisticated city, he replaced the Ballade with a fantasie on operatic themes.[38] Louis Moreau Gottschalk, too, generally reserved his performances of Chopin for large cities.[39] Thus, at mid-century, much of Chopin's music—and European art music generally—was understood to be for the cultivated class.[40]

Otto Dresel, a German immigrant who had known Schumann and Mendelssohn in Leipzig, championed Chopin's works in Boston throughout the 1850s and 1860s.[41] Between December 1852 and December 1853 he played the Berceuse, the *Marche funèbre* (twice), Nocturnes op. 15 no. 2, op. 62 no. 2, and one in B major (given in *Dwight's Journal* as op. 12 no. 1[!]; perhaps op. 62 no. 1, the mate to op. 62 no. 2); two mazurkas, a prelude (possibly op. 28 no. 15), a polonaise; Etudes op. 10 no. 11 and one in A♭ major (perhaps the popular 25/1); and Waltzes op. 34 nos. 1, 2, op. 42, and op. 64 no. 2. Presenting the Nocturne op. 62 no. 2 was a bold move for the idealistic Dresel. This Nocturne, perhaps partly because of its severely contrapuntal, dissonant, and agitated midsection, has always been at the periphery of the Chopin repertoire performed in America. But Dwight, the only reviewer of the event, thought it "exquisite."[42]

Dwight's review of new publications on 9 April 1853 was devoted to a series of sheet music by George P. Reed of Boston. This series, "The Pianist's Album," was, according to Dwight,

> to contain . . . finer modern classics of the instrument. . . . Several pieces of CHOPIN figure in the list. This is in answer to the spirit of the times,—at least hereabouts. The past musical winter in Boston has been marked, among other things, by the development of an interest in the compositions of this most exquisite and individual, . . . most spiritually imaginative, poet of the piano, who, so far as depth and purity of sentiment and originality of ideas go, is far above all his modern contemporaries. . . . Until this season it has been a rare thing to get any work of Chopin

played here, beyond a mere Mazurka or two. But Dresel in his chamber soirées, and Jaëll even before the vast audiences in the Music Hall, have changed all that. Mazurkas, waltzes, polonaises, notturnes [*sic*], études, even his most difficult "Ballades" and Concertos, have had repeated hearing; and we have scarcely entered a private musical circle this winter where Chopin did not figure as principal.... Already published are: 1. The *Marche Funèbre* from the Sonate, op. 35, now an established favorite, and a creation almost as remarkable in its kind (which is not orchestral) as the two funeral marches of Beethoven. 2. A set of Mazurkas, ... op. 7. The first is *the* well known one for years past, which every body has played to us, in all sorts of time, from *andante molto* to *prestissimo*, and it took an artist like Mr. Dresel to restore its poor crazed life.[43]

The year 1853 also saw the first inclusion of a piece by Chopin in a piano method. Nathan Richardson selected the Waltz op. 64 no. 1 for his volume, *The Modern School for the Piano-forte*.[44] In March 1854 the *Boston Evening Transcript* reported that Richardson's *Modern School* "is becoming very popular among the professors and amateurs, and ... is making its way into most of the seminaries throughout the entire country.... We understand that the second edition is now ready."[45]

During the 1840s and early 1850s public taste in New York was more inclined to large musical performances such as the symphonic repertoire and opera, with its social corollaries.[46] The piano music played tended toward a more popular type—fantasies and variations on operatic themes,[47] which may explain why most American publication of Chopin's music up to 1855 occurred in Boston and Philadelphia. In October 1854 the *New York Times* noted that one of Chopin's compositions played by William Mason would be "an unusual treat. Not one performer in five hundred is capable of appreciating or rendering the solemn majesty of this great composer."[48] A brief note about that concert in the *Times* two days later further reveals the attitude toward piano recitals in opera-loving New York.

We were glad to observe a crowded attendance at Mr. Wm. Mason's second piano concert on Saturday evening. The entertainment was very fine, and merited not only the attendance but the applause bestowed by the attendants. It is a little difficult to popularize entertainments that depend mainly on the piano for their attractiveness, but Mr. Mason will, we think, undoubtedly do so.[49]

Also in New York in 1854 Richard Hoffman's performance of the Nocturne op. 32 no. 2 (titled "Consolation" in the program as in Wessel's edition) occasioned some informative criticism. The reviewer for *The Musical World* found the Nocturne lacking in "sufficient feeling, gentle inspiration, or anything else, suggestive of its being called the Consolation." But the editor of the journal, Richard Storrs Willis, added a footnote: the performance of the Nocturne had probably been too "ponderous. Chopin, who . . . always breathed rather than played, his exquisite creations upon the piano, . . . a soft *Pleyel*, . . . used to play this piece . . . with the most extreme sensibility and delicacy."[50] The American-born Willis had studied composition in Germany and apparently had heard Chopin play in Paris, an exposure that allowed him to suggest an appropriate performance style for the composer's more delicate, melancholic creations.

Crop failures and the revolutions of 1848 in Europe caused an increase in immigration, especially from Germany, which significantly increased the amount and quality of musical activity here. During the 1850s and 1860s interest in the performance of instrumental music developed at an accelerating pace. Concurrently there emerged the first group of able American-born concertizing pianists, which included—among many others—Gottschalk, Mason, and B. D. Allen—a pupil of Dresel, who introduced a tradition of Chopin playing in Worcester, Massachusetts. Not surprisingly, then, the years 1855–60 witnessed the documented spread of the public performance of Chopin's works to cities outside Boston, Philadelphia, and New York—mainly to those close to the eastern seaboard where rail transportation existed, but also to New Orleans, St. Louis, and Chicago, all on major waterways. In 1860 Jadwiga Brzowska premiered the Allegro of the Concerto op. 11 in New Orleans, where she lived for three years as a professor of piano. A report sent to *Ruch muzyczny* proclaimed her "the best pianist that we have ever heard" and recognized "the great feeling and sweetness" of the concerto movement.[51] Map 13.1 provides some idea of how Chopin playing in recital gradually moved westward as the country's growing economy supported the development of cultural interests. Railroad development between 1840 and 1870, as shown on Maps 13.2 and 13.3, enabled the spread of musical life. Many of the unfamiliar towns, such as rural Georgetown, Kentucky (twenty miles from the state capitol), had colleges, small

music schools, or private high schools—sometimes called seminaries—for young ladies.

Training ladies in music was considered important for the cultivation of musical taste in the population at large. Program notes
about Chopin for a student recital on 13 November 1857 at the
exclusive Miss Porter's School in Farmington, Connecticut, touch
on some major themes of American reception. The Chopin piece
played was an unidentified Impromptu.

> One of the most original writers for the pianoforte. His com-
> positions belong to the so-called "romantic" school. The strict-
> ness of the old forms of composition was not congenial to his
> nature; most of his works are in the free style, such as Etudes,
> Nocturnes, Mazurkas, and Polonaises. He never oversteps the
> boundaries of the Beautiful, not even when he is full of vehe-
> mence, of passion, as often in his Polonaises, where he seems to
> pour out his love of his native country and his deep, burning
> grief over the misfortunes of down-trodden Poland. . . . But he is
> not always sad and melancholy. Touches of caprice, playfulness,
> tenderness, and coquetry are frequently found even in his most
> serious works, especially in his Mazurkas—gems of composition
> for the parlor. The present piece is rather in his lighter style, a
> refined, salon conversation, impetuous, but not passionate, lan-
> guid but not trivial.[52]

References to mazurkas as "gems of composition for the parlor"
and to the unspecified impromptu on the program as a "refined
salon conversation" were codes for women's music and, by nineteenth-century male-imposed standards, of lesser value. Such opinions reveal a failure to recognize the degree of development that
Chopin brought to genres previously familiar in the salon.

The decade of the 1860s was welcomed with Ditson's publication of the complete Mazurkas and Waltzes in one volume in
April 1861. Following successful sales Ditson announced the preparation of all the Polonaises and all the Nocturnes in 1865.[53] The
less arduous pieces in these genres joined the Waltzes, Mazurkas,
and the *Marche funèbre* as part of the domestic repertoire. In November 1861 the American pianist Sebastian Bach Mills introduced
Chopin's Concerto in F Minor op. 21 to the New World in New
York City, and "played superbly." *The Albion*'s reviewer contrasted
that work with Henselt's Variations op. 1 on a theme from Doni-
zetti's *L'Elisir d'amore*, in which he found little merit.

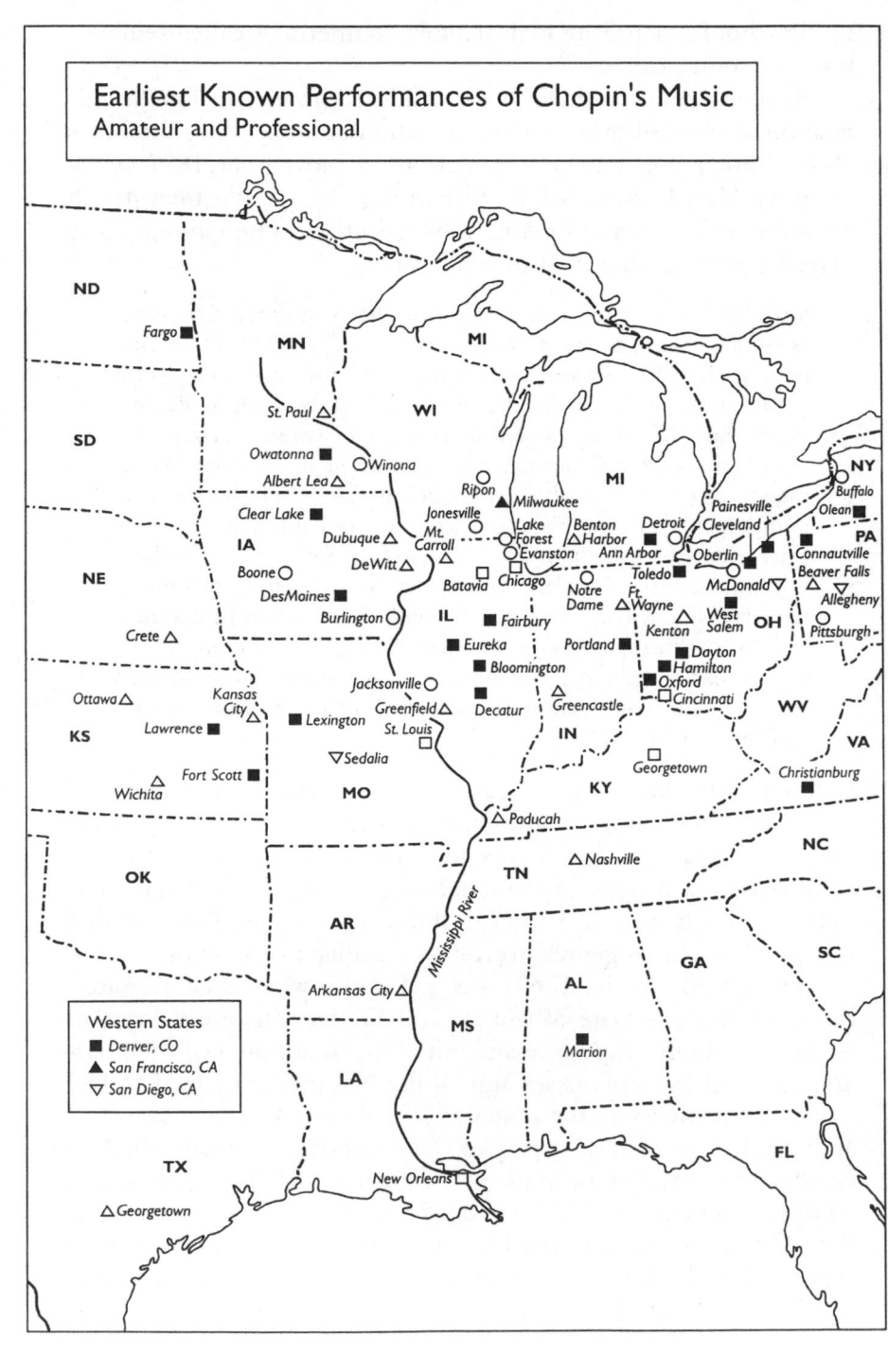

Earliest Known Performances of Chopin's Music
Amateur and Professional

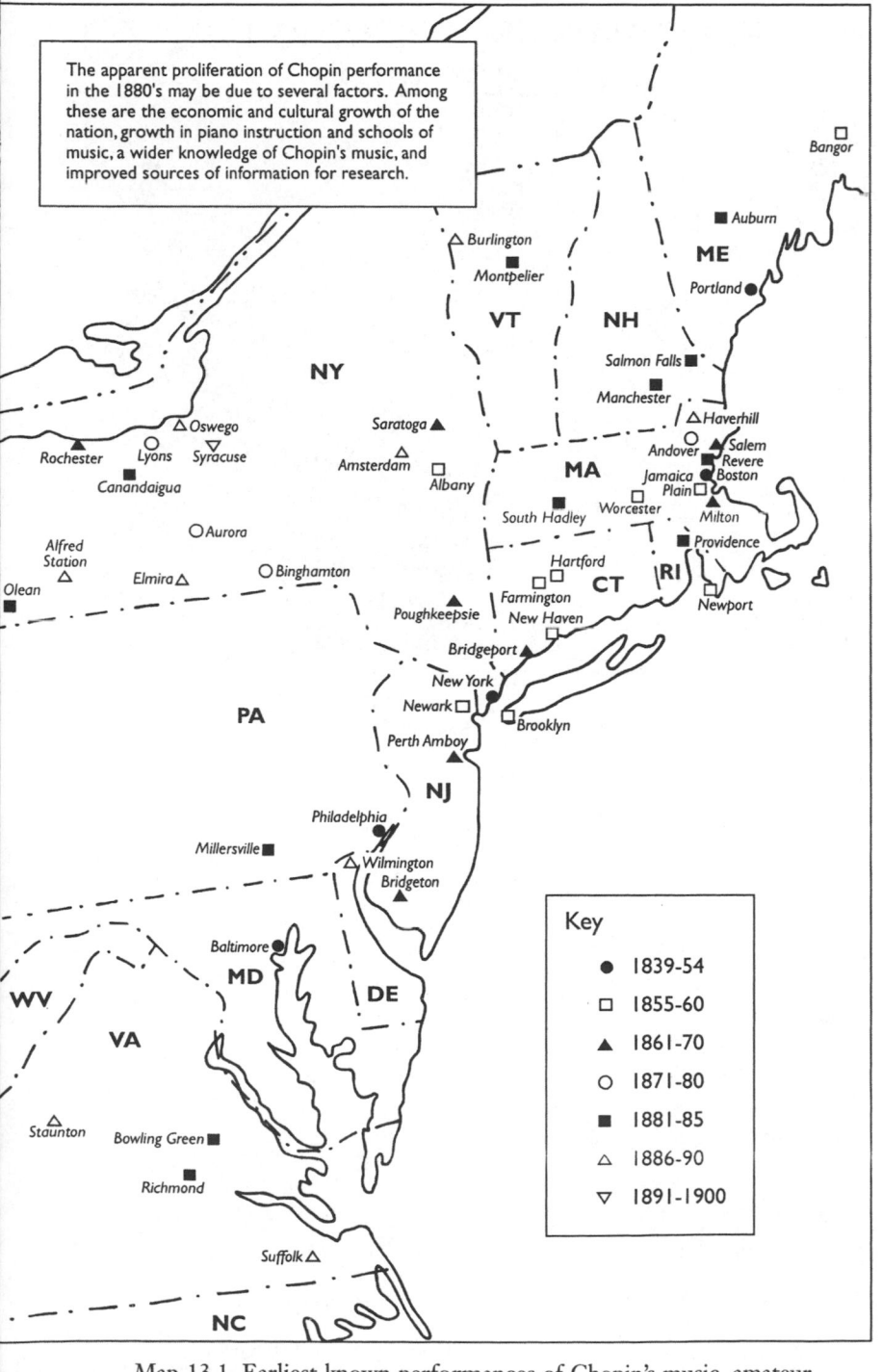

The apparent proliferation of Chopin performance in the 1880's may be due to several factors. Among these are the economic and cultural growth of the nation, growth in piano instruction and schools of music, a wider knowledge of Chopin's music, and improved sources of information for research.

Bangor

Auburn

ME

△ Burlington
■ Montpelier

Portland ●

VT    NH

Salmon Falls ■

Manchester

△ Haverhill

NY

Saratoga ▲

△ Oswego

Rochester ▲    ○ Lyons    ▽ Syracuse

■ Canandaigua

Amsterdam □

Albany

△ Andover    ○ Salem ▲

Revere

Jamaica ● Boston

Plain □ ●

Milton ▲

MA

South Hadley □

Worcester ■

Providence ■

○ Aurora

Alfred Station △

Olean ■    Elmira △    ○ Binghamton

Hartford □ □

Farmington

New Haven □

CT    RI

Newport □

PA

Poughkeepsie ▲

Bridgeport ▲

New York

Newark □ ●

Perth Amboy ▲    Brooklyn □

NJ

Philadelphia ●

Millersville ■

△ Wilmington

Bridgeton ▲

Baltimore ●

MD    DE

WV

VA

Staunton △

Bowling Green ■

Richmond ■

Suffolk △

NC

**Key**

| | |
|---|---|
| ● | 1839-54 |
| □ | 1855-60 |
| ▲ | 1861-70 |
| ○ | 1871-80 |
| ■ | 1881-85 |
| △ | 1886-90 |
| ▽ | 1891-1900 |

Map 13.1. Earliest known performances of Chopin's music, amateur and professional.

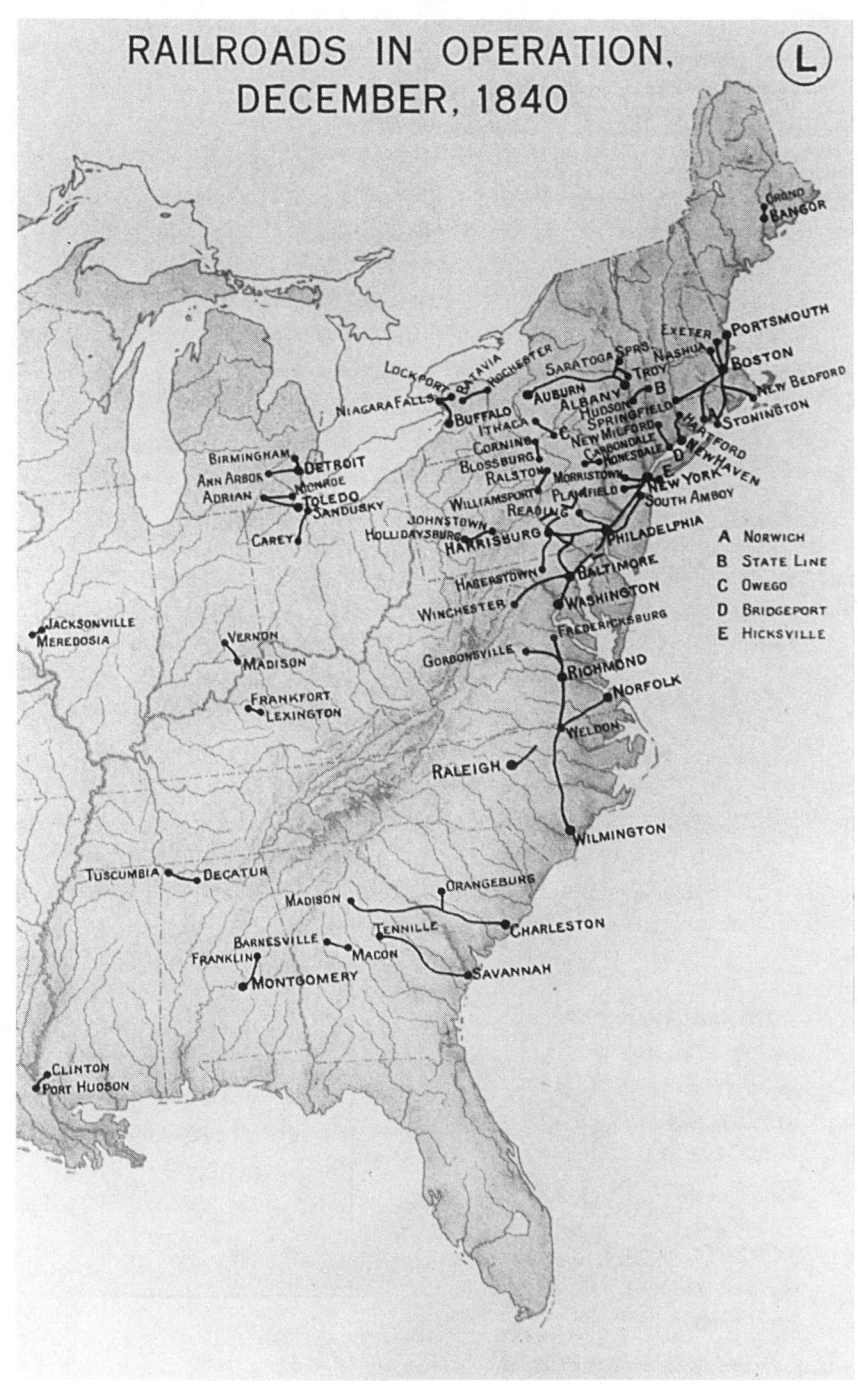

Map 13.2. Railroads in Operation, December 1840 (Charles O. Paulin, *Atlas of Historical Geography of the United States*, ed. John Wright [joint publication of the Carnegie Institution of Washington, D.C., and the American Geographical Society of New York, 1932] plate 138). Courtesy, American Antiquarian Society.

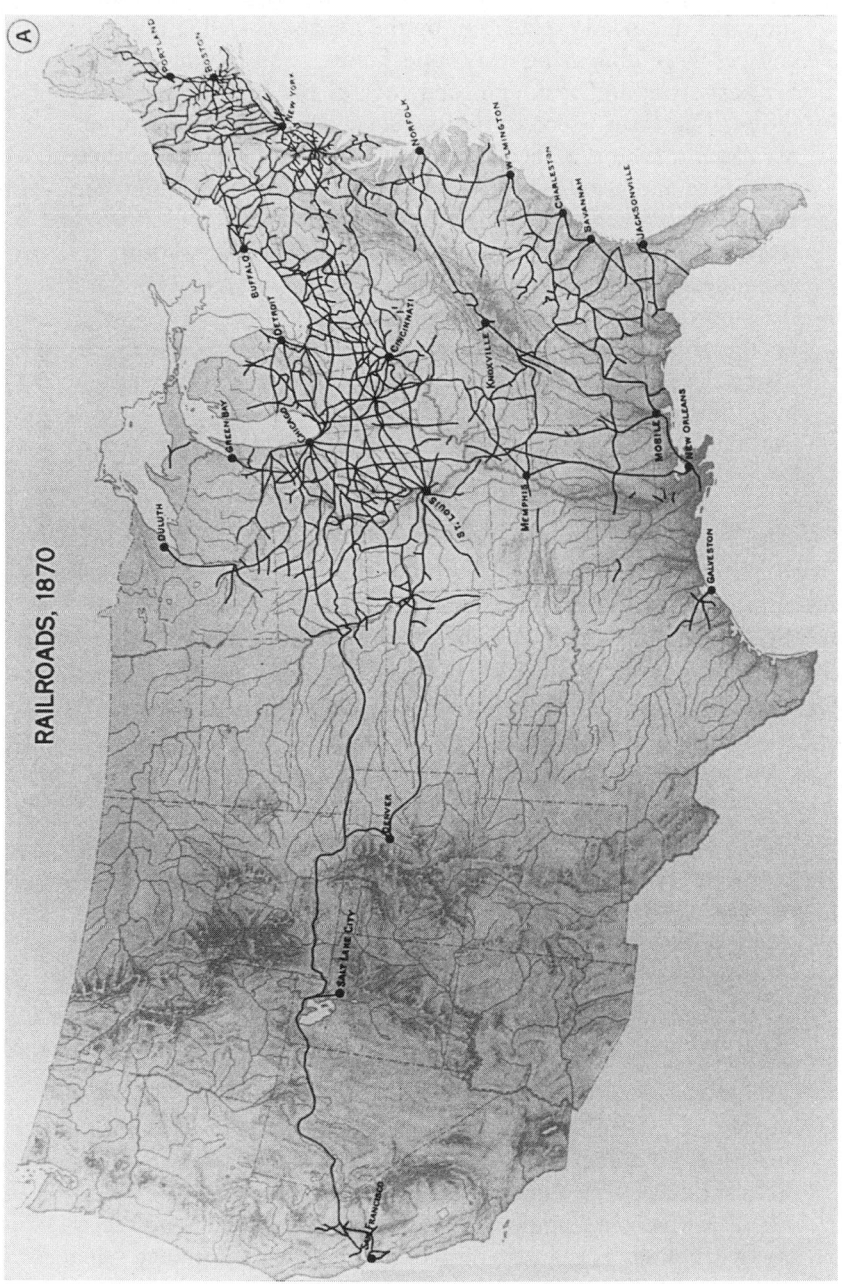

RAILROADS, 1870

Map 13.3. Railroads in 1870 (Paulin, *Atlas*, plate 140). Courtesy, American Antiquarian Society.

It was far different with Chopin's Concerto . . . which Mr. Mills played superbly. Here we have ideas that will bear elaboration; thoughts that need explanation by the master as well as the artist; and yet with fullness, nothing superfluous. . . . The concerto is in his best style; and although long, not in the faintest degree tedious. The form is somewhat peculiar, especially in the second movement, where a species of dramatic declamation has been attempted and not unsuccessfully. . . . It has been said, and sometimes with truth, that Mr. Mills lacks inspiration, aiming it would seem for mechanical perfection rather than poetic warmth and roundness. But in this movement, . . . he reproduced, we think, the composer's intention, and certainly left nothing to be desired by the most exigent stickler after style. The third movement, where the composer seems unwilling to leave his motive until he has reflected it in every possible contrapuntal light, was equally well done. . . . Mr. Mills was rewarded after each movement with a torrent of applause.[54]

George Templeton Strong, who had found the Concerto op. 11 a "pretty thing," recorded in his diary that op. 21 "did not interest me. Timm rates it very high."[55]

The growth of musical culture in the developing Midwest was materially aided by Easterners who either took up residence in the frontier cities or taught in short summer courses called Normal Music Schools or Teachers' Institutes. The critic C. H. Brittan sent Dwight a vivid description of the rationale for such courses.

As your Chicago correspondent has accepted an engagement to give instruction in a "Normal Music School" during part of the summer vacation, he takes the liberty of sending you a communication in regard to the workings of the school [in Princeton, Indiana]. . . . The Normal School for the study of music, if rightly conducted, becomes an important factor in the development of the musical talent of the West. For scattered throughout these smaller towns are numbers of music teachers who have little time, and, in most cases, not money enough, to come to the large cities during the musical season, and keep themselves abreast with the progress of the world. Thus we find a seeming necessity for these different musical elements,—from the large cities and the smaller inland towns,—to mingle with each other, imparting and receiving instruction, as the case may be. Oftentimes misguided talent is given a positive start in the true direction of development, and the seeds of a correct taste planted, which, after a season, bring forth fruit worthy of real art. . . .

The student who had devoted his time to commonplace music seems to find in the works of the old masters a new and
wonderful field for study. . . . a sonata of Beethoven will often
excite musical interest to such a degree that a long course of
technical *Etudes* are undertaken with the aim of reaching the
grand music of this master.[56]

William Mason, a leader in developing these schools, gave two
recitals a week wherever he taught, with a typical program consisting of a sonata by Beethoven, pieces by Schumann and Chopin,
and one of his own. By the end of a two-week course students
would have heard at least one nocturne, polonaise, waltz, and
ballade of Chopin plus others of the same or of other genres.[57]
For some students this would have been their first exposure to
Chopin.

The concert repertoire most often played in the 1860s demonstrates that the genres Ditson published in 1861 and 1865, and
those Mason introduced at summer institutes, were among the
standard concert fare, along with some large single-movement
works. Between 1861 and 1870 the most commonly heard pieces
were waltzes (especially op. 18), nocturnes (often op. 15 no. 2),
polonaises (opp. 53, 22), sometimes an etude or mazurka, the Ballades opp. 23 and 47, Scherzo op. 31, Impromptu op. 29, Berceuse,
Fantasie op. 49, *Fantasie-Impromptu*, *Marche funèbre*, and both Concertos. Works introduced but seldom played included the Allegro
de Concert, Ballade op. 38, Impromptu op. 36, Scherzos opp. 20,
39, and 54, and the Krakowiak op. 14. The Ballade op. 52,
Polonaise-Fantasie, Sonata for Cello and Piano, and Variations op.
2 each seem to have been played publicly only once, as far as I
have been able to discover. Works played in Philadelphia during
the season of 1868–69 might have passed as the "top eight" in the
United States at that time: both Concertos, the Fantasie op. 49,
Ballade op. 23, Scherzo op. 31, Nocturne op. 27 no. 2, and Etudes
op. 25 nos. 7 and 11.[58] The other piano music most frequently
played in that city (and in Boston) was by Mozart, Beethoven,
Mendelssohn, and Schumann.

Between 1870 and 1900 there was increased variety in the concert repertoire, particularly among the etudes, preludes, and mazurkas, and occasionally, too, there was an all-Chopin program.[59]
Favored works included waltzes (especially opp. 18, 42, 64 no. 1);
nocturnes (opp. 9 no. 2, 15 no. 2, 48 no. 1); polonaises (opp. 22,

40 no. 1, 53); Etudes op. 10 nos. 3 and 12, and op. 25 nos. 1 and 7; Prelude op. 28 no. 15; Ballades opp. 23 and 47; Scherzo op. 31; the Berceuse; Fantasie op. 49; Impromptu op. 29; Fantasie-Impromptu; Marche funèbre; and both Concertos. The Fantasie op. 49 was Anton Rubinstein's "big Chopin number" on his U.S. tour in 1872–73, and the Allegro de Concert was also played more widely than previously. Etudes, preludes, and mazurkas were now programmed in groups of four to six rather than singly, the mazurkas mainly by touring Europeans. The Sonata op. 35 was played occasionally.

Some late works were very seldom played: the Ballade op. 52, Scherzo op. 54, Sonata op. 58, Nocturnes op. 55 no. 2 and 62 no. 2, and the Polonaise-Fantasie. Beyond their formidable technical difficulties, those works contain enough that was novel in form, harmony, texture, and other elements of composition that they seemed inaccessible and met resistance from performers and critics. In a review of a recital by Charles Jarvis in Philadelphia in 1888, the anonymous critic "A" described Chopin's Sonata op. 58 as "a very brilliant work, but somewhat lacking in those qualities which go to the making of a great composition."[60]

By 1870 Chopin was increasingly included by American writers in the pantheon of otherwise German greats whose music had become part of the canon[61] and most publishers wanted a piece of the action. More effort was put into making Chopin the property of a larger group of amateurs. For those who wanted music without six flats, Ditson advertised: "Study in G [major], op. 25 no. 9. . . . Original key G♭."[62] The *Boston Conservatory Method for the Pianoforte* appeared in 1873 with a clumsily simplified and shortened version of the Waltz op. 18. That Waltz had become hugely popular and its inclusion was undoubtedly meant to attract those who had either heard it or knew the magic name of Chopin. In collections of mostly unpretentious music for teaching and for use by rural and urban families in the parlor, with titles such as *Little Classics for Little Players*, Chopin was now often represented by the Nocturne op. 9 no. 2, a waltz, or the Funeral March.

For professional pianists and the growing number of advanced students, G. Schirmer of New York issued a number of volumes and individual pieces in the 1880s and published Chopin's Complete Works, edited and fingered by Carl Mikuli, between 1894 and 1898.[63] Also in 1894, to secure their market share of intermediate to advanced players who wanted a sampling of works in

Table 13.2. Thirty-two Favorite Compositions by Frédéric Chopin

---

*Waltzes:* op. 18 E♭ Major; op. 34 no. 1 A♭ Major; op. 34 no. 2 A Minor; op. 42 A♭ Major; op. 64 no. 1 D♭ Major; op. 64 no. 2 C♯ Minor; Posth. E Minor

*Mazurkas:* op. 7 no. 1 B♭ Major; op. 7 no. 2 A Minor; op. 33 no. 1 G♯ Minor; op. 33 no. 3 C Major; op. 33 no. 4 B Minor

*Polonaises:* op. 40 no. 1 A Major; op. 26 no. 1 C♯ Minor

*Nocturnes:* op. 9 no. 2 E♭ Major; op.15 no. 2 F♯ Major; op. 15 no. 3 G Minor; op. 27 no. 2 D♭ Major; op. 32 no. 1 B Major; op. 37 no. 1 G Minor; op. 37 no. 2 G Major

*Ballades:* op. 47 A♭ Major; op. 23 G Minor

*Impromptu:* op. 29 A♭ Major

*Studies:* op. 25 no. 7 C♯ minor; op. 25 no. 9 G♭ Major; op. 25 no. 1 A♭ Major

*Prelude:* op. 28 no. 15 D♭ Major

*Scherzo:* op. 31 D♭ Major [given in the *Collection* as B♭ Minor]

*Fantasy-Impromptu:* op. 66 C♯ Minor

*Berceuse:* op. 57 D♭ Major

*Funeral March* from Sonata op. 35 B♭ Minor

---

many genres, Schirmer put out *A Collection of 32 Favorite Compositions* that are listed in Table 13.2. According to my survey of Chopin's music played in nineteenth-century America, almost all the pieces included are among either the ones most often played in concert or the ones most often studied.

Prepared to a degree by their earlier European experience of Chopin's music, American critics for the most part gave much of Chopin's work a favorable reception. There was nothing like the pockets of strong resistance found in England and Germany. But a few reviews of a popular favorite in a familiar style, op. 11, and of a later work in which Chopin broke many boundaries, op. 23, reveal a difference in reception as he moved away from the readily accessible *stile brillante* to a less comprehensible, more individual style.

Earlier I cited Watson's unalloyed praise of the second and third movements of op. 11 after its première in New York. Of that same performance the reviewer for the *Morning Courier* wrote:

> The music . . . is very beautiful, full of imagination and originality, . . . much less crude in its harmonies and more shapely in form than any other of Chopin's compositions which we know;

but it is not a concerto. It lacks the construction of a concerto; there is no working of the subjects between the pianoforte and the orchestra at all, and it seems rather a sonata with orchestral accompaniment. Mr. Timm's performance was received with enthusiasm.[64]

Although all newspaper reviews at this time were written anonymously, this was probably penned by Richard Grant White, who was generally admired for his criticism.[65]

Dwight had heard all three movements in the Boston première by Jaëll. The Concerto was "full of beauties . . . [he wrote]; and though that form required of [Chopin] more brilliancy, more popular effect than is his wont, yet repeatedly there fleet and smile across the bolder and more common passages some of those faint, exquisite *fioriture*, so steeped in finest sentiment, which reveal [his] inmost peculiarity." Here Dwight recognized the delicacy of detail and sensuousness in Chopin's melodic style that were often heard in a gendered role. Then he co-opted Liszt's opinion that "in [Chopin's] efforts to bring his thoughts into the limits of the strictly classic form, 'we discern rather the will, the purpose, than the inspiration.' "[66] Of this Concerto, generally only the form and sometimes the length of the first movement or the orchestration were criticized[67] but most critics thought it an excellent composition, "full of originality and peculiar [individual or distinctive] effects."[68] Audiences listened "most intently" and loved it.

William Henry Fry of the *New York Tribune*—a composer of symphonies and operas and no lover of the piano—occasionally carped at Chopin and was strongly prejudiced against recent developments in German music, which he found wanting in melody and tending toward chaos. After a performance in 1854 he appraised the Romance and Finale of op. 11 with a backhanded compliment followed by an insult: the solo part, particularly the slow movement, "is more Italian in its melody" than most of Chopin's works, "whose characteristics are national and salient. . . . The coda to the rondo would pass for the kind which Herz invented. The execution [by Richard Hoffman] was admirable and brought down the house"[69]

In the early 1870s the conservative critic of the *Boston Daily Advertiser* voiced stronger negative opinions of Chopin's works. After praising a "perfect" performance of op. 11 by Anna Mehlig, he demeaned this Concerto to a degree seldom reached in the American press:

There is in much of Chopin's music a whimsicality, almost amounting to sickliness, [some of which is] . . . exhibited in the *allegro* of this concerto. Many of Chopin's effects are but pretty conceits, pleasing by the richness of the coloring, lulling the sense with delight, astonishing by their mechanical difficulty very often, but hardly warming the hearer, hardly firing the mind with enthusiasm as Beethoven almost always does. It is *genre* painting; still-life with a strong national flavor.[70]

However, that feminizing and devalorizing review sounds almost neutral when compared to an anonymous review from the British *Musical Magazine* of July 1835, which calls the concerto a "heterogeneous mass, *and compound of filthy sounds.* . . . ludicrous and extravagant passages—modulations we cannot call them, for they *'Out Herod'* every thing of the kind we ever before heard; . . . It is altogether beneath criticism."[71]

By contrast with the Concerto, the Ballade op. 23—a work of daring originality—received a decidedly mixed reception from American critics and audiences, although it was a perennial favorite of pianists. Dwight found it "full of poetry and meaning" at its première, as cited above, and in 1855, played by Gustave Satter, he described it as "one of the most florid, dreamy, passion-fraught, and difficult of [Chopin's] compositions [though it] was played with wonderful ease and brilliancy."[72] But when Satter programmed the Ballade in New York shortly afterward, a lengthy review in *The Musical World* said not a word about it. Probably the critic found it too strange at first, as did G. W. Fink, who reviewed the work in *Allgemeine musikalische Zeitung* only after five hearings.[73] The *New York Times* admitted that the "ballad [!] . . . did not impress us so favorably. . . . The individuality of the composer was preserved too tenaciously, and the thin, thought-like outline of his ballad became lost in what should have been the subordinate characteristic coloring."[74] That critic's lamentable prose expresses his bewilderment all too well.

That Ballade was the only work prior to the Sonata op. 35 that reaped broadly negative reactions in America. Strong recorded in his diary, "gymnastic rather than musical: Truck, . . . unmeaning sequences of notes to show off a player's muscle. . . . What idiocy most of our fashionable piano music is!"[75] Carl Wolfsohn's performance in Philadelphia in 1865 caused "Mercutio" to report that although the work is "replete with beauties, [it] is not, to my fancy, one of [the composer's] best efforts; why Mr. Wolfsohn should have selected it, I can scarcely imagine."[76] When Anton Rubinstein played the Ballade in New York in 1872, the audience was less enthusiastic than Dwight's reporter. He noted the difference between the reaction to that piece and to Rubinstein's arrangement of Beethoven's March from *The Ruins of Athens*, a public favorite he considered "utterly commonplace." "Compare the applause which follows [the March] with the faint praise called forth by a rendering of Chopin's *Ballade*, in which the piano sings like a siren, where the true nature and greatness of the artist are clearly revealed."[77]

Reference to op. 23 as a work inspired by the plight of Poland and its émigrés was rare in America until Huneker's book, *Chopin: The Man and His Music*, appeared in 1900. However, Fanny Malone Ritter, one of the few women writers on music and a person who read widely in the European literature, remarked of the Ballade in 1879 that "every phrase [is] weighty . . . with concentrated anger, patriotic rage, and regret."[78] By 1890 no audience reserve was noted by the *Chicago Tribune* when Adele Aus der Ohe gave "an unusually excellent interpretation of this beautiful [Ballade]."[79] Fortunately the pianists had persisted, and by the end of the century the audience, too, found the beauty in Chopin's adventure.

*   *   *

There were, of course, expectations for fine Chopin performance by the end of the nineteenth century. Reviews of pianists considered important Chopin players reveal what critics were listening for and hoping to hear, what they actually heard, and what they were reacting against.

For American critics, Chopin's music required the utmost subtlety in performance. In 1861 Minos in Philadelphia stated that Mr. Jarvis "can play everything else and 'Chopin' into the bargain."[80] A decade later Dwight commented that Anton Rubinstein's playing of Mozart's Rondo in A Minor was "delicious" in Rubinstein's "nice and tender handling; he refined it to an almost Chopin-like subtlety and grace."[81] And in a report from New York to Dwight in 1876, A.A.C. wrote: "One who plays Chopin can play anything. But it is no mean test, for his music traverses the whole gamut of human emotions and experiences."[82]

How was this subtlety created? One phrase that reviewers of Chopin playing used was "the true spirit," coined in 1858 by the anonymous—t—when he wrote of a performance by Mr. Goldbeck in New York: the pieces "were correctly played, but without the true spirit."[83] The importance of reproducing "the composer's intention" was mentioned above in a review of Mr. Mills's première of the Concerto op. 21. What was "the true spirit" or "the real Chopinism of Chopin" that "very few . . . pianists . . . can interpret?"[84] One essential, according to A.A.C. in New York, was a poetic, "spiritual approach," to express "the true Chopin mood, that indefinable *żal,*"[85] a Polish melancholy tinged with grief, remembrance, or regret.

In a review dated 3 February 1857,—t—was "very much" disappointed in Mr. Goldbeck's performance of Chopin's Prelude op. 28 no. 15 and tells us how *not* to play Chopin. "He seemed not to have entered at all into the spirit of that tender, sighing first part, but played it in a really matter-of-fact manner, too fast, without the least delicacy, and with nothing of the 'rubato,' which . . . it so evidently requires. The second part, with its mysterious chords . . . he interpreted far better."[86]

The reviews of Rafael Joseffy, one of the premiere Chopin players of his time, provide more positive evidence. This quotation is from the *New York Tribune* following his debut in October 1879:

> When we hear of a phenomenal young pianist . . . we usually think of a "pounder." Joseffy is anything but that. He is brilliant, yet not noisy, dashing without clatter. Neither does he dazzle us with flashes of irregular splendor, or overcome us with outbursts of passion and tempest. His playing, full . . . of glowing color and of strong feeling, is justly measured and exquisitely symmetrical. . . . It is when Joseffy executes the softest passages of Chopin that we feel surest in declaring him the most dashing of all pianists. . . . There is perhaps no pianist now living whose work is so clean. . . . Every phrase is . . . clear; . . . his precision . . . seems . . . to be the simplest expression of a poetical nature highly endowed with a sense of the beauty of form and proportion. [Coupled with this elegance of expression is] a wonderful . . . beauty of touch. . . . his tone was a revelation. Few of us believed that the piano could produce sounds so sweet and varied.[87]

In Boston, Dwight had never heard "a more near approach to absolute perfection in every element of technique and of execution." He called attention to "the . . . penetrating power, always expressively graduated and shaded; . . . singularly soft and velvety *pianissimos;* . . . faultless style, proportion, unity throughout."[88] A correspondent from New York wrote to Dwight of Joseffy's "perfect use of the pedal (an art in itself) [which is a] peculiar qualification for the satisfactory performance of the exacting compositions of the greatest writer for the pianoforte . . . who has ever lived."[89] For C. H. Brittan in Chicago, however, Joseffy did not "represent the heroic side, after the manner of a Rubinstein, perhaps, nor the intellectuality of von Bülow."[90] But for most other critics, the only serious criticism leveled at Joseffy was for adding occasional octaves (à la Tausig) or embellishments in certain of Chopin's pieces: "this is simply atrocious, and as a display of impudence is unparalleled."[91] Unfortunately Joseffy left no recordings.

As just noted, both Anton Rubinstein and Hans van Bülow also gave concerts in America in the 1870s. Their divergent musical personalities provided critics the opportunity to discuss composer- and work-centered performance versus virtuosity and individuality in performance. Rubinstein was a powerful performer. In spite of "the beauty of his tone" and "the alternate might and delicacy of his touch," in 1873 the reviewer for the *New York Times* felt that he was

> not always at his best in Chopin's music. . . . The vigor and dash of his execution are sometimes detrimental to the effect of the vaguely beautiful and ever-changing harmonies, and the elaborate arabesques of the Polish artist's writings. We have to be grateful to Mr. Rubinstein for not using to excess the *tempo rubato*, and his playing yesterday was marked by a less injudicious recourse to the pedal than we have sometimes had cause to complain of; on the other hand, though his most rapid passages were generally clear, they were often too deftly done for the ear to catch the composer's intentions, and they dazzled rather then charmed.[92]

According to this review Rubinstein's playing included several an- tipodes of the qualities for which Joseffy was praised. He does not "dazzle" us but charms with his beauty of touch, tone, proportion, and poetical expression. His use of the pedal was "perfect."

Of Rubinstein's concerts in Boston in May 1873 Dwight re- ported very little "of that stormy exaggeration to which we have alluded on some former occasions," but he noted "passionate ex- pression alternating with the sweetest tenderness" in the Mozart Fantasia in C Minor.[93] A later all-Chopin program received high praise. His rendering of the *Berceuse* was "exquisitely perfect in its way; such purity and even delicacy of tone we never heard surpassed or equalled; the notes run like oil, yet are distinct as pearls.—And so on, through *Mazurkas*, *Valses*, the rousing *Polonaise* in A, . . . and several *Etudes*, some of terrific speed and intricacy, in which he calmly rides the whirlwind."[94] However, William Foster Apthorp, also Boston-based and writing for the *Atlantic Monthly*, was not so pleased.

> It has become too painfully evident that Rubinstein often plays works of the great masters not as they are, but as his momentary mood impels him to feel them. He either cannot or is often too careless to merge his own fiery individuality in that of the composer. It takes little acumen to see how utterly different Rubinstein's nature is from that of Beethoven, Bach, Schumann, Mendelssohn, and many other composers. . . . His hot Slavic blood . . . is ever liable to rebel against that moderation in expression and style which his great predecessors felt to be one of the highest elements in art. Schumann . . . becomes at times a perfect bull in a china-shop in Rubinstein's hands; Chopin . . . is often fit to turn the saints themselves into bacchantes when he speaks to us through Rubinstein's fingers. . . . Now Rubinstein's influence upon young musicians has been in many cases undeniably bad. Admiration prompts imitation. . . . Why should not I too be a thunderer? says the young pianist.[95]

Von Bülow's approach to interpretation resulted in his being considered an "intellectual" performer. Reviewing his concert of 18 January 1876 in Poughkeepsie, Fanny M. Ritter explained why he

> is the most unique of living artists. Unique, because, more than any preceding or contemporary pianist, he voluntarily abjures his own nature, in order to enter more fully into that of other artists. . . . Bülow is . . . a perfect pianist; one of extraordinary mental capacity, scholarship, mechanism, taste, correctness, and power of memory. He is too thoroughly intellectual a player ever to be carried by irresistible fervor of feeling over the boundaries of conscious self-possession; but it would be most unjust to stigmatize him therefore as cold and unfeeling, for such genuine artistic manifestations as those of Bülow necessarily combine deep emotion with high thought.[96]

Writing of another concert, Dwight concurred: "Dr. Von Bülow's *technique* is simply perfect." He has "mastery of the rare art of *phrasing*. . . . Where he astonished, startled, he did not break the spell of beauty. Proportion, measure, the *repose* of Art, pervaded all. . . . We were hearing Beethoven, as afterwards Chopin, far more than we were hearing Bülow."[97] Following his Boston appearance, von Bülow arrived in Philadelphia on the heels of Anton Rubinstein. In a very long article about von Bülow's background and first concert in that city, the critic for the *Philadelphia Inquirer* compared the playing of the two men. "Rubinstein [also a composer] represents the creative gift of genius, always wonderful, often magnificent, sometimes erring. Bülow represents the highest form of acquired taste, not always either wonderful or magnificent, but always satisfying."[98] Rubinstein put before the public *his* conception of the music; he was all virtuosic interpreter. With von Bülow, a work-oriented "subordination of player to composer" was almost always evident.

After his next concert the *Inquirer* had more to say about von Bülow's playing of Chopin.

> It has been understood for years that Bülow was most remarkable for interpreting Beethoven. But, judging by the past two concerts, Chopin's music is that which gains most at his hands. The consummate art and the faithful expression of the player give to Chopin a power and meaning which never appeared before. The Nocturne in G major . . . and the Valse Brillante, opus 42, were exceedingly fine. But they were fairly eclipsed by the "Berceuse" and the "Polonaise in A flat." Nothing equal to the grace and delicacy of the former or the splendid octave passages in the latter has been heard here before.[99]

Finally, a review of Bülow in the *Baltimore Bulletin* harks back to a comment by Richard Willis on Chopin's own playing, cited above.

> To our fancy he excels all others in [Chopin's] music; it is so exquisitely tender and poetic. Rubinstein played Chopin grandly; but Chopin is ethereal, capricious, morbid, not grand. . . . Von Bülow plays the wild arabesques that Chopin throws around his themes, with such a soft touch, so legato, yet so crisp, that they seem almost to be felt rather than heard, and through this the melody wails so sadly that it seems to call up the pale sad face of the composer before the listener. His is the very music of Chopin: von Bülow understands him best.[100]

Raoul Pugno, a student of Chopin's pupil Georges Mathias, and perhaps the leading exponent of the French school of pianism at the turn of the century, left some very early recordings.[101] His was playing of elegance, clarity, and controlled expression, al-though—judging from his recordings but even more from the re-views—he allowed himself, on occasion, greater abandon than usual in the French school, especially in regard to power. The main criticism of Pugno's playing by his contemporaries seems to have been his fondness for what the *New York Times* reviewer termed "harsh and unlovely [dynamic] contrasts."[102] However, his "almost superhuman technique"[103] provided accuracy, lightness, and deft-ness even at some incredibly fast speeds. The lighter action of the French pianos (in comparison with German and American instru-ments of the period) was ideal for such technique.

Pugno's programs of November 1905 in Boston and New York included—following Schumann's *Faschingschwank aus Wien*—Cho-pin's Ballade op. 23, the rarely played Nocturne op. 62 no. 2, *Fantasy-Impromptu* op. 66, and the Polonaise op. 22. The *Boston Evening Transcript* observed:

> He played the [*Faschingschwank*] with a vigor warmed with what was almost dash and enthusiasm—almost, but not quite. For Mr. Pugno never forgets his containment. That is the charm of [his] playing. To like him you must like that and look for it.
>
> His Chopin gains from this [containment] qualities and beau-ties that are generally absent from the playing of those who spoil Chopin with improving him. Mr. Pugno puts Chopin on the key-board and lets him play himself. In consequence we get a Chopin that is refreshingly new, until it strikes you as being the Chopin we ought always to hear; done without any sobbing, in perfect rhythm, and in a tone whose usual Chopin sugariness has been gratefully sent a-flying.[104]

That description echoes some characteristics of von Bülow's play-ing and is reminiscent of the comments of Mikuli, another of Cho-pin's students and his assistant for several years, who wrote that "Chopin's playing was always controlled, chaste, truly refined, and at times even severely reserved."[105]

The *Boston Daily Advertiser* amplified views related to those of the *Transcript:*

> At last we have a pianist who can play [Chopin] for men, as well as for women. . . . The average man is not overfond of candy as a steady diet. . . . Pugno is no confectioner. . . .

It is refreshing to hear such music played with a strong virility, clear, resonant, altogether different from the cloying sweetness which has been ladled out on a patient public ever since the
rush of foreign pianists set in. Nobody could mistake . . . that it
was a different artist from the old Liszt school. . . . There was no
blacksmith work either.[106]

Of his New York recital William James Henderson of the *New
York Times*—regarded by some as the most brilliant of the American critics at this time[107]—noted frequent disproportionate contrasts of dynamics, especially in Beethoven's Sonata op. 31 no. 2.
But, in his playing of Chopin,

> he seemed to practice a greater moderation in extremes, both of
> tempo and of dynamics. He works here with more delicate and
> more beautiful tone color, with subtler shades and half tints. It
> is a man's Chopin that he gives. He is not . . . a sentimentalist.
> . . . Yet there is in [his playing] a definite mood of poetry.[108]

Pugno recorded Chopin's *Marche funèbre* and the Berceuse on
disc in Paris in 1903 under extremely primitive conditions,[109] and
the Polonaise op. 22 (without orchestra) on a Welte-Mignon roll
in 1905.[110] The Trio of the *Marche* demonstrates what reviewers
described as Pugno's more straightforward, unsentimental yet sensitive manner of playing Chopin. But what is a surprise for listeners
now, although not unusual then, is that at the return of the *Marche*
Pugno took the liberty of turning Chopin's dynamics on their head.
He placed the band directly in front of us, with a powerful *fortissimo*, and let the sound diminish as the players move away—the
opposite of Chopin's plan, which repeats the dynamics as they had
been in the opening *Marche*.

The Polonaise op. 22 demonstrates Pugno's sensitive coloring
of tone, sometimes achieved with imaginative use of the *una corda*
in conjunction with the damper pedal (again reminiscent of what
we read about Chopin's playing)[111] and his famous *jeu perlé* passage-
work that he colored to a surprising degree with pedal. This Polonaise was among Chopin's works whose playing was praised in the
reviews of 1905 quoted above; and after Pugno's recital in December 1902, the *New York Times* reported that it was among the works
that "showed the best side of his art."[112]

Vladimir de Pachmann, born in the Ukraine, belonged to no
particular school of piano playing; his fame rested largely on his

own style of Chopin performance, which always seems to have been tonally beautiful and delicate, though by the time he made recordings, musical miscalculations of other types began to appear in his playing. "Probably nobody plays Chopin's music more nearly as Chopin himself played it, in scale of conception and quality and subtlety of tone," wrote one of Pachmann's severest critics, Richard Aldrich of the *New York Times*, in 1911.[113] The opinions expressed of his New York debut on 7 April 1890 in the *New York Times* and the *New York Tribune* were remarkably similar. Henry Krehbiel of the *Tribune* observed:

> M. de Pachmann is . . . a genre player, . . . listen to him attentively and one is transported into another musical atmosphere . . . where finesse . . . and genuine poetic feeling predominate. Pachmann's art is the art of the miniature painter, . . . He does not stun nor startle one, but the sensuous beauty of his touch, his subtle phrasing, his admirable rubato, and the absolute finish of his technical work, rank him at once as a pianist hors ligne, but one whose limitations are unusually well defined. . . . Pachmann's pianissimo appears to begin where other pianists end theirs. His coloring is most tender and evanescent, but [the amount of] tone was his weakest point. . . . He is wanting entirely in his appreciation of the Polish tone-poet on the virile side. But the brilliant elegancies, the tender morbidities, and that exotic atmosphere which envelops many of Chopin's compositions—for all these Pachmann seems to have the most intense appreciation.[114]

Of the same concert Henderson wrote:

> His tone color is very soft and agreeable. . . . His playing is full of delightful nuances, which are never forgotten even in the most rapid passages. His cantabile is sweet and well sustained. . . .
> On the other hand, his range of dynamic effects is not large. His limits appear to lie between an extremely delicate pianissimo and a fairly sonorous forte. . . . [O]n the whole, M. de Pachmann's playing of those numbers which represent the feminine side of Chopin's character was delightful. [But] the finale [of the Sonata op. 58] was deficient in force [as were] the latter part of the ballade [op. 23] and the allegro de concert [!]. . . . His conception of Chopin's music appears to be tinged chiefly with delicacy and tenderness. . . . It is pretty well established, however, that there was a masculine side to Chopin's nature, and, so far as yesterday's performance indicated, the new-comer will not teach his American hearers much about that.[115]

In a review of his second program, the *Times* opined that Pachmann's touch in Chopin's smaller works "is very much like what Joseffy's was in the days when he excelled as a Chopin player. There are some things of Chopin's that we should prefer to hear Joseffy play now rather than de Pachmann."[116] Henry Finck of the New York *Evening Post* remarked that, for him, Pachmann did "not sufficiently emphasize discords, on which the dramatic life of a composition depends. In this respect Mr. Joseffy is his superior"[117]

Chopin's Nocturne op. 27 no. 2 was very much in vogue at this time. In 1890 the *Tribune* wrote that Pachmann played the Nocturne "in a velvety fashion."[118] According to Aldrich in 1904, its performance "was truly poetic, melting in its delicious tonal quality, and as the carving of a cameo in the exquisite clarity of its outlines and gradations at the extreme vanishing point of pianissimo."[119] In Pachmann's recording from 1916, Chopin's inner voices—tucked into the rhythmically weak sixteenths of the left-hand accompaniment (e.g., mm. 32–33) but more obvious in the alto—are carried to the ear in sensuous tones that still fit among their neighbors.[120]

The Etude op. 25 no. 9, the "Butterfly," was another favorite of the period. After Pachmann's first performance of it in America in April 1890, Krehbiel thought it one of "the gems of the afternoon's performance."[121] In 1911, after wishing for more dramatic power and passion in the "Revolutionary" Etude, Aldrich described the Etude op. 25 no. 9, the Ballade op. 47, and the Nocturne op. 15 no. 1 as "flooded with beauty by Mr. de Pachman's playing. . . . [These works as Pachmann plays them] need raise no . . . feeling of loss of emotional power in his interpretation. . . . He can be accepted thus as a sensuous delight, for a time; but such art before long cloys. It cannot . . . make the music with which it concerns itself truly beautiful or noble in any of the deeper sense that is attached to beauty and nobility."[122] In his recording of the Etude, which dates from 1907, between the years of those two reviews, Pachmann used even less pedal than Chopin indicated, perhaps because of problems with pedaling in the recording techniques of those early years; but he did use Chopin's pedalings to help build his subtle climax, which is hardly the indicated fortissimo. Unfortunately at the end, instead of letting the "Butterfly" go free, Pachmann added his own stereotypical chordal cadence that grounds the hovering creature.[123]

In 1899 Pachmann played Chopin's Piano Concerto op. 21

with the Boston Symphony Orchestra. Apthorp's remarks reflect the performer's total absorption in the music at hand.

> The whole work is of the tender, moonlight sort; ineffably beautiful but not grand. . . . Pachmann takes it from this point of view. . . . Hardly ever have I heard . . . so homogeneous a piece of playing; . . . for artistic perfection of expression . . . it was simply a wonder. Here we had . . . the whole of the Chopin F-Minor Concerto, and nothing but the Chopin F-Minor Concerto! It was a great achievement.[124]

Yet, in spite of the beauty of tone and other aesthetic assets of Pachmann's playing, by 1900 the *New York Times* had marked him as an erratic player, but without specific details and no mention of his talking as he played and other bizarre behavior. In 1904 Richard Aldrich of the *Times* believed that it was "difficult for Mr. de Pachmann to carry conviction as a truly great artist; but as a wonderful one, as a worker of a magical spell of his own, there is no one like him."[125]

Finally, in the course of assessing Pachmann as a Chopin player in 1907, an anonymous reviewer for the *Indianapolis News* mentioned again his periodic lack of emotional connection with the music he was playing and posited an unusual opinion of the role of Chopin's polonaises and ballades among his works.

> One feels that the polonaise form . . . is not the one which best exposes the pianist's genius. The polonaise is essentially proclamatory and dramatic, and no one else ever looked upon the actual vicissitudes of life, personal or national, with all the indifference of Pachmann. This is no denial of the assertion of those that fix Pachmann's place as the most intimate interpreter of Chopin. . . . [But] it is not in the polonaises or the ballads [!] that Chopin expressed the most influential elements of his being. They are the products of his moments of boisterous reaction from his brooding reflection and searching emotionality. . . . It must be in the smaller pieces that Chopin did his most important work and it must be in these that Pachmann attains to his finest effects.[126]

On the interpretation of Chopin's virile or heroic side the critics were not always in agreement. Most thought Joseffy and Rubinstein succeeded and Pachmann was woefully lacking; about Eugen d'Albert's Chopin playing there was genuine disagreement, which reveals a difference in the attitude of the reviewers toward the concerto played. On 18 November 1889 d'Albert played Chopin's Concerto op. 11 in New York. Even though he "did not disclose his powers in their entire puissance" until later in the program, Henry Krehbiel opined:

> Mr. d'Albert is somewhat virile and masculine for so essentially sentimental a composition as the familiar Concerto, and though he endowed his characteristically sane reading of it with unmistakable charm, he nevertheless exhibited a sobriety of tone-color and occasional hardness of touch which gave a foothold to a fault-finding disposition.[127]

As a critic Krehbiel was conservative, sometimes imperious, and "gave the impression that he was in possession of the unchangeable laws of music."[128] Nevertheless, from our twenty-first-century vantage he was at times surprisingly perspicacious. Critics had asserted that Chopin "did not disclose any special ability as a writer for the orchestra." After commenting negatively on the resulting re-orchestrations of his concertos by Klindworth and Tausig, Krehbiel posed a question that is being addressed again now: "But suppose the essence of Chopinism lies in this unequal relationship—what then? Is it not better to take his music as he intended it?"[129] Although there may be more than one reason for the manner in which Chopin orchestrated his concertos, Halina Goldberg has recently suggested that Chopin may have had in mind the more intimate venues and small forces commonly used for concerto performance in the nineteenth century.[130]

Reviewing that same performance of op. 11 by d'Albert for the *New York Times*, Henderson dubbed d'Albert "the little giant of the pianoforte" and compared him to the "diminutive" Moritz Rosenthal, whose "technical ability" included everything "known to the virtuosity of today." D'Albert has all that, but in addition:

> There is a more intense and vital individuality, a deeper and broader temperament, a more highly-gifted and more thoroughly-developed intellectuality. D'Albert is . . . a great musician. He is a thinker, an analyzer, and an explicator. His choice of the Chopin E minor concerto . . . was a happy one. Local music lovers . . . have heard all kinds of pianists play it, from Rosenthal and Joseffy to Otto Hegner. . . . D'Albert's performance of the work was . . . the greatest ever heard in this city. It was a surpassingly lovely reading of an immortal composition, and stamped D'Albert as one of the master musicians of this time.[131]

D'Albert was of the Liszt school and in this first tour of America, from the autumn of 1889 to the spring of 1890, he was at the peak of his pianism. However, in May he arrived in Boston in the shadow of Pachmann, and Arthur Weld, of the Boston *Post*, going far beyond Krehbiel's criticism, thought d'Albert's decision to play a Chopin group was a mistake. Pachmann was a "specialist, . . . apparently born to play Chopin's music," and his interpretation has been "a revelation in every way."

> [This] rather boisterous Englishman . . . thumps out these graceful measures with all the unmeasured force which is the chief . . . fault of his playing, and . . . it seems as if the wonderful composer whom we had only just learned to know was being deliberately murdered before our eyes. [In addition, much of] his work was rough and careless, and most of the time exasperatingly noisy.[132]

During the early years of the century D'Albert became more interested in composition, which worked to the detriment of his piano playing. By the time he began to make recordings, from 1910 on, we hear reflections of his greatness but he was already past his prime. Looking back, his real strength seems to have been as an interpreter of Beethoven and the German repertory.

Of all these pianists, the two most widely recognized as "Chopin specialists" were Joseffy and Pachmann. Henderson's review of Pachmann's second recital in New York in 1890 assesses Chopin's position in the world of piano music and pianism in words that remain true to this day.

> [The recital] was attended by a large audience, which was generous . . . in its expressions of approval. It was natural that people should have a great curiosity to hear a specialist in Chopin, whose music is a prolific subject of discussion. Its technical peculiarities and the singular difficulty of achieving certain Chopinesque effects are subjects of constant debate among musicians, and its aesthetic qualities give rise to many differences of opinion.[133]

### NOTES

Sections of this essay are reprinted, with permission of the editor, from the online *Polish Music Journal* 3, no. 2 (2000).

1. *Evening Star*, 15 October 1839, 2. Among the few relevant facts that can be found about Rakemann is that he had studied with both Hummel and Thalberg.

2. As announced in the program published by the *Morning Courier* on 15 October 1839, 2. Although both the *Evening Star* and the *Morning Courier & New-York Enquirer* wrote glowing reminders to their readers to attend the concert, neither paper reviewed it!

3. *Boston Evening Transcript*, 5 November 1839, 2.

4. *The Musical Magazine* 23 (9 November 1839): 367. This review was probably by German-born H. Theodor Hach, one of the magazine's editors and Dwight's close friend.

5. John Sullivan Dwight, "Concerts of the Past Winter," *The Dial* 1, no. 1 (July 1840): 129–30. *The Dial* and *The Harbinger*, in which Dwight also wrote, were publications of the New England transcendental movement, in which he was an active participant. Dwight had been educated at Harvard College and Harvard Divinity School and later was a founding member of the Harvard Musical Association.

6. *Dwight's Journal of Music* 10, no. 2 (11 October 1856): 14; hereafter, *DJ*. This recollection was occasioned by Dwight's article on Thalberg upon his long awaited arrival in New York.

7. Anonymous but possibly by Richard Grant White, *Morning Courier & New-York Enquirer*, 16 October 1846, 2. The *Evening Post* did not mention the piano solo. Fontana's solos in his debut program on 3 January 1846 had included only selections by Liszt, Thalberg, and himself (*New York Daily Tribune*, 4 January 1846, 2). A report in *The Harbinger* entitled "Music in New York" comments that "Mr. Fontana's style is quiet and rich" (2, no. 9 [7 February 1843]: 140).

8. In *The Albion*, Henry Cood Watson referred to the piece as "variations" (5, no. 42 [17 October 1846]: 504).

9. The most complete analysis and discussion of this work is in Mieczysław Tomaszewski, *Muzyka Chopina na nowo odczytana* (Kraków: Akademia Muzyczna, 1996), 73–93. In 1860, after S. B. Mills's performance, the *New York Times* reported that "there are lovely episodes and poetic vagaries in [Chopin's Fantasie] which demand exquisite delicacy of appreciation to detect and lay bare" (13 February 1860, 4). Later Dwight described the Fantasie as "a work of rare power and beauty, rich in variety and contrast" (*DJ* 28, no. 2 [11 April 1868]: 222).

10. Edward Downes, "The Taste Makers: Critics and Criticism," in Paul H. Lang, ed., *One Hundred Years of Music in America* (New York: Schirmer, 1961), 230–44.

11. Henry Edward Krehbiel, *The Philharmonic Society of New York* (New York: Novello Ewer, 1892), 100.

12. Vera Brodsky Lawrence, *Strong on Music: The New York Music Scene in the Days of George Templeton Strong, 1836–1875*, 3 vols. (Oxford: Oxford University Press, 1988 [Vol. 1]; Chicago: University of Chicago Press, 1995 [Vol. 2], 1999 [Vol. 3]), 1:389–90.

13. *Evening Mirror*, 25 November 1846, 2. Watson also praised Timm for his "*feeling*" and for his articulation and accentuation that "rendered everything clear to the mind." A somewhat different review by Watson, but also full of praise for the Concerto and Timm's performance, which was characterized by "grace, delicacy, feeling, and expression," appeared in *The Albion* (5, no. 48 [28 November 1846]: 575). "[Timm] shows his . . . refined taste by performing the works of such masters as Beethoven, Mendelssohn and Chopin." Watson became a founder of the New York Philharmonic Orchestra and by 1846, as a reviewer for the *Evening*

*Mirror, The Albion,* and the *Evening Signal,* was a leading music critic in New York (*New Grove Dictionary of American Music,* ed. H. Wiley Hitchcock and Stanley Sadie [New York: Macmillan, 1986], 1:538). Neither the *New York Herald* nor the *Tribune* reviewed that program.

14. Zofia Chechlińska, "Chopin Reception in Nineteenth-Century Poland," in Jim Samson, ed., *The Cambridge Companion to Chopin* (Cambridge: Cambridge University Press, 1992), 209.

15. Letter of 27 March 1830, in *Chopin's Letters,* ed. Henryk Opieński, trans. E. L. Voynich (New York: Dover, 1988), 76–77.

16. J. S. Dwight, "Musical Review," *The Harbinger* 3, no. 5 (11 July 1846): 76. Dwight also referred to the melodies of Mendelssohn's *Songs without Words* as "delicious, delicate, aromal" (*The Harbinger* 3, no. 13 [5 September 1846]: 218) and to a "fairy kind of Waltz" by the "poetic" Stephen Heller (*DJ* 2, no. 22 [5 March 1853]: 175). According to Judith Tick, around 1900 the music of Chopin and Mendelssohn was still categorized as leaning toward the *ewige weibliche* [eternal feminine] (*American Women Composers before 1870* [Ann Arbor: University of Michigan Press, 1983], 227–28).

17. J. S. Dwight, "The Virtuoso Age in Music," part 2, *The Harbinger* 1, no. 24 (22 November 1845): 379. Liszt's review was published on 2 May 1841 in *Revue et gazette musicale,* one of the many journals that Dwight read.

18. Robert Schumann, "*Neue Sonaten für das Pianoforte,*" in *Neue Zeitschrift für Musik* (1841); reprinted in Schumann's *Gesammelte Schriften über Musik und Musiker,* 2 vols. (1854); 5th ed., ed. Martin Kreisig (Leipzig: Breitkopf & Härtel, 1914), 2:12–15. The translation of the section "Chopin's Sonata" by Henry Pleasants is in *Robert Schumann: Schumann on Music* (New York: Dover, 1988), 173–74.

19. Wessel published the pamphlet in 1843; it was reprinted in two parts in *DJ* 10, no. 8–9 (22, 29 November 1856): 57–59, 66–67. James William Davison displayed a chameleon-like attitude toward Chopin's works. From a highly critical stance he did an about-face (no doubt with compensation in mind) when Wessel, the London publisher of Chopin's music and of his own arrangements of Chopin, invited him to write the *Essay.* Around 1860 Davison wrote a much less enthusiastic preface to the complete Mazurkas published by Boosey and Sons of London, and in his obituary of Chopin he wrote: "Time will show . . . whether the high reputation he enjoyed as a composer . . . was wholly or partially merited, or whether . . . his genius and influence have been greatly overrated by his immediate circle of admirers" (*The Musical World* [London] 24, no. 45 [10 November 1849]: 705).

20. *DJ* 28, no. 7 (20 June 1868): 263.

21. The *Musical Courier* of 12 March 1890 carried an unsigned article, "Chopin's Virile Side," intended as an antidote to the widespread impression of femininity in his music (20, no. 11 (1890): 227). Based on a comparison of its content with some of his later writing, I judge this article to be by James Huneker, who was on the editorial board of the magazine.

22. *New York Times,* 29 January 1890, 4; possibly written by William James Henderson, the highly regarded music critic of that paper.

23. *DJ* 5, no. 26 (30 September 1854): 205. In a casual mention of this Impromptu in 1855, a critic for the *New York Times,* in a bit of hyperbole, wrote, "which five thousand pianists are probably playing at this moment" (29 November 1855, 4).

24. For a discussion and tabulation of dances in sheet music at this time, see Mark McKnight, "Morceaux de Salon, Elegant Polkas, and Grandes Variations Brillantes: Instrumental Forms in Nineteenth-Century American Sheet Music,"

in D. Hunter, ed., *Music Publishing and Collecting: Essays in Honor of Donald W. Krummel* (Urbana: University of Illinois Press, 1994), 96–111.

25. The *Marche funèbre* may have been the most published of Chopin's pieces in the United States. In the 1850s three other publishers brought it out in its original form after Ditson's edition of c. 1846. In 1859 Ditson published a simplified version by the well-known arranger G. F. West (*DJ* 15, no. 22 [27 August 1859]: 176). When the great American poet Henry Wadsworth Longfellow died in 1882, Chopin's March was played at the funeral; this occasioned an edition by an enterprising New York publisher with the title "In Memoriam: Henry Wadsworth Longfellow's Funeral March" by F. Chopin. The earliest simplified solo version that I have found in a published collection is in *Our Heart's Delight: A Vast Treasury of Choice Vocal and Instrumental Music* (Philadelphia: Smith, 1891).

26. See "Works of Great Composers," *DJ* 1, no. 3 (4 April 1853): 30–31; and Paul Charosh, " 'Popular' and 'Classical' in the Mid-Nineteenth Century," *American Music* 10, no. 2 (summer 1992): 117–35.

27. Lawrence, *Strong on Music*, 1:485.

28. Dwight's circular, as cited in George W. Cooke's *John Sullivan Dwight: Brook-Farmer, Editor, and Critic of Music* (Boston: Small, Maynard, 1898), 147. This last statement reflects the quasi-religious role that music played in the philosophy of Transcendentalism.

29. *Baltimore Sun*, 24 May 1852, 2.

30. From the "Editor's Easy Chair," possibly by George W. Curtis, *Harper's New Monthly Magazine* 63, no. 378 (November 1881): 947.

31. Franz Liszt, *F. Chopin* (Paris: Escudier, 1852). It is now widely believed that Liszt's Polish "companion," the Princess Caroline von Sayn-Wittgenstein, played at least some role in the writing of the book (e.g., Edward N. Waters, "Chopin by Liszt," *Musical Quarterly* 47, no. 2 [April 1961]: 170–94, esp. 172, 183).

32. For example, by Finck: "Life and Letters of Chopin," *The Nation*, no. 627 (5 July 1877): 11–12; *Chopin and Other Musical Essays* (New York: Scribner's, 1889).

33. *DJ* 1, no. 3 (24 April 1852): 22. The *Daily Advertiser* reported that "the performances appeared to be very acceptable to the audience, and many were of much merit" (19 April 1852, 2).

34. Compare also Henry T. Finck, *Chopin and Other Musical Essays*, 45.

35. Antoine F. Marmontel, *Virtuoses contemporains* (Paris: Huegel, 1882), 184–85; see also Bertrand Jaeger, "Quelques nouveaux noms d'élèves de Chopin," *Revue de musicologie* 64 (1978): 86. According to Hélène Klener, Jaëll was admired for his sensitive and soulful playing ("Alfred Jaëll," in Friedrich Blume, ed., *Musik in Geschichte und Gegenwart* [Kassel: Bärenreiter, 1949–67], 6, col. 1660).

36. Sources for all lists of concert repertoire were the daily press and music journals.

37. *DJ* 2, no. 16 (22 January 1853): 125. There seem not to have been any other reviews of this concert.

38. Outside Boston Jaëll had a reputation for playing showy "salon music"; he later "repented" and played a more "classical" repertoire (John S. van Cleve, "A Pianistic Retrospect," *MUSIC*, March 1892, 510–11). Van Cleve taught piano and theory at the Conservatory in Cincinnati, was music critic for the *Cincinnati Commercial* and later for the *News-Journal*, and gave many lecture-recitals (*Grove's Dictionary of Music, American Supplement* [New York: Macmillan, 1920], 395).

39. Louis Moreau Gottschalk, *Notes of a Pianist*, ed. Jeanne Behrend (New York: Knopf, 1964), xxviii.

40. See also Michael Broyles, *"Music of the Highest Class": Elitism and Populism in Antebellum Boston* (New Haven, Conn.: Yale University Press, 1992), chap. 9.

41. According to Dwight, Dresel was "anxiously loyal to an artistic ideal, caring mainly for the music and the master's thought" (*DJ* 2, no. 22 [5 March 1853]: 175).

42. *DJ* 4, no. 13 (31 December 1853): 102.

43. *DJ* 3, no. 1 (9 April 1853): 7.

44. Richardson's *Modern School* had a long life, finally entering the catalog of Oliver Ditson, probably around 1861. In 1859 the author published a simplified tutor, the *New Method for the Piano-Forte*. Planned for less sophisticated beginners, the little pieces, titled "Amusements," were chosen with an eye to a much larger market and contained nothing by Chopin.

45. *Boston Evening Transcript*, 4 March 1854, 2.

46. *The Musical World and New York Musical Times* 7, no. 13 (26 November 1853): 99. Although this journal received news from many cities in the United States and Europe, only the large works performed were named and even those performances were not commented on. See also Downes, "The Taste Makers," 235.

47. An interesting source for what was played in New York is Andrew C. Minor's "Piano Concerts in New York City, 1849–1865" (master's thesis, University of Michigan, 1947). Boston had fewer opera and symphony performances at this time and Bostonians were more receptive to piano and chamber music than New Yorkers were. Indeed, that seems to have been an important reason for Dresel's choice of Boston as his residence; he felt that his talents and interests would be more appreciated there (David Urrows, "Apollo in Athens," *American Music* 12, no. 4 [winter 1994]: 350).

48. *New York Times*, 14 October 1854, 4. The critic of the *Evening Post* went so far as to compare the early Christians—driven to worship in obscure places, with those who love the "great *tone prophets*, Mendelssohn, Chopin, and Beethoven [and] are generally obliged to assemble in obscure nooks . . . leaving the open concert hall to the . . . potpourris and fantasias" of the likes of Thalberg and Gottschalk (3 February 1857, 2).

49. *New York Times*, 16 October 1854, 4; probably written by Charles Seymour Bailey.

50. *The Musical World and New York Musical Times* 8, no. 15 (15 April 1854): 177.

51. *Ruch muzyczny*, 16 May 1860, cols. 335–36. A later review of Brzowska's playing in a concert of 11 May 1860, on the eve of her marriage, was effusive in its praise for her versatility of inspiration that "unites . . . performer with composer," among other things (*Ruch muzyczny*, 19 September 1860, cols. 622–23).

52. *DJ* 12, no. 8 (21 November 1857): 268. A much later article titled "Karl Klauser" by Leopold Damrosch leads me to believe that Klauser, who had taught at Miss Porter's School, was the author of the program notes (*DJ* 31, no. 26 [23 March 1872]: 203–4).

53. *DJ* 25, no. 12 (2 September 1865): 94.

54. *The Albion* 39, no. 46 (16 November 1861): 547. A growing awareness of the distinctiveness of composers' styles is revealed in a review of a concert in Philadelphia in which Carl Wolfsohn played Bach, Haydn, Schumann, Chopin, and Liszt. "[I]t is to his credit that he did not fall short in any of the requirements of the widely different schools and epochs" (*Evening Bulletin*, 24 November 1866; reprinted in *DJ* 26, no. 19 [8 December 1866]: 360).

55. Lawrence, *Strong on Music*, 3:431.

56. *DJ* 39, no. 18 (16 August 1879): 136.

57. *DJ* 33, no. 12 (20 September 1873): 96.

58. *DJ* 29, no. 5 (22 May 1869): 39–40. The list for the Boston seasons of 1867–69 consisted of the Concertos opp. 11 (played four times) and 21 (once); the Impromptu op. 29, *Fantasie-Impromptu*, Fantasie op. 49, *Andante spianato* op. 22 (twice) [the list does not mention the Polonaise here]; Rondo op. 16, Mazurkas, ten or more; Polonaises op. 22, op. 26 (the latter twice); Etudes, at least four; Scherzo from Sonata op. 35 (twice); Scherzo op. 54, and others; Ballades: op. 23 (twice), op. 47; Berceuse, "Notturnos, Valses, Preludes, etc. &c, &c." (*DJ* 29, no. 7 [19 June 1869]: 55).

59. Carl Wolfsohn gave a Chopin cycle in Philadelphia in one season between 1863 and 1866, which would have included a number of all-Chopin programs (George Kehler, *The Piano in Concert*, 2 vols. [Metuchen, N.J.: Scarecrow, 1982], 2:1405). Other such programs include Anton Rubinstein in New York on 19 May 1873 (*DJ* 33, no. 3 [17 May 1873]: 22); Hans von Bülow in Philadelphia, 1875, and in Boston on 8 April 1876 (Kehler, *The Piano in Concert*, 1:200, 202); Annette Essipoff in New York on 2 May 1877 (ibid., 1:357), and Boston on 9 May 1877 (*DJ* 37, no. 4 [26 May 1877]: 32); Carl Wolfsohn in Chicago on 12 May 1877 (Kehler, *The Piano in Concert*, 2:1406); Emil Liebling in Evanston, Illinois, in August 1878 (*DJ* 38, no. 11 [31 August 1878]: 295; and William H. Sherwood at a Normal Music Institute in Canandaigua, New York, on 14 August 1880 with a lecture by Max Piutti (*DJ* 90, no. 17 [14 August 1880]: 135).

60. *The Etude* 6, no. 4 (April 1888): 62.

61. For example, Henry Cood Watson, Review, *The Albion* 5, no. 48 (28 November 1846): 575; *New York Evening Post*, 3 February 1857, 2; *DJ* 26, no. 13 (15 September 1866): 310, 311; J. S. Dwight, "The Intellectual Influence of Music," *Atlantic Monthly* 26, no. 157 (November 1870): 615; William Smythe Babcock Mathews, "On the Use of Studies in Piano Teaching," *The Etude* 6, no. 4 (April 1888): 65.

62. *DJ* 30, no. 26 (11 May 1871): 416.

63. In *The Etude* of June 1884, Presser (the magazine's publisher) had advertised the imported Complete Piano Works of Chopin, edited by Klindworth and Scharwenka.

64. *Morning Courier & New-York Enquirer*, 25 November 1846, 2.

65. White was coeditor of the *Morning Courier* along with James Webb. A lawyer by training and a Shakespeare scholar, the sharp-tongued White had read widely in music and served as music critic for the paper (*New Grove Dictionary of American Music*, 1:538).

66. *DJ* 2, no. 11 (18 December 1852): 86. Cf. Liszt, *Chopin*, 10.

67. Chopin's other works that were presumed to be in sonata form were also criticized. A reviewer for the *Cincinnati Commercial* wrote of the Sonata op. 35 as played by Edwin Perry: "It was evident that the free, airy spirit of Chopin's genius felt itself somewhat fettered and imprisoned with the exact and inflexible forms of the sonata, so that the work seemed a singular mixture of two distinct styles— the florid impassioned with the downright thoughtful. Yet the sonata was full of intrinsic beauty" ([2 May 1880]: 6).

68. From Chicago for *DJ* 18, no. 13 (29 December 1860): 318.

69. *New York Daily Tribune*, 7 March 1854, 6. Fry had returned in 1852 from six years in Paris and London as a correspondent for the *New York Tribune*, then "the most powerful newspaper in the country." He became its general editor and music critic, one of the earliest on a daily paper to wield public importance

(*New Grove Dictionary of American Music*, 1:538). From this pulpit he was a crusader for the performance of American music, including his own.

70. From the *Boston Daily Advertiser*, 5 January 1872; reprinted in *DJ* 31, no. 21 (13 January 1872): 164. A review of the Nocturne op. 48 no. 1, probably by the same critic, in the *Daily Advertiser* admired its "quiet loveliness" but called attention to "the perverse oddities of form [!] which mark its latter portions" (21 March 1873, 1).

71. *Musical Magazine* (England), July 1835, 111. In Germany Ludwig Rellstab, editor of *Iris im Geliebte*, was a strident critic of Chopin's music.

72. *DJ* 7, no. 1 (7 April 1855): 6.

73. *Allgemeine musikalische Zeitung*, 11 January 1837, cols. 25–26. Georges Mathias recalled in 1897 that neither his father—"a very good musician"— nor he understood much of that Ballade on the first hearing. "At that time it was the music of the future" (Mathias's preface to Isidore Philipp, *Exercices quotidiens tirés des œuvres de Chopin* [Paris: J. Hamelle, c. 1897 based on the plate number], 6).

74. Probably by Charles Bailey Seymour, *New York Daily Times*, 20 March 1855, 4.

75. Lawrence, *Strong on Music*, 2:561–62.

76. *DJ* 24, no. 23 (4 February 1865): 389.

77. From A.A.C. to *DJ* 32, no. 15 (19 October 1872): [321].

78. *DJ* 39, no. 9 (26 April 1879): 67. Of op. 38 Ritter repeated what Chopin supposedly told Schumann: that "it was while perusing [Mickiewicz's poems] that the idea of this Ballade first awoke in his mind" (*DJ* 39, no. 10 [10 May 1879]: 73).

79. *Chicago Tribune*, 7 March 1890, 4.

80. *DJ* 18, no. 18 (2 February 1861): 360.

81. *DJ* 32, no. 15 (19 October 1872): 326. Dwight's review of a performance of the Concerto op. 21 by a young American pianist, George W. Sumner, makes the point another way. The "rendering was well conceived, clear, firm, carefully elaborated. Had it been Hummel's Septet the rendering would have been highly satisfactory. But it was Chopin, and required a kindred inspiration" (*DJ* 32, no. 20 [11 January 1873]: 366). At that time Hummel's Septet and Piano Concertos were valorized on a far higher rung of the hierarchy than they are today.

82. *DJ* 36, no. 17 (25 November 1876): 343.

83. *DJ* 12, no. 17 (23 January 1858): 340.—t—was a regular contributor to *DJ* from New York City.

84. *Boston Evening Transcript*, 5 May 1880, 6, in a review of a performance by Mr. [E. B.] Perry of the Sonata op. 35. "The sonata was full of intrinsic beauty, and these beauties were set before us in a bright light by the skilled fingers and intelligent head of the young virtuoso."

85. A.A.C. in New York to *DJ* 35, no. 24 (2 March 1876): 191.

86. *DJ* 10, no. 19 (7 February 1857): 150.

87. Henry E. Krehbiel, *New York Daily Tribune*, 14 October 1879, 4–5. A shorter review in the *New York Times* praised Joseffy's "perfect technique and exquisite taste," his "crisp and delicate touch and the easy grace with which he handled the instrument . . . he does not pound the piano to pieces" (14 October 1879, 5). Earlier Dwight had described Anna Mehlig's playing of Chopin's Concerto op. 11 in this same way (*DJ* 31, no. 21 [13 January 1872]: 166).

88. *DJ* 39, no. 23 (8 November 1879): 182.

89. Anonymous, from New York on March 8 to *DJ* 40, no. 6 (13 March 1880): 48.

90. C. H. Brittan from Chicago to *DJ* 39, no. 24 (22 November 1879): 192.

Brittan, a prolific writer on music for several newspapers, had studied with Otto Dresel, who inevitably had helped to form his taste in piano playing (William Smythe Babcock Mathews, *A Hundred Years of Music in America* [Chicago: Howe, 1889], 606).

91. F. in *DJ* 41, no. 1 (1 January 1881): 8.

92. *New York Times*, 20 May 1873, 4; possibly written by Frederick Schwab.

93. *DJ* 30, no. 3 (17 May 1873): 22.

94. Ibid., no. 4 (31 May 1873): 30.

95. *Atlantic Monthly* 39, no. 232 (February 1877): 253–54.

96. *Poughkeepsie Daily News*, 19 January 1876; reprinted in *DJ* 35, no. 22 (5 February 1876): 169.

97. *DJ* 35, no. 15 (30 October 1875): 118. See also n. 51, above.

98. *Philadelphia Inquirer*, 18 December 1875, 2. Curiously, these men were exact contemporaries; both were born in 1830—von Bülow in Germany, Rubinstein in Russia—and both died in 1894.

99. *Philadelphia Inquirer*, 20 December 1875, 7.

100. *Baltimore Bulletin*, 11 December 1875; reprinted in *DJ* 35, no. 19 (25 December 1875): 147.

101. The ensuing discussion of the playing of Pugno, de Pachmann, and Eugen d'Albert was illustrated in a lecture at the Eastman School of Music with sections of pieces available in the recordings listed below, which were compared to the reviews read of the same artists playing the same pieces in concert.

102. *New York Times*, 24 November 1905, 9, probably written by Richard Aldrich.

103. *Boston Journal*, 16 November 1905, 6.

104. *Boston Evening Transcript*, 23 November 1905, 13, most probably written by Henry Taylor Parker.

105. Carl Mikuli, *"Vorwort,"* in *Fr. Chopin's Pianoforte-Werke*, ed. Mikuli (Leipzig: Kistner, [1880]), iii.

106. Louis C. Elson, *Boston Daily Advertiser*, 23 November 1905, 5.

107. Downes, "The Taste Makers," 238.

108. *New York Times*, 29 November 1905, 9.

109. Other works by Chopin recorded on disc in 1903 were the Nocturne op. 15 no. 2, the Impromptu op. 29, and the Waltz op. 34 no. 1. All are available on Opal CD 9836. The turntable in the Paris studio was not level, which produced a waver in the pitch. The recording horn was fixed for the height of a singer, so an upright piano was placed on a small raised platform to accommodate to that. Finally, there is the inevitable hiss on the recording.

110. On the Welte-Mignon roll Pugno also recorded Chopin's *Fantasie-Impromptu* and again the Nocturne op. 15 no. 2, along with music of other composers. The recordings on this role were transferred to a long-playing record in a collection titled *The Welte Legacy of Piano Treasures* (North Hollywood: Recorded Treasures, 1977).

111. Sandra P. Rosenblum, "Some Enigmas of Chopin's Pedal Indications: What Do the Sources Tell Us?" *Journal of Musicological Research* 16, no. 1 (1996): 41–42 and n. 24.

112. *New York Times*, 11 December 1902, 9. Performances of the Ballade op. 23 and the Impromptu op. 36 were the other two praised.

113. Ibid., 21 October 1911, 13.

114. Henry Krehbiel, *New York Tribune*, 8 April 1890, 6.

115. *New York Times*, 8 April 1890, 14.

116. Ibid., 9 Apr. 1890, 4.

117. *Evening Post*, 9 April 1890, 9.
118. *New York Tribune*, 9 April 1890, 7.
119. *New York Times*, 9 November 1904, 9.
120. This recording has been reissued on Opal CD 9840.
121. *New York Tribune*, 10 April 1890, 7. Pachmann's performances of the Barcarolle and the B-Minor Scherzo were criticized for rhythmic liberties.
122. *New York Times*, 21 October 1911, 13.
123. The recording played of Etude op. 25 no. 9 is on a CD titled *The Piano G & Ts: Recordings from the Gramophone and Typewriter Era (1900–1907)*, vol. 1, Appian Publications and Recordings, APR 5531.
124. *Boston Evening Transcript*, 30 October 1899, 8–9.
125. *New York Times*, 9 November 1904. 9. Aldrich had studied music at Harvard and succeeded Henderson as chief music critic of the *New York Times*.
126. *Indianapolis News*, 3 October 1907.
127. Henry Krehbiel, *New York Tribune*, 19 November 1889, 6.
128. Downes, "The Taste Makers," 238.
129. Henry Krehbiel, *New York Tribune*, 19 November 1889, 6.
130. Halina Goldberg, "Chamber Arrangements of Chopin's Concert Works," *The Journal of Musicology* 19, no. 1 (winter 2002): 39–84.
131. *New York Times*, 19 November 1889, 4.
132. Arthur Weld, *Boston Post*, 5 May 1890, 4. D'Albert did not record much Chopin, but his interpretation of the Polonaise op. 53, "conceived in the most warlike spirit" and yet with "a certain proportion and balance" (*New York Times*, 8 February 1905, 9) is on a CD, *Great Pianists on Piano Rolls*, Phonographie, PH 5027.
133. *New York Times*, 9 April 1890, 4.

# Contributors

Zofia Chechlińska is Associate Professor of Musicology at the Institute of Art, Polish Academy of Sciences, Warsaw, and at the Institute of Musicology at the Jagiellonian University, Cracow (Poland).

Halina Goldberg is Assistant Professor of Musicology in the School of Music and REEI at Indiana University–Bloomington.

Marianne Kielian-Gilbert is Associate Professor of Music in the School of Music at Indiana University–Bloomington.

Eric McKee is Associate Professor of Music at the Pennsylvania State University.

John B. Nici is Adjunct faculty (Medieval and Romantic Art History) at Queens College, City University of New York.

Waldemar Okoń is Associate Professor of Art History at the Wrocław University (Poland).

James Parakilas is the James L. Moody, Jr. Family Professor of Performing Arts and chair of the Music Department at Bates College.

Irena Poniatowska is Professor of Musicology, Chair of the Division of General Music History in the Institute of Musicology at the Warsaw University (Poland).

Sandra P. Rosenblum is Chairperson Emerita of the Department of Performing Arts at Concord Academy (Mass.).

Carl Schachter is Distinguished Professor Emeritus of Music at Queens College and the City University of New York Graduate School, Mannes College since 1956 (Chair of the Techniques of Music Division, Dean of the College from 1962 to 1966). Since 1996 he has been on the faculty of the Juilliard School.

Bożena Shallcross is Associate Professor of Polish Literature at the University of Chicago.

Daniel Stone is Professor of History at University of Winnipeg (Canada).

Maja Trochimczyk is Research Assistant Professor and Stefan and Wanda Wilk Director, Polish Music Center, Thornton School of Music, University of Southern California, Los Angeles.

Whitney Walton is Professor of History at Purdue University.

# General Index

# Index of Names

*Page numbers in italics refer to illustrations.*